FUNDAMENTALS OF AGENCY IN TEXAS

1ST EDITION

PERFORMANCE
PROGRAMS
COMPANY

STEPHEN METTLING
RYAN METTLING
DAN HAMILTON

Material in this book is not intended to represent legal advice and should not be so construed. Readers should consult legal counsel for advice regarding points of law.

6810 190th Street East, Bradenton, FL 34211
info@performanceprogramscompany.com
www.performanceprogramscompany.com

ISBN: 978-1965482575

Fundamentals of Agency in Texas

Table of Contents

PREFACE

Welcome to ***Fundamentals of Agency in Texas*** published by Performance Programs Company. This course is one of the six required 30-hour prelicense education courses that every candidate for a Texas real estate salesperson license must complete before sitting for the state licensing examination administered by the Texas Real Estate Commission (TREC). Together, the six courses total 180 hours of qualifying education and are designed to give new licensees a thorough foundation in the law, ethics, and professional practice of Texas real estate.

About This Course

Agency is the foundation of professional real estate practice. Every relationship a licensee forms with a buyer, seller, landlord, or tenant is shaped by agency law, and every transaction a licensee conducts is governed by the duties, disclosures, and ethical obligations that flow from those relationships. Understanding agency is not one topic among many in real estate education. It is the organizing framework within which all other topics operate.

This course covers 14 chapters organized across four areas of study: the legal and practical foundations of agency; the full range of agency positions recognized under Texas law; the ethical and statutory obligations that govern licensee conduct; and the applied skills needed to represent buyers and sellers effectively from listing through closing.

Topics Covered

The course opens with the legal architecture of agency in Texas. You will study the Texas Real Estate License Act (TRELA) and the Texas Occupations Code, the three classifications of agency authority, the fiduciary duties licensees owe to clients, and the distinction between the duties owed to a client versus a customer. The course then examines each of the agency positions recognized under Texas law: seller's agent, buyer's agent, and intermediary, together with the non-representation status created by SB 1968, in depth, covering the unique obligations and disclosure requirements each position carries.

You will study how agency relationships are created and how they end, including the events that automatically terminate an agency and the obligations that survive termination. The course addresses how brokers and salespersons clarify their agency role to clients and customers, how brokerage firms develop and implement agency policies, and how employment relationships between brokers and licensees are legally classified and managed.

The ethics and legal compliance portion examines the relationship between morals, ethics, and law. It then covers the five Texas Administrative Code canons of professional ethics, the TREC complaint and advisory letter process, federal fair housing and lending laws, the Texas Deceptive Trade Practices Act, and the rules governing escrow accounts, residential service company disclosures, and the Real Estate Recovery Trust Account. Chapters 10 & 11 provide a thorough study of the NAR Code of Ethics, including the 2026 updates to Articles 1, 2, 3, and 10, the informal and formal dispute resolution processes available to REALTOR members, and the DTPA in both its substantive and procedural dimensions.

The final section of the course applies everything covered earlier to real-world practice. You will study how to service listings, communicate with sellers, manage showings and open houses, modify and extend listing agreements, counsel sellers through the offer and counteroffer process, and protect the transaction through closing. The buyer-side chapters cover qualifying buyers, planning and conducting showings using professional technique, recognizing buying signals, preparing offers, and presenting them. The course concludes with a practical guide to agency compliance, risk management, offer presentation procedures, and the post-2024 NAR settlement compensation framework that now governs how buyer broker compensation is structured, communicated, and paid.

How to Use This Text

Each chapter opens with a set of learning objectives and closes with a Snapshot Review summarizing the key rules, definitions, and principles introduced in the chapter. These summaries are useful for focused review and exam preparation.

About the Authors

For over forty years, Stephen Mettling has operated one of the nation's most successful custom training organizations specializing in real estate program development. Mr. Mettling has also served as vice president and author for a major real estate training and publishing organization. Under various capacities, he has managed the acquisition, development, and sale of national real estate textbooks and publications, as well as directed the country's largest affiliated group of real estate schools.

Ryan Mettling, partner and publisher of Performance Programs, is an experienced online curriculum designer, author, and course developer.

Dan Hamilton is recognized nationally as a real estate author, educator and broker. During a Texas career spanning over 25 years, he has owned and operated many brokerages and received numerous professional awards and honors. Dan has operated his own school of real estate and currently teaches courses throughout the state. He has served on the board of the national Real Estate Educators Association (REEA) and as President of the Texas Real Estate Teachers Association (TRETA).

CHAPTER 1

AGENCY CONCEPTS

Chapter Objectives

After completing this chapter, you should be able to:

1. Define agency and explain the precise legal meaning of the term in the context of Texas real estate.
2. Identify the three classifications of agency and describe how each applies in real estate practice.
3. Distinguish between a client and a customer, and explain the fiduciary duties a licensee owes to each.
4. Describe the agency positions recognized under Texas law and explain the rules governing intermediary representation.
5. Explain the agency disclosure requirements under Texas law, including when and how disclosures must be made and the consequences of failing to comply.
6. Identify the roles and responsibilities of the key parties in a Texas agency relationship.
7. Distinguish between a client and a customer and explain how each is treated by a licensee.
8. Compare and contrast general, special, and universal agency.
9. Recognize how agency can be created by written agreement, oral agreement, or by the actions of a licensee.
10. Describe uncommon agency relationships including gratuitous agency, ostensible agency, and agency after the fact.
11. Explain the authority a broker holds through an agency relationship and the rules governing intermediary representation in Texas.

Contents

Key Roles in Agency Relationships
The Broker–Salesperson Relationship
Types of Agency
The Principal–Agent Relationship in Practice
How Agency Is Created
Uncommon Agency Relationships
Broker Authority and Intermediary Representation

What Is Agency?

The word "agent" gets used loosely in everyday conversation, but it has a precise legal meaning in real estate. A licensee is only legally an agent when a formal agency relationship exists with one of the following parties:

- A seller or landlord
- A buyer or tenant
- A sponsoring broker

Agency law is the body of law that defines and governs these relationships. Before going further, it is important to understand the key terms below.

Key Terms

Agency: The legal relationship between a principal and a real estate broker, in which the broker is authorized to act on the principal's behalf.

Agent: The person (broker) authorized to represent and act on behalf of another person.

Brokerage Agreement: A written agreement that establishes the terms of brokerage services and compensation. Under Texas law and the post-2024 NAR settlement rules, buyer representation agreements must be in writing and signed before a licensee shows property to a prospective buyer.

Client: A person who has entered into an agency relationship and is being represented by a broker.

Consumer: Any person requesting or receiving licensed real estate services.

Customer: A person who is not represented by an agent but who may receive ministerial acts from a licensee.

Ministerial Acts: Informational or clerical services performed by a licensee for a customer, such as providing property information or scheduling showings, that do not constitute representation.

Fiduciary Relationship: A relationship built on special trust and confidence in which one party (the agent) must act in the best interest of the other (the client).

Principal: The person who hires the broker and grants the broker authority to act on their behalf.

Types of Agency

Agents are classified into three types based on the scope of authority granted to them by the principal.

Universal Agent

A universal agent is empowered to perform any and all legal acts on behalf of the principal. This broad authority is can be granted through a power of attorney. This type of agency is rarely used in standard real estate transactions.

General Agent

A general agent is authorized to handle ongoing tasks within a specific business or enterprise on behalf of the principal. This may include the authority to enter into contracts. An example would be a property manager who handles day-to-day operations of a rental portfolio. Also, the relationship between an agent and the sponsoring broker is considered a general agency relationship.

Special Agent

A special agent (also called a specific agent) is authorized to carry out one specific task or transaction. Once that task is complete, the agency relationship ends. In most cases, a special agent cannot bind the principal to a contract without explicit authorization.

> *Most real estate brokerage relationships are special agency relationships. The broker is hired to complete one transaction, procuring a ready, willing, and able buyer or seller. When that goal is achieved, the relationship ends, though certain fiduciary duties continue to apply even after the transaction closes.*

Agency Coupled with an Interest

An agency coupled with an interest exists when the agent holds a personal financial interest in the subject property. This type of agency cannot be revoked by the principal, and it survives the death of the principal. For example, if a broker finances a development project in exchange for the exclusive right to sell the finished units, the developer cannot later revoke that agreement because the broker's interest is tied to the property itself.

Characteristics of Agency Relationships

Who Is the Agent?

In real estate, the supervising broker is always the legal primary agent of the client, not the individual salesperson, even if a salesperson handled the transaction from start to finish. The broker of record is responsible for all actions taken by every licensee in the office.

This means the broker must create office policies and training programs that help every licensee meet client needs and comply with the law. The broker is also liable for the conduct of the salespeople they sponsor, which is a strong incentive to be selective during hiring and diligent about ongoing training.

Agency in Other Professions

Agency relationships are not unique to real estate. Attorneys are agents of their clients and must place the client's interests above their own. Insurance agents are expected to do the same, though clients sometimes doubt this when premiums increase. A court-appointed guardian managing the affairs of a minor or incapacitated adult also functions as an agent. Understanding these parallels helps illustrate what a true fiduciary obligation looks like in practice.

Client Responsibility

One principle that often surprises people is that a client can be held liable for the wrongful acts of their agent, if the client knew about those acts and did nothing to correct them. For example, if a seller's agent tells a buyer that a roof is in better condition than it actually is, and the seller hears this statement and stays silent, the seller may share in the liability for that misrepresentation.

The practical takeaway for licensees: only state facts you can verify, always cite your sources, and never allow a misleading statement to go uncorrected in your presence.

The Agent's Authority to Act

Agency is always established at the broker level. Every licensee in the office, whether a broker associate or a salesperson, carries out agency duties on behalf of the supervising broker. This means that when a property is listed with a brokerage, every licensee in that office has a duty to represent the seller's best interests. Similarly, if a buyer signs a representation agreement with that same brokerage, every licensee in the office represents the buyer, which is why the intermediary framework described later in this chapter exists.

How Sellers Become Clients

A seller becomes a client by signing a listing agreement with a broker. This written agreement creates the agency relationship and defines the terms of the broker's authority to market the property and negotiate on the seller's behalf. Until the listing agreement is signed, the seller is a consumer, not a client, and the broker's obligations are more limited.

How Buyers Become Clients

Buyers typically first contact a licensee by calling on a yard sign, responding to an advertisement, or reaching out online. During that initial conversation, the licensee's goal is to schedule a face-to-face meeting or property showing.

Under the 2024 NAR settlement rules adopted in Texas, a licensee must have a signed written agreement in place before showing a buyer any property. This requirement makes it more important than ever for licensees to clearly explain the value of buyer representation early in the relationship. The agreement may be a full representation agreement or, where showing is the only service provided, a showing-only agreement without representation. In addition, subagency was eliminated in all Texas real estate transactions by SB 1968, effective January 1, 2026, and is no longer recognized under TRELA.

Once the buyer becomes a client by signing a representation agreement, the buyer receives the full benefit of the licensee's fiduciary duties, including skilled negotiation on the buyer's behalf.

How Licensees Treat Customers

Before an agency relationship is established, a buyer or seller is treated as a customer. Customers receive honest, factual information and fair treatment, but they do not receive strategic advice or negotiation advocacy. A licensee working with a customer must still disclose known property defects, title issues, and any material facts that could affect the customer's decision.

Because licensees may not be aware of every issue affecting a property, it is good practice to strongly recommend that buyers obtain a professional property inspection, a survey, and a title search before closing.

Duties to Clients

Texas licensees owe their clients a set of legally recognized duties known as fiduciary duties. These duties exist to ensure that the client's interests are placed above the licensee's personal interests at all times. Failing to meet these duties can result in client complaints to the Texas Real Estate Commission (TREC) and potential disciplinary action.

The core fiduciary duties owed to clients in Texas include:

Loyalty: Act solely in the client's best interest.

Confidentiality: Protect information the client shares during the relationship.

: Share all material information relevant to the transaction with the client.

Obedience: Follow the client's lawful instructions.

Reasonable Care and Diligence: Apply professional skill and effort to every aspect of the transaction.

Accounting: Safeguard all funds and property entrusted to the licensee.

The goal of fiduciary representation is to achieve the best possible outcome for the client, not the best outcome for the licensee. When both parties to a transaction are represented by licensees, the result is usually not a victory for one side, but rather a negotiated agreement that both parties consider acceptable. This is the professional standard in Texas real estate.

The Importance of Understanding Agency

You may wonder why it matters who exactly a licensee represents, as long as the transaction closes successfully. The answer is that it matters a great deal, for legal, ethical, and professional reasons.

Consumer Representation

Buyers and sellers today are more informed and more demanding than ever. Because Texas requires licensees to be educated and licensed, consumers expect a higher level of expertise and ethical conduct. Numerous consumer protection laws have been enacted in recent decades, and the era of "buyer beware" is over. Consumers on both sides of a transaction rely heavily on their agents for skilled guidance.

Intricacy of the Transaction

For most Texans, buying a home is the largest financial transaction of their lifetime. Many consumers also view homeownership as an investment strategy, buying, holding, and reselling over time. The more experience a consumer has, the better they understand the difference between receiving raw information and receiving strategic advice. Clients, those with signed representation agreements, receive the full benefit of an agent's expertise. Customers receive basic facts, but nothing more.

Multiple Brokers

Most residential transactions involve two licensees: a listing broker and a buyer's broker. Historically, many buyers assumed the broker who showed them homes was looking out for their interests, when in fact that broker may have been representing the seller. The post-2024 changes to the industry, driven by the NAR lawsuit settlement, were designed in part to address this confusion by requiring explicit buyer representation agreements and clearer compensation disclosures upfront.

Industry Professionalism

The role of the real estate professional has evolved significantly. Sellers no longer just want someone to find a buyer; they want counseling and strategic advice. Buyers want advocates who will protect their interests throughout the transaction. Today's licensees are expected to have broad knowledge across taxation, contract law, finance, investment analysis, appraisal, and property management. Texas continues to raise the bar on required competency, and licensees who understand agency are better positioned to meet those standards.

Public Perception of the Industry

Media portrayals of real estate professionals are not always flattering. Licensees who take agency seriously, who disclose their representation clearly, and who genuinely advocate for their clients play an important role in restoring and maintaining public trust in the profession.

Increased Litigation

The rise in real estate litigation makes agency compliance more critical than ever. Even the appearance of undisclosed dual agency (which is not permitted in Texas) can escalate a complaint into a full trial rather than a quick dismissal. Trials are expensive for all parties, and a broker's Errors and Omissions (E&O) insurance carrier may pressure a settlement that damages the broker's reputation. No licensee can completely eliminate the risk of litigation, but following agency disclosure rules consistently is the best defense.

Agency and the License Act

The Texas Real Estate License Act (TRELA) and the Texas Occupations Code define the legal framework for agency relationships in Texas. Under Texas law, a broker may take one of three representation positions in a real estate transaction, or may work with a party without representing them:

- Seller's agent (single agent)
- Showing without representation (non-representation status)
- Buyer's agent (single agent)
- Intermediary

> ***Important:*** *Undisclosed dual agency is not permitted in Texas. Any intermediary representation must be properly disclosed and consented to in writing by all parties.*

Single Agency

In a single agency relationship, a broker represents either the seller/landlord or the buyer/tenant, but not both. The relationship is established through a written agency agreement (a listing agreement for sellers, or a buyer representation agreement for buyers) that defines the scope and duration of representation.

The single agent owes full fiduciary duties to their client, and owes the parties on the other side of the transaction only basic honesty and fair dealing (the customer duties described earlier). Legally, only the supervising broker holds the formal agency relationship with the client; all salespeople and broker associates in the office carry out agency duties as representatives of the supervising broker.

Intermediary Agency

Intermediary agency occurs when a single brokerage firm represents both parties to the same transaction, specifically the seller and the buyer, through an intermediary. This can happen in two ways:

- The supervising broker (or a single licensee) represents both parties directly.
- One licensee in the office represents the seller, while a different licensee in the same office represents the buyer.

In the second scenario, since all licensees are acting under the authority of the supervising broker, the broker is technically representing both sides. An intermediary must act fairly and impartially and may not advocate for one party over the other.

Broker as Intermediary

A broker may act as an intermediary only when both of the following conditions are satisfied:

- The broker obtains written consent from each party authorizing the broker to act as an intermediary.
- The written consent identifies the source of any expected compensation to the broker.

A written listing agreement or a written buyer representation agreement that authorizes intermediary representation is sufficient written consent, provided the agreement also states that the broker or any associated licensee may not do the following:

- disclose to the buyer that the seller will accept a price lower than the asking price.
- disclose to the seller that the buyer will pay a price higher than the amount in a written offer.
- disclose any confidential information, or any information a party has instructed the broker in writing not to share, unless one of the following exceptions applies:
  - the party instructs the broker otherwise in a separate written document.
  - the broker is required by law to disclose the information.
  - the information materially affects the condition of the property.

Appointing Associated Licensees as Intermediary Representatives

When a broker is acting as an intermediary, the supervising broker may appoint one associated licensee to represent the seller and a different associated licensee to represent the buyer. Written notice of these appointments must be provided to all parties.

Once appointed, each associated licensee may provide opinions and negotiation advice to the party they have been designated to represent, a right that the undesignated intermediary broker does not have.

> ***Remember:*** *Undisclosed intermediary agency is illegal in Texas. Disclosed intermediary agency is legal when properly documented and when the brokerage's written policy permits it. Dual agency (representing both parties without proper intermediary disclosure) is never permitted in Texas.*

Compensation Disclosures Under the 2024 NAR Settlement

Beginning in 2024, changes resulting from the NAR lawsuit settlement require that compensation offered to a buyer's broker no longer be communicated through the MLS. Instead, compensation arrangements must be:

- Negotiated and documented in the buyer agreement before any properties are shown.
- Disclosed clearly to the buyer so they understand what they are agreeing to pay and what, if anything, the seller has agreed to contribute.
- Not tied to MLS offers of compensation, which are no longer permitted.

This shift places a much greater emphasis on early, transparent conversations between buyers and their agents about compensation. Texas licensees must be prepared to explain their value proposition clearly and enter into written representation agreements with buyers for the long-term benefit of both parties.

Agency Disclosures

Disclose Upon First Substantive Dialogue

Texas law requires that a licensee provide a written disclosure statement to any party to a real estate transaction at the time of the first substantive dialogue. This written statement (TREC form IABS 1-2 Information About Brokerage Services) explains in general terms the representation options available under Texas law: seller's agent, buyer's agent, and intermediary, and when a license holder may work with a party without representing them.

This form requires License Holder Contact Information including Sponsoring Broker, Designated Broker, Supervisor of Sales and Sales Agent

The disclosure is not required in either of the following situations:

- The transaction involves a residential lease of one year or less and a sale is not being considered.
- The licensee is meeting with a party who is already represented by another licensee.

"Substantive dialogue" means any meeting or written communication involving a substantive discussion about a specific property. It does not include:

- A meeting that occurs at an open house as long as the dialogue does not become substantive.
- A meeting or communication that takes place after the parties have already signed a contract to buy, sell, or lease the property (because the IABS should already have been presented)

Seller and Landlord Agents

The listing agent is ultimately required to fulfill the disclosure obligation in writing. The initial disclosure may be made orally, but it must be followed by written confirmation which the agent is required to maintain as a record.

Buyer and Tenant Agents

Buyer or tenant agents must disclose their agency relationship at the first point of contact with a represented seller, landlord, or either party's agent. This disclosure can be made orally. If the disclosure is made to a listing agent, that listing agent is then responsible for conveying the disclosure to their principal.

As with seller agents, the buyer agent's disclosure may be made orally at first but must be followed by a written disclosure (the actual IABS) prior to any substantive discussion.

Agents in an Intermediary Transaction

Licensees acting under an intermediary transaction must make disclosures consistent with both buyer agency and seller agency requirements:

- If the licensee initially represents the buyer, disclosure to the seller
- If the licensee initially represents the seller, disclosure to the buyer must be made upon first substantive dialogue.

In addition, both parties must provide written consent to the intermediary arrangement (Intermediary Authorization Agreement) before or at the time any transaction document is signed. This written consent constitutes informed consent and allows the intermediary representation to proceed.

Failure to Disclose

Licensees who fail to properly and timely disclose their agency relationship are in violation of Texas license law. Penalties may include:

- Suspension or revocation of the real estate license.

- Other sanctions as determined by TREC on a case-by-case basis.

Key Roles in Agency Relationships

Real estate transactions involve a network of legal relationships. Before diving into how these relationships are formed and managed, it is essential to understand who the key players are and what each term means under Texas law.

Terminology: Who Is Who?

The following terms describe the roles real estate professionals and the people they serve play in Texas transactions.

Licensee: Any person licensed in Texas as either a salesperson or a broker.

Broker Licensee: A person who holds a Texas broker's license and is qualified to operate a real estate office and supervise others.

Salesperson Licensee: A person who holds a Texas salesperson's license and must work under the supervision of a sponsoring broker.

Sponsoring Broker (Employing Broker): The broker who takes legal responsibility for the real estate activities of all salespersons and broker associates working under their supervision.

Agent: Either (1) a broker who has an established agency relationship with a seller, buyer, landlord, or tenant; or (2) a licensee who has an agency relationship with their employing broker.

Subagent: A licensee who is not affiliated with the client's broker but who represents the same client as a cooperating broker.

Seller's Agent (Listing Agent): A broker licensee who represents the seller in a transaction.

Buyer's Agent (Cooperating Broker): A broker licensee who represents the buyer in a transaction.

Intermediary: A broker licensee who represents both the seller and the buyer in the same transaction. This is a legally recognized form of representation in Texas when properly disclosed and consented to in writing by all parties.

Client (Principal): A person who is formally represented in a real estate transaction. The terms "client" and "principal" are used interchangeably in Texas real estate.

Customer: A person who receives some brokerage services but does not have a formal agency relationship with a broker.

Client vs. Customer: An Important Distinction

One of the most important distinctions in Texas real estate is whether a person is a client or a customer.

A **customer** is anyone a licensee works with before an agency relationship is established. The customer receives honest, factual information and fair treatment, but does not receive strategic advice, negotiation advocacy, or the benefit of the broker's full fiduciary duties.

A **client** is a customer who has entered into a formal agency agreement with the broker. Once the client relationship is created, the broker is obligated to pursue the best possible transaction for that client, whether the client is buying or selling.

> ***Key Rule:*** *All agency relationships in Texas are created at the broker level, never at the salesperson level. The broker is legally the agent of the client, even if a salesperson handles the day-to-day work of the transaction.*

The broker is also responsible to the Texas Real Estate Commission (TREC), the public, and the clients. Failure to provide adequate service to a client can result in disciplinary action by TREC or the local board of REALTORS® if the broker is a member.

The Broker–Salesperson Relationship

How Salespersons Derive Their Responsibilities

A salesperson in the office may be the one who locates and initiates an agency relationship with a seller or buyer, but the broker is ultimately responsible for everything that follows. This clear line of liability is good for the industry: when it is understood that the broker is responsible for all activity in the office, there is less room for confusion about accountability.

Salespersons derive their responsibilities directly from their sponsoring broker. Generally, those responsibilities are to find buyers and sellers, explain agency relationships, and enter into agency agreements on the broker's behalf. It is illegal in Texas for a licensee to perform real estate functions without a sponsoring broker.

This structure creates a strong incentive for brokers to invest in quality training programs. When salespeople are well-trained, they are less likely to make costly mistakes and more likely to deliver excellent service to every client the office represents. A well-run office with satisfied clients generates referrals and builds the broker's reputation in the community, an investment that pays dividends for years.

The Independent Contractor Agreement

The agency relationship between a broker and their salespeople is formalized through an independent contractor agreement. This document defines the duties of both the broker and the salesperson during the working relationship.

As a result of this relationship, salespeople have the authority to commit the broker to sellers and buyers in agency relationships. In many cases, a broker may never personally meet a client because the salesperson handles every step of the transaction. The broker remains legally responsible throughout.

Important: If a salesperson violates the Texas Real Estate License Act, the sponsoring broker can be held responsible along with the salesperson. This is why ongoing education, supervision, and clear office policies are essential in every brokerage.

Hiring a Broker: The Client's Perspective

Sellers tend to be deliberate when selecting a broker. They often ask neighbors, friends, and family for recommendations, looking for a licensee known for honesty and a track record of successful, stress-free transactions.

Buyers are sometimes less systematic about their search. In many cases, a buyer contacts a licensee while looking at a particular property, and the licensee introduces the idea of buyer representation during that conversation.

Whether the person is a buyer or a seller, they have the right to interview more than one licensee before choosing who will represent them. Encouraging this process is a sign of professionalism.

The Broker's Decision: Should I Take This Client?

Just as buyers and sellers choose their broker, brokers also make a business decision about whether to take on a particular client. While licensees do not routinely turn down clients, there are situations where pursuing an agency relationship may not be in either party's best interest. Examples include:

1. The seller is asking for a listing price the broker believes is far above market value.
2. The buyer does not appear to qualify for financing to complete a purchase.
3. The seller refuses to make repairs that are likely to derail the sale.
4. The buyer is legally unable to contract (e.g., a minor).
5. The seller is uncooperative or unreasonable to work with.
6. The buyer repeatedly views properties without taking any steps toward making a decision.

These are business decisions. Real estate involves significant time and expense, and a licensee who is selective about their clientele is better positioned to deliver high-quality service to the people they do represent.

Creating the Agency Relationship: Written Agreements

The best way to establish an agency relationship is through a written agreement, either a **listing agreement** for sellers or a **buyer representation agreement** for buyers. Under Texas law and the rules adopted following the 2024 NAR settlement, buyer agreements must be signed before the broker shows a buyer any property.

A written agreement accomplishes several important things:

1. Both the client and the broker have a copy of the document that outlines their respective duties, if any.
2. The act of signing a document reinforces the client's commitment to the relationship.
3. The existence of the agreement provides clear evidence in court if a dispute arises over commissions or services.
4. The written document defines the scope of the broker's authority, giving the client or customer a clear reference point if they believe the broker is overstepping or falling short.

In short, a written agreement serves as a beginning for the entire professional relationship. It protects both parties and eliminates ambiguity about who is responsible for what.

Types of Agency

Agency is not a single, one-size-fits-all concept. The type of agency that exists in a given situation depends on the scope of authority granted to the agent and the nature of the tasks involved. Texas real estate involves three primary classifications: general agency, special agency, and universal agency.

General Agency

A **general agency** exists when a principal delegates broad, ongoing authority to an agent to perform a wide range of tasks within a particular business or enterprise. In real estate, the most common example of general agency is the relationship between a broker and their salespeople.

Under a general agency, the broker authorizes salespeople to perform the full range of tasks necessary to serve clients: showing property, negotiating contracts, preparing documents, and so forth. The broker's fiduciary duties flow through to each salesperson in the office, meaning that each licensee owes the same duties to the client as the broker does.

General agency also arises when a broker takes on property management responsibilities for a client. In that role, the broker handles numerous ongoing tasks, including collecting rent, arranging maintenance, and managing tenant relationships, which goes beyond what is typical in a one-time sales transaction.

Special Agency

A **special agency** (also called specific agency) is the most common type of agency in Texas real estate transactions. In a special agency, the principal authorizes the broker to perform one specific task. Once that task is complete, the agency relationship ends.

For a seller-client, the broker's special agency task is to find a ready, willing, and able buyer for the property. Although the broker performs many activities in pursuit of that goal, including pricing, marketing, advertising, showing, and negotiating, and the singular objective of the relationship is to procure a buyer.

For a buyer-client, the broker's special agency task is to locate a suitable property and negotiate the best possible transaction. Once the purchase closes, the agency relationship concludes.

Under special agency, the client is responsible for the actions of the broker, but only for what the client has specifically authorized and only for what the client knew the broker was doing. The broker may not bind the client to a contract without the client's explicit authorization.

> ***Important:*** *When a salesperson leaves a brokerage, their listing agreements and buyer representation agreements belong to the broker, not the salesperson. The clients stay with the broker. The departing salesperson must begin building a new client base at their new brokerage.*

Universal Agency

Universal agency grants an agent the broadest possible authority, essentially full control over another person's life and property. This type of agency can be established through a **power of attorney** and is almost never encountered in standard real estate practice.

Universal agency typically arises in situations such as when a person becomes incapacitated and cannot manage their own affairs. A court may appoint a guardian, or a trusted individual may be given power of attorney, allowing them to make medical decisions, sign real estate contracts, pay bills, and handle all other legal matters on behalf of the incapacitated person. The person who receives this authority is called the attorney-in-fact.

Even in a universal agency, the agent owes fiduciary duties to the client. The agent must act in the client's best interest and must never place the client at unnecessary risk.

Universal agency is uncommon in real estate because standard brokerage never gives the broker full control over a client's decision-making. Even in an active agency relationship, the client always retains the right to make the final decisions. The broker provides advice and options, but the choice belongs to the client.

Express Agency vs. Implied Agency

Express agency is the clearest and safest form of agency for everyone involved. In an express agency, both the broker and the client have a thorough, mutual understanding of their roles, rights, and responsibilities and that understanding is expressed. Express agency can be created by either a written or an oral agreement, as long as the terms are clear and both parties understand what is expected.

Implied agency is created not by a formal agreement, but by the actions and behavior of the licensee. When a licensee gives a customer strategic advice, shares an opinion about what the customer should do, or negotiates on the customer's behalf, the licensee may inadvertently be creating an agency relationship, even without a signed document.

Implied agency creates serious problems. It is unintentional, undefined, and unprotected by any written record. The best way to prevent implied agency is to create all agency relationships in writing before providing any services that go beyond basic factual information.

The Principal–Agent Relationship in Practice

Understanding the Principal–Agent Relationship

A seller who lists exclusively with a broker is that broker's client, but only at that broker's office. The seller is a customer to every other broker in the market. Similarly, a buyer who has a signed an exclusive representation agreement with one broker is that broker's client, but is a customer to all other brokers.

A broker can represent multiple clients simultaneously: several sellers with active listings, several buyers searching for homes, or both. Handling multiple transactions at once is a normal part of the business and must always be done scrupulously and meticulously.

A person should not be referred to as a client or principal until an actual agency relationship has been created. Until that point, they are a customer. Once they become a client, the broker and the full resources of the office are working to secure the best possible outcome for them.

Broker Responsibilities to the Buyer-Principal

When a buyer becomes a client by signing a buyer representation agreement, the level of service they receive increases significantly. As a client, the buyer is entitled to:

1. Advice and professional opinions about properties and market conditions.
2. A comparative market analysis (CMA) or broker's price opinion to help evaluate a property's value.
3. Active negotiation on their behalf to achieve the lowest price and best terms.
4. Guidance throughout the offer, counteroffer, and negotiation process.
5. Full broker services from the signing of the representation agreement through the closing of the transaction.

The buyer's broker also benefits from this formalized relationship: with a signed exclusive agreement in place, the broker can be confident the buyer is committed and will not simply move to a competing brokerage.

Broker Responsibilities to the Seller-Principal

The broker's most critical first task with a seller-client is to conduct a thorough market analysis so the seller has a realistic understanding of what their property is worth. Many sellers overestimate their property's value; some underestimate it. Either way, it is the broker's job to help the seller set a price that is competitive in the current market.

Once the listing price is agreed upon and the listing agreement is signed, the broker undertakes a comprehensive marketing effort, which typically includes:

1. Entering the property in the Multiple Listing Service (MLS).
2. Placing advertising and marketing materials.
3. Installing a yard sign and, where appropriate, a lockbox.
4. Scheduling and facilitating showings.
5. Presenting all offers to the seller and advising on whether to accept, counter, or reject each offer.

When an offer is presented, the seller has four choices: accept the offer as written, submit a counteroffer, reject the offer entirely or fail to act (do nothing). The broker's role is to help the seller evaluate each option clearly and make an informed decision.

How Agency Is Created

Agency Created by Written Agreement

As discussed earlier, the written agency agreement, either a listing agreement or a buyer representation agreement, is by far the most reliable way to establish an agency relationship. A written agreement leaves no doubt about the existence of the relationship, the scope of the broker's authority, the duration of the agreement, and the compensation arrangement.

A written agreement protects both parties. The broker can enforce their right to a commission in court. The client can seek damages if the broker fails to perform. And both parties have a clear document to refer to if questions arise about what was, and was not, authorized.

Agency Created by Oral Agreement

It is legally possible to create an agency relationship through a verbal agreement, but this approach carries significant risks. Verbal communication is imprecise: tone, body language, and word choice can all lead to different interpretations of what was said. Without a written record, it may be impossible to establish exactly what duties each party agreed to, when the relationship was supposed to end, or whether compensation was discussed at all.

Texas courts generally will not hear real estate disputes based solely on verbal agreements. Most brokers prohibit verbal-only agency agreements as a matter of office policy. As a practical matter, a licensee should always seek a written agreement before providing any services that go beyond basic factual information.

Agency Created by the Actions of a Licensee (Implied Agency)

Agency can also be created unintentionally, simply by what a licensee says or does. This is called implied agency, and it is a significant risk for licensees who are not careful about the distinction between customers and clients.

When a licensee provides strategic advice, shares an opinion about what a customer should offer or accept, or negotiates on a customer's behalf, they may be creating an implied agency relationship, even without any written or oral agreement. Providing these services is appropriate for clients; providing them to customers crosses a legal line.

If a licensee accidentally creates implied agency with a buyer while simultaneously holding a written listing agreement with the seller, the result is a form of undisclosed dual agency, a serious violation of Texas license law. Any licensee who finds themselves in this situation must correct it as quickly as possible.

The takeaway is simple: always create agency relationships intentionally, in writing, before providing advice, opinions, or negotiation services to anyone.

Uncommon Agency Relationships

While most agency in Texas real estate is created through written listing or buyer representation agreements, there are several less common forms of agency that every licensee should be able to recognize.

Gratuitous Agency

Gratuitous agency occurs when a broker provides agency services without receiving compensation. Choosing to work for free does not eliminate the broker's legal and fiduciary obligations to the client. The duty to act in the client's best interest and to pursue the best possible transaction applies regardless of whether the broker is being paid.

Examples include a broker who handles the sale of a family member's home as a personal favor, or a broker who sells property donated to a civic organization of which they are a member.

A cautionary note: licensees should be careful about agency arrangements where they perform services in a role they were not authorized to fill. A salesperson from an outside office who shows a listing as a non-agent and then submits an offer may find that the listing broker refuses to share the commission, unless the two brokerages have some type of written compensation agreement.

Ostensible Agency

Ostensible agency (also called apparent agency) occurs when a court determines that a licensee was acting so much like an agent that they should be held legally responsible as one, even if no formal agency agreement existed.

These cases are almost always brought by members of the public who believe they were harmed by a licensee's actions. For example, a buyer-customer who received unsolicited advice from a licensee about the condition or value of a property, and who later suffered financial harm as a result, might argue in court that the licensee's behavior created an agency relationship, and that the licensee and their broker are therefore liable for the harm.

The most effective protection against ostensible agency claims is the same as for implied agency: always establish agency relationships in writing before providing any advice or opinions. When a written agreement exists, there is no need for a court to infer whether agency did or did not exist.

Agency After the Fact (Agency by Ratification)

Agency after the fact, also known as agency by ratification, occurs when a broker performs actions on behalf of a party before that party has agreed to be represented, and the party later accepts the benefit of those actions without objecting.

Consider this example: a salesperson walks a tract of land with a potential buyer, estimates a value, writes up a draft offer, and then contacts the owner to see if they are interested in selling, all before the owner has agreed to anything. If the owner does not object to what the licensee has done and ultimately benefits from the transaction, a court may find that an agency relationship was ratified after the fact.

For agency by ratification to be established, four elements are generally present:

1. The licensee performed an unauthorized act (e.g., entering the property without the owner's permission).
2. The owner learned of the unauthorized act.
3. The owner did not reject or deny what the licensee had done.
4. The owner received a benefit from the unauthorized act (e.g., the land was sold and converted to cash).

The lesson: always obtain authorization before acting on anyone's behalf.

The Texas Real Estate Commission states that a real estate broker cannot sue for a commission under ratification.

Broker Authority and Intermediary Representation

The Authority of the Broker Through Agency

When an agency relationship is established, the broker acquires **implied authority** to perform tasks on behalf of the client. For a seller-client, this includes showing the property, marketing and advertising, and presenting and negotiating offers. For a buyer-client, this includes showing homes, preparing and submitting offers, and negotiating on the buyer's behalf.

In all cases, however, the client retains the right to make the final decisions. The broker advises; the client decides. The broker may offer a list of options and a professional recommendation, but they may not commit the client to a course of action without the client's authorization.

The one exception is when the client grants the broker a **power of attorney**, which allows the broker to make binding decisions on the client's behalf. This is an unusual arrangement and would only be appropriate in very specific circumstances.

As with all aspects of agency, the scope of the broker's authority is clearest when it is spelled out in a written agreement. Verbal authority creates uncertainty for both the broker and the client. A written agreement that defines exactly what the broker is and is not authorized to do eliminates the potential for misunderstanding.

Broker Acting as an Intermediary

An **intermediary** is a broker who represents (limited representation) both the seller and the buyer in the same transaction. Intermediary representation is a unique feature of Texas real estate law and is legally permitted, provided it is properly disclosed and consented to in writing by all parties involved.

A broker may only act as an intermediary if both of the following conditions are met:

1. The broker obtains written consent from each party to act as an intermediary in the transaction.

2. The written consent identifies the source of any expected compensation to the broker.

A written listing agreement or buyer representation agreement that authorizes intermediary representation is NOT sufficient consent. To prove consent, the Intermediary Agreement must be used. The rule also states that the broker or any appointed licensee may not do the following:

1. Disclose to the buyer that the seller will accept a price less than the asking price, unless the seller has authorized the disclosure in writing.
2. Disclose to the seller that the buyer will pay a price greater than the price in a written offer, unless the buyer has authorized the disclosure in writing.
3. Disclose any confidential information or any information a party has instructed the broker in writing to keep confidential, unless authorized in writing by the disclosing party, required by law or court order, or if the information materially relates to the condition of the property.

Appointing Associated Licensees in an Intermediary Transaction

When acting as an intermediary, a supervising broker may appoint one licensee in the office to represent the seller and a different licensee to represent the buyer. Written notice of these appointments must be provided to all parties.

Once appointed, each licensee may provide opinions and advice during negotiations to the party they have been designated to represent, something the undesignated intermediary broker is not permitted to do.

> ***Remember:*** *Undisclosed dual agency, where a broker represents both sides of a transaction without proper disclosure and written consent, is illegal in Texas. Intermediary representation is the Texas-approved method for handling transactions where the same brokerage represents both parties, and it requires strict adherence to the written consent and disclosure requirements described above.*

Snapshot Review – Chapter 1

Key Terms to Know

Agency: The legal relationship between a principal and a real estate broker.

Agent: The broker authorized to represent and act on behalf of a principal.

Brokerage Agreement: A written agreement establishing the terms of representation and compensation.

Client: A person who has entered into an agency relationship with a broker.

Consumer: Any person requesting or receiving licensed real estate services.

Customer: A person receiving ministerial acts without an agency relationship.

Ministerial Acts: Informational or clerical services provided to customers.

Fiduciary Relationship: A trust-based relationship requiring the agent to act in the client's best interest.

Principal: The person who hires the broker and grants authority to act on their behalf.

Key Rules

1. Agency is always formed at the broker level, never at the salesperson level.
2. A buyer or seller is treated as a customer until a signed representation agreement creates an agency relationship.
3. Under Texas law and post-2024 NAR settlement rules, buyer representation agreements must be signed before a licensee shows property to a buyer.
4. Fiduciary duties require the agent to place the client's interests above their own at all times.
5. Dual agency is not permitted in Texas; intermediary agency is permitted only with proper written disclosures and consent.
6. Texas licensees must provide the TREC Information About Brokerage Services form at the time of first substantive dialogue.
7. Failure to make required agency disclosures is a violation of Texas license law and may result in suspension, revocation, or other sanctions.

Agency Positions Under Texas Law

Seller's agent (single agent)

Showing without representation (non-representation status)

Buyer's agent (single agent)

Intermediary

Why Agency Knowledge Matters

Consumer Representation: Clients expect licensed professionals to provide skilled, ethical representation.

Transaction Complexity: Real estate transactions involve large sums of money and require expert guidance.

Multiple Brokers: Buyers and sellers can be confused about who represents them; clear disclosures help.

Industry Professionalism: Today's licensees are counselors and problem-solvers, not just salespeople.

Public Perception: Ethical agency practice builds trust in the profession.

Litigation Risk: Even the appearance of undisclosed dual agency can trigger expensive litigation.

Agency Fundamentals

1. All agency relationships in Texas are created at the broker level, not the salesperson level. The broker is the legal agent of the client.
2. A customer is anyone who receives brokerage services without a formal agency agreement. A client is a customer who has signed a representation agreement.
3. Salespersons derive their responsibilities from their sponsoring broker and must work under the broker's supervision. It is illegal in Texas to perform real estate activities without a sponsoring broker.
4. Written agency agreements, including listing agreements for sellers and buyer representation agreements for buyers, are the best way to establish an agency relationship. Under post-2024 NAR settlement rules adopted in Texas an agreements must be signed before a buyer is shown any property.

Types of Agency

1. General agency: broad, ongoing authority, used between broker and salesperson, or in property management.
2. Special agency: authority to complete one specific task, and the most common type in Texas real estate transactions.
3. Universal agency: full authority over a person's affairs, created by a power of attorney and uncommon in real estate.
4. Express agency: clearly defined, whether in writing or orally.
5. Implied agency: created unintentionally by the actions or statements of a licensee. Avoid by always creating agency in writing first.

Uncommon Forms of Agency

1. Gratuitous agency: agency without compensation. Fiduciary duties still apply.
2. Ostensible agency: court-declared agency based on how a licensee behaved. Avoid by creating agency in writing.
3. Agency after the fact (ratification): agency established when a principal accepts the benefit of an unauthorized act.

Intermediary Representation in Texas

1. A broker may represent both the seller and the buyer as an intermediary, but only with the written consent of both parties.
2. The intermediary broker must treat both parties honestly and impartially.
3. The broker may appoint different licensees in the office to represent each side of the transaction, and must provide written notice to all parties.
4. Undisclosed dual agency is illegal in Texas. Intermediary representation is the approved alternative when both parties are clients of the same brokerage.

CHAPTER 1 QUIZ — AGENCY CONCEPTS

1. In Texas real estate, the term "agent" refers to which of the following?

a. A broker who has a formal legal relationship with a principal such as a buyer or seller
b. Any licensee who has completed the required pre-license education
c. A salesperson who has been sponsored by a broker for at least one year
d. Any person who assists in a real estate transaction for compensation

2. Which of the following best describes a "principal" in an agency relationship?

a. The supervising broker who oversees all licensees in an office
b. The person who hires the broker and grants authority to act on their behalf
c. The Texas Real Estate Commission official who issues licenses
d. The salesperson who obtained the listing agreement

3. A buyer who contacts a licensee for information about a specific property but has NOT signed a representation agreement is best described as which of the following?

a. A client
b. A principal
c. A customer
d. A fiduciary

4. Which type of agency relationship grants the agent the broadest authority to act on behalf of the principal, including the power to perform any legally delegable act?

a. Special agency
b. General agency
c. Intermediary agency
d. Universal agency

5. Most Texas real estate brokerage relationships are based on which type of agency?

a. Special agency, because the broker is hired to complete one specific transaction
b. General agency, because the broker handles ongoing tasks for the client
c. Universal agency, because the broker can act on all matters for the client
d. Intermediary agency, because two parties are always involved in a transaction

6. An "agency coupled with an interest" differs from a standard agency relationship in which important way?

a. It requires approval from TREC before it can be created
b. It cannot be revoked by the principal and survives the principal's death
c. It can be revoked by the principal at any time with 30 days' notice
d. It is only valid for commercial transactions, not residential ones

7. Agency in a real estate brokerage is always formed at which level?

a. The salesperson level, because salespeople have the most direct client contact
b. The transaction coordinator level, because they manage the paperwork
c. The broker level, with salespeople acting as representatives of the broker
d. The MLS level, because listings are registered there

8. Under the NAR settlement rules adopted in Texas, when must a buyer representation agreement be signed?

a. Before the buyer makes an offer on a property
b. At the time of closing
c. Within three business days of the first showing
d. Before the licensee shows the buyer any property

9. A seller hears the listing agent tell a potential buyer that the roof is in better condition than it actually is, but the seller says nothing to correct the statement. Which of the following is most accurate?

a. The seller may share in the liability for the agent's misrepresentation
b. Neither party is liable because it was a verbal statement only
c. Only the agent is liable because the agent made the statement
d. The seller is fully protected because they did not directly speak to the buyer

10. Which of the following best describes the fiduciary duty of "loyalty"?

a. Following the client's lawful instructions throughout the transaction
b. Acting solely in the client's best interest above all others, including the agent's own interests
c. Keeping the client's personal information confidential after the transaction ends
d. Providing the client with a full accounting of all funds received and disbursed

11. In Texas, which of the following agency arrangements is NOT permitted?

a. Single agency representing only the seller
b. Intermediary agency with proper written disclosure and consent
c. Dual agency in which the broker secretly represents both parties without disclosure
d. Buyer's single agency with a signed representation agreement

12. When a Texas broker acts as an intermediary, which of the following is the broker prohibited from doing?

a. Collecting compensation from both parties with written consent
b. Appointing different licensees in the office to represent each party
c. Providing written notice of licensee appointments to all parties
d. Disclosing to the buyer that the seller will accept a price lower than the listing price

13. Texas law requires that a licensee provide the Information About Brokerage Services form to a party at what point?

a. At the time of the first substantive dialogue about a specific property
b. At the time of contract execution
c. Only after a representation agreement has been signed
d. At the first open house the prospective buyer attends

14. Under Texas agency disclosure rules, which of the following situations does NOT require a licensee to provide the written agency disclosure?

a. A buyer's first in-person meeting to discuss purchasing a home
b. A meeting at an open house with a prospective buyer
c. A written email exchange about a specific property with a prospective seller
d. A phone call discussing the specific features and price of a listed property

15. Following the NAR settlement changes, how must buyer's broker compensation now be handled in Texas?

a. It must be offered through the MLS so all cooperating brokers can see it
b. It is set by TREC as a standardized percentage and cannot be negotiated
c. It must be negotiated and documented in the agreement before properties are shown
d. It must be paid exclusively by the seller at closing regardless of agreement

16. A licensee who fails to make required agency disclosures properly and on time is subject to which of the following under Texas law?

a. A mandatory civil lawsuit filed by the injured party
b. Automatic loss of E&O insurance coverage
c. A fine of no less than $5,000 per violation as set by statute
d. Suspension or revocation of their license and other sanctions as determined by TREC

17. Which of the following best describes a "sponsoring broker" in Texas?

a. A broker who represents the seller exclusively in a real estate transaction

b. A broker who holds a power of attorney on behalf of an incapacitated client

c. A broker who has been licensed in Texas for at least five years

d. A broker who takes legal responsibility for the real estate activities of salespersons working under his or her supervision

18. In Texas real estate, the terms "principal" and "client" are considered which of the following?

a. Interchangeable, both refer to a person formally represented by a broker

b. Distinct terms with different legal meanings under TRELA

c. Interchangeable only when the client is the buyer, not the seller

d. Terms that apply only after a transaction has closed

19. A licensee gives a customer an opinion on whether a property is priced fairly and advises the customer on what to offer. Which of the following has most likely occurred?

a. The licensee has fulfilled their ministerial duties to the customer

b. The licensee may have unintentionally created an implied agency relationship with the customer

c. The licensee has created an express agency relationship with the customer

d. The licensee has acted appropriately because all customers deserve advice

20. The agency relationship between a broker and his or her salespeople is formalized through which document?

a. A listing agreement

b. A buyer representation agreement

c. An independent contractor agreement

d. A power of attorney

21. A salesperson leaves a brokerage and moves to a new firm. Which of the following is true regarding the listing agreements and buyer representation agreements the salesperson had been working on?

a. The salesperson may take the agreements to their new broker with the clients\' written consent

b. The agreements are voided automatically when the salesperson leaves

c. The salesperson retains the agreements but must notify TREC within 10 days

d. The agreements belong to the broker, so the clients and agreements stay with the original brokerage

22. Which type of agency is most commonly used in Texas real estate transactions between a broker and their clients?

a. Special agency, because the broker is authorized to complete one specific task
b. Universal agency, because the broker must handle all aspects of the transaction
c. General agency, because the broker has many ongoing tasks to complete
d. Gratuitous agency, because no compensation is required until closing

23. Under special agency, which of the following correctly describes the client's responsibility for the broker's actions?

a. The client is responsible for all actions the broker takes, regardless of authorization
b. The client is responsible only for actions they specifically authorized and knew the broker was taking
c. The client bears no responsibility for any of the broker's actions
d. The client is responsible only if the broker is also a salesperson licensee

24. A broker handles the sale of their neighbor's home as a personal favor without charging a commission. Which type of agency does this describe?

a. Ostensible agency
b. Universal agency
c. Gratuitous agency
d. Agency after the fact

25. Ostensible agency (also called apparent agency) is most accurately described as which of the following?

a. An agency relationship created when a broker works without charging a fee
b. An agency relationship created by a written listing agreement that has not yet been signed by all parties
c. An agency relationship that is automatically terminated when the transaction closes
d. An agency relationship declared by a court based on how a licensee behaved, even without a formal agreement

26. Agency by ratification, also known as agency after the fact, requires which of the following elements?

a. An unauthorized act by the licensee, followed by the principal accepting the benefit without objection
b. A written agreement executed before the agent begins performing any tasks
c. The principal's advance approval of all actions the agent plans to take
d. TREC approval of the agency arrangement before the transaction proceeds

27. When a broker holds a written listing agreement with a seller and all agency is properly disclosed, which of the following best describes the broker's authority?

a. The broker has express authority to make all final decisions on the seller's behalf

b. The broker has implied authority to show, market, and negotiate on the seller's behalf, while the client retains final decision-making authority

c. The broker has universal authority to act on all matters relating to the seller's affairs

d. The broker's authority is limited to entering the property into the MLS only

28. When a Texas broker acts as an intermediary and appoints separate licensees to represent each party, what must the broker provide to all parties?

a. A comparative market analysis prepared by each appointed licensee

b. A copy of the MLS listing agreement signed by both parties

c. Written notice of the licensee appointments

d. Verbal confirmation of the appointments at the first showing

29. Which of the following is a valid reason a licensee might choose NOT to pursue an agency relationship with a prospective client?

a. The prospective client wants to use a standard TREC contract form

b. The prospective client requests that the licensee present all offers, including low ones

c. The buyer is legally unable to contract because they are a minor

d. The seller wants to list the property at exactly the appraised value

CHAPTER 2

BASIC AGENCY RELATIONSHIPS, DISCLOSURES AND DUTIES TO THE CLIENT

Chapter Objectives

After completing this chapter, you should be able to:

1. Define agency and describe the three classifications of agency used in Texas real estate.
2. Explain the responsibilities of each party in an agency relationship, including the broker, affiliated licensees, sellers, and buyers.
3. Describe the scope of the broker's authority and the practical limits of that authority.
4. Identify the broker's responsibilities to affiliated licensees, the community, the industry, and TREC.
5. Explain when and how an agency relationship should be terminated, and when the broker's authority ends.
6. Identify and explain each of the five fiduciary duties a Texas licensee owes to a client.
7. Describe an agent's disclosure obligations, including what must be disclosed for both seller and buyer clients.
8. Distinguish between the level of service provided to a client and the level of service provided to a customer.
9. Explain the principal's duties to the agent and the scope of the broker's authority under a listing agreement.
10. Identify additional disclosure requirements, including disclosure of relationships, multiple offers, commission splits, and the recommendation to retain an attorney.

Contents

Limitations of Broker's Authority

Client Liability

Broker Non-Responsibility

Broker Responsibility to Others

When to Withdraw from Agency

When Authority Ends

Fiduciary Duties

Disclosure Duties

Levels of Service

Buyer-Client Disclosure

Principal's Duties to the Agent

Agency Disclosure

Broker Authority

Seller's Expectations

Buyer's Expectations

Disclosure of Relationships

Disclosure of Multiple Offers

Disclosure of Commission Splits

Recommendation to Retain an Attorney

Agency Defined

An agent is any person who represents the interests of another person, called the client or principal, in dealings with third parties. Agency relationships allow people to hire a professional to accomplish tasks they either lack the expertise to do themselves or simply prefer to delegate to someone more qualified.

All agency relationships share two foundational characteristics:

Expert Reliance: The principal trusts the agent as a professional whose advice and counsel can be relied upon.

Fiduciary Responsibility: Because the relationship involves money or property, the agent must always act in the principal's best financial interest. The agent is often referred to simply as a fiduciary.

In real estate specifically, a salesperson may be an agent for a broker, and a broker may be an agent for a buyer, a seller, or, under specific conditions, both. To navigate this complexity clearly, it helps to understand the three recognized classifications of agency.

> ***Important:*** *A licensee is NOT an agent simply by virtue of holding a license. A licensee only becomes an agent when an agency relationship is formally established. Even then, it is the broker*

> *who is the legal agent of the client. All licensees in the office are agents of the broker and, as such, share the same obligations to the principal as the broker does.*

Classifications of Agency

Agency in Texas real estate is classified into three categories: universal, general, and special. Each classification carries its own set of duties, responsibilities, and liabilities for both the agent and the principal. Understanding the scope of each classification will help you conduct your business clearly and within the boundaries the law requires.

Universal Agency

Universal agency is the broadest form of agency. In a universal agency, a person or a court grants an agent full control over another person's life and property to meet a specific need. This authority is created through a power of attorney, and the person receiving that authority is called the attorney-in-fact.

A common example: a person becomes medically incapacitated and has no family available. A court may appoint a guardian with power of attorney to sign medical documents, pay bills, and sell real estate on the person's behalf. Similarly, an aging parent might grant a child power of attorney to manage the parent's affairs.

A principal may have only one universal agent. The duties a universal agent may carry out include:

- Acquiring and disposing of assets
- Disbursing the principal's funds
- Entering into contracts on the principal's behalf

The principal is accountable for the actions of their universal agent, and the agent owes a fiduciary duty to act in the principal's best interest without placing the principal at unnecessary risk. Universal agency is rare in standard real estate practice because brokers never hold full control over a client's decision-making. All final decisions remain with the client.

General Agency

In a general agency, the principal delegates broad, ongoing authority to an agent to handle a range of tasks within a particular business or enterprise. This delegation may include the authority to enter into certain contracts. In Texas real estate, general agency is most commonly seen in the relationship between a broker and their affiliated licensees, and it is formalized through the independent contractor agreement.

Under a general agency, a broker authorizes their licensees to perform a wide range of activities on behalf of the brokerage and its clients, including:

- Listing properties
- Showing properties to prospective buyers
- Conducting marketing and advertising activities on the firm's behalf
- Entering into buyer representation agreements
- Preparing, presenting, and negotiating offers to purchase
- Initiating and preparing documents needed for closing
- Maintaining transaction files for all completed or terminated transactions

The scope of authority granted under general agency is significant. As the principal in this relationship, the broker is liable for the actions of all their licensees. If a licensee performs any act that is illegal or improper while operating under the authority of the general agency relationship, the broker bears responsibility for that act. Texas law explicitly holds brokers accountable for the conduct of their affiliated licensees acting within the scope of their independent contractor agreements.

General agency also arises in property management. A property management agreement specifies what tasks the property manager is authorized to perform for the owner, typically including negotiating leases, contracting for maintenance, and initiating eviction proceedings when necessary.

Special Agency

Special agency, also called limited agency, is the most common form of agency in Texas real estate transactions between a broker and their clients. In a special agency, the principal authorizes the broker to accomplish one specific task. Once that task is complete, the agency relationship terminates. In most cases, a special agent may not bind the principal to a contract.

Listing agreements and buyer representation agreements both create special agency relationships, because the broker's authority is limited to what is defined within those agreements.

For a **seller-client**, the broker's task is to procure a ready, willing, and able buyer. In pursuit of that goal, the broker may market the property, conduct showings, advise on staging, and negotiate offers. However, the broker has no authority to sign any contracts on the seller's behalf, accept an offer for the seller, authorize changes to an offer, or allow a buyer to move into the property before closing.

For a **buyer-client**, the broker's task is to locate a suitable property and negotiate the best possible price and terms. The broker assists throughout the process but, again, has no authority to sign or accept contracts on the buyer's behalf. All final decisions rest with the client.

Authority of the Agent

In most real estate transactions, two types of agency exist simultaneously within a brokerage:

- The broker holds **special agency** relationships with clients, created through listing agreements and buyer representation agreements.

- The broker holds **general agency** relationships with their affiliated licensees, created through independent contractor agreements.

Because the licensees are general agents of the broker, the authority created by the broker's special agency with a client flows down to every licensee in the office. When a client hires a brokerage, they are, in effect, being served by the entire team operating under the broker's authority.

Broker Responsibility to Clients

When a special agency is created with a client, the broker is obligated to prioritize the client's needs above all others, including the broker's own interests. The Texas Real Estate License Act (TRELA) places the burden of accountability squarely on the broker, even when a licensee in the office is the primary point of contact with the client.

Specifically, the broker must:

- Deal fairly and honestly with all parties, including customers who are not clients.
- Negotiate on behalf of the client throughout the transaction.
- Proactively communicate material information the client may not know they need in order to make an informed decision.
- Communicate with licensees and customers who present offers on a seller-client's property.
- Negotiate on behalf of a buyer-client when the broker represents the buyer.

The broker can be held accountable for problems that arise within the transaction, but only for those things within the broker's control. For example, TREC will not hold a broker responsible for the actions of a loan officer, but it will hold the broker responsible for the conduct of affiliated licensees, the quality of training provided to them, and the adequacy of the broker's supervisory practices.

Licensee Responsibility

Although the broker is ultimately responsible for all office activity, every licensee represents the broker and therefore carries the same responsibilities to the client that the broker does. In many transactions, the licensee is the only person from the office who has direct contact with the client, and in some cases the broker never personally meets the client being represented.

The licensee must inform and guide the client throughout the entire transaction, with the goal of securing the best possible outcome. Even when interacting with a customer (a party not represented by the broker), the licensee must still conduct themselves in a manner consistent with their role as the client's representative.

If a client files a complaint with TREC, both the licensee and the broker face potential disciplinary consequences. The range of possible sanctions runs from a written warning placed in the licensee's file all the way to full license revocation, depending on the severity of the violation.

Seller-Client Responsibility

The agency relationship is a two-way street. The broker relies on the seller-client to provide accurate, truthful information about the property. When the seller completes the Seller's Disclosure Notice of Property Condition, the broker should be able to trust that the information is complete and honest. That said, a careful licensee will always walk through the property and compare their own observations with the disclosure form, in case the seller overlooked or omitted something significant.

The seller is also expected to negotiate in good faith and avoid making unreasonable demands of the buyer or the listing agent.

The seller has a financial obligation to the broker as well. Once the broker fulfills the terms of the listing agreement, typically by producing a ready, willing, and able buyer, the seller owes the agreed commission. If that promise to pay was made in writing (as it always should be, and as Texas listing agreements require), the broker can pursue the commission through the courts if necessary. An oral promise to pay commission carries no legal weight in Texas courts.

> ***Practical Note:*** *Standard Texas listing agreements include a provision for the broker's compensation. An oral-only commission agreement should never occur in a properly documented Texas real estate transaction.*

Buyer-Client Responsibility

When a buyer enters into a buyer representation agreement in Texas, they are agreeing to an exclusive arrangement with the broker. This means the buyer may not simultaneously enter into another representation agreement with a different broker for the purpose of purchasing a home.

The buyer representation agreement specifies how the broker's compensation will be calculated, typically as a percentage of the sales price. Under the agreement, the broker will first seek to obtain that compensation from the seller and the listing broker. If, for any reason, the listing side does not pay the full amount, the buyer-client is responsible for covering any shortfall up to the agreed amount.

Under the 2024 NAR settlement rules adopted in Texas, compensation offered to a buyer's broker may no longer be communicated through the MLS. **All compensation arrangements must be negotiated and documented in the buyer representation agreement before any properties are shown.** This makes it essential that the licensee clearly explain the compensation terms, and the exclusive nature of the agreement, before the buyer signs.

Buyers often do not read every line of the agreement carefully and depend on the licensee to walk them through the key provisions. A licensee who fails to explain the compensation and exclusivity terms clearly should not be surprised if confusion later leads to a complaint filed with TREC. Clear, upfront communication is both a professional obligation and a practical protection.

Practical Applications of Authority

Understanding what a broker can and cannot do under special agency is essential to avoiding liability. Even when an offer is perfect, such as full price with no contingencies, the broker does not have the authority to accept it on the seller's behalf. The client is always the decision maker. The following actions are outside the broker's authority under a standard special agency arrangement:

- Accepting any offer on a listing, regardless of price. Only the owner has that authority.
- Allowing a buyer to move into the property before closing without the owner's explicit permission.
- Submitting an offer on a property on a buyer-client's behalf without the client's prior authorization.

The only circumstance under which a broker could take these kinds of actions is if the client granted the broker a power of attorney, which would convert the relationship to a universal agency. This is an unusual arrangement and would typically only occur if the client were a close family member or faced a situation preventing them from participating directly.

The broker's role is to present the client with a clear set of options and, where appropriate, offer a professional recommendation. But the decision always belongs to the client. There will be times when a broker disagrees with a client's choice, for example when a buyer-client wants to accept a counteroffer the broker believes leaves money on the table. After providing advice, the broker must set their personal feelings aside and carry out the client's decision.

Broker's Authority in Property Management

When a broker takes on a property management role, their agency relationship is with the property owner, who is the client. The tenant is a customer, a third party outside the agency relationship, and not a client.

The property management agreement defines what the broker is authorized to do on the owner's behalf. Typical authority granted to a property manager includes:

- Marketing the property and taking applications for leases.
- Committing the owner to a particular tenant, provided the tenant meets criteria previously established with the owner (such as rent amount, financial qualifications, and rental history).
- Ordering emergency repairs before notifying the owner when immediate action is needed, such as a burst pipe.

For larger properties or portfolios, the property manager may also have authority to:

- Supervise a maintenance crew or on-site management office.

- Budget income and pay operating expenses on the owner's behalf, including debt service, utilities, insurance, and property taxes.

Full budgeting authority is less common when managing individual single-family residences, and more typical for larger multi-unit or commercial properties.

Broker's Authority When Representing Buyers

In the early stages of a buyer representation relationship, the broker's primary task is simply to show properties that match the buyer's needs, the same activity the broker would perform for a buyer-customer. The difference becomes significant once the buyer-client has identified a property they want to pursue.

At that point, the broker shifts into active advocacy mode. The broker will:

- Prepare a comparative market analysis (CMA) on comparable sold properties to help the buyer understand current market value.
- Help the buyer develop a negotiation strategy designed to get the property under contract at favorable terms.
- Adjust the strategy as the negotiation evolves, responding to the listing agent's and seller's positions.
- Continue searching for alternative properties if negotiations break down.

Both the buyer's agent and the listing agent understand the negotiation dynamic well: the listing agent has typically built some flexibility into the asking price, and the buyer's agent is not expected to open with a full-price offer. Through the back-and-forth of negotiation, guided by the decision-making authority of their respective clients, both agents work toward a meeting of the minds.

> ***Important:*** *Once a transaction closes, the broker's authority ends. The one exception is the duty of confidentiality, which continues indefinitely. Information shared by a client during the agency relationship must be kept confidential even after the transaction is complete.*

Limitations of Broker's Authority

The broker's duty to represent the client does not extend to doing whatever the client asks. Some client requests cross ethical and legal boundaries that no licensee may fulfill, regardless of the client's wishes.

Limitations When Working with Seller-Clients

A seller may occasionally ask the broker to take actions that are prohibited by law or professional ethics. The following are clear examples of requests a broker must refuse:

- A seller may ask the broker to conceal a known defect in the property. The broker cannot do this. Material defects must be disclosed.
- A seller may ask the broker to refuse offers from buyers of a particular race, religion, national origin, sex, disability, or familial status. The broker cannot do this. Such discrimination is a direct violation of the Federal Fair Housing Act and Texas law.
- A seller may ask the broker to hide the transaction from the IRS. This falls outside the broker's responsibility and is not something the broker should assist with.

Limitations When Working with Buyer-Clients

Buyers sometimes make requests that are also outside the bounds of what a broker may legally do. For example, some buyers do not want a sale to appear in the local Multiple Listing Service (MLS), concerned that it might prompt the tax office to reassess the property and raise taxes. Most MLS systems impose monetary fines on agents who withhold required sale information.

There is one action a buyer's agent is permitted to take that may seem unusual: concealing the buyer's identity from the seller. This is done by writing another name as the buyer in the contract, followed by the phrase "and/or assigns." This means the named buyer may assign the contract to another party before closing. This technique is legally permissible in Texas and may be used when the buyer has a legitimate reason for privacy.

Client Liability

Clients can be held liable for the actions of their broker and the broker's licensees, particularly when the client was aware of misconduct and failed to correct it. If a seller knew that a licensee was misrepresenting the condition of the property and said nothing, the seller may share liability alongside the licensee.

This underscores an important obligation for both sellers and buyers: correct your agent immediately when they say something that is inaccurate or potentially misleading. Doing so benefits everyone, as it ensures the licensee is working with accurate information and protects the client from later claims that they knowingly allowed false information to stand.

A client may also bear responsibility for paying the broker's commission even if a transaction falls through, depending on the circumstances. If the broker presents the seller with a ready, willing, and able buyer, or presents the buyer with the property they have been seeking, and the transaction fails for reasons unrelated to the broker's performance, the client may still owe the commission.

The extent of a client's liability is largely shaped by their own honesty and the professional competence of the licensee they chose to work with.

Broker Non-Responsibility

While brokers carry significant responsibility, there are clear circumstances under which a broker is not held accountable for problems that arise in a transaction.

Statements Made by Third Parties

A broker is not responsible for information communicated to a client or customer by someone else, such as a neighbor, another professional, or a party to the transaction, unless a reasonable person in the broker's position should have known that the information was inaccurate. The "reasonable person" standard is the key: if the broker had no way of knowing the information was wrong, they are generally not liable for it.

Protecting Confidential Client Information

A broker is not only not required to share confidential client information. Doing so would actually be a breach of fiduciary duty. For example, if a listing agent knows the seller will accept $20,000 less than the listed price, that agent is under no obligation to share that with a buyer. In fact, volunteering that information would be a serious violation of the agent's loyalty to the seller.

Relying on Published Sources

When a broker provides information that comes from a published source, such as the MLS, an appraisal district record, or a tax statement, and cites that source clearly, the broker is generally protected if the information later proves to be inaccurate. For example, if a buyer asks about the square footage of a home and the broker responds, "According to the appraisal district, the square footage is 1,500 square feet," the broker has acted appropriately. If the figure is wrong and no reasonable person would have detected the error, liability does not attach to the broker.

Client Misrepresentations During Showings

A broker cannot be held responsible for false or inaccurate statements made directly by the client during a showing. For example, if a buyer asks the seller, who happens to be present at the showing, about the age of an appliance, and the seller gives incorrect information, that error cannot reasonably be attributed to the broker. The broker is entitled to rely on the truthfulness of their client.

Broker Responsibility to Others

A broker's professional obligations extend beyond their clients. Texas licensees also carry responsibilities to the people they work with, the communities they serve, the broader real estate industry, and the regulatory body that governs the profession.

Responsibility to Affiliated Licensees

The broker is responsible for adequately training and supervising every licensee working under their sponsorship. This responsibility does not end after initial onboarding. It is ongoing.

Practical ways a broker can fulfill this responsibility include:

- Staying current with industry publications and sharing relevant articles with affiliated licensees, such as by email or through a shared bulletin board.
- Reviewing listing agreements, buyer representation agreements, MLS entries, and contracts for accuracy and potential errors.
- Monitoring affiliated licensees' license expiration dates and reminding them of upcoming renewals and continuing education requirements.

Responsibility to the Community

Real estate professionals have both the opportunity and the informal obligation to strengthen the communities where they work. Licensees who are active in their community build goodwill and reputation. Examples include organizing neighborhood cleanup efforts, volunteering at local organizations, adopting a highway section for trash pickup, or helping homeowners in a specific area make basic improvements that raise property values.

These activities benefit the community and, in return, build the licensee's and the brokerage's reputation throughout the market area.

Responsibility to the Industry

The real estate industry depends on the engagement and investment of its practitioners. Brokers and salespersons have opportunities to participate at the local board level, through the Texas Association of REALTORS®, and even at the national level through the National Association of REALTORS®.

Serving on committees, contributing to political action committees, or simply being an active member of a professional organization helps improve standards, protect consumer rights, and shape the laws and rules that govern the industry. Active participation should generally be pursued once a licensee is financially stable enough to dedicate time away from their primary business activities.

Responsibility to TREC

Every Texas licensee is responsible for keeping their license current, complying with license laws and statutes, and responding to any complaints filed against them.

Brokers have additional TREC obligations, which may include:

- Maintaining a corporate license for an "S" corporation or LLC if the brokerage operates under that structure.
- Filing a "doing business as" (DBA) name with TREC if applicable.

- Staying current with changes in Texas real estate law and the TREC forms used in the office.
- Responding promptly to any complaint filed against the brokerage or affiliated licensees.
- Submitting sponsorship forms to TREC as soon as a new licensee joins the office.
- Returning a licensee's license to TREC immediately when the independent contractor agreement ends or when the licensee requests their license be released.

When to Withdraw from Agency

Once an agency relationship is established, it is not easily or casually ended. However, there are circumstances where continuing the relationship would require the broker or licensee to violate the law, and in those cases, termination of the agency is not just appropriate but necessary.

When a Client Requests Illegal Actions

If a client asks the broker or licensee to break the law, the first step is education, clearly explaining what the licensee can and cannot do, and why. If the client persists in demanding illegal conduct, the broker must seriously consider withdrawing from the agency relationship. This applies equally to sellers and buyers.

Common examples where withdrawal may be required:

- A seller insists the licensee conceal a material defect from prospective buyers.
- A buyer asks the licensee to violate Fair Housing laws by filtering out certain types of sellers or neighborhoods based on protected class characteristics.

When a Buyer Refuses to Cooperate

A broker may also have grounds to end a buyer representation relationship if the buyer consistently refuses to take basic steps necessary for the transaction to move forward. The most common example is a buyer who will not seek pre-qualification for a loan. Some buyers claim they have cash funds to purchase and therefore do not need lender pre-qualification, but even in those cases, a broker should request a letter confirming availability of certified funds so that negotiations can proceed with credibility.

If a buyer refuses even that basic request, the licensee must make a practical judgment: is this person genuinely committed to purchasing a property, and are they likely to remain with this broker when they do? If the answer to either question is no, it may be time to end the relationship.

When Authority Ends

The broker's authority, and the agency relationship itself, ends when the transaction is complete. At that point, the broker has no ongoing obligation to continue providing services to the former client.

There is one important exception: the duty of confidentiality survives the end of the agency relationship permanently. Information the client shared during the representation must be kept confidential forever, even after the transaction has closed and the agency has ended.

After a transaction closes, good brokers take several additional steps:

- Enter the former client into a long-term marketing plan to maintain the relationship, generate referrals, and position the brokerage for future transactions.
- Securely file all transaction records to prevent unauthorized access. Transaction files contain sensitive property and financial information that could be misused to fraudulently sell or lease a property.
- If a member of the MLS, enter the completed sale into the system so that other licensees can use the data for future market analyses. This sale information may also be transmitted to the county tax assessor's office, potentially triggering a reassessment of the property's value.

Fiduciary Duties

An agency relationship imposes fiduciary duties on both the client and the agent, though the heavier burden falls on the agent. These duties are moral and ethical in nature, but they are also legal obligations enforceable under the law of agency.

The five duties a Texas licensee owes to their principal are commonly referred to by the acronym COALD:

Care: Reasonable care, skill, and diligence in representing the client.

Obedience: Following the client's lawful instructions in good faith.

Accountability: Accounting for all money, documents, and property received from the client.

Loyalty: Placing the client's interests above all others, including the agent's own.

Disclosure: Informing the client of all facts that could affect the client's interests.

Each of these duties is explained in detail in the sections that follow.

Care

Texas law requires that an agent perform their duties with a reasonable degree of care, skill, and diligence. Because the client hires a licensee specifically for their professional expertise, the client is entitled to have that expertise applied fully on their behalf.

When representing a seller, exercising reasonable care includes:

- Helping the seller set a realistic and competitive asking price.
- Discovering and disclosing facts that could affect the seller's position.

- Presenting contracts properly and completely.
- Marketing the property effectively.
- Helping the seller evaluate and respond to purchase offers.

When representing a buyer, exercising reasonable care includes:

- Helping the buyer locate housing that fits their needs.
- Evaluating property values and identifying property condition issues.
- Researching and presenting financing alternatives.
- Preparing and presenting offers and counteroffers with the buyer's best interests in mind.

A licensee who fails to exercise reasonable care in representing a client may be found guilty of negligence and held liable for any resulting financial loss to the client.

Obedience

The duty of obedience requires the agent to act in good faith and follow the client's instructions as set out in the agency agreement, provided those instructions are legal.

For example, an agent may honor a seller's instruction that the property not be shown on Sundays. However, the agent may not follow instructions that violate Fair Housing laws or that direct the agent to conceal a known defect in the property. No agency agreement can authorize illegal conduct.

If a client insists on a directive that is illegal and refuses to remove it, the agent should withdraw from the relationship rather than comply.

Accountability

The duty of accountability requires the agent to maintain a full and accurate accounting of all money, documents, and other property received on behalf of the client.

Brokers are also required to provide copies of all relevant documents to everyone affected by them and to retain those documents for at least three years, in compliance with Texas law.

Loyalty

The duty of loyalty requires the agent to place the client's interests above all others, including their own financial interests. When negotiating on a client's behalf, the licensee must not allow their compensation to influence their recommendations or actions. A licensee is also required to disclose any personal interest they hold in a property involved in a transaction.

Confidentiality is a key component of loyalty. What an agent learns about a client during the course of the relationship must be protected. Specifically:

For a seller-client, the agent may not disclose without the seller's express permission:

- The seller's willingness to accept an offer lower than the asking price.
- The seller's urgency or anxiety to sell.

For a buyer-client, the agent may not disclose without the buyer's express permission:

- The buyer's willingness to pay more than the asking price.
- The buyer's urgency or desire to move quickly.

In both cases, however, the agent is still required to disclose material facts about the property itself. When confidentiality conflicts with the legal duty to disclose, the agent must inform the client of the conflict. If the conflict cannot be resolved, the agent must withdraw from the relationship.

> ***Important:*** *The duty of confidentiality does not end when the transaction closes. Personal information learned during the agency relationship must remain confidential permanently, long after the agency itself has terminated.*

Disclosure

The duty of disclosure requires the agent to inform the client of all facts that might affect the client's interests in the transaction. This includes facts the agent knows and facts the agent should have known through the exercise of reasonable care.

The agent is responsible for actively discovering information that a client would consider important to an informed decision, regardless of whether that information favors the client's position. Failure to disclose such information can result in liability for damages.

A common "should have known" scenario: a crack in a foundation or wall that the agent failed to notice during a walkthrough. If the defect later causes damage, a court may find that a reasonably skilled agent would have noticed and disclosed it.

Disclosure Duties

The specific items an agent must disclose depend on whether they are representing the seller or the buyer.

Disclosure Duties When Representing a Seller

An agent representing a seller has a duty to disclose to the seller:

- All purchase offers received on the property.
- The identity of prospective buyers and any relationship the agent may have with them.

- The buyer's financial ability to complete the transaction.
- Any indication that the buyer may be able to offer a higher price.
- The buyer's intention to resell the property for a profit.

Disclosure Duties When Representing a Buyer

An agent representing a buyer has a duty to disclose to the buyer:

- Known deficiencies in the property.
- Any contract provisions or financing terms that are not in the buyer's best interest.
- How long the property has been listed on the market.
- The seller's reason for selling, if known.

There is no obligation to obtain or disclose information about a party's race, creed, color, religion, sex, or national origin. Anti-discrimination laws make such information entirely immaterial to any real estate transaction.

Texas requires sellers to provide prospective buyers with a written disclosure of property condition using the **Seller's Disclosure of Property Condition** form. This disclosure may reduce but does not necessarily eliminate the agent's own disclosure obligations.

Levels of Service

Licensees work with two types of people: clients, who are represented by the broker under a written agency agreement, and customers, who receive services but are not represented. The level of service provided to each is significantly different.

A client relationship is created through a written agreement, typically a listing agreement with a seller or a buyer representation agreement with a buyer. Under that agreement, the agent owes the client full fiduciary duties and can provide professional advice, counsel, and strategic guidance.

A customer, by contrast, receives factual information from the licensee but does not receive advice, opinions, or advocacy. The licensee provides facts to a customer and strategy to a client.

> ***One important limit:*** *A licensee may not provide legal advice to anyone, client or customer, unless the licensee also holds a separate license to practice law. Recommending that clients and customers consult an attorney is not only appropriate but required.*

In short: the agent works for the client and with the customer.

Buyer-Client Disclosure

A buyer who is represented as a client receives everything a buyer-customer receives regarding property condition, plus a great deal more. The expanded disclosure and service that come with client representation include:

- A comparative market analysis showing what similar properties have recently sold for in the area.
- A negotiation strategy designed to achieve an acceptable purchase price.
- Information on how long the property has been listed, whether the seller may accept less than the asking price, and the seller's reason for selling, if known.
- Active attention to every detail of the transaction, managed in a way that is designed to save the buyer money, time, and effort.

When a buyer has signed a representation agreement, the buyer becomes the agent's primary focus. The buyer is in a stronger negotiating position and can make decisions with confidence, knowing the agent is proactively disclosing everything relevant to the purchase.

There is also a practical benefit for the licensee. With a signed buyer representation agreement in place, the licensee can invest their time and energy in this client without concern that the buyer will quietly move on to another broker before the transaction closes.

Principal's Duties to the Agent

The agency relationship is not one-sided. Just as the agent owes duties to the principal, the principal has obligations to the agent that are necessary for the relationship to function effectively.

Availability: Because a special agency limits the agent's decision-making authority, the principal must remain available for consultation and decision-making throughout the transaction. If the principal is unreachable when decisions need to be made, the agent cannot complete the job.

Information: The principal must give the agent enough information to carry out the agreed tasks effectively. This typically includes property data, financial information, and the client's timing requirements or deadlines.

Compensation: If the agency agreement includes a compensation provision and the agent performs as agreed, the principal is obligated to pay. Note, however, that compensation is not inherent to the agency relationship itself. Gratuitous agency is possible, though fiduciary duties still apply.

Agency Disclosure

Texas law requires that a licensee provide a written disclosure statement to any party to a real estate transaction at the time of the first substantive dialogue. This statement, known as the Information About

Brokerage Services, explains in general terms the representation options available under Texas law: seller's agent, buyer's agent, and intermediary, and when a license holder may work with a party without representing them.

The form does not require signatures, dates, or the licensee's name, but it must be printed in at least 10-point type.

When the Disclosure Is Not Required

The written disclosure is not required in two situations:

- The transaction involves a residential lease of one year or less and a sale is not being considered.
- The licensee is meeting with a party who is already represented by another licensee.

What "Substantive Dialogue" Means

"Substantive dialogue" means any meeting or written communication involving a meaningful discussion about a specific property. It does not include:

- A meeting that occurs at an open house.
- A meeting or written communication that occurs after the parties have already signed a contract to buy, sell, or lease the property.

Broker Authority

An agent is authorized to perform only those activities the principal permits. In most Texas real estate transactions, the broker is a special agent, meaning the scope of authority does not extend beyond what is defined in the listing or buyer representation agreement.

What the Broker Is NOT Authorized to Do

Even when representing a seller, the broker generally does not have authority to:

- Sign any contract on the seller's behalf.
- Initial changes to an offer.
- Permit a buyer to take early occupancy of the property.

What the Broker IS Authorized to Do

The listing agreement typically authorizes the broker to:

- Place a sign on the property.
- Advertise the property.
- Show the property to prospective buyers.
- Cooperate with other brokers.
- Enter the property into a Multiple Listing Service (MLS).
- Accept earnest money deposits.

Brokers also have implied authority to perform customary tasks not explicitly listed in the agreement, when those tasks are reasonably necessary to achieve the agreement's purpose. Holding an open house through a salesperson is a common example.

Seller's Expectations

Many sellers begin a listing relationship without a clear picture of everything a broker actually does on their behalf. What most sellers are certain of is that they want the property sold and they want the proceeds available for their next move. When asked directly, most sellers say the same thing: they want top dollar and they want it quickly. Most licensees align with that goal, since their commission is tied to both the price and the speed of the sale.

What sellers also want, even if they do not articulate it directly, is protection. No seller wants to end up defending their actions in a courtroom, receiving demand letters from attorneys, or returning part of their proceeds to settle a lawsuit. The seller's own honesty in completing the Seller's Disclosure of Property Condition is a major factor in whether problems arise after closing. A seller who discloses everything they know about the property's condition significantly reduces their exposure to post-closing claims.

The licensee plays an equally important role in this protection. A professional who handles every step with skill and integrity is the seller's best defense against complaints and litigation. Doing the job right is not just good ethics; it is the most effective risk management available.

Buyer's Expectations

Every buyer, whether a customer or a represented client, wants to find a property that meets their needs at a fair price. When a buyer becomes a client by signing a representation agreement, their expectations rise accordingly. Most buyers have limited experience with formal buyer agency, but they understand clearly that they want professional guidance and they want to avoid overpaying.

Much of what a buyer's agent does on the client's behalf happens behind the scenes during negotiations. The buyer may not always see or fully appreciate the agent's work. There is also an interesting dynamic in buyer representation: a highly skilled negotiator who secures a lower purchase price for the buyer may actually earn a slightly lower commission, since many commission structures are tied to the sales price. A lower price means a lower commission.

This is simply the nature of the work. Buyers who feel they were well-represented and received a fair deal become the most valuable referral sources an agent can have. The professional standard is to focus on the client's outcome, not the commission figure. In virtually every transaction, a skilled licensee takes steps on the client's behalf that the client never fully sees, and that is exactly how it should be.

Disclosure of Relationships

A client has the right to know if the licensee has a personal or professional relationship with any other party to the transaction. Any relationship that could reasonably be perceived as a conflict of interest must be disclosed.

Examples of relationships requiring disclosure include:

- The listing agent is related to the prospective buyer.
- The buyer's agent is writing an offer on a property owned by someone they know personally, such as a former spouse or business associate.
- The agent is representing the buyer and the seller happens to be the broker who owns the office where the agent works.
- The listing agent is also representing the buyer in the same transaction.

In every case, both parties affected by the relationship have the right to know about it. Transparency protects the client, protects the licensee, and demonstrates the professionalism the public expects from licensed real estate practitioners.

Disclosure of Multiple Offers

When more than one offer is received on the same listing, the listing agent must notify all buyers that competing offers exist, without revealing the specific terms or content of any individual offer. This notification gives each buyer an opportunity to strengthen their bid if they choose to do so, and gives their agents time to develop a strategy.

The listing agent must present all offers to the seller-client promptly and advise the seller on how to evaluate each one. Together, the agent and seller develop a plan for how to respond, whether by accepting one offer, countering one offer, or allowing the competition to continue.

A critical rule: the seller may not issue counteroffers to all buyers simultaneously. If every buyer accepted, the property would effectively be sold multiple times, which is not legally permissible.

Equally important: sharing the content or terms of one buyer's offer with a competing buyer is called "shopping an offer" and is a serious breach of the listing agent's fiduciary duty to the seller. All buyers must be treated fairly and kept on equal footing throughout the process.

Disclosure of Commission Splits

Brokers are required to inform their clients about how the commission will be divided with other brokers involved in the transaction. This is not a disclosure about the internal split between the broker and their affiliated licensees; it is a disclosure about how the listing broker will share the commission with a cooperating broker who represents the buyer.

Historically, an informal 50/50 split between the listing and selling offices was standard practice. That norm has shifted considerably, and brokers today make their own decisions about how much of the commission to offer to cooperating brokers.

Under the NAR settlement rules adopted in Texas, compensation offered to a buyer's broker may no longer be advertised through the MLS. **Instead, buyer broker compensation must be negotiated and documented in the buyer representation agreement before any properties are shown.** This change places greater responsibility on licensees to have transparent compensation conversations with their clients at the beginning of the relationship.

The seller has the right to know how the commission will be distributed before signing a listing agreement. This allows the seller to make an informed decision about which broker to hire, understanding how competitive that broker's cooperation structure will be with buyers' agents in the market.

Recommendation to Retain an Attorney

Texas licensees are prohibited from providing legal advice unless they are also licensed attorneys. This prohibition exists even when a licensee has processed many transactions and has become familiar with contract language over time. Practical familiarity with contract forms is not the same as the legal training required to interpret and advise on legal matters.

Licensees are required to recommend to all buyers and sellers that they consult a licensed attorney. This recommendation is built into the transaction process through the Texas earnest money contract, which includes a designated line for the buyer's attorney and a corresponding prompt for the seller's attorney when the offer is presented. These fields serve as a reminder for the licensee to raise the topic with each party at the appropriate time.

Most standard contract provisions are straightforward. Issues with down payment, loan amount, pricing, survey responsibilities, and title policy coverage are familiar ground for experienced licensees. The most common source of confusion arises in the Special Provisions paragraph, where buyers sometimes make non-standard requests that do not fit any pre-printed section of the contract. When unusual language appears in a Special Provisions paragraph, the wise listing agent will seek clarification from the buyer's agent before presenting the offer to the seller, to ensure the seller fully understands what is being proposed.

Chapter 2 Snapshot Review

Agency Defined

1. An agent represents a principal's interests in transactions with others. All agency relationships rest on two foundations: the principal's trust in the agent's expertise, and the agent's fiduciary duty to act in the principal's best financial interest.
2. A licensee is not an agent simply by holding a license. Agency only exists once a formal relationship is established. The broker is the client's agent; licensees are agents of the broker.

The Three Classifications of Agency

Universal Agency: Created by power of attorney; grants the agent full control over a principal's affairs. Rare in real estate. The person holding this authority is the attorney-in-fact.

General Agency: Broad, ongoing authority. Most common between brokers and affiliated licensees, formalized through the independent contractor agreement. Also used in property management.

Special Agency: Authority to complete one specific task; the most common form in Texas real estate transactions. Created by listing agreements and buyer representation agreements. Terminates when the task is complete.

Broker and Licensee Responsibilities

1. The broker must prioritize the client's needs above all others, negotiate on the client's behalf, and disclose material information the client needs to make informed decisions.
2. Licensees carry the same responsibilities to the client as the broker does, because they act as agents of the broker.
3. If a complaint is filed with TREC, both the licensee and the broker are at risk of disciplinary action, up to and including license revocation.

Limits of Broker Authority

1. The broker cannot accept offers, authorize a buyer to move in before closing, or submit an offer without client authorization. All final decisions belong to the client.
2. The broker cannot conceal property defects, discriminate against buyers based on protected class characteristics, or assist in hiding a transaction from the IRS.
3. The broker is not liable for statements made by third parties (unless a reasonable person should have known the information was wrong), for keeping client information confidential, or for a client's own misrepresentations during showings.

Broader Responsibilities

1. Brokers are responsible for training and supervising affiliated licensees, reviewing their agreements and documents, and monitoring license renewal deadlines.

2. Licensees have responsibilities to the community they serve, to the real estate industry, and to TREC.
3. If a client requests illegal conduct, the broker must educate the client about legal limits. If the client persists, the broker should withdraw from the agency.
4. When a transaction closes, the agency ends, but the duty of confidentiality continues permanently.

The Five Fiduciary Duties (COALD)

Care: Perform all duties with reasonable skill, diligence, and expertise. Failure to exercise reasonable care can result in a finding of negligence.

Obedience: Follow the client's lawful instructions in good faith. Do not follow instructions that are illegal, discriminatory, or that require concealing a defect.

Accountability: Account for all funds, documents, and property received. Retain copies of all transaction documents for at least three years.

Loyalty: Place the client's interests above all others, including your own. Keep client information confidential, both during and after the agency relationship.

Disclosure: Inform the client of all known and reasonably discoverable facts that could affect the client's decision-making.

Key Disclosure Rules

1. The duty of confidentiality survives the end of the agency relationship permanently.
2. Agents representing sellers must disclose all offers, buyer identities, buyer relationships, and buyer financial capacity to the seller.
3. Agents representing buyers must disclose known property deficiencies, unfavorable contract terms, time on market, and the seller's reason for selling.
4. Agents provide advice and counsel to clients. They provide factual information to customers, but no advice or strategic guidance.
5. The Texas Seller's Disclosure of Property Condition form is required in Texas. It may reduce but does not eliminate the agent's own disclosure obligations.

Agency Disclosure Requirements

1. The TREC Information About Brokerage Services form must be provided at the time of first substantive dialogue.
2. The form does not require signatures or dates but must be printed in at least 10-point type.
3. The disclosure is not required for short-term residential leases or when the party is already represented by another licensee.
4. Substantive dialogue means a meaningful discussion about a specific property. It does not include open house conversations or communications after a contract is already signed.

Broker Authority

1. Brokers operating under special agency may not sign contracts, initial offer changes, or permit early occupancy without explicit client authorization.
2. Standard listing agreement authority includes placing signs, advertising, showing the property, cooperating with other brokers, using the MLS, and accepting earnest money.
3. Brokers also have implied authority for customary tasks not listed in the agreement, such as holding open houses.

Additional Disclosure Requirements

1. Any personal or professional relationship with another party to the transaction must be disclosed to the client.
2. When multiple offers exist, all buyers must be notified of competing offers without revealing specific terms. Shopping an offer is a serious violation.
3. Sellers must be informed of how the commission will be split with cooperating brokers. Under 2024 NAR settlement rules, buyer broker compensation must be negotiated in the buyer representation agreement, not advertised through the MLS.
4. Licensees are required to recommend that all buyers and sellers retain a licensed attorney.

CHAPTER 2 QUIZ — BASIC AGENCY RELATIONSHIPS, DISCLOSURES AND DUTIES TO THE CLIENT

1. Which of the following best describes a fiduciary relationship in a real estate agency?

a. The agent is obligated to act in the principal's best financial interest because the relationship involves money or property.

b. The agent is required to share all client information with cooperating brokers.

c. The agent may make final decisions on behalf of the client when the client is unavailable.

d. The agent's duty ends as soon as the listing agreement expires.

2. A licensee becomes an agent of the client when:

a. The licensee passes the Texas real estate exam.

b. The licensee is sponsored by a broker.

c. The licensee shows a property to a prospective buyer for the first time.

d. A formal agency relationship is established, such as through a listing or buyer representation agreement.

3. Which classification of agency is most commonly used in Texas real estate transactions between a broker and a buyer or seller client?

a. Universal agency

b. General agency

c. Special agency

d. Subagency

4. A broker has been granted power of attorney by an elderly client who cannot manage her own affairs. This arrangement is an example of:

a. Universal agency

b. Special agency

c. General agency

d. Dual agency

5. Under a standard special agency arrangement, which of the following actions may a listing broker take without specific client authorization?

a. Accept a full-price, no-contingency offer on behalf of the seller.

b. Market the property, conduct showings, and negotiate offers.

c. Allow the buyer to move into the property before closing.

d. Sign the sales contract on the seller's behalf if the seller is out of town.

6. The relationship between a broker and their affiliated licensees in Texas is most accurately classified as:

a. Special agency created by the listing agreement.

b. Universal agency created by a power of attorney.

c. Subagency created by the MLS cooperation rules.

d. General agency created by the independent contractor agreement.

7. A seller asks the listing agent to avoid presenting offers from buyers of a particular religion. The agent's correct response is to:

a. Honor the seller's request since the seller is the client.

b. Agree to filter offers but document the seller's written request first.

c. Refuse the request because it violates the Federal Fair Housing Act, and explain the legal limits to the seller.

d. Refer the matter to TREC for a ruling before taking any action.

8. Under the 2024 NAR settlement rules now in effect in Texas, how must compensation for a buyer's broker be communicated?

a. Through the buyer representation agreement, negotiated and documented before any properties are shown.

b. Through the MLS as part of the listing information.

c. By verbal agreement between the buyer and broker before the first showing.

d. By the seller at closing based on the final sales price.

9. A buyer's agent provides the seller with a client's financial information in order to encourage the seller to accept a lower offer. This action would most likely be considered a:

a. Reasonable negotiation strategy.

b. Violation of the agent's fiduciary duty of confidentiality to the buyer-client.

c. Required disclosure under TRELA.

d. Permitted action if the buyer gave verbal approval.

10. Which of the following statements about the broker's duty of confidentiality is correct?

a. Confidentiality ends when the transaction closes.

b. Confidentiality applies only to buyer-clients, not seller-clients.

c. Confidentiality can be waived by the broker's managing attorney.

d. Confidentiality continues permanently, even after the agency relationship ends.

11. A seller is present at a showing and tells the buyer that the roof is only two years old. The broker later learns the roof is actually twelve years old. In this situation, the broker is most likely:

a. Fully liable because the showing occurred under the broker's authority.

b. Not liable for the client's direct misrepresentation during the showing, as the broker is entitled to rely on the truthfulness of their client.

c. Liable because the broker should have disclosed the roof age independently.

d. Required to withdraw from the listing immediately upon learning of the discrepancy.

12. An agent working with a buyer-client discovers the buyer consistently refuses to seek pre-qualification for a loan or provide proof of funds, despite repeated requests. The most appropriate course of action is to:

a. Continue showing properties and attempt to secure pre-qualification on the buyer's behalf.

b. File a complaint with TREC against the buyer.

c. Evaluate whether the buyer is genuinely committed to purchasing and, if not, consider ending the representation relationship.

d. Present offers without pre-qualification since pre-qualification is optional under Texas law.

13. The acronym COALD is used to remember the five fiduciary duties a Texas licensee owes to a client. Which of the following correctly identifies all five duties?

a. Confidentiality, Obedience, Accountability, Loyalty, Disclosure

b. Care, Obligation, Accountability, Loyalty, Diligence

c. Confidentiality, Obligation, Accuracy, Loyalty, Disclosure

d. Care, Obedience, Accountability, Loyalty, Disclosure

14. A listing agent shows a property and notices a significant crack running along the base of the living room wall but does not mention it to prospective buyers. Later, the crack is found to indicate a serious foundation problem. The agent is most likely liable under which fiduciary duty?

a. Disclosure, because the agent should have identified and disclosed a condition that could affect a buyer's decision.

b. Obedience, because the agent failed to follow the seller's instructions.

c. Accountability, because the agent failed to keep accurate transaction records.

d. Loyalty, because the agent failed to place the buyer's interests above the seller's.

15. A seller instructs the listing agent not to show the property on Sundays. The agent must also refuse to follow a seller's instruction that:

a. Requires the property to be shown by appointment only.

b. Directs the agent to conceal a known water intrusion problem from prospective buyers.

c. Requests that only qualified buyers with pre-approval letters be scheduled for showings.

d. Prohibits the use of open house events during the listing period.

16. During a transaction, the seller's agent learns that the seller is under financial pressure and will accept significantly less than the asking price. Under the duty of loyalty, the agent:

a. Should disclose this information to the buyer's agent to help facilitate a quicker sale.

b. May share this information if the buyer requests it directly.

c. Must keep this information confidential and may not disclose it without the seller's express permission.

d. Must disclose it to the buyer because material facts must always be shared.

17. The duty of confidentiality that arises from the fiduciary duty of loyalty:

a. Ends when the transaction closes and the commission is paid.

b. Applies only to financial information shared by the client.

c. Can be waived by the broker if the client moves out of the state.

d. Continues permanently, even after the agency relationship has ended.

18. A buyer working with a licensee has not signed a buyer representation agreement. Under Texas agency law, this buyer is classified as a:

a. Customer, who receives factual information but not professional advice or advocacy.

b. Client, because the licensee is helping them search for property.

c. Principal, because they have a fiduciary relationship with the licensee.

d. Subagent, because the listing broker ultimately represents all parties.

19. Under Texas law, the Information About Brokerage Services form (TREC IABS 1-2) must be provided to a party:

a. Only after a listing agreement or buyer representation agreement has been signed.

b. At the time of first substantive dialogue about a specific property.

c. At the closing table before the deed is signed.

d. Only when the licensee is acting as an intermediary.

20. Which of the following situations does NOT require the licensee to provide the TREC Information About Brokerage Services disclosure?

a. A seller calls the office to inquire about listing their home.

b. A buyer meets with the listing agent at the property for a scheduled showing.

c. A buyer visits an open house and asks general questions about the property.

d. A tenant asks about available commercial space for lease for longer than one year.

21. A listing agent receives two offers on the same property on the same day. Which of the following best describes the agent's obligations?

a. Present only the higher offer to avoid confusion, then notify the other buyer if that offer falls through.

b. Issue counteroffers to all buyers simultaneously to create urgency.

c. Disclose the full terms of both offers to each buyer so they can compete fairly.

d. Notify all buyers that competing offers exist without revealing specific terms, present both offers to the seller promptly, and advise the seller on how to respond.

22. Sharing the terms of one buyer's offer with a competing buyer in order to encourage a higher bid is known as:

a. Shopping an offer.

b. Dual agency.

c. Procuring cause.

d. Intermediary disclosure.

23. Under the 2024 NAR settlement rules now in effect in Texas, how must compensation for a buyer's broker be handled?

a. Listed in the MLS so all cooperating agents are aware before showing.

b. Negotiated and documented in the buyer representation agreement before any properties are shown.

c. Determined by the listing broker after the offer is accepted.

d. Set by TREC at a standard percentage of the sales price.

24. A buyer client asks their agent to explain whether a special provisions paragraph in the purchase contract creates any legal obligations. The agent's correct response is to:

a. Explain the legal implications based on their experience with similar contracts.

b. Tell the buyer the provision is standard and no further review is needed.

c. Recommend that the buyer consult a licensed attorney, as licensees are prohibited from providing legal advice.

d. Contact the listing agent for an explanation of what the seller intended.

CHAPTER 3

DUTIES AND DISCLOSURES TO THIRD PARTIES

Chapter Objectives

After completing this chapter, you should be able to:

1. Describe the non-fiduciary duties a licensee owes to customers and third parties.
2. Explain the duties of honesty and fairness when working with customers, including disclosure of material facts.
3. Define "third party" and explain how customers differ from clients in a Texas real estate transaction.
4. Identify obligations and disclosure requirements when interacting with third parties, including disclosure of agency relationships, multiple offers, and property conditions.
5. Recognize safety considerations and prohibited conduct when working with customers.
6. Explain the three types of misrepresentation and describe how to avoid liability for each.
7. Define material facts and explain the broker's responsibility to discover and disclose them.
8. Distinguish between latent and patent defects, and explain how fraudulent misrepresentation is established under Texas law.
9. Explain title defects, boundary disclosure obligations, and the requirements for completing and using the Seller's Disclosure of Property Condition form.
10. Describe the rules governing stigmatized property, sex offender disclosure, and AIDS-related disclosure under Texas and federal law.

Contents

Third Party Obligations
Customer Obligations
Third Party Disclosure Obligations
Third Party Safety
Misrepresentation
Avoiding Innocent Misrepresentation Liability
Avoiding Negligent Misrepresentation Liability
Avoiding Fraudulent Misrepresentation Liability
Material Facts Defined
Material Facts and Broker Responsibility
Fraudulent Misrepresentation
Latent Defects
Patent Defects
Title Defects
Boundary Disclosures
The Seller's Disclosure of Property Condition Form
Stigmatized Property

Non-Fiduciary Duties

A customer is a person the licensee is not representing. Another agent may be representing that customer, but this particular licensee is not. Even so, the licensee still has obligations to customers that must be met whenever they come into contact.

Licensees must not only understand what they can and cannot do for a customer; they must also communicate those limits clearly to the customer. Every customer has the right to know whether the licensee is already representing someone else in the transaction:

The seller has the right to know if the licensee is already representing a buyer.
The buyer has the right to know if the licensee is already representing the seller.

A common situation involves a buyer who hires a licensee to help purchase a For Sale By Owner (FSBO) property. In that case, there is no agency relationship between the licensee and the seller. The agency runs to the buyer, and the seller becomes a customer. In this situation, the licensee must disclose their buyer agency status to the FSBO seller at the outset.

Working with a Buyer-Customer

The most common way a licensee comes into contact with a buyer-customer is when that buyer is interested in a property listed with the licensee's brokerage. If the listing belongs to the sponsoring broker, then every licensee in that office is representing the seller.

The salesperson who has the first contact with the buyer-customer should make that representation clear immediately: the licensee represents the seller, not the buyer. The buyer should also be cautioned to be thoughtful about what they say in the presence of the seller's agent, since anything the buyer discloses could be information the agent is obligated to pass along to the seller.

Customer Notice and the Effective Date of a Contract

A question that frequently arises during negotiations is: when exactly did the contract become effective? This is particularly important when a buyer has purchased a termination option, which gives the buyer a set number of days to reconsider the transaction. If the parties cannot agree on when the option period began, they cannot agree on when it ends.

In Texas, the effective date of a contract is established by a specific rule: the contract is official when the last licensee whose client or customer signed the final counteroffer contacts the agent on the other side of the transaction and communicates that everything has been accepted. It is that act of communication, not the act of signing, that makes the contract binding.

This rule carries an important practical consequence. When a salesperson is notified of acceptance, it is legally the same as notifying the client or customer directly. This means the licensee must communicate that acceptance to their client or customer immediately. A delay of even a few days means the party has been under a binding contract without knowing it, which is a serious problem. Prompt communication of acceptance is not optional; it is a professional and legal obligation.

Types of Customers

There are two categories of customers a licensee will encounter. The first is a customer the licensee is working with directly, such as a buyer being shown properties by a seller's agent. The second is a customer being represented by another agent, who is simply a customer to this particular licensee.

In both cases, the customer is entitled to certain disclosures: information about the condition of the property and, critically, a clear statement of who the licensee represents. A buyer who understands who the agent works for can make better decisions about what to say, what to ask, and whether to seek representation of their own.

Customer Disclosure

Anyone participating in a showing, a discussion about a property, or a transaction has the right to know whether the agent across the table already has an agency relationship with someone on the other side.

The simplest way to handle this is direct verbal disclosure. Licensees should become comfortable saying clearly: "I am representing the seller" or "I am representing the buyer." This brief statement removes any ambiguity and allows the customer to make informed decisions about what information to share and how to proceed.

While TREC has not developed a standardized written form specifically for this disclosure, individual brokers may work with an attorney to create a written disclosure document for their office. A written disclosure has an obvious advantage: it creates a record that the disclosure was made. Verbal disclosures, while standard practice, leave the licensee without proof if the customer later claims they were not informed. Either way, the disclosure must happen.

Honesty

Honesty is not optional in real estate. It applies in every interaction with every customer and client. There will be pressure, at times, to stay quiet about something unflattering about a property or to guess at an answer rather than admit uncertainty. Neither approach serves anyone well.

If a licensee discovers new information after a showing, such as realizing that a property boundary is not where they thought it was, the right course of action is to go back to the buyer with the corrected information, even if it means scheduling a second visit to the property.

When a licensee does not know the answer to a question, the honest response is: "I will find out for you" or "Let's get an expert to answer that." Real estate professionals are not expected to know everything. Admitting that something is outside your knowledge and finding a reliable answer is far more professional than guessing, and far safer legally.

Honesty Regarding Material Facts

A material fact is any information that a customer would likely not discover on their own and that would influence their decision about whether to proceed with a transaction. Material facts include things like survey irregularities, title problems, liens against the property, and known physical defects.

Rumors do not need to be disclosed; documented facts do. The standard is the "reasonable person" test: if a reasonably competent agent in the same situation would have noticed or discovered the information, then this agent is expected to have noticed it too.

For example, if a significant crack in a garage floor would be visible to any agent conducting a reasonable walkthrough, failure to point it out to the buyer could be treated as an attempt to conceal a potential foundation issue. The buyer is entitled to enter any transaction with as complete a picture as possible, and it is the responsibility of every licensee involved to make sure material facts reach the buyer, even if that buyer is a customer rather than a client.

Honesty Regarding Title

Licensees should advise both clients and customers to obtain a title search before closing on any property. In practice, this is rarely a problem because virtually all lenders require a title search and a lender's title insurance policy before funding a loan.

When a licensee helps a buyer write an offer, they do not present title insurance as an option. Instead, the licensee confirms that a title policy will be obtained and asks the buyer whether they want to pay for it or request that the seller cover the cost. Most buyers ask the seller to pay for the owner's title policy, which is a standard negotiating point in Texas transactions.

> ***Practical Note:*** *Advising a buyer to obtain a title search or title insurance policy is one of the requirements a broker must have satisfied in order to pursue a commission claim in court. It is both a disclosure obligation and a business protection.*

Recommending an Attorney

Licensees must recommend to all buyers and sellers that they retain a licensed attorney to represent them in the transaction. This requirement applies regardless of whether the party is a client or a customer.

In practice, many Texas buyers and sellers proceed without a personal attorney. The attorneys at the title company and lending institution handle the legal mechanics of transferring the property and executing the loan documents. Even so, having personal legal counsel can be valuable, particularly when unusual or non-standard terms are being negotiated.

Attorneys involved in real estate transactions do not derail deals. They review and refine the terms, sometimes striking language that is unfavorable to their client or drafting new language for the Special Provisions paragraph to address unique circumstances such as a final walkthrough or custom construction terms. Their role is not to stop a transaction but to ensure their client enters it on sound terms.

Fairness

Fairness does not mean treating a client and a customer identically. A licensee representing a seller cannot negotiate equally on behalf of both the seller and the buyer. That would be a conflict of interest, not fairness.

True fairness in agency means being as honest and even-handed as possible with the customer, while still fulfilling the full duty of advocacy owed to the client. A buyer-customer who feels the dynamic is unbalanced has a straightforward remedy: hire an agent of their own.

One important expression of fairness is disclosure. The listing agent should inform the buyer-customer directly that the licensee's loyalty is to the seller. This is not a discouragement; it is transparency. The buyer who understands the relationship knows to be thoughtful about what information they volunteer, since anything shared with the seller's agent may find its way to the seller and affect the negotiation.

Definition of a Third Party

A third party is any person who is not in an agency relationship with a licensee in a given transaction. Customers are considered third parties unless and until they enter into a representation agreement and become clients.

The first contact most licensees have with a third party is often through an inquiry: a phone call about an advertisement, a response to a yard sign, or an online message about a listing. From that first contact, the professional goal is to help the customer understand the value of representation and, where appropriate, to convert that customer into a client.

Some people resist committing to a representation agreement regardless of how clearly the benefits are explained. At that point, the licensee has a practical decision to make. Dropping the customer guarantees no commission. Continuing to work with the customer as a non-represented party means the buyer could choose another agent at any time, since there is no agreement requiring loyalty. The licensee who works with a customer accepts that risk as part of the relationship.

Tracking Customers

Customers are easy to lose track of. In the middle of an active pipeline of transactions, it is easy to forget the seller who received a market update last week or the buyer who toured homes last month and has gone quiet since.

Every licensee should develop and maintain a consistent follow-up system for every customer contact until either a transaction is completed or the customer asks not to be contacted further. This does not require expensive software. A simple log of names, contact information, and recent interactions is enough to keep customers from slipping away unnoticed.

Prepared communications, including letters and email templates covering common real estate topics, are widely available online and can be personalized quickly. Consistent, professional follow-up converts customers into clients and clients into referral sources.

Customers to Avoid

Not every customer is one a licensee should pursue. There are three categories of customers that require special caution:

Underage Customers

A minor lacks the legal capacity to enter into a real estate contract. A licensee should not proceed with a transaction involving an underage buyer or seller. That said, the minor should be treated with respect. Real estate professionals invest in long-term relationships, and a teenager who is not yet old enough to buy may become a client in just a few years.

Customers with Diminished Capacity

There will be occasions when a buyer or seller displays signs of cognitive impairment or diminished capacity. When this occurs, the licensee should discuss the situation with their broker and consider involving the person's family members before proceeding. A title company closing officer is also trained to observe signers for signs of incapacity and will stop a closing if there is a genuine concern. It is better to pause and resolve the issue than to complete a transaction that could later be challenged or voided.

Customers Who Present a Safety Risk

Licensees occasionally encounter individuals who raise personal safety concerns. This is one of the primary reasons experienced agents prefer to meet new, unverified buyers at the office before taking them to a property. It is also why some licensees bring a colleague along when showing property to someone they have not previously met.

Any decision to carry a personal protection device must be discussed with and approved by the broker, and must be carried legally and in full compliance with applicable law.

When a Customer Becomes a Client

A situation that tests a licensee's professional judgment occurs when a property expires off a listing and relists with a different broker, and then the original listing agent is contacted by someone who wants to see it. There is nothing preventing the original agent from showing the property through the new listing office.

The complication arises because the original listing agent may have learned confidential information about the seller during the prior listing, such as the seller's willingness to accept a price below the asking price. That information was obtained while representing the seller and remains confidential, even after the listing has expired. It cannot be shared with a buyer, even if doing so would help close a deal.

If the interested party then asks the original listing agent to represent them as a buyer's agent, a conflict arises. The agent must disclose to the buyer that they may have confidential information from the prior listing that they are not permitted to share. If the buyer is uncomfortable with that limitation, the appropriate solution is to connect the buyer with a different licensee in the office who has no prior connection to the property. This protects the buyer's interests and respects the confidentiality obligation that survives the end of the original agency.

Third Party Obligations

Customers often ask questions that go beyond what a licensee can answer with certainty. Crime statistics in a neighborhood are a common example. A licensee may have a general impression of an area, but impressions are not statistics, and providing a vague assurance about neighborhood safety is not appropriate. The correct response is to direct the customer to the local law enforcement agency's website or, if no website exists, to the agency directly. The buyer should conduct their own research and make their own assessment.

Licensees showing property should also be mindful of the security risks that accompany home showings. Items of value occasionally disappear during property tours. Sellers should be advised to secure or remove valuables before showings. Buyers should be reminded to stay together as a group when touring a home, though this is admittedly difficult when children are involved. A licensee who is alert to these dynamics reduces the risk of an uncomfortable situation for everyone.

Customer Obligations

There are certain types of information that a licensee is prohibited from sharing with customers, even when asked.

Concealing Property Defects Is Not an Option

A seller may instruct the listing agent not to disclose a known defect, such as a roof that leaks. This instruction cannot be followed. If the agent knows about a material defect, they are obligated to disclose it. If the seller continues to insist on concealment after being informed of the legal requirements, the broker should seriously consider terminating the agency. A client who asks the licensee to violate the law is asking the licensee to put their license and livelihood at risk.

Fair Housing Information Is Off Limits

Information relating to any Fair Housing protected class, including race, color, religion, sex, national origin, familial status, and disability status, must not be discussed with any party to a transaction, even if a customer asks directly. This information is legally immaterial to any real estate transaction and discussing it creates significant legal exposure for the licensee.

Do Not Weaken Your Client's Negotiating Position

Licensees must never share information that undermines their client's position in negotiations. A listing agent who tells a buyer-customer that the seller is desperate to sell, has already purchased another property, or is under pressure to close quickly is handing the buyer a negotiating advantage at the seller's expense. These statements are a direct breach of the duty of loyalty.

The same applies to buyer's agents. Telling a listing agent that the buyer is qualified to spend far more than their offer amount gives the seller leverage the buyer did not authorize the agent to provide. Every disclosure during negotiations should be evaluated against one question: does sharing this information serve my client, or does it serve someone else?

Third Party Disclosure Obligations

Every Texas licensee should keep in mind what experienced agents call the "15 Minute Rule." The idea is simple: within 15 minutes of the moving van leaving, a neighbor will introduce themselves to the new owners and begin sharing everything about the property and the neighborhood, including things the agent should have disclosed but did not.

The rule is not literally about 15 minutes. It is a vivid reminder that buyers will learn the truth about a property one way or another. The only question is whether they learn it from the licensee before closing, or from a neighbor after. When there is any doubt about whether something should be disclosed, the better practice is to disclose it.

A useful real-world example: at a listing appointment, a seller mentioned that someone had drowned in a nearby lake and the body washed up in the backyard the following day. They asked whether that needed to be disclosed. The answer was maybe, and the recommended approach was to prepare a brief written statement summarizing the event that could be shared with any interested buyer. Full disclosure, clearly documented, is always the safer and more professional path.

Third Party Safety

A licensee showing property has a responsibility to be aware of, and warn buyers about, potential physical hazards on or near the property.

Residential and Rural Property Hazards

Some hazards are not immediately obvious. An older property may have been connected to the city sewer system for years but still have an abandoned septic tank on the lot that was never properly filled and sealed. Old wells that have been capped but not filled present similar risks. These are the kinds of conditions the 15 Minute Rule was made for: a neighbor may know about them even when the seller has long forgotten.

When showing rural or agricultural properties, additional hazards apply:

- Livestock, including bulls and other large animals, can be unpredictable and dangerous.
- Electric wire fences may not be visible and buyers must be warned before walking a property perimeter.
- In dry conditions, open flame or cigarette smoking near fields or brush presents a fire risk.
- Roads that pass close to the property may present collision risks for the structure itself, especially on rural curves or steep grades.

Commercial Property Hazards

Commercial showings present their own safety requirements. Some active facilities require hard hats or safety glasses in certain areas. Hazardous chemicals may be present on site, and operating machinery can be dangerous. A licensee showing occupied commercial property should find out in advance what safety protocols apply and communicate those requirements to the buyers before the showing.

Misrepresentation

Misrepresentation lawsuits are the most common type of legal action brought against real estate brokers. Historically, a majority of suits against practitioners have involved misrepresentation, with a significant additional percentage involving failure to disclose. The financial and reputational consequences can be severe, which is why every Texas licensee must understand what misrepresentation is, how it occurs, and how to prevent it.

Misrepresentation involves either making an inaccurate statement about a material feature of a property or failing entirely to disclose an important fact about it. The most frequently misrepresented conditions involve foundations and building structures, followed by property boundaries, HVAC systems, roofs, and pest infestations.

Texas law recognizes three categories of misrepresentation:

Innocent Misrepresentation: The agent made a false statement while genuinely believing it to be true, based on reasonable grounds.

Negligent Misrepresentation: The agent failed to disclose a significant property flaw due to a lack of knowledge that reasonable diligence would have uncovered.

Fraudulent Misrepresentation: The agent or seller knowingly concealed or misrepresented a material fact in order to complete the transaction.

Avoiding Innocent Misrepresentation Liability

As a listing agent, the most effective way to reduce the risk of innocent misrepresentation is to ensure the seller understands the importance of completing the Seller's Disclosure of Property Condition form thoroughly and honestly. The disclosure should not be treated as a formality.

Walk through the disclosure with the seller. Ask about the source of information for any major repairs or known issues. If the roof was replaced, find out when the work was done and whether a licensed contractor completed it. The goal is to feel confident that every entry on the form is an accurate reflection of the property's actual condition.

As a buyer's agent, read the seller's disclosure carefully and walk the property with your client before the option period expires. If any disclosures seem inconsistent with what you observe during the walkthrough, discuss those concerns with your client and, where appropriate, recommend that a qualified contractor or inspector evaluate the area in question. Do not assume everything is fine because the disclosure says so.

Avoiding Negligent Misrepresentation Liability

Negligent misrepresentation most often occurs when a licensee offers an opinion on a technical matter without the expertise to back it up. Issues involving asbestos, lead-based paint, radon, groundwater contamination, and structural integrity are all areas that require professional evaluation. An agent who offers a casual opinion on these topics risks having that opinion treated as a statement of fact by the buyer.

A common example: a buyer notices hairline cracks in a garage floor during a showing and raises a concern. An agent who responds by saying "those are just normal expansion and contraction cracks, nothing to worry about" has just given a structural opinion without any engineering qualifications to support it. If a foundation problem develops later, that offhand comment becomes a significant liability.

The correct response is simple and professional: "If you have any concerns about the structural integrity of the floor, I recommend consulting a structural engineer before you proceed." A real estate licensee's job is to facilitate the transaction, not to diagnose property conditions. Knowing where your expertise ends is itself a form of professional competence.

Avoiding Fraudulent Misrepresentation Liability

Fraudulent misrepresentation is straightforward to avoid: never make up an answer to appear more knowledgeable than you are, and never conceal a known fact to close a deal.

During showings, buyers frequently ask questions the agent cannot immediately answer with certainty: Where exactly are the fence lines? How old is the roof? Has there been any water damage? What are the average utility bills? How old is the water heater? An agent who invents answers to these questions to appear confident and capable is creating serious legal exposure.

The professional approach is to check whether the seller's disclosure statement answers the question. If not, write down the specific questions, tell the buyer you will find accurate answers, and follow up with the most reliable source available. Some answers will come from public records. Others will come directly from the seller. Technical questions may require an expert. Whatever the source, document your research, report back to the buyer with the answer, and note where the information came from. That documentation protects everyone involved.

Material Facts Defined

A material fact is any piece of information that a reasonable person would consider significant when deciding whether to proceed with a transaction, on what terms, and at what price. "Material" means the information is relevant and important to the decision, not trivial or incidental.

To illustrate the difference: a cracked window discovered during a showing is likely a minor, easily repaired issue that would not significantly affect a buyer's decision. A broken heating system, by contrast, is a material fact, because it affects the habitability and value of the property in a meaningful way.

Under Texas law, both the seller and the listing broker are specifically required to disclose material facts related to the property's physical condition and legal status. Examples of material facts that must be disclosed include:

- A history of flooding or a basement that takes on water.

- Known problems with HVAC systems.
- Accurate square footage of the home.
- Environmental hazards, including mold, lead-based paint, asbestos, and radon.
- Planned developments in the area that could affect the property, such as a new highway.
- Presence of wood-destroying insects.
- Existing easements, encroachments, or boundary disputes.

Sellers are required to disclose in writing all known information about their property. Usually this is done using one of several types of seller's disclosure forms. Beyond the required items, sellers should also consider disclosing anything they know that is not legally required but that could reasonably become a point of dispute after closing. Proactive disclosure of questionable conditions is almost always less costly than litigation.

The broker's obligation runs alongside the seller's. A real estate broker is required to conduct a reasonably competent and diligent visual inspection of the property offered for sale and to disclose to a prospective buyer all facts that materially affect the property's value or desirability.

Material Facts and Broker Responsibility

Litigation in the real estate industry is common, but most lawsuits are preventable. An agent who knows the law and exercises due diligence significantly reduces their exposure. The foundational rule is clear: never conceal a material fact, under any circumstances. A cooperating agent, as well as the listing agent, shares the obligation to disclose material facts honestly.

When conducting an inspection walkthrough with the sellers, take time to go through the entire property systematically and note every visible condition that could reasonably be interpreted as a defect. Once that list is prepared, provide a copy to the sellers to aide them in filling in a seller's disclosure notice. .

In addition, maintain a transaction log that records significant events throughout the transaction, including:

- Meaningful telephone conversations.
- Inspection records and findings.
- Face-to-face meetings and key decisions made.

When a real estate dispute ends up in litigation, the outcome frequently comes down to one party's word against another's. The agent with thorough documentation nearly always has the stronger position. Written records are not just good practice; they are a professional protection.

Fraudulent Misrepresentation

When a seller or agent knowingly conceals or misrepresents a material fact, the legal standard for fraud may be met. Common law imposes a duty on sellers to disclose facts that:

- Materially affect the value or desirability of the property.
- Are known or accessible only to the seller.
- The seller knows are not accessible or obvious to a buyer using reasonable diligence.

For a statement to rise to the level of fraudulent misrepresentation under Texas law, the following elements generally must all be present:

1. The statement is false.
2. The statement concerns a material fact.
3. The person making the statement knows it to be false.
4. The buyer believed and relied on the statement.
5. The statement was made to induce the buyer to act.
6. The buyer suffered actual damages as a result.

Fraud can take the form of a verbal statement, a written statement, or a deliberate action that conceals a defect. Courts have generally held that silence alone does not constitute active concealment; there must be an affirmative act or statement to support a fraud claim. However, when a person has a legal duty to speak and instead stays silent, that silence can itself support a fraud claim.

Latent Defects

A latent defect is a flaw that is not readily observable or discoverable through reasonable inspection. The traditional rule of property law is caveat emptor, meaning "let the buyer beware," which places the burden on the buyer to inspect the property before purchase. Buyer beware does NOT work in Texas, the seller must disclose any latent defect they know.

That said, there are limits to what a standard inspection can uncover. The condition of interior brickwork, for example, cannot be fully assessed without some form of destructive testing, which no seller would reasonably be expected to permit simply to satisfy a buyer's due diligence. The law acknowledges this reality.

A claim for failure to disclose latent defects is not automatic. But when a latent defect is discovered, there is generally a presumption that the seller misrepresented the property's condition. The seller must then demonstrate that they genuinely could not have known about the defect. Sellers who made any representation, however indirect, about the affected portion of the property face a more difficult defense.

Patent Defects

A patent defect is a problem that is visible and obvious to anyone conducting a reasonable inspection. Examples include cracks in a sidewalk, peeling paint, non-functional light fixtures, and similar conditions that do not require specialized knowledge or equipment to notice.

Even though the buyer should have seen a patent defect, they do not need to show due diligence in the buyer's inspection. The sellers are obligated to disclose all latent and patent defects, in all situations.

Sellers occasionally go to considerable lengths to mask patent defects. One documented example: a seller placed a paint can over a bathtub drain. Buyers who toured the home assumed the can had been left there after some touch-up work. After closing, when the paint can was removed, gases from a defective septic tank flooded the bathroom. The seller had effectively hidden a serious problem in plain sight.

When a seller actively misrepresents or conceals a patent defect, the buyer will almost always prevail in litigation unless it can be shown that the buyer knew about the defect independently and chose to proceed with the purchase anyway.

Title Defects

Some properties are difficult to transfer because of problems with the chain of title. Title issues are often not discovered until a title search is ordered, which typically happens only after the property is under contract. There are three common categories of title defects:

Divorce

When a property is acquired during or after divorce proceedings, the ex-spouse may still appear on the deed. Before the title can pass, that individual must sign a quit claim deed formally releasing their interest in the property. The current owner must locate the ex-spouse and obtain the required signature before the closing can proceed.

Death

Properties that have been inherited sometimes have title complications. A title search may reveal that an heir or relative must sign off to clear the chain of title. Affidavits of Heirship are a common tool title companies use to resolve these situations. The listing agent may not be aware of the potential problem until the title search is completed.

Fraud

Fraudulent activity can cloud a title in several ways: a seller attempts to convey the same property to two different buyers on the same day; a developer creates mortgage fraud that encumbers the title; a tenant attempts to "sell" a property they do not own. All of these scenarios can complicate or prevent a closing and represent situations where the title company and legal counsel must be involved to resolve the defect.

Boundary Disclosures

Survey and boundary issues are material facts that must be disclosed. Sellers and buyers are often unaware of discrepancies between what they believe the property boundaries to be and what a formal survey reveals. Common boundary-related disclosure situations include:

Acreage Discrepancies

A seller may genuinely believe they are selling 20 acres, only to have a survey reveal the actual acreage is 16. Once this is discovered, the buyer must decide whether to proceed at the agreed price or to renegotiate to reflect the reduced land area.

Fence Not on the Property Line

When the fence between two neighboring properties does not sit on the actual property line, the sliver of land between the fence and the true boundary must be disclosed and addressed. The parties can agree to move the fence, accept the property as it stands, or the buyer may choose to walk away from the transaction.

Setback Violations and Encroachments

An improvement such as a garage may be built closer to a side lot line than the deed restrictions for the subdivision allow. In most cases the structure does not have to be removed, but the encroachment must be disclosed and the buyer must accept it knowingly.

Other common encroachment issues include buildings constructed too close to the road, tool sheds near the property line, a neighbor's driveway crossing a corner of the lot, or in a commercial context, inadequate ingress and egress for the buyer's intended use. All of these are material facts and must be disclosed before closing.

The Seller's Disclosure of Property Condition Form

Texas law requires residential sellers to complete a written disclosure of the property's condition before entering into a contract with a buyer. The seller has lived in or owned the property and is in the best position to know things about it that would not be apparent to a visitor or buyer.

The Texas Real Estate Commission has for this purpose. Texas REALTORS also has its own version of the seller's disclosure form, which is available to members through the local Board of REALTORS. The broker determines which form is used in their office. Any form used must contain all items required by Section 5.008 of the Texas Property Code

Key requirements under Texas Property Code Section 5.008 include:

- The disclosure is required for residential real property comprising not more than one dwelling unit.
- The notice must be executed by the seller
- The seller must complete the form to the best of their knowledge and belief as of the date it is signed. If a fact is unknown, the seller must indicate that on the form, which constitutes compliance.
- The seller is not required to disclose whether a death by natural causes, suicide, or accident unrelated to the property's condition occurred on the property, or whether a prior occupant had or may have had AIDS or HIV.

The disclosure form is comprehensive and includes questions about systems and features that may not exist on every property, such as attic fans, French drains, and various mechanical systems. The form uses a "Yes / No / Unknown" format on its first page. The second page instructs sellers to mark "Yes" if they are aware of an issue and "No" if they are not, which is a slightly different framing. This inconsistency can confuse sellers, and the licensee may need to explain the difference in format between the two pages.

> ***Important:*** *The licensee must never fill out any portion of the Seller's Disclosure form on behalf of the seller, even if the seller requests it due to a physical limitation. Friends, family members, or a personal attorney may assist the seller, but not the listing agent. If the licensee fills out the form and any information turns out to be incorrect, the licensee may be personally liable for misrepresentation. The seller must complete and sign the form themselves.*

When a Seller's Disclosure Is Not Required

Texas law exempts certain types of transfers from the seller's disclosure requirement. A disclosure notice is not required for:

- Court-ordered transfers or foreclosure sales.
- Transfers through bankruptcy proceedings.
- Transfers to a mortgagee by a mortgagor, or to a beneficiary of a deed of trust.
- Transfers by a mortgagee or deed of trust beneficiary who acquired the property through a court-ordered foreclosure or deed in lieu of foreclosure.
- Transfers of property acquired through a will or trust.
- Transfers from one co-owner to another co-owner.
- Transfers to a spouse or to persons in the direct line of ancestry of a transferor.
- Transfers between spouses resulting from a divorce or legal separation.
- Transfers to or from any governmental entity.
- Sales of new residences by the builder.

- Transfers where the value of any dwelling on the property does not exceed five percent of the total property value.

> ***Practical Note:*** *If a contract is executed without the seller providing the required disclosure, the buyer may terminate the contract for any reason within seven days of receiving the notice.*

Blank Answers and Fraud

The Seller's Disclosure form requires a "Yes" or "No" response for each item. Leaving an answer blank is not acceptable and is not a neutral act. A blank response, particularly when everything else on the form is completed, strongly suggests the seller was aware of a problem in that area and chose to avoid answering.

For example, if a seller answers "No" to a question about the septic system and a defect is later discovered, the seller can maintain they had no knowledge of the problem. But if the seller leaves that line blank, they have deliberately disregarded the instructions on the form. The only reasonable inference is that the omission was intentional, which can support a claim of fraud.

Stigmatized Property

A stigmatized property is one that a buyer may reject for reasons unrelated to its physical condition. The property is not defective in a structural or mechanical sense; it is associated with an event, history, or reputation that some buyers find objectionable or concerning.

Stigmatized property falls into several recognized categories:

Public Stigma: The property is widely known to the public for a notorious event. Any reasonable person would be expected to know about it. Examples include properties that became subjects of major news coverage.

Criminal Stigma: The property was used in the ongoing commission of crimes, such as serving as a drug house, chop shop, or similar illegal enterprise.

Murder or Suicide Stigma: Some jurisdictions require disclosure if a violent death occurred on the premises. Requirements vary by state.

Debt Stigma: Debt collectors who are unaware that a debtor has moved continue to contact and harass the new owners.

Phenomena Stigma: The property has a reputation for paranormal activity. Some jurisdictions require disclosure if a property is known for reported ghost activity.

Minimal Stigma: Information known to many but taken seriously by only a small group. Often involves the property's location, such as neighborhood characteristics or an unusual lot configuration.

Buying and Selling Stigmatized Property

There are many conditions that affect a home's marketability that are not legally required to be disclosed but that a buyer might consider significant, including:

- Airport noise or flight path proximity.
- Known geological hazards such as landslides, sinkholes, or unstable soil.
- Lead-based paint in older structures.
- History of significant weather damage.

When working with a stigmatized property, agents should:

1. Verify that the stigmatizing event is based on fact, not rumor.
2. Obtain a written legal opinion from an attorney regarding disclosure obligations.
3. If disclosure is legally required, make it upfront and in writing.
4. Advise the client and be prepared to discuss a price adjustment.
5. Consider an appraisal from an experienced professional who can assess the impact on value.
6. Be open and honest throughout the process.

Some buyers actively seek stigmatized properties because they can often be purchased at a significant discount. These buyers calculate that they can outlast the stigma and ultimately realize a profit. Others specifically seek out properties with unusual histories to market them to niche audiences. Most buyers, however, prefer to avoid stigmatized properties entirely, believing that the risk to long-term value is not worth the reduced purchase price.

Sex Offender Disclosure

Texas law requires sex offenders to register with law enforcement upon release from incarceration, including providing photographs and fingerprints. This framework is derived from the federal Sexual Offender (Jacob Wetterling) Act of 1994, commonly referred to as Megan's Law, which requires persons convicted of sex crimes against children to notify local authorities of any change of address or employment after release. The notification requirement may last a fixed period, typically at least ten years, or it may be permanent.

In Texas, owners of single-family homes and real estate agents are specifically exempt from any duty to disclose information about registered sex offenders living in the area to prospective buyers. The law does not require this disclosure.

Even so, many agents choose to advise buyers to conduct their own research. A practical approach is to direct buyers to the local law enforcement agency's sex offender registry, which is publicly available online, and encourage them to review it as part of their due diligence before making a decision.

AIDS Disclosure and Fair Housing

The Fair Housing Act Amendments of 1988 established that individuals diagnosed with AIDS are members of a protected class under federal fair housing law. Discrimination based on disability status, including AIDS and HIV, is illegal, just as discrimination based on race, color, religion, sex, national origin, or familial status is illegal.

The Department of Housing and Urban Development (HUD) has stated that it is illegal for real estate agents to make unsolicited disclosures that a current or former occupant of a property has or had AIDS. If a prospective buyer directly asks whether a former occupant had AIDS, and the agent knows that to be true, HUD advises that the agent should not respond to the question.

The National Association of REALTORS recommends the following response in such situations:

> *"It is the policy of our firm not to answer inquiries of this nature in either direction, as we consider this information to be immaterial to the transaction. Any response could also constitute a violation of federal fair housing law. If you believe this information is relevant to your decision, you will need to pursue that inquiry on your own."*

Snapshot Review – Chapter 3

Non-Fiduciary Duties and Customer Rights

1. A customer is a person not represented by this licensee. Non-fiduciary duties to customers still apply.
2. Every customer has the right to know who the licensee represents. Verbal disclosure is standard; written disclosure is stronger.
3. In a FSBO purchase where the buyer hires a licensee, the seller is a customer and the licensee must disclose their buyer agency status to the seller.
4. When a salesperson is notified of contract acceptance, it is legally the same as notifying their client or customer. Prompt communication is required.

Honesty and Material Facts

1. Material facts must be disclosed to buyers, whether they are clients or customers.
2. A material fact is anything the buyer could not discover independently that would affect their decision.
3. The reasonable person standard applies: if a competent agent would have noticed it, this agent is expected to have noticed it too.
4. When a licensee does not know the answer to a question, the honest response is to find a reliable source rather than guess.
5. Licensees must recommend that all buyers and sellers retain a licensed attorney.

Fairness and Third Parties

1. Fairness does not mean equal treatment of clients and customers. It means honest, transparent conduct while fulfilling full fiduciary duties to the client.
2. A third party is any person not in an agency relationship with the licensee. Customers are third parties until they sign a representation agreement.
3. Customers to avoid: those who are underage, those who show signs of diminished capacity, and those who present a personal safety risk.
4. A licensee who previously represented a seller as a listing agent cannot share confidential information from that prior representation with a new buyer client, even after the listing has expired.

Prohibited Conduct and Disclosure Obligations

1. A licensee may not conceal a known property defect, even at the client's request. Persistent client demands to conceal a defect are grounds to terminate the agency.
2. Fair Housing protected class information, including race, color, religion, sex, national origin, familial status, and disability, must not be discussed with any party.

3. Licensees must not share information that weakens their client's negotiating position, whether the client is the seller or the buyer.
4. The "15 Minute Rule": when in doubt, disclose. Buyers will learn the truth about a property eventually. It is better they learn it from the agent before closing.

Third Party Safety

1. Licensees must identify and disclose physical hazards on or near a property, including abandoned wells, old septic tanks, dangerous road conditions, livestock, electric fences, and combustion risks.
2. Commercial property showings may require hard hats, safety glasses, or other precautions. Know the site requirements before bringing buyers to the property.
3. Advise sellers to secure valuables before showings, and remind buyer groups to stay together during property tours.

The Three Types of Misrepresentation

Innocent: A false statement made while genuinely believing it to be true. Reduce risk by thoroughly reviewing the seller's disclosure and documenting sources.

Negligent: Failure to disclose a significant flaw due to lack of knowledge. Avoid by referring buyers to qualified experts for technical questions rather than offering personal opinions.

Fraudulent: Knowingly concealing or misrepresenting a material fact to close a deal. Never fabricate answers; document all responses and their sources.

Material Facts and Broker Responsibility

1. A material fact is any information a reasonable person would consider significant to their decision. Both the seller and the listing broker are required to disclose material facts.
2. Brokers must conduct a reasonably competent visual inspection and disclose all material conditions to prospective buyers.
3. Maintain a transaction log documenting all significant conversations, inspections, and meetings. Documentation wins disputes.
4. Fraud requires a false statement of material fact, knowledge of its falsity, buyer reliance, intent to induce action, and resulting damages.

Defect Definitions

Latent Defect: Not visible or discoverable through reasonable inspection. Buyers should protect themselves contractually. When discovered post-closing, the seller bears the burden of proving they could not have known.

Patent Defect: Visible and obvious to any reasonable inspection. The seller is generally not liable unless they actively concealed it.

Title Defects and Boundary Disclosures

1. Title defects commonly arise from divorce (ex-spouse still on deed), death (heirs must sign off), or fraud (clouded title).
2. Survey discrepancies, fences not on property lines, setback violations, and encroachments are all material facts requiring disclosure.

Seller's Disclosure of Property Condition (Form OP-H)

1. Required for residential property of not more than one dwelling unit in Texas.
2. Must be provided to the buyer before the effective date of the contract.
3. The seller, not the licensee, must complete and sign the form.
4. Blank answers in Section 3 are not acceptable and may be treated as evidence of fraud.
5. If the disclosure is not provided before contract, the buyer may terminate within seven days of receiving it.
6. Exemptions include foreclosures, bankruptcy, court-ordered transfers, inherited property, new construction, co-owner to co-owner transfers, and transfers to or from governmental entities.

Stigmatized Property and Special Disclosures

1. In Texas, violent deaths and murders must be disclosed. Non-violent deaths are not required to be disclosed.
2. Texas agents and single-family homeowners are exempt from disclosing the proximity of registered sex offenders. Direct buyers to public law enforcement resources for their own research.
3. Unsolicited disclosure that a prior occupant had AIDS is illegal under federal fair housing law. If directly asked, the agent should decline to respond and advise the buyer to conduct their own inquiry.
4. When in doubt about disclosure, err on the side of disclosing. The "15 Minute Rule" applies: neighbors will tell the new owners what the agent did not.

CHAPTER 3 QUIZ — DUTIES AND DISCLOSURES TO THIRD PARTIES

1. A buyer hires a licensee to help purchase a For Sale By Owner (FSBO) property. In this situation, the FSBO seller is considered a:
    a. Customer, and the licensee must disclose their buyer agency status to the seller at the outset.
    b. Client, because a contract will be written on the property.
    c. Principal, because the seller controls the property.
    d. Subagent, because the MLS rules apply to all cooperating brokers.

2. Under Texas law, the effective date of a real estate contract is established when:
    a. Both parties have signed the final counteroffer.
    b. The earnest money has been deposited with the title company.
    c. The title company receives the executed contract and opens the file.
    d. The last licensee whose client signed the final counteroffer contacts the other agent and communicates that everything has been accepted.

3. A salesperson is notified by phone that the seller has accepted the buyer's offer. Under Texas law, this notification:
    a. Has no legal effect until the broker also receives written confirmation.
    b. Is legally the same as notifying the buyer-client directly, requiring the salesperson to communicate acceptance to the buyer immediately.
    c. Starts the option period only after the buyer signs an acknowledgment of acceptance.
    d. Is effective only if the salesperson responds in writing within 24 hours.

4. A buyer-customer asks the listing agent whether the neighborhood is safe. The most appropriate response is to:
    a. Confirm that the neighborhood is generally safe based on personal experience showing homes there.
    b. Decline to answer because safety questions are outside the scope of real estate practice.
    c. Direct the buyer to the local law enforcement agency's website or office to research crime statistics independently.
    d. Provide a general assessment based on the listing price and surrounding property values.

5. A material fact in a real estate transaction is best defined as:
    a. Information that a buyer could not discover independently and that would likely influence their decision about the transaction.
    b. Any information that the seller is required to list on the Seller's Disclosure Notice.
    c. Any fact about a property that reduces its market value below the asking price.
    d. Information shared by neighbors or third parties that has not been independently verified.

6. A listing agent is showing a property and notices a large crack running across the garage floor. The agent does not mention it to the buyer-customer. This failure is most accurately described as:

a. Acceptable, because the crack is visible and the buyer could have noticed it independently.

b. Acceptable, because the agent's duty to disclose material facts applies only to represented clients, not customers.

c. A violation only if the crack was reported on the Seller's Disclosure Notice.

d. A violation of the duty to disclose material facts to the buyer, applying the reasonable person standard.

7. Which of the following correctly describes the difference between "fairness" to a customer and "loyalty" to a client?

a. Fairness requires the agent to negotiate equally for both the customer and the client.

b. Fairness means honest, transparent conduct with the customer while still providing full fiduciary advocacy for the client.

c. Fairness and loyalty are the same obligation applied to different parties.

d. Fairness to the customer overrides loyalty to the client when there is a conflict between the two.

8. A seller instructs the listing agent not to disclose that the basement floods during heavy rain. The agent's correct course of action is to:

a. Honor the instruction since the seller is the client and the agent must follow lawful client directions.

b. Disclose the condition only if a buyer asks directly about the basement.

c. Disclose the flooding condition to buyers regardless, and inform the seller that concealing known defects is not permitted.

d. Add a general disclaimer to the listing that the property is sold as is.

9. A licensee who previously represented a seller as a listing agent is later contacted by a buyer who wants to purchase that same property, which has since expired and relisted with another broker. The licensee:

a. Must disclose to the prospective buyer that confidential information from the prior listing cannot be shared, and may refer the buyer to another licensee if the buyer is uncomfortable with that limitation.

b. May freely share all information learned during the prior listing because the agency relationship has ended.

c. Cannot show the property at all because of the prior agency relationship.

d. Is required to represent the buyer and disclose all prior information as part of the fiduciary duty of disclosure.

10. Which of the following types of customers should a licensee avoid proceeding with in a real estate transaction?

a. A customer who has not yet obtained a pre-approval letter from a lender.

b. A customer who is representing themselves without a buyer's agent.

c. A customer who is purchasing an investment property rather than a primary residence.

d. A customer who is a minor and lacks the legal capacity to enter a real estate contract.

11. The "15 Minute Rule" in Texas real estate practice refers to:

a. The maximum time a licensee has to notify a client after receiving an accepted offer.

b. A reminder that buyers will eventually learn the truth about a property, and it is better for the agent to disclose known issues before closing than for the buyer to discover them afterward.

c. A TREC requirement that property disclosures be delivered at least 15 minutes before a scheduled showing.

d. The standard follow-up interval for contacting customers after an initial inquiry.

12. A listing agent tells a buyer-customer that the seller has already purchased another home and is under significant pressure to close quickly. This statement is:

a. Appropriate, because customers are entitled to know the seller's motivation.

b. Appropriate, because the information might help the buyer decide whether to make an offer.

c. A violation of the duty of loyalty, because it gives the buyer a negotiating advantage at the seller's expense.

d. Required under the duty of honesty owed to all parties in the transaction.

13. During a showing, a buyer asks the listing agent whether hairline cracks in the garage floor indicate a foundation problem. The agent responds, "Those are just normal settling cracks, nothing to worry about." This response is most likely an example of:

a. Innocent misrepresentation, because the agent believed the statement to be true.

b. Fraudulent misrepresentation, because the agent intentionally concealed a known defect.

c. An acceptable response, because agents are permitted to offer general opinions about cosmetic conditions.

d. Negligent misrepresentation, because the agent offered a structural opinion without the expertise to support it.

14. Which of the following is the best example of a material fact that must be disclosed to a prospective buyer?

a. A history of basement flooding that the seller has known about for several years.

b. A cracked window in a guest bedroom that can be replaced for under one hundred dollars.

c. The seller's personal opinion that the neighborhood is improving.

d. The color the prior owners painted the kitchen before the current owners repainted it.

15. For a statement to constitute fraudulent misrepresentation under Texas law, which of the following elements must be present?

a. The agent made the statement in writing rather than verbally.

b. The buyer suffered actual damages as a result of relying on a false statement of material fact made to induce the transaction.

c. The statement was made at a public open house rather than a private showing.

d. The seller was represented by a licensed attorney at the time the statement was made.

16. A latent defect differs from a patent defect in that a latent defect is:

a. Always required to be disclosed on the Seller's Disclosure form, while a patent defect is not.

b. One that the seller intentionally concealed, while a patent defect was simply overlooked.

c. Not visible or discoverable through a reasonable inspection, while a patent defect is obvious to anyone who looks.

d. Related to title issues, while a patent defect relates only to physical condition.

17. A seller places a paint can over a drain in the master bathroom before showings. After closing, the buyer removes the can and discovers that sewer gases enter the bathroom due to a defective septic connection. This situation is best described as:

a. A latent defect, because the buyer could not discover it through a normal inspection.

b. An acceptable seller action, because the Seller's Disclosure form does not include septic system questions.

c. A latent defect for which the seller bears no liability because the property was sold as is.

d. A patent defect that the seller actively concealed, which would likely support a buyer claim against the seller.

18. Which of the following transfers is exempt from the Texas requirement to provide a Seller's Disclosure of Property Condition?

a. A transfer of property acquired through a court-ordered foreclosure sale.

b. A sale of a three-bedroom home by a seller who has owned the property for five years.

c. A sale of a condominium listed through the MLS.

d. A sale of a duplex where the seller has lived in one unit for two years.

19. A seller asks the listing agent to fill out the Seller's Disclosure of Property Condition form on the seller's behalf because the seller has a hand injury. The agent's correct response is to:

a. Complete the form based on the agent's own inspection of the property.

b. Decline to complete the form and explain that the seller must complete and sign it, suggesting a family member, friend, or personal attorney assist instead.

c. Complete the form by asking the seller each question verbally and recording the answers.

d. Complete the form and have the broker co-sign it to share the liability.

20. Under Texas law, which of the following events on a property must a seller disclose to prospective buyers?

a. A prior occupant's death from natural causes in the home.

b. A prior occupant's suicide on the property.

c. A prior occupant who had AIDS living in the home.

d. A murder that occurred on the property.

21. A prospective buyer directly asks the listing agent whether any previous occupant of the home had AIDS. According to HUD guidance and NAR recommendations, the agent should:

a. Answer honestly, since buyers have a right to all material information.

b. Decline to respond, explain that the firm's policy is not to answer such inquiries as the information is immaterial to the transaction, and advise the buyer to pursue the inquiry independently if desired.

c. Disclose only if the occupant lived in the home within the last three years.

d. Confirm or deny based on information in the Seller's Disclosure form.

22. A survey of a property reveals that the seller's fence does not sit on the actual property line, leaving a strip of land between the fence and the true boundary. Under Texas disclosure requirements, this situation:

a. Does not need to be disclosed because fences are personal property, not real property.

b. Is automatically resolved by the title company as part of the standard closing process.

c. Is a material fact that must be disclosed, and the parties must decide how to address the discrepancy before closing.

d. Only requires disclosure if the disputed strip of land exceeds one acre.

CHAPTER 4

SELLER AGENCY

Chapter Objectives

After completing this chapter, you should be able to:

1. Identify the different types of listing agreements and explain when each is appropriate.
2. Distinguish between express and implied agency in the context of seller representation.
3. Describe the key components of a listing agreement, the Multiple Listing Service, and the listing presentation.
4. Explain the advantages and disadvantages of exclusive seller agency, in-house sales, and cooperating with other brokers.
5. Explain marketing strategies, ethical conduct during listing appointments, and required disclosures to both sellers and buyers.
6. Define subagency and explain how it is created and terminated in a Texas real estate transaction.
7. Describe the liability risks associated with subagency for listing brokers, sellers, and subagents.
8. Explain why brokers formerly had to set company policy on subagency, and what replaced that decision.
9. Compare the advantages and disadvantages of subagency for sellers, buyers, and licensees.
10. Explain confidentiality rules in subagency and how a licensee should handle conflicts between prior subagent knowledge and current buyer representation.

Contents

Disadvantages of Exclusive Seller Agency

Marketing for Listing Appointments

Ethics During the Listing Appointment

Ready, Willing, and Able Buyer

Questions to Ask Sellers

Disclosure Issues

Buying Your Own Listing

What Is Subagency?

How Subagency Begins

Representing the Seller or the Buyer: Two Clear Paths

Subagency: Eliminated Effective January 1, 2026

Note: subagency was eliminated in all Texas real estate transactions by SB 1968, effective January 1, 2026, and references to it were removed from TRELA and from the Information About Brokerage Services form. It is presented here because licensees encounter it in older files and in other states, and because understanding it explains why Texas moved to the intermediary framework.

The Liability of Subagency

Company Policy

Subagency and the MLS

Rejecting Subagency

How Subagency Is Offered or Declined

Seller Liability in Subagency

Deciding Whether to Act as a Subagent

Advantages of Subagency

Disadvantages of Subagency

Working with Investors as a Subagent

Working with Another Broker as a Subagent

Being Denied Subagency Can Be an Opportunity

Confidentiality and Subagency

Seller Agency

Seller agency is the foundation on which Texas real estate practice was built. In the early days of Texas real estate, transactions were informal and unregulated. The formal system that eventually developed focused on the broker as a matchmaker: find a seller with property, find a buyer who wants it, negotiate the transaction, and earn a commission. That basic model remains the core of the business today.

Among experienced, high-producing agents, listings remain the engine of the business. An old saying captures it well: "If you don't list, you won't last." When a licensee has active listings, buyers respond to the advertising, which generates more contacts, more showings, more offers, and more closings. Listings create momentum.

Express Agency

Agency with a seller can be created in two ways: expressly, through a written agreement, or impliedly, through the conduct of the parties. Express agency is by far the clearer and more protective approach for everyone involved.

A written listing agreement, signed by the seller and initialed on each page, leaves no ambiguity about whether an agency relationship exists, what the broker is authorized to do, how long the agreement lasts, or how the broker will be compensated. Both the seller and the broker have a signed document to refer to if questions arise.

Implied Agency

Implied agency with a seller occurs when the licensee begins working on a seller's behalf without a written agreement in place. This might happen if a seller refuses to sign a formal document, or if the licensee chooses to keep the arrangement informal because of concerns about the relationship. However, once agency is created, whether in writing or by conduct, all fiduciary duties apply to the client in full. An agent cannot hold a client at arm's length and still claim to be that client's fiduciary.

In practice, implied seller agency is uncommon today. Licensees are understandably reluctant to spend money on advertising and marketing a property without a written agreement that protects their right to a commission. Implied agency is a more significant risk on the buyer side, where a licensee can inadvertently create an agency relationship through the advice and advocacy they extend to a buyer-customer.

Listing Agreements

When meeting with a seller, a licensee can structure the representation in one of three ways:

Exclusive Right to Sell

This is the listing type that best protects the broker. Under an exclusive right to sell agreement, the broker is entitled to the agreed commission regardless of who actually procures the buyer, including the seller. Because the broker's commission is guaranteed once the property sells, the broker can invest confidently in marketing, advertising, and time without risk of losing the commission to the seller's own efforts. This is the most common listing type in Texas residential real estate.

Exclusive Agency

An exclusive agency agreement authorizes one broker to market the property, but the seller retains the right to sell the property themselves without owing the broker a commission. This arrangement typically comes up when the seller has one or two specific prospective buyers in mind and wants to reserve the right to sell to those individuals without broker involvement, while still having the broker pursue other buyers on the open market.

Open Listing

An open listing is a unilateral contract that allows the seller to engage any number of brokers simultaneously. All contracted brokers may market the property at the same time, but only the broker who produces the ready, willing, and able buyer earns the commission. Open listings offer the least protection to any individual broker and are generally avoided by experienced agents because of the high likelihood of doing significant work without receiving compensation.

Completing the Listing Agreement

TREC does not promulgate a specific form for residential listing agreements. The Texas Association of REALTORS provides the Residential Real Estate Listing Agreement, Exclusive Right to Sell, which is the standard form used by most Texas brokers who are REALTOR members. The key sections of the listing agreement include:

Seller: The complete legal names of all persons with ownership interest in the property.

Broker: All identifying information about the brokerage firm entering into the agreement.

Type of Listing: A statement confirming the agreement is an exclusive right to sell.

Property: The full legal description of the property, along with any items specifically included in or excluded from the sale.

Price: The asking price the sellers have authorized the broker to advertise.

Term: The beginning and ending dates of the listing agreement.

Broker's Fee: The commission the seller agrees to pay, either as a flat fee or a percentage of the sales price, negotiated between the parties.

Protection Period: The period after the listing expires during which the broker is still entitled to a commission if the property is sold to a buyer the broker introduced during the listing term.

Cooperation with Other Brokers: The compensation the listing broker will offer to any cooperating broker who brings a buyer.

Broker's Authority: The specific marketing and advertising activities the broker is authorized to perform.

Seller's Representations: The seller's certification that there are no known defects or adverse claims and that the seller has the legal right to convey the property.

Limitation of Liability: The seller's agreement to hold the broker harmless for personal injury or property loss that occurs during the listing.

Addenda: Any additional documents attached to and incorporated into the listing agreement.

The paperwork itself is the easier part of the listing appointment. The real challenge is earning the seller's confidence and commitment before the forms come out. Good preparation, including a thorough comparative market analysis, goes a long way toward making the appointment go smoothly. When a seller raises an objection or asks a difficult question, the right response is either a factual answer or an honest acknowledgment that you will find out.

The Multiple Listing Service

The Multiple Listing Service (MLS) is not a type of listing agreement. It is a shared database that allows licensees to publish listing details and search available properties across a broad network of participating brokers. It remains the fastest and most effective way to connect sellers with buyers in the market.

Once a property is entered into the MLS, any member can search it by price, location, bedroom count, school district, and many other criteria. The system is internet-based and accessible from any device.

The MLS is also the primary resource for preparing a Comparative Market Analysis (CMA). The three data sets used in a CMA are:

- Active listings currently on the market (showing competition).
- Recently sold properties (showing actual market values).
- Expired listings (showing prices the market did not accept).

MLS membership is tied to local board membership. A licensee must belong to a board of REALTORS somewhere in order to join an MLS. Many agents belong to a single board but participate in multiple MLS systems, depending on the geographic area they serve.

The Listing Presentation

When a licensee arrives at a listing appointment, the primary objective is to earn the seller's confidence and secure the listing agreement. In most markets, the seller is interviewing more than one licensee, which means the presentation must be strong, specific, and professional.

A complete listing presentation typically includes:

- A detailed overview of the marketing plan, covering yard signage, MLS entry, online advertising, broker cooperation, and any print or social media marketing the office uses.
- The broker's internet presence and the specific websites and platforms where the listing will be promoted.
- A thorough Comparative Market Analysis showing the seller what similar homes have sold for and what the current competition looks like.
- Letters of recommendation or testimonials from satisfied past clients and customers.

Recommendation letters are most effectively obtained by asking for them at closing or when delivering a closing gift. A licensee who consistently requests feedback from satisfied clients builds a library of credible, specific endorsements that are far more persuasive than anything the licensee can say about themselves.

Exclusive Seller Agency

Seller agency was the original model for Texas real estate. The concept of buyer representation did not exist in the early days of the industry. The prevailing rule was caveat emptor, meaning "let the buyer beware." It was the buyer's responsibility to evaluate the deal, assess the property, and decide whether to proceed. The broker represented the seller, period.

Some brokers and agents still operate under an exclusively seller-focused policy today. Under this model, the agent always knows who their client is, the fiduciary obligations never shift between parties, and there is no risk of the role confusion that can arise in dual or intermediary situations. Commission structures within the office are also straightforward and consistent.

There is, however, a practical limitation. Sellers frequently ask at the listing appointment, "Where are you moving when your home sells?" The opportunity to represent that seller in the purchase of their next property is a natural extension of the listing relationship. A broker whose policy prohibits buyer representation cannot take advantage of that opportunity. Every such situation represents a commission that must go to another office.

In-House Sales

An in-house sale occurs when both the seller and the buyer are connected to the same brokerage. The buyer may be a customer of the listing agent, a client of another agent in the same office, or a customer working directly with someone in the office while a different agent holds the listing.

From the broker's perspective, an in-house sale is highly desirable because the brokerage retains the full commission rather than sharing a portion with an outside cooperating broker. The commission is then distributed entirely within the office, whether to the listing agent, the buyer's agent, or both.

That said, the broker's first obligation is to the client, not to the commission structure. Getting the seller's property sold at the best possible price and terms is the goal, whether that sale is completed by someone in the office or by a cooperating broker from another firm.

Cooperating with Other Brokers

Listing brokers are generally willing to cooperate with other brokers who bring buyers to their listings. Cooperation serves the seller's interest by expanding the pool of potential buyers, which is ultimately more important than keeping the entire commission within one office.

When a broker is a member of a local board and MLS, they agree as a condition of membership to cooperate with and compensate other member brokers. The listing broker publishes the cooperation offer in the MLS, specifying the amount, whether a percentage or flat fee, that a buyer's broker will receive.

> ***2024 NAR Settlement Update:*** *Under rules adopted in Texas following the 2024 NAR settlement, offers of buyer broker compensation may no longer be communicated through the MLS. Compensation must be negotiated and disclosed in the buyer representation agreement before any property is shown. Brokers who wish to offer cooperative compensation to a buyer's broker do so outside the MLS system, through direct negotiation documented in writing.*

When no MLS system is involved, cooperating brokers negotiate and document their commission arrangement directly before the property is shown. The agreement specifies what each broker will receive, who will pay it, and when payment will occur.

Benefits of Seller Agency

Operating as an exclusively seller-focused brokerage or agent offers several practical advantages:

- The risk of dual agency conflicts is minimized or eliminated, since buyers are always customers and never clients of the same firm that represents the seller.
- The seller receives undivided loyalty from the brokerage, with no concern that buyer interests are being considered alongside their own.
- For experienced agents who have operated this way for most of their careers, the consistency of always representing the seller simplifies every transaction.
- Commission structures within the office are clear and consistent, with no need to adjust splits based on whether a buyer or seller is being represented.

Disadvantages of Exclusive Seller Agency

There are real drawbacks to representing only sellers:

- Buyers who want representation must go elsewhere. The portion of the commission that would have gone to a buyer's agent in-house goes to a competing broker instead.
- Agents in an exclusively seller-side office are at a higher risk of inadvertently creating implied agency with buyers, who may not understand they are not being represented. Clear communication about the nature of the relationship is essential and ongoing.

- When the seller is ready to buy their next home, the listing agent cannot legally help them, because that would require the agent to represent a buyer. The seller must go elsewhere, and the potential commission from the next transaction is lost entirely.

Marketing for Listing Appointments

More listings produce more business. When active listings are on the market, buyers call in response to yard signs, online ads, and MLS entries. Those buyer inquiries can be converted into more clients and more listings. The pipeline feeds itself.

Most brokerages have defined marketing systems for obtaining listings, including referral networks, geographic farming, direct mail, and digital marketing. Agents should take ownership of their marketing activity rather than waiting for the broker to generate it. The relationship between listings and income is direct: listings generate showings, showings generate offers, offers generate contracts, contracts generate closings, and closings generate commissions and referrals.

Marketing directly to buyers is possible, but less efficient in most markets. Buyers tend to call the listing agent when responding to property advertising. The agent who holds the listing is already positioned to capture that inquiry.

Ethics During the Listing Appointment

Sellers frequently ask, "How long have you been in real estate?" This is a reasonable question and deserves an honest answer. Misrepresentation is never appropriate, even when the truth feels unflattering.

One new agent, when asked this question on their very first listing appointment, responded: "This is my third day in the business. If you hire me, there is no agent in this market who will devote more time to selling your home, because this will be my first listing." The seller appreciated the honesty and the obvious commitment. The agent got the listing and earned their first commission.

The lesson is not that inexperience is an advantage. The lesson is that honesty, combined with a clear value proposition, is always more effective than a vague or inflated answer. Sellers are perceptive. They are making a significant financial decision and they recognize authentic engagement when they encounter it.

Ready, Willing, and Able Buyer

Under Texas listing agreements, a broker earns the commission when they produce a ready, willing, and able buyer. In practice, licensees almost always wait for the closing to receive payment, but the listing agreement itself does not require the closing to occur before the commission is earned.

Each of the three elements has a specific meaning:

Ready: The buyer is prepared to proceed without contingencies that prevent moving forward. A buyer who makes an offer contingent on selling another property first is not ready.

Willing: The buyer intends to complete the transaction. A buyer who needs to wait and see whether a job transfer comes through before committing is not willing.

Able: The buyer has the financial capacity to complete the purchase. A buyer who cannot obtain a mortgage and has no alternative financing is not able.

If a broker presents the seller with a buyer who meets all three criteria and the seller refuses to accept the offer for a reason not permitted under the listing agreement, the broker has earned the commission. In that situation, the broker may need to pursue the commission through legal action. Only a broker, not a salesperson, has standing to sue for a commission in Texas, since it is the broker who is the legal agent of the client.

Questions to Ask Sellers

The listing appointment should include a thorough fact-finding conversation. The licensee who asks the right questions at the beginning of the relationship is far better equipped to represent the seller, market the property accurately, and disclose material facts to buyers. The following questions are a practical starting point:

1. Did both of you acquire this property together, or did one of you own it before the relationship?
2. What negative information do you have about the condition of the property?
3. Are there any problems with utility service in the area?
4. What repairs have been done on the property, and by whom?
5. Are there any easements on the property?
6. Are there any deed restrictions that apply?
7. Are there any encroachments on or from adjacent properties?
8. If tenants are in place, how long do they have remaining on their lease?
9. Are there any zoning issues that affect the property?
10. Are there any liens against the property?
11. Are there any known environmental issues, such as proximity to a landfill or presence of protected species?
12. Is there a homeowner's association, and if so, what are the fees and restrictions?
13. Have there been any termite, rodent, or pest problems?
14. Is there anything else about the property I should know before we begin marketing?

Take thorough notes during this conversation and treat everything that surfaces as a potential material fact that will need to be disclosed to prospective buyers.

Disclosure Issues

Before signing the listing agreement, the listing agent must provide the seller with the TREC Information About Brokerage Services form which describes the services and obligations associated with seller representation, buyer representation, and intermediary status. This disclosure can be incorporated into the listing agreement itself or attached as an addendum.

Disclosure of the Seller's Agent to the Buyer

The seller's agent has a clear obligation to disclose to every buyer they interact with that the licensee represents the seller, not the buyer. This disclosure should happen at the first substantive contact with the buyer, along with delivery of the form.

Many brokerages reinforce this with a written acknowledgment form that the buyer reads and signs, confirming they understand the licensee represents the seller and that the buyer is a customer, not a client. This document typically explains what the seller's agent can and cannot do for the buyer.

Buyers who are not represented by their own agent should be advised clearly: treat every conversation with the seller's agent the same way you would treat a conversation directly with the seller. The seller's agent is not neutral. Anything the buyer shares with the listing agent may be passed to the seller and used in negotiations. By the same token, the listing agent will not provide the buyer with information that would not also come directly from the seller.

The seller's agent must remain professional throughout: honest and fair with the buyer-customer, while maintaining full loyalty and advocacy for the seller-client.

Buying Your Own Listing

A licensee may wish to purchase a property they currently have listed. There is nothing inherently wrong with this, but it comes with specific disclosure obligations.

First, the licensee must have provided the seller with an honest market value opinion when the listing was taken. A thorough CMA at the time of listing makes this straightforward to demonstrate.

Second, when the licensee decides to make an offer on the property, they are no longer acting as the seller's agent. They are acting as a buyer pursuing their own interest. This conflict must be disclosed in writing in the purchase contract. A clear and commonly used disclosure statement is:

> *"Buyer is a licensed real estate agent and is purchasing the property in hopes of making a profit."*

This statement puts everyone who reads the contract on notice that the licensee is acting as a buyer, not as the seller's representative. The licensee must also check the appropriate representation box on the signature page of the earnest money contract to confirm who they represent in the transaction.

Purchasing investment property is a natural opportunity for active licensees. Being positioned in the market gives licensees early access to properties before they receive wider attention, and the due diligence skills developed in practice make them well-equipped to evaluate investment opportunities quickly and accurately.

Snapshot Review – Chapter 4

Seller Agency Basics

1. Listings are the foundation of real estate production. When a licensee has active listings, buyers respond and the transaction pipeline fills.
2. Express agency, created through a signed listing agreement, provides the strongest protection for both the seller and the broker.
3. Implied agency with a seller can arise from conduct alone, but it is uncommon in practice because brokers require a written agreement before investing in marketing.
4. Once agency is created, whether express or implied, all fiduciary duties apply to the client in full.

The Three Types of Listing Agreements

Exclusive Right to Sell: The broker earns a commission regardless of who finds the buyer, including the seller. Provides maximum protection to the broker and is the most common listing type in Texas.

Exclusive Agency: One broker is authorized, but the seller retains the right to sell without owing a commission. Used when the seller has specific buyers in mind they wish to pursue directly.

Open Listing: Any number of brokers may be engaged simultaneously. Only the broker who produces the buyer earns a commission. Provides the least protection to any individual broker.

MLS and Market Analysis

1. The MLS is a shared information system, not a listing type. It is the primary tool for connecting sellers and buyers across a broad network of brokers.
2. A CMA for listing preparation draws on three MLS data sets: active listings, recently sold properties, and expired listings.
3. Under 2024 NAR settlement rules adopted in Texas, buyer broker compensation may no longer be advertised through the MLS. It must be negotiated and documented in the buyer representation agreement.

In-House Sales and Cooperation

1. An in-house sale occurs when both parties in a transaction are connected to the same brokerage. The broker retains the full commission.
2. Cooperation with other brokers is required by MLS membership and serves the seller's interest by expanding the buyer pool.

Ready, Willing, and Able

1. A broker earns the commission under a Texas listing agreement when they present the seller with a buyer who is ready (no blocking contingencies), willing (genuinely intending to close), and able (financially qualified).

2. Only a broker, not a salesperson, has legal standing to sue for a commission in Texas.

Disclosure and Ethics

1. The TREC IABS 1-2 form must be delivered to the seller before signing the listing agreement. This disclosure may be included in the listing agreement or in an addendum.
2. The seller's agent must disclose their representation status to every buyer at the first substantive contact, along with delivery of the IABS 1-2 form.
3. A buyer-customer dealing with the listing agent should treat every interaction as if they were speaking directly with the seller. Nothing shared with the seller's agent is confidential from the seller.
4. When a licensee buys their own listing, they must disclose in the contract that they are a licensed agent purchasing for profit and are no longer acting as the seller's representative.
5. Honesty at the listing appointment, including about experience level, is non-negotiable. Misrepresentation at any point in the relationship is unacceptable.

CHAPTER 4 QUIZ — SELLER AGENCY

1. Which type of listing agreement provides the greatest protection to the listing broker by guaranteeing the commission regardless of who finds the buyer, including the seller?

a. Exclusive right to sell

b. Open listing

c. Exclusive agency

d. Net listing

2. A seller wants to list their home with a broker but insists on reserving the right to sell the property to a neighbor without owing a commission. The listing type that best fits this situation is:

a. Exclusive right to sell, because it is required for MLS entry in Texas.

b. Open listing, because multiple brokers can compete for the commission.

c. A verbal agreement, which protects both parties equally.

d. Exclusive agency, which authorizes one broker while allowing the seller to sell to specific buyers without a commission.

3. A licensee begins showing a seller's property and negotiating with prospective buyers before a written listing agreement is signed. If the seller later disputes whether an agency relationship existed, the court would most likely find:

a. No agency relationship, because Texas requires all agency to be established in writing.

b. That the licensee acted as a buyer's agent, not a seller's agent.

c. That an implied agency was created by the conduct of the parties, and full fiduciary duties apply.

d. That the licensee is entitled to no compensation because no written agreement exists.

4. The Multiple Listing Service is best described as:

a. A type of listing agreement that allows multiple brokers to cooperate on a single transaction.

b. A shared database that allows participating brokers to search and publish listing information across a broad network.

c. A TREC-promulgated form used to document cooperative compensation arrangements.

d. A marketing agreement between the listing broker and the seller that authorizes internet advertising.

5. When preparing a Comparative Market Analysis for a listing presentation, the three categories of MLS data a licensee should use are:

a. Active listings, recently sold properties, and expired listings.

b. Active listings, pending sales, and new construction starts.

c. Expired listings, withdrawn listings, and cancelled contracts.

d. Sold properties, tax appraisal records, and current rental rates.

6. Under the 2024 NAR settlement rules adopted in Texas, which of the following correctly describes how buyer broker compensation must be handled?

a. Listing brokers must post the buyer broker compensation offer in the MLS before the property can be shown.

b. Buyer broker compensation is set by the local board of REALTORS and cannot be negotiated between the parties.

c. Buyer broker compensation is paid directly by the buyer at closing and does not require disclosure in the representation agreement.

d. Buyer broker compensation must be negotiated and documented in the buyer representation agreement before any property is shown, and may no longer be advertised through the MLS.

7. A broker presents a seller with a buyer who has been pre-approved for a mortgage, has no contingency requiring a prior home sale, and has signed an offer at the listing price. The seller rejects the offer for personal reasons not permitted under the listing agreement. Under Texas law, which of the following is most accurate?

a. The broker has not earned the commission because the transaction did not close.

b. The salesperson who showed the property may sue the seller directly for the commission.

c. The broker has earned the commission by producing a ready, willing, and able buyer, and may need to pursue it through legal action.

d. The broker forfeits the commission because the listing agreement requires the seller's consent to all offers.

8. An unrepresented buyer who is working with the listing agent asks the agent whether the seller would take less than the asking price. The agent's correct response is to:

a. Share what is known about the seller's flexibility, since honesty is owed to all parties.

b. Decline to share that information, because the duty of loyalty requires the agent to protect the seller's negotiating position.

c. Recommend that the buyer make a low offer to test the seller's response.

d. Tell the buyer the seller's bottom line so the transaction can close efficiently.

9. A licensee who wishes to purchase a listed property must:

a. Disclose in the purchase contract that they are a licensed agent purchasing the property for their own account and are no longer acting as the seller's representative.

b. First withdraw as the listing agent and allow another broker to represent the seller before submitting any offer.

c. Obtain written permission from TREC before submitting an offer on their own listing.

d. Reduce their commission by the amount of any profit anticipated on the resale of the property.

10. At a listing appointment, the seller asks the agent how long they have been in real estate. The agent was licensed three months ago. The most appropriate response is to:

a. Describe the broker's overall experience, since the broker is ultimately responsible for all transactions.

b. State that they have been in the business for several years to avoid creating doubt about their qualifications.

c. Redirect the conversation to the CMA and avoid answering the question directly.

d. Answer honestly, acknowledge the limited experience, and emphasize the commitment and effort they will bring to the listing.

11. Under the 2024 NAR settlement rules now in effect in Texas, buyer broker compensation:

a. May no longer be advertised through the MLS and must instead be negotiated and documented in the buyer representation agreement before any property is shown.

b. Must be published in the MLS listing so cooperating agents can review it before showing.

c. Is set by TREC at a standard percentage and may not be negotiated between the parties.

d. Is paid directly to the buyer and applied as a credit toward the purchase price.

CHAPTER 5

BUYER AGENCY

Chapter Objectives

After completing this chapter, you should be able to:

1. Explain buyer agency, describe when and how to offer it, and identify the benefits it provides to both buyers and licensees.
2. Discuss company policy considerations regarding buyer representation, including offices that represent buyers exclusively.
3. Describe the buyer representation agreement, its key provisions, and how compensation is structured under Texas rules.
4. Identify potential conflicts of interest in buyer agency and explain how to handle them professionally.
5. Explain the fiduciary duties of a buyer's agent, procuring cause, and common misconceptions about buyer representation.
6. Describe the consulting role of the buyer's agent and the elevated level of service a buyer-client receives compared to a buyer-customer.
7. Explain how a buyer's agent works through each stage of a purchase transaction, from property analysis through contract negotiations.
8. Identify the compensation structures available to a buyer's broker and explain the advantages and disadvantages of each.
9. Describe the disclosures a licensee must make to the buyer before entering into a representation agreement and to the seller or listing broker at first contact.
10. Explain the property condition disclosure process and identify additional contract benefits a buyer's agent may negotiate for the buyer-client.

Contents

Explaining Compensation to the Buyer
Expanding the Property Search
Perceived Conflicts of Interest
Tenant Representation
Representing Two Buyers
Terminating Buyer Agency
Misuse of the Termination Form
Representation Agreements
Exclusive Right to Purchase
Key Provisions of the Buyer's Representation Agreement
Limitations of Exclusive Buyer Agency
Fiduciary Duties of the Buyer's Agent
Procuring Cause
Single-Property Agreements
Common Misconceptions About Buyer Agency
Counseling the Buyer-Client
Tailoring the Representation Agreement
Access to the Full Marketplace
Benefits of Buyer Agency for the Licensee
The Purchase Agreement
A Buyer Agency Case Study
Written Compensation Agreements
Buyer Agency Fee Arrangements
Retainer Fees
Seller-Paid Commission
Commission Splits
Buyer-Paid Fees
Gross Price Compensation
Advantages and Disadvantages of the Seller Paying the Commission
Disclosures to the Buyer
Disclosures to the Seller and Listing Broker
Buyers Who Prefer Customer Status
Better Disclosure, Better Service
Property Condition Disclosure
Additional Contract Benefits for the Buyer-Client

Buyer Agency

Buyer agency exists when a broker represents the buyer exclusively in a real estate transaction. For most of Texas real estate history, buyers were treated as customers, with no formal representation and no agent acting on their behalf. That changed as residential consumers recognized that the same professional representation available to sellers could work equally well for buyers.

A buyer agency relationship may be created verbally, in writing, or through the conduct of the parties. A written agreement remains the most protective option for both sides. Some express buyer agency relationships are initially oral, with written confirmation incorporated into the sales contract, but a signed agreement is always the stronger approach.

When working with a buyer, the licensee should determine early whether to offer buyer agency, disclose the nature of the relationship, and obtain the necessary signatures to formalize it. Licensees can act as agents for the buyer, as subagents for the seller, or under the intermediary framework if both parties are clients of the same broker.

When to Offer Buyer Agency

Not every buyer who walks through the door is ready to be a client. Before offering buyer agency, the licensee should take a moment to evaluate whether the buyer has genuine capacity and intent to purchase. Three questions frame that assessment:

1. Is this person actually going to buy?
2. Are they likely to continue working with me?
3. Do they have the financial ability to obtain a mortgage?

The third question is best answered by having the buyer meet with a loan officer for pre-qualification before the property search begins. Pre-qualification establishes a realistic price range, saves time for everyone involved, and gives the licensee confidence that the buyer can actually close.

Once pre-qualification is confirmed, the licensee can proceed to form agency with the buyer. The only remaining disqualifiers would be legal incapacity, such as being under the age of majority or being legally incompetent to contract.

If the evaluation is not favorable, the licensee has three options: convert the buyer to a client regardless and invest in the relationship, continue working with the buyer as a customer without a representation agreement, or refer the buyer to a different licensee.

Company Policy

Every brokerage has a policy on buyer representation, and licensees must understand that policy before working with buyers. Most offices are willing to work with both buyer clients and buyer customers, cooperating with any licensee regardless of the representation structure.

A small number of offices operate exclusively as buyer-only brokerages, never representing sellers. While this model simplifies the agent's role and eliminates the risk of dual representation, it also removes a significant source of income: commissions from the listing side of the business. These offices rely on word-of-mouth referrals from satisfied buyer clients, since they have no listings to attract new prospects through advertising.

There are also a handful of independent offices that do not belong to a local board or MLS and decline to cooperate with outside brokers in any capacity. A buyer who wants to see one of those office's listings must work directly with that office, regardless of who their agent is.

Representing Buyers Only

Brokers who choose to represent buyers exclusively see distinct professional advantages in limiting their practice to one side of the transaction. When every client is a buyer, there is no ambiguity about who the agent represents. The buyer receives complete loyalty because there is never a seller in the same office whose interests could compete. The agent's fiduciary obligations are uncomplicated and consistent across every transaction.

These brokers typically refer sellers to trusted listing agents in exchange for an agreed referral fee, documented in writing before any work is done. The arrangement allows the buyer-only broker to stay within their area of focus while maintaining professional relationships across the industry.

In practice, representing buyers exclusively is rare. The income lost by not handling listing transactions can be substantial, and the MLS infrastructure makes it straightforward for most brokers to serve both buyers and sellers competently.

Working a Target Territory

Texas licensees are authorized to practice throughout the entire state. In practice, most agents define a geographic focus that allows them to serve clients efficiently without excessive travel time or cost. In urban markets, the buyer representation agreement typically identifies specific counties as the defined search territory.

The geographic scope of the agreement can be amended if the buyer's search expands. If a buyer becomes interested in a property outside the original area, both parties can agree to an amendment extending the territory into the new location. That amendment should be signed before the licensee begins showing properties in the new area.

In some cases the territory is extremely narrow. A buyer may approach a licensee specifically to purchase a single For Sale by Owner (FSBO) property, preferring to have professional representation even though the seller has no agent. In that situation, the buyer representation agreement can be drafted to cover only that one physical address. If negotiations fall apart, the agency relationship ends automatically, and the buyer is free to search for other properties independently or with a different licensee.

Creating Buyer Agency

Agency with a buyer can be created in three ways: in writing, orally, or through the conduct of the parties. A written agreement remains the most reliable approach and the only form that gives the broker a clear basis for pursuing a commission if the need arises.

Some licensees resist using a written buyer representation agreement, reasoning that a buyer who is happy with the service will not leave for another agent. That reasoning misses the point. The agreement protects both parties. It gives the buyer a clear picture of what services to expect, what the compensation arrangement is, and what geographic area the relationship covers. It gives the broker enforceable rights. And it gives the buyer a reason to feel professionally committed to the relationship.

TREC does not promulgate a buyer representation form. The Texas Association of REALTORS and local MLS associations provide approved forms available to their members. Some brokers, working with their own attorneys, have developed shorter one-page versions. Whatever form is used, it must be specific enough to minimize ambiguity and protect both parties in the event of a dispute.

If a licensee begins working with a buyer verbally before a written agreement is in place, the written form should follow as soon as possible. If a buyer consistently refuses to sign any form of representation agreement, the licensee should decide whether to continue the relationship as a customer arrangement or refer the buyer elsewhere.

The Buyer's Negotiating Advantage

The most compelling reason a buyer should want representation is the negotiating advantage it creates. A buyer without an agent has no professional advocate. A buyer with a representation agreement has a licensee whose job is to negotiate the lowest possible price and the most favorable contract terms on the buyer's behalf.

The gap between no representation and full representation is not trivial. A buyer-customer receives factual information. A buyer-client receives professional analysis, strategic guidance, and active advocacy during every phase of the negotiation. Any buyer who genuinely understands this distinction will often seek out buyer representation before the licensee even suggests it.

The licensee's role is to explain this dynamic clearly and help the buyer recognize what is at stake. A well-informed buyer who understands the difference between being a customer and being a client will almost always choose client status.

Why Licensees Value Buyer Agency

Buyer agency benefits the licensee as well as the buyer. Before buyer representation agreements became standard practice, buyers had no professional obligation to stay with any particular agent. A buyer could look at properties with one licensee on Monday and walk into a competing office on Tuesday without any notice or consequence. The agent who invested hours in showing properties had no meaningful claim on the eventual commission.

A signed buyer representation agreement changes that dynamic entirely. The buyer has made a professional commitment, and the licensee can invest time, research, and resources in the relationship with reasonable confidence that they will be the agent sitting at the closing table when the transaction is complete. That security changes how a licensee approaches the work. It justifies a deeper investment in understanding the buyer's needs and delivering a higher level of service.

When buyer agency first became available in Texas, some listing brokers were reluctant to cooperate with buyer's agents. That resistance has long since disappeared. Today, every listing broker expects to cooperate with buyer's agents and would not think of refusing.

Explaining Compensation to the Buyer

When completing the buyer representation agreement, the licensee must explain clearly how the buyer's agent will be compensated. There are three possible sources of payment:

1. The seller pays the buyer's broker commission directly.
2. The buyer pays the commission.
3. The seller and the buyer share the commission between them.

Most buyers prefer the first option. However, the buyer representation agreement specifies that if the seller or listing broker does not cover the full agreed commission, the buyer is responsible for making up the difference. For example, if the agreement specifies a four percent buyer broker commission and the listing broker offers only three percent to cooperating agents, the buyer would owe the remaining one percent.

> ***NAR Settlement Update:*** *Under rules adopted in Texas following the 2024 NAR settlement, buyer broker compensation must be negotiated and clearly disclosed in the buyer representation agreement before any properties are shown. This requirement applies regardless of how the commission is ultimately sourced. Licensees must have this conversation with buyers at the outset of the relationship and document the agreed compensation in writing.*

Expanding the Property Search

One of the practical benefits of buyer agency is access. Because a buyer who has not signed a representation agreement is limited in the services a licensee may provide, a buyer who is a customer may find that a meaningful portion of available inventory is simply off-limits. A buyer who becomes a client, represented by a buyer's agent, gains access to the full cooperative market.

When the buyer's search expands beyond the geographic area specified in the representation agreement, the agreement must be amended before the licensee shows properties in the new area. An amendment identifying the additional territory and signed by both parties protects the licensee's commission rights and keeps the agreement current with the actual scope of the search. If no separate amendment form is available, the new territory can be added directly to the original agreement with the buyer's initials confirming the change.

Perceived Conflicts of Interest

A buyer-client may raise a concern when they learn that the broker also represents the seller of a property the buyer wants to pursue. This is a legitimate issue and deserves a direct, professional response.

The first step is education. Once the buyer understands how the intermediary framework operates in Texas, many conclude the concern is manageable. If the buyer remains uncomfortable, several paths are available:

1. **Convert the buyer to customer status.** The buyer gives up representation and proceeds without an agent. This is rarely an attractive option once a buyer has experienced the benefits of representation.
2. **Convert the seller to customer status.** The broker shifts full representation to the buyer and the seller proceeds without representation. The seller may actually prefer this if it means no commission obligation on their end.
3. **Refer the buyer to another broker.** The buyer obtains independent representation through a different office, entirely eliminating the conflict. The original broker continues representing the seller without any dual-representation concern.

The broker's job is to present these options clearly and let the buyer decide how to proceed. None of the options is inherently correct; the right choice depends on what the buyer values most.

Tenant Representation

A licensee can represent a tenant in finding commercial or residential space to lease. The representation relationship is the same in structure: the broker forms agency with the tenant and negotiates the most favorable lease terms possible on the tenant's behalf. Commission can be paid by the landlord, the tenant, or split between them.

Tenant representation is most common in commercial real estate. A corporation searching for office space, a retailer looking for a storefront, or a distribution company evaluating warehouse options all benefit from having a professional advocate who understands market rates, lease structures, and negotiating leverage. The broker's job in commercial tenant representation is to identify properties that meet the tenant's criteria for size, visibility, parking, accessibility, and storage, then negotiate the best possible lease terms.

In residential leasing, tenant representation is far less common. Commission amounts on residential leases are typically modest, making the investment of time and effort difficult to justify as a standalone business model. Most residential agents who do any tenant work focus on commercial leasing rather than residential rentals.

Representing Two Buyers

Brokers routinely represent multiple buyers and sellers simultaneously. Occasionally, two buyer-clients represented by the same broker will want to make offers on the same property. When this happens, the situation must be handled with transparency and care.

The best preparation is proactive: when completing the buyer representation agreement with each client, the licensee should review the paragraph that addresses competing clients. This sets the expectation clearly at the beginning, before any conflict arises.

When two clients do pursue the same property, both should be offered the choice to continue with the current broker or transfer to representation at a different office. In practice, most buyers prefer to stay with their original agent. The emotional investment in the property, combined with concern that switching brokers could cost them time and the property itself, keeps most clients in place.

When the negotiation concludes, one buyer will be under contract and the other will not. The licensee's protection throughout this process is thorough documentation and consistent honesty with both parties. Detailed notes on every communication, every showing, and every offer provide a clear record if any party later questions how the situation was handled.

Terminating Buyer Agency

Buyer agency may be terminated at any time by either the broker or the client. In practice, the most common way buyer agency ends is the most natural one: the buyer finds a property, closes the transaction, and the purpose of the agreement is fulfilled.

Other common termination scenarios include expiration of the agreement's term, a mutual decision to end the relationship, or a buyer who stops communicating entirely. If a buyer has gone silent and is no longer returning calls or messages, the licensee should notify the broker, complete a termination form, and send it to the buyer's address of record along with a written explanation. Documenting the termination protects the licensee if questions arise later about whether the agency was still active.

Some brokers prefer to simply let the agreement expire rather than terminate it formally. This approach keeps the door open during the remaining term in case the buyer re-engages, while ensuring the relationship ends cleanly on the agreed date without any additional action required.

Misuse of the Termination Form

When a buyer-customer walks into an office, the licensee should ask two threshold questions: whether the buyer is already working with someone in that office, and whether the buyer is currently represented by another agent elsewhere. If the buyer says they have an existing agent but want to make a change, the licensee must be careful about how they handle the transition.

Some licensees have attempted to help the buyer exit the prior relationship by completing the termination form themselves and sending it to the other office. This is problematic. When the form arrives at the other office bearing the new agent's contact information and brokerage number, it can appear that the second office is actively soliciting the first office's client. A formal complaint under the Code of Ethics with the local board may follow.

The proper approach is straightforward: if the buyer wants to end their relationship with their current agent, tell them to contact that agent directly by phone or send a letter to the other office themselves. Once the prior agreement is terminated by the parties to it, the buyer is free to enter into a new representation agreement with a different licensee. The new agent's role is to advise the buyer on the process, not to execute the paperwork on the other side of it.

Representation Agreements

Before entering into a buyer representation agreement, the licensee should explain clearly what services the buyer-client can expect. These typically include:

- Assistance in evaluating and selecting favorable financing options.
- Market value analysis to support informed offer decisions.
- Strategic advice during contract negotiations.
- Preparation and structuring of purchase offers.
- Referrals to related service providers such as inspectors, insurance agents, and lenders.

The licensee should also advise the buyer to consult outside experts when appropriate, including a CPA for tax implications and a licensed attorney for any legal questions the transaction raises.

Buyer representation agreements vary in format. Some are the standard forms provided by the Texas Association of REALTORS or the local MLS. Others are developed by individual brokers with the assistance of legal counsel. Whatever the format, the agreement should address, at minimum:

- The agent's role and scope of services.
- How conflicts of interest will be handled.
- The term of the agreement and conditions for early termination.
- Whether the representation is exclusive.
- Compensation structure and source of payment.

Even when a licensee chooses not to form a formal agency with a buyer, having some written record of the working relationship is good practice. A clear written understanding, even if it falls short of a full representation agreement, reduces the likelihood of disputes and provides a reference point for both parties.

Exclusive Right to Purchase

The exclusive right to purchase agreement gives the broker the right to a commission if the buyer acquires any property during the term of the agreement, even if the broker did not personally show the buyer the property that was ultimately purchased. This is the buyer-side equivalent of the exclusive right to sell listing.

Less experienced buyer's agents sometimes hesitate to ask buyers to sign an exclusive agreement, preferring a non-exclusive arrangement with an easy termination option. More experienced agents treat securing an exclusive buyer representation agreement with the same professional confidence they bring to securing a listing. They understand that an open, non-exclusive agreement creates the same procuring cause complications on the buyer side as an open listing creates on the seller side: multiple agents may claim the commission when the transaction closes.

The buyer who signs an exclusive agreement faces a straightforward trade-off: a deeper commitment to one agent in exchange for that agent's full investment of time, knowledge, and professional resources. An open arrangement offers less commitment from both sides. The buyer must decide which arrangement better serves their interests.

> ***Important:*** *TREC has not promulgated a state-approved buyer representation form. The Texas Association of REALTORS and local REALTOR associations provide forms for their members. Brokers who draft their own agreements without legal counsel take on unnecessary risk. Consult an attorney before developing or modifying any buyer representation form.*

Key Provisions of the Buyer's Representation Agreement

The Texas Realtor's Buyer's Representation Agreement is a comprehensive document. The following are its principal provisions:

Parties: Complete identifying information for the buyer-client and the broker, including contact details.

Appointment: The client grants the broker the exclusive right to act as their agent in acquiring property.

Definitions: Key terms are defined and the geographic territory of the property search is specified.

Term: The start and end dates of the agreement.

Broker's Obligations: A description of the services the broker will provide.

Client Obligations: The buyer's duties, including notifying other licensees of the existing representation agreement.

Representations: The client's confirmation that they can legally enter into the agreement and are not already bound by another representation agreement.

Intermediary: The client's election regarding whether the broker may show them the broker's own listings, and the terms under which the broker would act as intermediary in that event.

Competing Clients: The client's acknowledgment that the broker may simultaneously represent other buyers interested in the same properties.

Confidential Information: A description of what the broker may not disclose during and after the representation.

Broker's Fees: The full compensation structure, including how the commission is calculated, its source, when it is earned and payable, the protection period following expiration, and escrow authorization.

Mediation: The parties' agreement to attempt good-faith negotiation before pursuing formal legal remedies.

Default: The definition of default and the client's resulting obligations.

Limitation of Liability: The scope of conduct for which the broker will not be held liable.

Special Provisions: Space for any additional terms not addressed elsewhere in the agreement.

Additional Notices: Required disclosures regarding fair housing, non-discrimination, and the prohibition on legal advice from a non-attorney licensee.

Limitations of Exclusive Buyer Agency

Brokerages that limit their practice entirely to buyer representation face a distinct set of trade-offs. The advantages include:

- Buyers gain confidence that they will have access to all available inventory from every source, since the broker has no competing seller interests.
- Buyer loyalty increases because the exclusive commitment the broker makes mirrors the commitment the buyer makes in return.
- The exclusive buyer broker may more readily charge retainer fees, since buyers understand the depth of the broker's commitment.
- The risk of inadvertently representing more than one party in the same transaction is nearly eliminated when the broker holds no listings.

- Role confusion in negotiations is reduced when the agent always represents the same type of client.

The disadvantages are equally real:

- Clients who later want to sell their property must seek a different broker. The exclusive buyer brokerage cannot take listings and loses the opportunity to represent the transaction on both sides.
- When two buyer-clients want to make competing offers on the same property, a genuine conflict of interest arises that is difficult to resolve within the same office.
- Without listings, the broker loses all commission income from the listing side of the market, which can represent a substantial reduction in overall revenue.

Fiduciary Duties of the Buyer's Agent

Texas licensing law and common law both hold a buyer's agent to a higher standard of care than a licensee working with a buyer-customer. The buyer's agent has an affirmative duty to investigate and disclose all facts relevant to the buyer's decision to purchase, including facts that may not be favorable to the transaction.

While the buyer's agent must be honest and fair with the seller, the agent owes no duty to advise or counsel the seller. The fiduciary obligation runs entirely to the buyer-client.

In terms of the quality and depth of service owed, the buyer's agent is held to the same professional standard as a listing agent working with a seller-client. There is nothing unique about the fiduciary framework; the duties of care, loyalty, obedience, accountability, and disclosure apply fully, directed toward the buyer. What is different is not the structure of the obligations but the person to whom they are owed.

Buyers do not receive this standard of service automatically. It is available only to buyers who retain their own licensed representative. A buyer-customer working without representation receives honest and fair treatment, but nothing more.

Procuring Cause

Procuring cause refers to the agent whose efforts were the direct cause of the buyer's decision to purchase a specific property. In most cases this is clear: the agent who showed the property, wrote the offer, and guided the transaction to closing is the procuring cause. In some cases it is not.

A buyer might sign an exclusive representation agreement with one agent, but if a second agent is the one who ultimately facilitates the closing, that second agent may be deemed the procuring cause and entitled to the commission, depending on the specific facts. This type of dispute occasionally proceeds to arbitration when the parties cannot resolve it on their own.

When a buyer is represented under a properly executed buyer representation agreement, procuring cause disputes are largely eliminated. The agreement defines who the buyer's agent is and establishes the broker's claim to the commission under the terms of that agreement, even if the buyer was first introduced to the property by a listing agent and even if negotiations had already begun before the buyer representation agreement was signed.

Creating a formal agency relationship does not prevent a competing licensee from filing a procurement claim. However, a well-drafted representation agreement provides strong documentation of the broker's entitlement to compensation.

Single-Property Agreements

A buyer representation agreement does not have to cover a broad geographic territory or an extended period of time. In some situations, a single-property agreement is the most appropriate structure.

This typically arises when a buyer has already identified a specific property they want to pursue, such as a FSBO property or an unlisted commercial building. The buyer wants professional representation for that one transaction and has no interest in a broader or ongoing agency relationship.

In these situations the broker prepares a representation agreement limited to the one address. The agent does not disclose the property's location until the agreement is signed, which protects the broker's right to a commission if the buyer proceeds. If the buyer first confirms they have not been shown similar properties in the area, this arrangement is clean and straightforward.

For a FSBO showing to proceed under this structure, the licensee must contact the seller, obtain a one-time showing authorization, and make clear to the seller how the commission will be structured and who will pay it. The buyer's agent discloses their representation status to the FSBO seller at the outset.

Common Misconceptions About Buyer Agency

Several misconceptions have historically slowed the adoption of buyer representation. Most of these have been resolved as buyer agency has become the standard practice in Texas. A few still surface occasionally:

- Buyer agency must be in writing to be legally valid. This is false. Buyer agency can be created verbally or through conduct, though written agreements are strongly preferred.
- Buyer agency is too complicated for buyers and sellers to understand. This is false. The concept is straightforward, and most buyers grasp it readily once it is explained.
- Lenders do not recognize buyer agency. This is false. Buyer agency is fully recognized by lenders and does not affect loan qualification.
- Buyer agency increases the risk of procuring cause disputes. This is false. A signed representation agreement reduces procuring cause risk by clearly documenting the agency relationship.
- Buyer agency is illegal or prohibited by MLS rules. This is false. Buyer agency is legal in Texas and supported by MLS rules.

- The seller cannot pay the buyer's broker commission, or the listing broker cannot split a commission with the buyer's agent. This is false. Compensation arrangements of this kind are standard practice, subject to the disclosure requirements established by the 2024 NAR settlement.

In most Texas markets today, the great majority of buyers are represented. The licensed professional who understands buyer agency, communicates its value clearly, and executes representation agreements consistently will be better positioned to serve clients and build a sustainable practice.

Counseling the Buyer-Client

When a buyer retains a broker under an exclusive right to represent agreement, the agent's role shifts from selling to advising. The focus is no longer on persuading the buyer to purchase a particular property. It is on helping the buyer evaluate properties objectively, weigh alternative courses of action, and ultimately secure the best possible outcome.

A buyer's agent actively investigates conditions the listing agent or seller may not feel obligated to disclose: high utility costs, reported neighborhood issues, traffic congestion, nearby noise sources, or improvements made without required permits. This kind of proactive inquiry is part of the fiduciary duty owed to the buyer-client.

The buyer-client can also expect the agent to review proposed contracts and flag any provisions that may be unfavorable or that require review by a licensed attorney before signing. The difference between customer treatment and client treatment is substantial. A buyer-customer gets property showings and basic information. A buyer-client gets analysis, advocacy, and professional guidance through every step of the transaction.

Tailoring the Representation Agreement

One of the practical advantages of a buyer representation agreement is its flexibility. The buyer and broker can structure the scope of services and the compensation arrangement to fit the specific nature of the transaction and the buyer's needs. A buyer acquiring a single investment property has different needs than one purchasing a primary residence, and the agreement can reflect that.

In some large brokerages with extensive listing inventories, agents occasionally enter into written customer service agreements rather than full agency agreements, in order to avoid any suggestion that the firm is representing more than one party inappropriately. Under such an arrangement, the licensee continues to function as the seller's agent and is compensated accordingly. This approach requires transparent disclosure to the buyer so the customer clearly understands the nature and limits of the relationship.

Comprehensive buyer agency agreements reduce the most common source of conflict between clients and licensees: unclear expectations. The better the agreement is drafted, the fewer the misunderstandings. Brokers who develop their own representation forms are advised to work with a real estate attorney to ensure the document is both legally sound and professionally thorough.

Access to the Full Marketplace

A buyer's agent whose compensation is established and protected in a signed representation agreement has no reason to limit the property search to any particular source. The agent is motivated to present the buyer with every available option that meets the buyer's criteria, regardless of where those properties originate.

A fully represented buyer has access to properties from all of the following sources:

- Properties expected to come on the market in the near future.
- Real estate owned (REO) properties held by mortgage companies, banks, and savings institutions.
- Foreclosure and courthouse sales.
- For Sale by Owner (FSBO) properties.
- Open listings.
- Sales by trustees or pension plans.
- Properties offered by government agencies.
- Properties listed with cooperating brokers.

The buyer's agent evaluates the entire market from the buyer's perspective, maintaining undivided loyalty throughout. When a buyer is dealing directly with an unrepresented seller or a FSBO, having a professional advocate is especially important. Some buyers assume that unlisted properties are less desirable or that something is wrong with them. An experienced buyer's agent can investigate such properties objectively and advise the buyer accordingly.

Benefits of Buyer Agency for the Licensee

Buyer agency benefits the licensee, not just the buyer. Before representation agreements became standard practice, working with a buyer was a speculative investment. An agent could show properties for weeks with no guarantee that the buyer would return or that a commission would ever materialize. Buyers drifted from office to office with no professional obligation to stay with any agent.

A signed buyer representation agreement changes that entirely. The agent now has a committed client, the ability to ask more substantive questions, confirmation of pre-qualification, and the assurance that the buyer is not simultaneously working with competing brokers. The agent can negotiate on behalf of a known client with a clear mandate and a reasonable expectation of being present at the closing.

Beyond price, a buyer's agent negotiates a wide range of contract terms that affect the buyer's outcome, including:

- Earnest money amount and deposit structure.
- Financing contingencies and seller financing terms where applicable.

- Interest rate locks, commissions, and loan terms.
- Home warranty coverage, termite inspections, repair requests, and inspection contingencies.
- Assessments, appraisal requirements, closing costs, and title provisions.
- Possession date, hazard insurance, and extension rights.
- Personal property items that will or will not remain with the property.

Each of these items is a potential point of conflict between buyer and seller. A skilled buyer's agent manages that conflict in the buyer's favor.

The Purchase Agreement

Preparing and presenting the offer to purchase is one of the core responsibilities of the buyer's agent, but it comes with important professional limitations. The agent assists and advises but does not make decisions for the client. Every significant choice in the offer belongs to the buyer.

Key guidelines for the buyer's agent when assisting with the purchase agreement include:

- Guide the client through the analysis; let the client make all final decisions. The agent's role is to inform and advise, not to dictate what is best.
- Avoid any unauthorized practice of law. The agent is not a licensed attorney and must not alter the written language of a contract form. Complicated drafting questions should be referred to a real estate attorney.
- Structure the offer to be realistic and fair. A one-sided offer may reduce the probability of a successful agreement and can harm the buyer's position if the seller perceives it as unreasonable.
- Suggest negotiating strategies and financing options that reflect the buyer's goals, but leave the legal drafting of non-standard provisions to an attorney.

Two contract concepts the buyer's agent and client should understand before entering negotiations:

Assignable Contract: A contract whose rights may be transferred to another party. Both buyer and seller should confirm whether a contract is assignable before entering into negotiations.

Contract Acceptance: The seller's acceptance of an offer is valid only when communicated in writing to the buyer or the buyer's agent. The buyer retains the right to withdraw the offer at any time before that written acceptance is delivered. The acceptance must be dated and the time noted.

A Buyer Agency Case Study

The following example illustrates how a buyer's agent applies their responsibilities across the key components of a real estate transaction. Marcus has engaged Denise, a licensee with a local brokerage, to represent him in acquiring investment rental properties. They have signed an exclusive buyer representation agreement, with the seller designated as the source of Denise's commission. Denise has disclosed to the listing agent at first contact that she represents the buyer.

As Marcus identifies a property he wants to pursue, Denise works through each of the following elements with his interests as the consistent priority:

Price and Appraised Value

Denise analyzes the property and the seller's apparent position to identify the lowest realistic offer price. She prepares a CMA focused on comparable sales from the prior year, reviews any existing appraisals on the property, and may recommend an independent appraisal to support Marcus's pricing strategy.

Earnest Money

Denise advises Marcus on the appropriate earnest money amount. A modest deposit may preserve cash while still advancing the offer. A larger deposit can signal serious intent to the seller, which may be strategically valuable in a competitive situation.

Contingencies

Denise explains each contingency in the purchase agreement to Marcus, including the financing contingency and the inspection contingency, ensuring he understands the purpose and effect of each before signing. She is careful not to add or modify contract language without attorney involvement, which would constitute unauthorized practice of law.

Fixtures and Inventory

Denise may advise Marcus to request that certain personal property items remain with the property, such as appliances, window treatments, or storage systems. She helps him identify what to ask for and how to document it clearly in the contract.

Seller Financing

If seller financing is part of the deal, Denise recommends Marcus consult a real estate attorney to review the financing terms. Default provisions, prepayment penalties, grace periods, and late charges often favor the seller in seller-carried notes. Independent legal review protects the buyer's long-term interests.

Property Condition

Denise recommends that Marcus's offer includes an option with a property inspection, and she advises him on engaging qualified inspectors for the roof, plumbing, termite, and any other systems warranting evaluation. The goal is to ensure Marcus is not contractually committed to a property whose true condition he does not fully understand.

Written Compensation Agreements

Every commission agreement must be in writing. A broker has no enforceable legal claim against a seller or buyer who refuses to pay a commission if that obligation was not documented in a signed written agreement. This applies to buyer and seller commission agreements and to fee-split arrangements between cooperating brokers.

The TREC standard contract form includes a "Broker Information and Ratification of Fee" section that specifies the conditions and amount of any compensation flowing from the listing broker to the buyer's broker. Licensees should be familiar with this section and ensure it is completed accurately in every transaction.

> ***NAR Settlement Update:*** *Under rules adopted in Texas following the 2024 NAR settlement, buyer broker compensation must be agreed upon in the buyer representation agreement before any properties are shown. Offers of buyer broker compensation may no longer be published through the MLS. All fee arrangements between cooperating brokers must be negotiated directly and documented in writing outside the MLS system.*

Written compensation agreements also limit procuring cause disputes. When a buyer is under a signed representation agreement, the identity of the buyer's broker is documented and the commission entitlement is established. This does not prevent another licensee from filing a procurement claim, but it significantly strengthens the buyer broker's position.

Buyer Agency Fee Arrangements

There is no single required method for compensating a buyer's broker. The appropriate structure depends on the type of transaction, the services being provided, and what the buyer and broker have agreed upon. Generally, the buyer's broker fee is paid at closing, either through a commission split or through a seller credit to the buyer that is then paid to the broker.

All fee arrangements should be established and documented in writing before any properties are shown. Commission disputes between brokers should be resolved between the brokers themselves. Clients should not be drawn into compensation disagreements unless the client's actions or interests are directly at the center of the dispute.

Retainer Fees

A retainer fee is an advance payment for services. Some brokers require a retainer before beginning a buyer search, both as a practical screening tool to assess the buyer's seriousness and as partial compensation for services that will be rendered before any transaction closes.

Texas does not restrict how or when a broker may withdraw retainer funds, unlike some other states. However, the retainer must be linked to actual services. If a broker accepts a retainer and then conducts no search, shows no properties, and provides no advice, they would have difficulty justifying retention of the fee.

When a retainer is collected and the transaction closes with the broker also being paid by the seller, the broker is receiving compensation from two sources. Many brokers choose to credit the retainer toward the final commission or refund it at closing, both to avoid double compensation issues and to preserve the buyer's available cash for closing costs.

Retainer policies must be applied consistently. A broker should not require a retainer from some buyers while waiving it for others without a principled, documented basis for the distinction.

Seller-Paid Commission

There is no legal prohibition in Texas against the seller paying the buyer's broker commission. Paying the buyer's agent does not compromise the buyer's agent's loyalty to the buyer, as long as the agency relationship is clearly established in writing and both parties understand who represents whom.

The compensation arrangement should be addressed explicitly in both the listing agreement and the buyer representation agreement. When the agency relationship is unambiguous, the source of the payment does not alter it. Courts have generally held that the source of compensation is one factor, among others, in determining an agent's principal, so clarity in the written agreements is essential.

When the buyer broker's compensation arrangement differs from the listing broker's standard split, the buyer's agent should include a written explanation with the offer. Without this, the listing agent and seller may be confused by the commission structure, which can introduce unnecessary friction into the negotiation.

Commission Splits

In most Texas residential transactions, the buyer's broker is compensated through a split of the commission the seller pays to the listing broker. The specific percentage or amount must be negotiated between the brokers and documented in writing before the transaction proceeds.

The preferred approach in Texas is a formal written buyer representation agreement that addresses compensation, scope of services, term, exclusivity, and conflict of interest provisions. TREC does not promulgate a state-approved form for buyer representation. The Texas REALTORS and local boards provide forms for their members, and brokers may also develop their own with legal counsel.

When a buyer's broker approaches a listing broker about cooperating on a transaction, confirming the commission split arrangement at initial contact is sound professional practice. Most sellers are far less interested in how the commission is divided between the brokers than they are in receiving a solid offer at an acceptable price.

Buyer-Paid Fees

In some transactions, the buyer pays the broker's fee directly. Three common structures exist:

Hourly Rate

The broker charges a non-contingent hourly fee for consulting services, payable regardless of whether a transaction closes. This structure is most common when the client is seeking advice rather than transaction services, for example, whether to acquire a particular type of commercial property, how to evaluate a proposed development site, or how to assess the risks of a specific deal.

Percentage Fee

The broker receives a percentage of the property's final purchase price. This structure is familiar to both clients and licensees and aligns the agent's compensation with the transaction outcome. The potential drawback is an inherent tension: a higher purchase price produces a higher commission, which could create a perceived conflict with the buyer's interest in paying less. This tension should be acknowledged and addressed clearly in the representation agreement.

Flat Fee

The broker agrees to a fixed dollar amount for the engagement. The amount is typically based on the agent's estimate of the work involved, the likelihood of a successful outcome, and what the seller might otherwise have contributed to the commission. Flat fees provide cost predictability for the buyer and remove the purchase price tension that can arise with percentage-based arrangements.

Gross Price Compensation

The gross price method is an alternative compensation structure in which the buyer pays the full contract price and the seller pays the buyer's broker commission from the sale proceeds. The seller acknowledges that the buyer's broker represents the buyer exclusively, notwithstanding the fact that the seller is the source of the payment.

This approach simplifies the transaction for lenders and appraisers, who see a clean purchase price without embedded commission adjustments. It reduces confusion about double compensation and makes the seller's net proceeds more straightforward to calculate.

When structured properly, the net result to all parties is essentially equivalent to a conventional transaction: the buyer pays market price, the seller nets a comparable amount, the buyer's broker commission is built into the contract economics, and the financing amount reflects the actual purchase price. The gross price method works cleanly for both listed and unlisted properties.

Advantages and Disadvantages of the Seller Paying the Commission

When the seller is the source of the buyer's broker compensation, there are both advantages and limitations worth understanding:

Advantages

- Does not interfere with the listing broker's existing commission agreement with the seller.
- Eliminates the most common basis for procuring cause disputes between cooperating brokers.
- Clarifies the relationship between who is representing whom and who is paying whom.
- Protects the buyer from an unexpected out-of-pocket commission obligation at closing, while preserving that option if the seller declines to pay.
- Shields the buyer's agent from liability if the seller breaches the listing agreement or the listing is poorly drafted.
- Applies equally to listed, unlisted, MLS, and non-MLS properties.
- Does not trigger TRELA provisions concerning undisclosed dual compensation, since both parties are aware of and have consented to the arrangement.
- Places the obligation to compensate the buyer's broker with the party whose transaction interests were directly served.

Disadvantages

- May alter the tax treatment of the transaction for one or both parties.
- The legal framework for buyer-paid commission structures is less extensively tested in Texas courts than the traditional commission split model.
- Lender confusion about the commission source or structure may occasionally cause processing delays.

Disclosures to the Buyer

Before entering into a buyer representation agreement, the licensee must disclose to the buyer any existing agency relationships the broker has with sellers or landlords whose properties the buyer may wish to consider. This disclosure may be oral or written, but a written disclosure with the buyer's signed acknowledgment is strongly preferred.

The broker is also required to provide the buyer with a written statement describing seller agency, buyer agency, and intermediary representation under Texas law. This is satisfied in most transactions by delivery of the TREC Information About Brokerage Services form

With respect to the property's condition, the seller is generally responsible only for disclosing what is within their personal knowledge. Buyers should not rely solely on the seller's disclosure. A professional inspection provides independent evaluation and often surfaces issues the seller may have overlooked or not recognized as relevant. A seller's disclosure of a problem does not mean the seller is obligated to fix it; the disclosed item becomes a point of negotiation.

For any property built before 1978, the Residential Lead-Based Paint Hazard Reduction Act requires the seller and their agent to:

- Disclose all known lead-based paint hazards in the home.
- Retain signed buyer acknowledgments for a minimum of three years as proof of compliance.
- Provide the buyer with the EPA pamphlet titled "Protect Your Family from Lead in Your Home."
- Allow the buyer a ten-day window to conduct lead testing before the contract becomes binding.

Disclosures to the Seller and Listing Broker

The NAR Code of Ethics requires the buyer's agent to disclose their representation status to the listing agent at first contact, whether that contact is a phone call to schedule a showing, a written inquiry, or any other initial communication. Written confirmation of that disclosure must be provided no later than the execution of the purchase agreement.

TRELA independently requires every licensee to disclose their representation status to all other parties and their agents at first contact. For a buyer's agent, this means clearly stating at the outset of any interaction with the listing side that the licensee represents the buyer and is not acting as a subagent of the listing broker.

When the property is not listed with a broker and the buyer's agent is dealing directly with a seller, the same disclosure obligation applies. The buyer's agent identifies themselves as the buyer's representative at first contact and makes any commission requests at that time.

The seller will typically require financial qualification documentation as part of the purchase process, including pre-approval confirmation and, in many cases, a financing contingency with a defined approval deadline. Additional seller-requested disclosures may arise after the initial offer is submitted.

Buyers Who Prefer Customer Status

Representation is not universally desired. Some buyers actively prefer to operate as customers, choosing flexibility over commitment. They may work with multiple brokers simultaneously, gathering market information from each, and make their purchase decision without formal ties to any single agent.

Other buyers prefer dealing directly with the listing broker, believing it gives them faster access to information or a strategic edge in making an offer. In a competitive seller's market, some buyers worry that routing an offer through a buyer's agent may slow the process or put them at a disadvantage compared to a buyer going directly through the listing office.

These are legitimate considerations. The buyer's agent's role in this situation is to explain the representation options clearly and let the buyer decide. Not every buyer relationship becomes a formal agency. A licensee who understands this can serve customers professionally while also recognizing the situations where pursuing a formal agreement is worth the additional effort.

Better Disclosure, Better Service

For most of Texas real estate history, sellers received professional representation and buyers did not. Evolving disclosure rules, licensing regulations, and professional standards have changed that. Today, buyers can access the same caliber of professional advocacy that sellers have long received, and most choose to take advantage of it.

The decision to enter into formal buyer representation is significant. The agent becomes a fiduciary, accountable for the quality of their advice and the thoroughness of their investigation. All disclosures should be documented in writing.

The lead-based paint disclosure is one of the most consequential required disclosures. The buyer's agent's role is to ensure the seller provides the required materials, that the buyer has the opportunity to conduct testing, and that the buyer understands the implications of any disclosed hazards. Failing to facilitate this disclosure carries civil penalties of up to $11,000 per violation, enforced by HUD's Lead Programs Enforcement Division. Beyond liability, the underlying purpose of the requirement is to protect children and elderly residents from lead contamination that causes serious and lasting illness.

Property Condition Disclosure

The seller submits a property condition disclosure as required by the Texas Property Code, and the buyer's agent should review it carefully with the client. The agent may counsel the buyer on what items to address in the purchase contract, which can include requests that the seller confirm:

- All known adverse environmental conditions have been disclosed and remediated where required.
- All required building permits for improvements have been obtained and closed.
- The property will be in the same condition at closing as when it was contracted, or in the improved condition required by the agreement.
- The property will be clear of debris, and all major systems, including HVAC, plumbing, electrical, and appliances, will be in working order at closing.
- No personal property items included in the sale will be substituted or removed before closing.

The disclosure form does not obligate the seller to repair any disclosed condition. When a buyer requests repairs, the contract moves into counteroffer status. The seller may refuse, and the buyer must then decide whether to proceed with the property as-is or withdraw from the transaction. A licensee who fails to make a buyer-client aware of the disclosure requirement and its implications risks client damages and potential license disciplinary action.

Additional Contract Benefits for the Buyer-Client

A skilled buyer's agent may negotiate a range of contract provisions beyond price that benefit the buyer-client. These can include:

- Credit to the buyer for any funded escrow accounts on assumed mortgages.
- A right of first refusal to purchase any adjoining property the seller also owns.
- Reasonable pre-closing access for inspections by the buyer's chosen contractors, including termite inspectors, engineers, roofers, plumbers, and home inspectors.
- Permission to show the property to prospective tenants before closing, in the case of an investment acquisition.
- Pre-closing occupancy rights, typically accompanied by a separate rental agreement and an agreed daily rate.
- The right to lock in interest rate points on the buyer's loan before closing.
- Seller payment of the appraisal fee and origination points.
- Seller coverage of the buyer's additional costs if the seller fails to close on the agreed date.
- Permission to substitute collateral on any seller-carried financing.
- The right of first refusal if the seller later discounts any purchase money mortgage they carried back.

The buyer's agent must use judgment in which concessions to pursue. Each additional request reduces the likelihood of the seller accepting the offer without a counteroffer, and some requests may signal to the seller that the buyer is either inexperienced or negotiating in bad faith. An experienced buyer's agent helps the client prioritize the concessions that matter most and present them in a way that keeps the deal moving forward.

Snapshot Review – Chapter 5

Buyer Agency Fundamentals

1. Buyer agency exists when the broker represents the buyer exclusively in the transaction. It may be created in writing, orally, or through conduct. A written agreement is always preferable.
2. Before offering buyer agency, evaluate whether the buyer is genuinely ready, willing, and able to purchase. Pre-qualification by a lender provides the clearest answer to the financial readiness question.
3. A signed buyer representation agreement creates client loyalty, enables a deeper level of service, and gives the broker an enforceable right to compensation.
4. TREC has not promulgated a buyer representation form. Use the TXR form, a local board form, or a form developed by the broker with legal counsel.

Compensation

1. The buyer's broker commission may be paid by the seller, the buyer, or shared between them. The buyer representation agreement must specify the amount and source.
2. Under 2024 NAR settlement rules adopted in Texas, buyer broker compensation must be negotiated and disclosed in the buyer representation agreement before any properties are shown. It may no longer be communicated through the MLS.
3. If the listing broker offers less than the agreed buyer broker commission, the buyer may be responsible for covering the difference.

Conflicts of Interest

1. When a buyer-client wants to offer on a property also listed with their broker, the conflict can be resolved by converting one party to customer status, referring the buyer to a different broker, or proceeding under the intermediary framework with full disclosure.
2. When two buyer-clients compete for the same property, both should be offered the option to continue with the current broker or seek representation elsewhere. Document all communications carefully.

Exclusive Right to Purchase

1. The exclusive right to purchase entitles the broker to a commission if the buyer purchases any property during the agreement term, even one the broker did not show.
2. Open buyer agreements create the same procuring cause risks as open listings. Exclusive agreements provide better control and clearer commission rights.

Key Provisions of the Buyer's Representation Agreement

Parties and Appointment: Identifies the buyer and broker; grants the broker the exclusive right to act as buyer's agent.

Term and Territory: Sets the agreement's duration and the geographic scope of the property search.

Intermediary: Specifies whether the buyer consents to the broker showing the broker's own listings and acting as intermediary.

Broker's Fees: Covers commission calculation, source, when earned, protection period, and escrow authorization.

Competing Clients: Acknowledges the broker may represent other buyers pursuing the same properties.

Limitation of Liability: Defines the scope of conduct for which the broker is not liable.

Fiduciary Duties and Procuring Cause

1. The buyer's agent owes the full COALD fiduciary duties to the buyer-client, including an affirmative duty to investigate and disclose all relevant facts.
2. The buyer's agent must be honest and fair with the seller but owes no duty to advise or counsel the seller.
3. Procuring cause is the agent whose efforts directly caused the buyer's decision to purchase. A signed representation agreement is the strongest protection against procuring cause disputes.

The Buyer's Agent Role

1. The buyer's agent counsels and advocates rather than selling. The focus is on helping the client evaluate properties, negotiate effectively, and make informed decisions.
2. The buyer-client receives professional analysis, strategic guidance, and active advocacy. The buyer-customer receives only honest and fair treatment with no representation.
3. The buyer's agent investigates conditions the seller may not disclose: utility costs, permit history, neighborhood issues, noise, and traffic.
4. The agent reviews proposed contracts for unfavorable provisions and recommends attorney review for complex or non-standard drafting.

Purchase Agreement Guidelines

1. The buyer makes all decisions. The agent advises and presents options but does not determine what is best for the client.
2. The agent must not alter written contract language. Non-standard provisions require a licensed attorney.
3. Offers should be realistic and balanced. An offer structured entirely in the buyer's favor may provoke rejection and harm the buyer's negotiating position.

Assignable Contract: A contract whose rights may be transferred to a third party. Parties should confirm assignability before negotiations begin.

Contract Acceptance: Effective only when communicated in writing to the buyer or buyer's agent. The buyer may withdraw the offer at any time before that written acceptance is delivered.

Compensation Structures

Retainer Fee: An advance payment for services. Must be tied to actual services rendered. Applied consistently across all buyers in the office. May be credited or refunded at closing if the seller also pays a commission.

Seller-Paid Commission: No legal barrier exists to the seller paying the buyer's broker. The agency relationship must be clearly documented so the source of payment does not create ambiguity about who the agent represents.

Commission Split: The most common residential structure. The buyer's broker receives a negotiated portion of the listing broker's commission at closing. Must be agreed upon in writing before properties are shown.

Hourly Rate: A non-contingent consulting fee payable regardless of whether a transaction closes.

Percentage Fee: Based on the final purchase price. Familiar to clients and licensees; requires disclosure of the inherent tension between a higher price and a higher commission.

Flat Fee: A fixed dollar amount for the engagement, based on estimated work, probability of success, and expected seller contribution.

Gross Price Method: The buyer pays the full contract price; the seller pays the buyer's broker commission. This method simplifies the transaction for lenders and appraisers while producing equivalent economics for all parties.

Required Disclosures

1. Before signing a buyer representation agreement, the licensee must disclose any existing agency relationships with sellers whose properties the buyer may consider, and provide the TREC IABS 1-2 form.
2. TRELA requires disclosure of representation status to all parties and their agents at first contact.
3. NAR Code of Ethics requires the buyer's agent to disclose representation to the listing agent at first contact and confirm in writing no later than contract execution.
4. For homes built before 1978, the Residential Lead-Based Paint Hazard Reduction Act requires disclosure of known hazards, delivery of the EPA pamphlet, signed buyer acknowledgments, and a ten-day testing window. Civil penalties for non-compliance reach $11,000 per violation.

Property Condition Disclosure

1. The seller's disclosure does not obligate the seller to repair anything. Repair requests by the buyer trigger counteroffer status.
2. The disclosure must be provided within the timeline required by the Texas Property Code. Failure to do so may allow the buyer to rescind the contract.
3. A licensee who fails to inform a buyer-client of the disclosure requirement risks client damages and license disciplinary action.

CHAPTER 5 QUIZ — BUYER AGENCY

1. Which of the following best describes how a buyer agency relationship may be legally created in Texas?

a. Through a written agreement, orally, or through the conduct of the parties, though a written agreement is strongly preferred.

b. Only through a written agreement signed by both the buyer and the broker.

c. Only through the TREC-promulgated buyer representation form.

d. Automatically, when the broker shows the buyer any property for the first time.

2. Before offering buyer agency, a licensee should evaluate three threshold questions about the prospective buyer. Which of the following is one of those questions?

a. Has the buyer previously worked with a licensed real estate agent?

b. Does the buyer have the financial ability to obtain a mortgage?

c. Does the buyer intend to purchase new construction or an existing home?

d. Is the buyer a Texas resident for at least six months of the year?

3. A buyer signs a buyer representation agreement with a licensee. The primary benefit this agreement provides to the licensee is:

a. The licensee is required to get written acceptance from any company listed properties.

b. The licensee is entitled to both the listing and selling commission if the buyer purchases a property the broker also listed.

c. The buyer has made a professional commitment, allowing the licensee to invest time and resources with confidence of being at the closing table.

d. The licensee no longer needs to provide the TREC Agency disclosure form to the buyer.

4. Under 2024 NAR settlement rules now in effect in Texas, when and how must buyer broker compensation be disclosed and documented?

a. In the MLS listing before the property is shown to any buyer.

b. At the closing table once the buyer and seller have agreed on a purchase price.

c. Through a separate compensation disclosure form submitted to TREC within three business days of the first showing.

d. In the buyer representation agreement, negotiated and documented before any properties are shown.

5. A buyer representation agreement specifies a four percent buyer broker commission. The listing broker offers three percent to cooperating agents. Under the terms of the buyer representation agreement, who is responsible for the remaining one percent?

a. The buyer is responsible for covering the difference between what the listing broker offers and the agreed commission amount.

b. The listing broker must match the agreed amount or the sale cannot proceed.

c. TREC's Recovery Trust Account covers the shortfall.

d. The buyer's agent waives the difference as a professional courtesy.

6. A buyer-client learns that the broker also represents the seller of a property they want to purchase. The buyer is uncomfortable with this arrangement. Which of the following is NOT a valid option for resolving the conflict?

a. Convert the buyer to customer status so the broker represents only the seller.

b. Proceed with the transaction and disclose the dual representation to TREC within 48 hours.

c. Convert the seller to customer status so the broker represents only the buyer.

d. Refer the buyer to a different broker who has no conflict with the seller.

7. Which TREC form is the approved, promulgated buyer representation agreement for Texas residential transactions?

a. TREC Form IABS 1 – 2, the Information About Brokerage Services form.

b. TREC Form OP-H, the Seller's Disclosure of Property Condition adapted for buyers.

c. There is no TREC-promulgated buyer representation form. Licensees use TR (Texas Realtor) forms, local board forms, or broker-developed forms reviewed by legal counsel.

d. TREC Form BRA-1, available through the TREC website to all licensed agents.

8. An exclusive right to purchase agreement entitles the buyer's broker to a commission if:

a. The broker personally shows the buyer the property that is ultimately purchased.

b. The seller agrees in writing to cooperate with the buyer's broker before closing.

c. The buyer submits a written offer on a property the broker identified and presented.

d. The buyer purchases any property during the agreement term, even one the broker did not show.

9. A buyer who has signed a representation agreement with one licensee walks into a competing office and asks a second licensee to help them end their current agreement by completing a termination form. The second licensee should:

a. Advise the buyer to contact their current agent directly or send a letter to the first office themselves, and not complete the termination paperwork on the buyer's behalf.

b. Complete the termination form as a courtesy to the buyer and send it to the first office.

c. Contact the first broker directly to negotiate a release on the buyer's behalf.

d. Ask the buyer to sign a new representation agreement immediately, which automatically supersedes the prior one.

10. Procuring cause refers to:

a. The broker who first contacted the seller about listing the property.

b. The agent whose efforts were the direct cause of the buyer's decision to purchase a specific property.

c. The licensee whose name appears on the buyer's pre-qualification letter from the lender.

d. The broker who submitted the first written offer on the property, regardless of whether it was accepted.

11. Two buyer-clients represented by the same broker both want to make offers on the same property. The broker's best course of action is to:

a. Present only the stronger offer to avoid creating a conflict of interest.

b. Withdraw from both representation agreements and refer both buyers to other agents.

c. Offer both clients the choice to continue with the current broker or transfer to representation at a different office, and document all communications carefully.

d. Disclose both buyers\' offer amounts to each other so they can make informed decisions.

12. A buyer who wants professional representation for a single FSBO property but has no interest in a broader representation relationship should be offered:

a. A standard buyer representation agreement covering the buyer's entire county of residence.

b. A verbal agency agreement, since FSBO transactions do not require written documentation.

c. No representation, because FSBO sellers are not required to cooperate with buyer's agents.

d. A single-property buyer representation agreement limited to that one address.

13. The fiduciary duties of a buyer's agent in Texas differ from those of a listing agent primarily in that:

a. The buyer's agent owes the same full COALD fiduciary duties but directed toward the buyer-client rather than a seller-client.

b. The buyer's agent owes a reduced level of care because buyers are more sophisticated than sellers.

c. The buyer's agent has an additional duty to advise and counsel the seller about the transaction.

d. The buyer's agent is not required to maintain confidentiality after the transaction closes.

14. Which of the following is a true statement about buyer agency in Texas?

a. Buyer agency must be in writing to be legally valid.

b. A signed buyer representation agreement reduces procuring cause risk by clearly documenting the agency relationship.

c. Lenders do not recognize buyer agency agreements for loan qualification purposes.

d. Buyer agency is prohibited on properties listed in the MLS because subagency rules take priority.

15. A buyer's search expands beyond the geographic territory defined in their buyer representation agreement. Before showing properties in the new area, the licensee should:

a. Show the properties first and amend the agreement afterward to avoid delaying the buyer's search.

b. Prepare a new buyer representation agreement covering only the expanded territory and have the buyer sign it in place of the original.

c. Execute an amendment to the representation agreement identifying the additional territory, signed by both parties, before showing any properties in the new area.

d. Proceed without an amendment because the original agreement implies authority to show any property that meets the buyer's criteria regardless of location.

16. A buyer-client working with a buyer's agent under an exclusive representation agreement receives which of the following that a buyer-customer does not?

a. Professional analysis, strategic advocacy, and guidance through every stage of the transaction.

b. Access to MLS listings and scheduled showings.

c. The right to attend open houses without the agent present.

d. A written summary of the seller's asking price and days on market.

17. A buyer's agent discovers during their investigation that a home's garage addition was built without a permit. The agent's duty to the buyer-client is to:

a. Keep this information confidential so as not to interfere with the seller's listing.

b. Report the permit violation to the local building authority before advising the buyer.

c. Ignore the issue because permit records are the buyer's responsibility to research independently.

d. Disclose this finding to the buyer-client as part of the proactive inquiry the fiduciary relationship requires.

18. Under the 2024 NAR settlement rules adopted in Texas, buyer broker compensation must be:

a. Posted in the MLS listing before the property is shown to any buyer.

b. Negotiated and documented in the buyer representation agreement before any properties are shown, and may no longer be advertised through the MLS.

c. Set by the local board of REALTORS at a standard percentage and applied uniformly.

d. Determined by the listing broker after the offer is accepted and disclosed to the buyer at closing.

19. A broker accepts a retainer fee from a buyer before beginning the property search. The transaction later closes and the seller pays the buyer's broker commission in full. In most cases, the broker should:

a. Retain both the retainer and the full commission because both were earned through separate agreements.

b. Apply the retainer to the seller's closing costs as a good faith gesture.

c. Credit the retainer toward the final commission or refund it at closing to avoid double compensation and preserve the buyer's available cash.

d. Transfer the retainer to the title company and let them determine how it should be applied.

20. A buyer's agent is assisting a client in completing an offer to purchase. The buyer wants to include a non-standard financing clause that does not appear in any pre-printed section of the TREC contract form. The buyer's agent should:

a. Refer the drafting of any non-standard clause to a licensed real estate attorney to avoid unauthorized practice of law.

b. Draft the clause in the Special Provisions paragraph based on the agent's experience with similar transactions.

c. Decline to include any additional terms and instruct the buyer that only pre-printed forms may be used.

d. Ask the listing agent to draft the clause since the listing agent is more familiar with the property.

21. A seller accepts a buyer's offer verbally and calls the listing agent to confirm. Under Texas contract law, this acceptance:

a. Creates a binding contract because both parties have agreed to the same terms.

b. Is binding only if the buyer was present during the verbal confirmation.

c. Becomes effective when the listing agent relays the verbal acceptance to the buyer's agent.

d. Is not yet legally effective because acceptance must be communicated in writing to the buyer or the buyer's agent.

22. A buyer's broker is paid by the seller under a commission split arrangement. Which of the following correctly describes the effect of this arrangement on the buyer's agent's fiduciary duties?

a. The seller's payment compromises the buyer's agent's loyalty because the seller controls the commission.

b. The source of payment does not alter the agency relationship as long as it is clearly documented in writing and both parties understand who represents whom.

c. The buyer's agent becomes an intermediary because they are receiving compensation from both sides of the transaction.

d. The buyer's agent must refund the commission to the buyer if the purchase price exceeds appraised value.

23. Under the gross price compensation method, the buyer pays the full contract price and the seller pays the buyer's broker commission from the sale proceeds. The primary advantage of this structure is that it:

a. Allows the buyer's broker to receive compensation from both the buyer and the seller.

b. Eliminates the need for a buyer representation agreement because compensation is handled through the listing contract.

c. Presents a clean purchase price to lenders and appraisers without embedded commission adjustments, while producing equivalent economics for all parties.

d. Requires TREC approval before the structure can be used in a Texas residential transaction.

24. Before entering into a buyer representation agreement, the licensee is required to disclose to the buyer:

a. Any existing agency relationships the broker has with sellers whose properties the buyer may wish to consider, along with the TREC IABS 1-2 form.

b. The seller's original purchase price and property tax history.

c. The full commission the listing broker will receive on any property the buyer might purchase.

d. Whether the buyer's pre-approval letter will be shared with the listing agent.

25. Under the Residential Lead-Based Paint Hazard Reduction Act, which of the following is required for all homes built before 1978?

a. The seller must remove all lead-based paint before the property can be listed.

b. The buyer must sign a waiver acknowledging they accept the property in its current condition.

c. The listing broker must arrange and pay for a lead inspection before accepting any offer.

d. The seller and their agent must disclose known hazards, provide the EPA pamphlet, retain signed buyer acknowledgments for three years, and allow a ten-day testing window.

26. The civil penalty for each violation of the Residential Lead-Based Paint Hazard Reduction Act, enforced by HUD, is up to:

a. $1,000

b. $11,000

c. $5,000

d. $25,000

27. A seller's property condition disclosure reveals that the HVAC system has a known refrigerant leak. The seller states they do not intend to repair it before closing. Under Texas contract law, this disclosed condition:

a. Automatically voids the purchase contract because the seller is required to deliver the property in working order.

b. Must be corrected before the option period expires under Texas Property Code requirements.

c. Does not obligate the seller to make any repairs; if the buyer requests a repair, the contract moves into counteroffer status and the seller may refuse.

d. Allows the buyer to terminate the contract and receive a full refund of earnest money without any further negotiation.

28. A buyer's agent is negotiating a contract for a client purchasing a small rental property. In addition to price, which of the following is an example of an additional contract benefit the buyer's agent might negotiate for the client?

a. Permission to show the property to prospective tenants before closing.

b. A reduction in the listing broker's commission to free up funds for closing costs.

c. Seller agreement to maintain the property listing in the MLS until the transaction closes.

d. A requirement that the seller purchase a home warranty covering the buyer for five years.

CHAPTER 6

INTERMEDIARY BROKERAGE

Chapter Objectives

After completing this chapter, you should be able to:

1. Trace the evolution of real estate representation from subagency through dual agency to the intermediary brokerage model required by Texas law.
2. Explain the legal requirements for a broker to act as an intermediary, including written consent and written compensation.
3. Distinguish between intermediary with appointments and intermediary without appointments, and describe the duties and restrictions of each.
4. Describe how appointments are made, who may and may not be appointed, and what happens when a broker is absent.
5. Explain confidentiality obligations in intermediary transactions and the impact of intermediary relationships on broker policy and office operations.
6. Explain how intermediary brokerage applies in specialized real estate transactions, including 1031 exchanges, syndications, and commercial lease agreements.
7. Describe the paperwork and steps involved in a 1031 exchange and identify the fraud risks associated with certain exchange-related investment products.
8. Distinguish between intentional undisclosed dual agency and accidental dual agency, and identify the conduct and circumstances that most commonly lead to each.
9. Explain the disclosure requirements when a licensee is involved in an in-house sale, purchases a FSBO property on behalf of a buyer-client, or sells their own property.

Contents

Problems with Subagency

Subagency and Commission Splitting

Subagency as a Flawed Model

The Dual Agency Model

Dual Agency Restrictions

Undisclosed Dual Agency

Transaction Brokerage

Representing More Than One Party in Texas

The Intermediary Model

Written Consent

Written Compensation

Intermediary with Appointments

Restrictions on Appointed Agents

Intermediary without Appointments

Confidentiality in Intermediary Transactions

Common Law and Statutory Law

How Appointments Are Made

Appointment Options

The Broker Cannot Be Appointed

When Appointments Take Place

Pre-Appointment Systems

The Notification of Intermediary Relationships Form

In-House Sales and Intermediary

Branch Offices

Non-Agency in Texas

Client Objections to Intermediary

Broker Policy

Impact on Brokers

Intermediary in Specialized Transactions

Intermediary Agent Review

Intermediary and 1031 Exchanges

1031 Exchange Documentation

Steps in a 1031 Exchange

1031 Exchange Fraud Risks

Intermediary and Syndications

Intermediary and Lease Agreements

Unintended Dual Representation

Avoiding Unintended Dual Representation

In-House Sales

Buying an In-House or MLS Listing

Representing a Buyer in a FSBO Purchase

Selling Licensee-Owned Property

From Dual Agency to Intermediary Brokerage

Since September 2005, Texas law no longer permits brokers to act as common law dual agents. When a broker represents more than one party in the same transaction, that broker must operate under the intermediary framework established by the Texas Real Estate License Act (TRELA). Understanding why this change occurred requires a look at how agency relationships in real estate evolved over time.

The foundation of all real estate agency is common law, which developed through court decisions rather than through legislation. Common law originated in medieval England and spread throughout countries with English legal heritage. Unlike statutes, which require legislative action to change, common law can be refined incrementally through judicial interpretation. In the United States, common law forms the bedrock of business and commercial relationships, and real estate transactions have always been heavily grounded in it.

Agency Law and Fiduciary Duties

Agency law governs the relationship between a principal, the party being represented, and an agent, the party authorized to act on the principal's behalf. This is a fiduciary relationship, meaning the agent is bound to act in the principal's best interest with the highest degree of trust and loyalty.

The fiduciary duties owed by an agent to a principal are:

- Loyalty
- Diligence
- Confidentiality
- Obedience
- Disclosure
- Accounting
- Reasonable Care

An agent must follow the client's lawful instructions and act within the bounds of the representation agreement. Over time, both common law and statutory law have shaped how these duties are applied in real estate transactions, and the frameworks for agency representation have evolved as the market and legal environment changed.

The History of Subagency

For most of Texas real estate history, agents represented only the seller. Even when a licensee was actively helping a buyer search for property, the fiduciary duties ran entirely to the seller. The buyer received services but had no representation.

This structure was formalized through subagency. The listing broker, with the seller's permission, could extend the seller's representation to cooperating brokers at other firms. Those cooperating brokers became subagents of the listing broker, working with buyers while legally representing the seller.

The system functioned reasonably well as long as buyers understood they were unrepresented. The problem was that most of them did not. A 1983 Federal Trade Commission study found that more than 70 percent of buyers believed the agent they worked with was representing their interests. In reality, three out of four buyers were sharing confidential information with agents who were legally obligated to use that information in the seller's favor. This report triggered nationwide disclosure reform. By 1988, most states had enacted disclosure laws requiring agents to identify who they represented.

The Rise of Buyer Representation

As awareness grew, buyers began asking a logical question: if sellers can have an agent working exclusively for them, why can't buyers have the same? Buyer agency developed in response to that demand.

Under buyer agency, all fiduciary duties shift to the buyer. The buyer can speak freely with their agent about price strategy, negotiating priorities, and property concerns without worrying that the information will be passed to the seller. Buyer agency created a symmetrical transaction model: one agent working exclusively for the seller on one side, one agent working exclusively for the buyer on the other.

A survey conducted in 2001 found that 45 percent of home buyers were using buyer representation. Today, buyer representation is the norm in most Texas markets.

What a Buyer's Agent Does

A buyer's agent provides the buyer with professional guidance throughout the entire purchase process. Core responsibilities include:

- Advising the client from initial consultation through closing.
- Identifying the buyer's needs, priorities, and motivating factors.
- Educating the buyer on current market conditions, pricing trends, and comparable sales.

- Searching all available inventory that meets the buyer's criteria.
- Arranging and coordinating property access and showings.
- Helping the buyer narrow choices and evaluate options.
- Managing the negotiation process in the buyer's interest.
- Preparing and delivering all required transaction forms.
- Coordinating inspections and advising on how to address repair requests.
- Scheduling and managing the closing process.

Exclusive Buyer Firms

An exclusive buyer firm is a brokerage that represents only buyers, never sellers. These firms take no listings and never place themselves in a position where they represent both sides of a transaction. Their sole purpose is to advocate for buyers without any competing loyalties.

Exclusive buyer firms show buyers all available inventory from cooperating brokers as well as unlisted sources such as FSBO properties, and then guide the buyer through evaluation and negotiation. Exclusive buyer firms represent a very small fraction of all real estate brokerages in the United States, well under one percent, but they reflect a clearly defined philosophy about how buyer representation should work.

The Rise of the MLS

The original listing model had an obvious limitation: a broker could only sell what their own firm had listed. If a buyer wanted a property listed with a different firm, they had to start the process over with that firm. The agent who had invested time with the buyer earned nothing.

The multiple listing service (MLS) solved this problem. By pooling all listed properties into a shared database and allowing any member broker to show and sell any listing, the MLS created a cooperative marketplace that served buyers, sellers, and agents simultaneously. The buyer could access all available inventory through a single agent. The seller reached the entire agent network. Every participating broker had the opportunity to earn a commission on any listed property.

The roots of MLS cooperation trace back to the late 1800s, when real estate brokers in local markets began sharing property information informally. The term "multiple listing" was coined in 1907, and MLS systems expanded rapidly through the 1920s and became nearly universal after World War II. By 1980, 95 percent of real estate firms belonged to at least one MLS.

How the MLS Works

The MLS operates on a foundational principle of mutual cooperation: help me sell my property and I will help you sell yours. A listing broker enters property details into the shared MLS database. Member brokers can access those listings and show them to their own buyer-customers.

> ***2024 NAR Settlement Update:*** *Under rules adopted in Texas following the 2024 NAR settlement, offers of buyer broker compensation may no longer be advertised through the MLS. Buyer broker compensation must be negotiated and documented in the buyer representation agreement before any properties are shown, and cooperative compensation arrangements must be handled outside the MLS system.*

The Role of the Subagent

When a cooperating broker showed a property under the original MLS framework, that broker was not representing the buyer. The MLS rules required compensation to be based on the cooperating broker acting as a subagent of the listing broker. The cooperating broker helped a buyer view and purchase a property while legally representing the seller throughout. Brokers owed no fiduciary duties to buyers under this model.

Subagency had one significant advantage: it allowed a listing broker to work with both buyers and their own seller without creating what would later be called dual agency. Both brokers in the transaction were on the same side. The conflict-of-interest question did not arise.

Over time, buyers became frustrated with having no representation and legal challenges mounted. Disclosure requirements were introduced as a partial fix, but disclosure alone did not solve the underlying problem: informed buyers now knew they were unrepresented, and many wanted representation of their own. Calls for regulatory reform intensified.

Problems with Subagency

The real estate industry initially defended subagency as essential to broker cooperation. Disclosure requirements were offered as a compromise, but they proved insufficient. In many cases disclosure actually increased litigation by making buyers aware they had been operating without representation. Buyers who felt outmaneuvered in a transaction began filing lawsuits in growing numbers.

The Department of Justice awarded over $500 million in class action settlements involving subagency and dual agency misrepresentation during the 1990s. The scale of that liability made clear that the subagency model had structural flaws that could not be patched with disclosure alone.

Key problem areas included:

- Buyers consistently preferred client status over customer status once they understood the difference. Subagency made them customers by default.
- Agents were trained to secure exclusive listing agreements from sellers but had no equivalent training or culture around securing representation agreements from buyers. Subagency preserved a system that treated buyers as incidental to the transaction.

- Most standard forms were drafted with subagency assumptions built in, favoring the seller's position by design.
- Earnest money practices were structured to protect the seller. When buyer agency became common, agents needed new training to advise buyers on whether earnest money terms were appropriate for their interests.

Subagency and Commission Splitting

A secondary concern with subagency was the practice of commission splitting itself. When the listing broker sets the cooperating broker's compensation in the MLS, several problems follow:

- The listing broker dictates the fee the selling agent will earn, with no input from the buyer's broker.
- The listing broker effectively prevents the buyer's agent from negotiating a fee directly with the buyer.
- By accepting the split, the cooperating broker accepts a subordinate position in the transaction structure.

Some brokers responded by structuring listing agreements to include compensation to the listing firm only on the seller's side, removing subagency and cooperating broker provisions entirely. The buyer and buyer's agent then negotiate the fee independently, through a buyer representation agreement or a separate commission agreement. When executed correctly, this model makes representation clear to everyone: the seller knows who is representing them, and the buyer knows who is representing them, without any commission confusion.

Subagency as a Flawed Model

Co-brokerage under subagency placed both agents on the seller's side of the transaction, leaving the buyer without any advocate. This worked as long as buyers felt the process was fair. When buyers felt disadvantaged or deceived, the legal consequences were severe. The real estate industry needed a better model, one that acknowledged buyers as full participants entitled to professional representation.

Several reform paths were proposed. Some brokers advocated abandoning agency representation entirely in favor of a neutral facilitator role. Others argued for formalizing buyer representation as a distinct and equal practice. The emergence of buyer agency addressed the representation gap, but it created a new question: what happens when the same brokerage represents both the buyer and the seller in the same transaction?

The Dual Agency Model

Dual agency emerged as a framework for situations where one brokerage represented both the buyer and the seller. Under dual agency, the broker steps back from exclusive advocacy for either party and instead attempts to serve both simultaneously. Dual agency is not a relationship between two individual agents; it describes the status of the brokerage itself when representing both sides.

The key features of dual agency include:

- Neither the broker nor any agent in the firm may advocate exclusively for either party.
- Both parties must give informed written consent to the arrangement.
- Confidential information about price, motivation, competing offers, and negotiating terms must be kept strictly confidential from the other party.
- The dual agent may not take actions that benefit one party at the expense of the other.
- Subject to these constraints, the broker owes the same fiduciary duties to both the buyer and the seller.

Two common dual agency scenarios illustrate how the relationship arises: a listing agent who also ends up representing the buyer directly, or two agents within the same firm who are separately representing the buyer and seller in the same transaction. Because brokers and all agents under their license are legally treated as a single entity, either situation creates dual agency for the brokerage.

Dual Agency Restrictions

Dual agency imposes meaningful limitations on what the agent can and cannot do. The agent must treat both parties honestly and equally. Full property condition disclosure to the buyer is still required. However, the agent cannot share one party's confidential information with the other.

The most significant practical restriction: when an offer is made, the dual agent cannot advise the buyer on how much to offer, and cannot advise the seller whether to accept, reject, or counter. Both parties must make their own strategic decisions without guidance from the agent. This limitation frustrated buyers, sellers, and agents alike and ultimately drove Texas toward a different statutory solution.

Undisclosed Dual Agency

Dual agency is not inherently illegal, but undisclosed dual agency is. When an agent's conduct creates the impression in a buyer's mind that the agent is representing the buyer, without any actual representation agreement in place, the agent has created an undisclosed dual agency.

Courts apply a high standard to dual agency disclosure. For dual agency to be lawful, the agent must explain carefully to both the buyer and the seller that a fiduciary relationship exists with both parties simultaneously. Both parties must sign acknowledgment forms confirming they understand the arrangement and that by consenting, they each waive their right to the agent's undivided loyalty.

Transaction Brokerage

Transaction brokerage emerged in some states as an alternative to both subagency and dual agency. A transaction broker serves as a neutral professional coordinator rather than a fiduciary for either party. The transaction broker assists with the mechanics of the transaction, including preparing offers, facilitating communication, and coordinating the closing, while owing no fiduciary duties to either side.

A transaction broker typically charges a flat fee rather than a percentage commission. The duties that do apply include honest dealing, disclosure of all known material facts affecting property value, and timely presentation of all offers and counteroffers. Transaction brokerage is not legal in all states. Texas has adopted transaction brokerage and has established the intermediary framework as a solution for dual-client situations.

Representing More Than One Party in Texas

When dual agency first appeared in Texas, there was no statutory framework governing how a broker should handle it. Brokers fell back on common law practices, which essentially required them to withhold advice from both clients. The problem played out in every negotiation: the buyer would ask how much to offer and the broker could not say. The seller would ask whether to accept and the broker could not advise. The counteroffer would come back and neither party could get guidance. All three parties found this unsatisfying.

Texas eventually resolved the problem through legislation. Section 1101.561 of TRELA now makes clear that if a broker is going to represent both a buyer and a seller in the same transaction, the broker must do so as an intermediary under the statutory framework. Common law dual agency is no longer a permissible model in Texas. Intermediary relationships are the required approach.

The Intermediary Model

Section 1101.559(a) of TRELA authorizes a broker to act as an intermediary between parties to a real estate transaction, provided two conditions are met: the broker must have written consent from each party, and that written consent must identify who will pay the broker.

At the broker level, intermediary looks much like the old dual agency restriction: the broker cannot give advice or express opinions to either party. The real benefit of intermediary over dual agency is what happens next. The broker may appoint one or more agents to represent the seller and a different agent or agents to represent the buyer. Once appointments are made, each appointed agent is freed to give full advice and advocacy to their respective client, even if that advice is not helpful to the other party in the same transaction. This is called intermediary with appointments, and it is the model that most effectively serves both clients.

Written Consent

For a broker to act as an intermediary, written consent is required from each party. The cleanest way to satisfy this requirement is through the standard agency agreements: paragraph 9 of the TR listing agreement and paragraph 8 of the TR buyer representation agreement each contain the necessary intermediary consent language. When a client signs the agreement and initials the relevant paragraph, they have authorized the broker to act as intermediary if the occasion arises.

Consent to intermediary does not mean intermediary will occur. It simply means the possibility has been authorized. Intermediary only becomes relevant when the broker ends up representing both a buyer and a seller in the same transaction. Many signed agency agreements never give rise to an intermediary situation at all. Common scenarios where intermediary does not apply include an offer from an outside broker, the buyer pursuing a property listed elsewhere, or a buyer-customer situation where only one party is a client.

Written Compensation

Written consent alone is not sufficient. The intermediary authorization must also identify the source and structure of the broker's compensation. The standard listing agreement and buyer representation agreement both address compensation, so using these forms satisfies both the consent and compensation requirements in a single document.

An agent operating under an oral listing or a verbal buyer agency arrangement has neither written consent for intermediary nor a documented compensation agreement. If such an agent becomes involved in a transaction where the other party is also represented by the same broker, the intermediary relationship exists without the required documentation. The agent must go back to the client and obtain the appropriate written agreement before negotiations can proceed properly. Starting every agency relationship with a signed written agreement prevents this situation entirely.

Intermediary with Appointments

Intermediary with appointments is the preferred structure in most in-house transactions. The broker appoints one agent to represent the seller and a different agent to represent the buyer. In most cases the appointments follow naturally from the pre-existing relationships: the agent who listed the property is appointed to the seller, and the agent who brought the buyer is appointed to the buyer.

Once appointments are made, each appointed agent may give their client full advocacy and advice, including advice that works against the interests of the other client in the transaction. This is the key advantage of intermediary with appointments over both common law dual agency and intermediary without appointments: each client has a dedicated professional working exclusively for them, even though both agents work under the same broker.

Many brokers implement a standing pre-appointment policy: if one agent in the office has the seller as a client and a different agent has the buyer as a client, those agents are automatically appointed to their respective clients when an in-house transaction begins. The agent writing the offer documents the appointment on the Notification of Intermediary Relationships form.

Restrictions on Appointed Agents

Intermediary with appointments has one important confidentiality restriction. Each appointed agent may advocate fully for their own client, but they may not share certain information across the appointment divide:

- The agent appointed to the buyer may not disclose to the buyer how low the seller is willing to accept.
- The agent appointed to the seller may not disclose to the seller how high the buyer is willing to go.

Each agent may share information about the property's condition and any information their client has expressly authorized them to share with the other side. What neither agent knows, they cannot share. But what they do know and that falls into the confidential category must be protected.

The broker's role during intermediary with appointments is administrative. The broker may assist the agents in process matters but cannot give strategic advice or express opinions to either party. For example, if the agent appointed to the buyer asks whether a home inspection is a good idea, the broker may confirm that inspections are generally advisable. If the agent appointed to the seller asks whether it is acceptable to negotiate on the title insurance split, the broker may confirm that it is a negotiable item. Neither response constitutes advice that favors one party over the other.

Intermediary without Appointments

Intermediary without appointments applies when one agent has both the buyer and the seller as clients in the same transaction. Nothing in Texas law forces the broker to make appointments in this situation, and the same agent can legally continue working with both clients. The trade-off is that without appointments, the agent cannot give advice or express opinions to either party.

The agent must explain to both clients that in this structure each will need to take greater personal responsibility for their own decisions. Neither client will receive strategic advice from the agent during negotiations. If either client objects to this, the broker has three options: make appointments so each client has a dedicated agent, convert one client to customer status, or refer one client to representation at another office.

In practice, intermediary without appointments is uncommon and often short-lived. By the time both clients are engaged in a transaction together, each typically has an emotional investment in the deal and is willing to accept the limitation rather than risk losing the opportunity. Both the agent and the broker must stay in close communication throughout, and the governing principle is simple: what the client wants, the client gets.

Confidentiality in Intermediary Transactions

Confidentiality in an intermediary relationship, like all agency relationships, survives forever. It does not end when the transaction closes. The only confidential information that may ever be shared is information the client has specifically authorized the agent to disclose to the other side.

Confidentiality demands extra vigilance in intermediary transactions because two clients with opposing interests are in active negotiations under the same broker. The potential for one client to feel that confidential information was shared or that they were treated less favorably is real. A useful professional standard to internalize is this: talk about the property, never about the person.

When an agent is uncertain whether a particular piece of information is confidential or whether it may be shared, the right course is to consult the broker before saying anything. After that consultation, a conversation with the client may also be warranted. Keeping the broker, the agent, and the client aligned before any disclosure is made eliminates the most common source of intermediary disputes.

Common Law and Statutory Law

When buyer agency first appeared in Texas, no statute governed how a broker should handle the situation of representing both a buyer and a seller. Brokers worked from common law, which was later endorsed by court decisions as a recognized way to practice. Dual agency, even in its limited form, became an accepted model.

Section 1101.561 of TRELA changed that. The statute explicitly provides that when a broker will represent both the buyer and the seller, the broker must act as an intermediary. The same section states that a broker may not agree to act as a dual agent while also complying with TRELA. Common law dual agency is no longer a valid operating model in Texas, regardless of what some brokers may have practiced in the past. Intermediary relationships are the legally required framework for any in-house transaction where both parties are clients.

How Appointments Are Made

Appointments are typically handled through one of two mechanisms: a standing pre-appointment system embedded in office policy, or a case-by-case decision by the broker when an intermediary situation arises.

Under a pre-appointment system, the broker's standing instruction is: if one agent in this office listed the property and a different agent in this office represents the buyer, both agents are automatically appointed to their respective clients when the buyer makes an offer. The agent preparing the offer documents this on the Notification of Intermediary Relationships form and includes it with the offer as an addendum.

If the broker wants to handle appointments personally rather than through a system, the broker must be available when the appointment decision is needed. If the broker is unavailable, a designated person in the office may make the appointment in the broker's absence. However, the person making appointments in the broker's absence faces the same restriction as the broker: they cannot appoint themselves into the transaction on either side.

Appointment Options

In most cases, the appropriate appointments are obvious: the listing agent goes to the seller and the buyer's agent goes to the buyer. When a broker does not allow intermediary without appointments and there is only one agent working with both clients, the broker must assign a second agent from the office to take over one of the client relationships.

The broker has wide latitude in deciding which client to reassign and to whom. No specific rule dictates the choice, although practically it is often easier to reassign the seller, particularly when the buyer's agent is already preparing the offer. The broker should distribute appointments reasonably across the available agents to avoid the appearance of favoritism within the office.

The broker may also appoint more than one agent to the same side of the transaction. This most commonly arises with agent teams, where two licensees regularly work together and share commissions. If both team members are already involved on one side of the transaction, the broker may appoint both of them to that client.

The Broker Cannot Be Appointed

When appointments are made in an intermediary transaction, the broker is never one of the appointed agents. The reason is structural: if the broker were appointed to represent one side, the broker would be providing full advocacy to that party while remaining neutral with the other. That disparity would undermine the integrity of the intermediary framework.

The broker's role during intermediary with appointments is to step back from negotiations and allow the appointed agents to handle communications with their respective clients. The broker may provide administrative guidance to the agents but does not give advice or opinions to either party in the transaction.

This restriction does not prevent the broker from participating in an intermediary transaction. The broker may communicate with both parties directly, including taking the lead role in negotiations, but only if doing so as intermediary without appointments. In that mode, the broker applies the same no-advice, no-opinion standard to both sides, ensuring that neither party receives a level of service the other does not.

When Appointments Take Place

Appointments become relevant at the moment an in-house buyer-client decides to make an offer on a property listed by the same brokerage. Up to that point, the buyer may be looking at any number of properties, including company listings, without triggering an intermediary relationship.

When the buyer selects a company listing and the buyer's agent begins preparing the offer, the intermediary situation is live. The buyer's agent completes the Notification of Intermediary Relationships form, checks the box indicating that appointments will be made, writes in the buyer's agent's name as appointed to the purchaser, and writes in the listing agent's name as appointed to the seller. This form is attached to the offer as an addendum before submission.

If only one agent is working with both the buyer and seller, the form reflects intermediary without appointments, and neither party receives strategic guidance from the agent during negotiations.

Pre-Appointment Systems

A pre-appointment system is a standing policy that automates the appointment process without requiring the broker to be present and active for each transaction. The broker trains the salespeople on the policy in advance: when an agent who listed the property and a different agent representing the buyer are both in-office, each is automatically appointed to the client they are already working with.

This approach keeps the transaction moving efficiently and removes uncertainty about who is appointed to whom. The agent writing the offer knows exactly what to put on the notification form without needing to contact the broker first.

Pre-appointment systems work well for brokers who are willing to allow intermediary without appointments as a fallback when one agent holds both sides. For brokers who require a separate agent on each side in every intermediary situation, a more active approach to appointment management is necessary.

The Notification of Intermediary Relationships Form

The Notification of Intermediary Relationships is a TR form used to document and communicate that an intermediary relationship has been activated. TREC does not have a comparable promulgated form. This TR form is available only to members of the Texas REALTORS.

Licensees who are not TR members must accomplish the same purpose by having an attorney draft a comparable form for office use.

The form does not need to be delivered while the buyer is still searching. Its purpose is specific: to notify both clients that the intermediary relationship that was authorized in their original agency agreements has now been activated in this particular transaction. Once the form is signed and delivered with the offer, both the listing agent and the buyer's agent can proceed to give full advice and advocacy to their respective appointed clients.

In-House Sales and Intermediary

Not every in-house transaction is an intermediary transaction. If the seller is a client and the buyer is a customer, both connected to the same office, there is only one client. An intermediary relationship requires two clients. When the buyer is a customer, it is simply an in-house sale. The seller's agent owes full fiduciary duties to the seller without restriction, and the buyer receives only honest and fair treatment.

The commission structure is identical whether the in-house transaction is an intermediary sale or a non-intermediary sale. The total commission earned by the brokerage and how it is divided among the agents does not change based on intermediary status. The difference is about the type of service each party receives and about company policy, not compensation.

Branch Offices

A broker who operates multiple office locations must understand that all branch offices under the same broker's license are treated as one entity for intermediary purposes. If a seller is a client at one branch and a buyer is a client at a different branch of the same brokerage, the transaction is still intermediary. The separate physical locations do not change the analysis; it is the broker's identity that determines whether intermediary applies.

This is different from independently owned franchises. Two separately owned offices operating under the same franchise brand have different brokers. A buyer represented by one independently owned franchise office and a seller represented by a different independently owned franchise office are not in an intermediary transaction, even if they share the same brand name.

Brokers who operate multiple locations should train all agents across all branches on intermediary procedures and ensure that agents know to verify whether the other side of any transaction is also represented within the same brokerage umbrella.

Non-Agency in Texas

Some brokers, finding intermediary relationships complicated to administer, have explored whether they can simply operate outside the agency framework entirely. Non-agency is a legally recognized practice model in Texas.

The practical alternative for a broker who wants to avoid intermediary is a clear office policy: when one party in a transaction is a client, the other will be a customer. This eliminates the two-client scenario that triggers intermediary. The trade-off is that one side of every in-house transaction will be unrepresented.

An individual licensee may adopt a similar personal policy, but it must align with the broker's company policy. A licensee who wants to avoid representing both sides in any transaction should have that conversation with their broker to ensure the approach is consistent with office practice.

Client Objections to Intermediary

Not all clients are comfortable with intermediary representation, even when they originally consented to it in their agency agreement. A buyer or seller who has had a negative experience with intermediary in a previous transaction may refuse to proceed and ask to be referred to another firm.

When a client objects and leaves the brokerage, the transaction can still close. The listing broker retains a share of the commission. The listing agent in the original firm earns their portion. The departing client engages a new broker and proceeds. The agent who initiated the relationship with the departing client typically receives nothing unless the office policy provides for a referral fee. A well-designed policy can address this outcome in advance, protecting agents who lose a client due to a principled client objection rather than a failure of service.

Broker Policy

All of the intermediary structures discussed in this chapter are legally available. The broker decides through company policy which of them will be used and which will not. Most broker policies center on the question of intermediary without appointments.

Brokers who do not permit intermediary without appointments require that whenever one agent holds both the buyer and seller as clients, a second agent must be brought in to take one client. This produces better representation for both parties. It also produces a practical side effect: the original agent knows that if they end up with both sides of a transaction, they will share the commission with whoever is appointed to the other client. This creates an inadvertent incentive to keep the buyer as a customer rather than a client, which results in the buyer receiving no representation at all. Brokers who adopt this policy should be aware of that dynamic and provide explicit guidance to agents about it.

Impact on Brokers

Intermediary relationships have had a greater impact on brokers than on any other license holder. Salesperson responsibilities have remained largely the same: find buyers and sellers, convert customers to clients, negotiate contracts, and earn commissions. Salespeople encounter intermediary transactions occasionally, and how they are affected is often more a function of company policy than of the law itself.

The broker bears the structural weight of the intermediary framework. The broker is the one who cannot be appointed, who must stay neutral across both sides, who must administer the appointment process, and whose license is the pivot point for determining whether any given transaction is an intermediary situation. Small-office brokers who also practice day-to-day sales feel this constraint most directly.

Experienced brokers who received their licenses before intermediary became law in 2005 often learned the system after the fact, through continuing education and application. Newer licensees encounter intermediary in pre-licensing coursework. The result is that newer agents sometimes have stronger conceptual grounding in the intermediary framework, while experienced brokers have the practical context that comes from working through the situations the law was designed to address.

Intermediary in Specialized Transactions

Dual agency issues and intermediary obligations are not confined to residential home sales. A broker must be equally prepared to navigate representation questions in exchanges, syndications, commercial and industrial property sales, farm transactions, and lease agreements. These are collectively referred to as specialized real estate transactions.

A specialized transaction typically involves three or more parties, each with their own representatives, goals, and assumptions about who is working for whom. A common error in these settings is for one participant to assume that every other party already understands each agent's role. That assumption is often wrong and can create serious liability. The broker's responsibility is to know every player in the transaction, understand each person's role, and make disclosures proactively rather than waiting to be asked.

All provisions of Sections 1101.558 and 1101.559(a) of TRELA apply equally to specialized property transactions and to residential transactions. There is no exemption for commercial, industrial, farm, or exchange transactions. In addition, under TRELA Section 1101.651, any agreement that authorizes the possibility of an intermediary relationship must be in writing, and the intermediary disclosure language must appear in bold print.

Intermediary Agent Review

Before examining specialized applications, a brief review of the core intermediary rules is useful. When acting as an intermediary, a broker must:

- Obtain written consent from each party to act as an intermediary. That written consent must also state who will pay the broker and must set forth the broker's obligations as an intermediary in conspicuous bold or underlined print.
- Treat all parties honestly and fairly and comply with TRELA throughout the transaction.
- Refrain from disclosing that the seller will accept less than the asking price unless the seller has authorized that disclosure in writing.
- Refrain from disclosing that the buyer will pay more than the price stated in a written offer unless the buyer has authorized that disclosure in writing.
- Keep all confidential information confidential, including any information a party has specifically instructed the broker not to share, unless the disclosure is authorized in writing by the party, required by court order, required by TRELA, or concerns the physical condition of the property.
- With the consent of both parties, appoint one in-house licensee to communicate with and carry out the instructions of the seller and a different in-house licensee to communicate with and carry out the instructions of the buyer.

Intermediary and 1031 Exchanges

Section 1031 of the Internal Revenue Code (26 U.S.C. Section 1031) allows certain property owners to defer recognition of capital gains when they exchange one qualifying property for another of like kind. Rather than paying capital gains tax at the time of sale, the taxpayer rolls the proceeds into a replacement property and defers the tax obligation. Section 1031 exchanges are particularly common in rental and investment property transactions.

Because 1031 exchanges can involve large sums of money and significant commissions, they create financial incentives that can tempt a broker toward shortcuts or toward compromising one party's interests in order to close the deal. The intermediary framework is the appropriate professional tool for handling an in-house 1031 exchange transaction fairly. Using intermediary with appointments allows the broker to maintain integrity across all parties while ensuring that each client has a dedicated agent working on their behalf.

Transparent, thorough disclosure to all parties is the non-negotiable foundation of any 1031 exchange. A broker who cuts corners, omits a required step, or fails a fiduciary duty in a complex exchange transaction faces the prospect of unhappy clients, legal disputes, and license jeopardy after the deal closes.

1031 Exchange Documentation

Even a straightforward 1031 exchange generates a substantial number of required documents. The following list represents the core paperwork for a basic exchange transaction:

- Exchange Agreement
- Real Estate Contract to Sell the Relinquished Property
- Assignment of the Relinquished Property
- Notice of Assignment of the Relinquished Property
- Deed to Convey the Relinquished Property
- Settlement Statement on the Sale of the Relinquished Property
- IRS Form 1099 on the Sale of the Relinquished Property
- Identification of the Replacement Property
- Real Estate Contract to Purchase the Replacement Property
- Assignment of the Replacement Property
- Notice of Assignment of the Replacement Property
- Deed to Receive the Replacement Property
- Settlement Statement on the Purchase of the Replacement Property
- IRS Form 1099 on the Purchase of the Replacement Property
- IRS Form 8824 (Like-Kind Exchanges) to report the transaction

This list reflects only the basic exchange. Commercial transactions frequently involve additional layers of documentation. A single broker attempting to represent all parties in a complex commercial 1031 exchange without the intermediary structure in place carries an elevated risk of missing a step, overlooking a fiduciary duty, or inadvertently favoring one side. The volume and complexity of these transactions make proper representation structure essential, not optional.

Steps in a 1031 Exchange

A standard 1031 exchange proceeds through the following sequence:

1. The taxpayer signs a real estate sales contract for the sale of the relinquished property.
2. The taxpayer enters into an Exchange Agreement with a qualified intermediary.
3. The taxpayer assigns the sales contract for the relinquished property to the qualified intermediary.
4. The net sale proceeds from the closing are paid to the qualified intermediary at closing and held or invested in a short-term account on the taxpayer's behalf.
5. The taxpayer conveys title to the relinquished property directly to the buyer at closing.
6. Within 45 days of the transfer, the taxpayer identifies the replacement property and notifies the qualified intermediary in writing.
7. The taxpayer enters into a purchase contract with the seller of the replacement property.
8. The taxpayer assigns the purchase contract for the replacement property to the qualified intermediary.
9. The closing on the replacement property must occur within 180 days of the transfer of the relinquished property, or by the due date of the taxpayer's return for the year of transfer, whichever is earlier.
10. The seller of the replacement property conveys title directly to the taxpayer.
11. The qualified intermediary transfers the sale proceeds from the relinquished property to the seller of the replacement property. Any remaining funds are returned to the taxpayer.

> *The 45-day identification period and the 180-day closing deadline are strict IRS requirements. Missing either deadline disqualifies the exchange and triggers the deferred capital gains tax immediately. Licensees working with clients in a 1031 exchange should ensure the client is working with a qualified intermediary and a tax advisor, and should not attempt to provide tax or legal guidance themselves.*

1031 Exchange Fraud Risks

Licensees should be aware of a category of securities fraud that has emerged in connection with tenants-in-common (TIC) real estate investments, which are often marketed under the 1031 exchange label.

In these schemes, financial professionals misrepresent the risks and potential returns of TIC investments to attract buyers. Investment firms sell these products without conducting adequate due diligence, often driven by extremely high commission structures that create a financial incentive to close sales regardless of suitability. These schemes are frequently targeted at conservative or retired investors who are seeking a straightforward way to defer capital gains.

A licensee who participates in or facilitates such an arrangement, even unknowingly, faces significant legal exposure. The prudent course is to refer clients to independent legal and tax counsel before any exchange-related investment decision is made and to avoid any arrangement where the commission structure creates an obvious conflict with the client's best interest.

Intermediary and Syndications

A real estate syndicate is a group of investors who pool capital to acquire or develop a property that would be impractical or impossible for any single investor to handle independently. Syndication is not unique to real estate; similar structures exist in underwriting, banking, and insurance. In real estate, syndicates typically involve a general partner who manages the investment and limited partners who contribute capital.

Representation problems arise when the general partner of a syndicate is also a licensed real estate broker. When the same person who manages the partnership also acts as the broker in a transaction involving that partnership, a potential conflict of interest exists. The specific circumstances that require careful disclosure include:

- The general partner-broker sells property owned by the partnership and receives a commission.
- The general partner-broker sells property to the partnership and receives a commission.
- The general partner-broker purchases property listed by another firm for the partnership and receives compensation.
- The general partner-broker acquires unlisted property and seeks compensation from the seller.

In each of these situations, the broker owes fiduciary duties to all partners in the syndicate. A commission paid by the partnership to the general partner-broker is appropriate only if full and transparent disclosure is made to all partners. Disclosure does not neutralize the underlying conflict of interest, but it removes the element of concealment. Failing to disclose in any of these situations constitutes a breach of fiduciary duty.

Intermediary and Lease Agreements

Lease transactions, particularly in commercial real estate, frequently involve representation questions as complex as any purchase transaction. Many commercial leasing agents work under exclusive leasing arrangements with developers or property owners, placing them in a position similar to a listing agent. Unlike a standard residential lease, a commercial lease negotiation involves numerous terms and concessions, including base rent, escalation clauses, tenant improvement allowances, lease term options, and exclusivity provisions. The leasing agent is often in the middle and must clearly understand the role of every participant.

In some commercial lease transactions, both the landlord and the tenant have their own legal counsel handling the negotiations directly. In that setting the broker may function primarily as a coordinator, facilitating communication rather than advocating for either side.

In other situations, a tenant without representation may approach a leasing agent and ask for negotiating help. If the same firm represents the landlord, an intermediary situation exists. The broker must disclose the intermediary relationship to all parties before any substantive negotiation begins. The rule in all lease and purchase transactions is the same: every person in the deal must know who represents whom, and the agent must know every person in the deal. Disclosure is not a formality. It is the foundation of every legitimate representation relationship.

Unintended Dual Representation

Dual agency is not a permissible model in Texas. It has been replaced by the intermediary framework. A competent agent will identify any potential intermediary situation and make the required disclosures before negotiations advance.

Two distinct situations involving dual representation require attention:

> **Undisclosed Dual Agency**: An intentional act in which an agent represents both sides of a transaction without informing either party. This is illegal in every state. The agent is treating both sides as clients without any required notice or consent.
>
> **Accidental Dual Agency**: An unintentional situation in which an agent's conduct creates a dual agency relationship without any deliberate intent to deceive. It may arise from carelessness, a misunderstanding of fiduciary obligations, or from becoming too helpful to the opposing party in pursuit of a completed deal.

Both forms are illegal. The distinction matters not because accidental dual agency is treated more leniently in court, but because it identifies a different source of risk. Undisclosed dual agency is a character and ethics failure. Accidental dual agency is a training and awareness failure. Both expose the licensee and the broker to discipline and civil liability.

A common path to accidental dual agency is the seller's agent who begins offering the buyer strategic advice. For example, suggesting to a buyer that the seller will accept below the asking price, advising on offer strategy, or making statements that suggest the agent is working in the buyer's interest can create an implied agency relationship. Once a buyer reasonably believes the agent represents them, accidental dual agency has occurred.

Avoiding Unintended Dual Representation

Common circumstances that can give rise to unintended dual representation include:

- A listing broker who ends up representing both the buyer and seller without following the intermediary process.
- Any in-house transaction that proceeds without proper intermediary notifications and written consent from both parties.
- A written agreement with one party combined with only a verbal understanding with the other, leaving the nature of representation unclear.

An agent can also create an implied agency relationship with the opposing party by taking on tasks that should belong to the other party's representative. When a customer in a transaction asks the seller's agent for advice, the agent should refer the customer to seek their own professional counsel rather than answering in a way that might be construed as representation.

The following types of statements by an agent can create an implied agency with the other party and should be avoided:

- "You can count on me to take care of all the details in the sale."
- "Let me see if I can get you a better price from the seller."
- "This property is overpriced. You should offer significantly less."
- "Trust me, I'll get you the best possible deal."
- "The seller is not going to respond with a counteroffer."

Each of these statements signals to the other party that the agent is working in their interest. Even a well-intentioned agent who genuinely wants the transaction to close can inadvertently step into dual representation by trying too hard to move both sides toward agreement.

In-House Sales

When two licensees from the same brokerage represent opposing parties in the same transaction, the brokerage is operating as an intermediary. When an independent broker personally represents both parties, that broker is also functioning as an intermediary. In either situation, the proper notifications and written consents must be in place before negotiations proceed.

Intermediary is not the same as dual agency. Intermediary is the Texas statutory framework designed to replace dual agency. The critical distinction is that intermediary with appointments allows each appointed agent to give full advocacy and guidance to their respective client, which dual agency did not permit.

Some brokers overlook the timing requirement: written consent to intermediary must be obtained well before the transaction closes, not as an afterthought when a dispute arises. Retroactive intermediary consent is not valid. If the required documentation is not in place before negotiations begin, the broker is in an unauthorized dual representation situation, which creates liability regardless of how the transaction ultimately concludes.

Buying an In-House or MLS Listing

Situations occasionally arise where a licensee wishes to purchase a property that is listed by their own firm or by another member of the same MLS. Both situations require careful handling.

A licensee purchasing a property listed by their own firm is in a position of informational advantage. The agent knows the terms of all other offers submitted on that property. Texas law prohibits dealings in bad faith and dishonest conduct. Using knowledge of competing bids to gain a purchasing advantage is a violation of those principles. If the licensee intends to purchase an in-house listing, they should reveal the price and terms of their own offer to any other competing buyers to level the playing field.

When a licensee purchases a property listed in the MLS by a different firm, a different concern applies. The seller may perceive the licensee-buyer as holding fiduciary duties toward the seller by virtue of their license status. Texas Administrative Code Rule 535.144 requires that a licensee disclose their licensed status in writing when purchasing real property. This disclosure should appear in the sales contract itself and should make clear that the licensee is the buyer, not an agent acting on the seller's behalf. It should also recommend that the seller seek independent professional representation.

Representing a Buyer in a FSBO Purchase

When a buyer-client wants to purchase a property being sold directly by the owner without a listing agent, the buyer's agent must take several specific steps to protect both the buyer and themselves:

1. **Confirm the buyer representation agreement is in place.** If the buyer has signed the TR Residential Buyer/Tenant Representation Agreement (TXR 1501), Paragraph 11B makes clear that if the seller declines to pay the commission, the buyer may be responsible for it. The buyer should understand this before any offer is made.
2. **Deliver and discuss the Information About Brokerage Services form (TREC IABS 1-2).** This form must be provided to the seller before or at the first substantive contact. It explains the types of representation available in Texas.
3. **Complete the Registration Agreement Between Broker and Owner (TXR 2401).** Check the section indicating that the licensee represents only the buyer. Have the seller sign this document to confirm they understand the representation arrangement.
4. **Provide the Seller's Disclosure Notice (TXR 1406).** Give this form to the seller to complete and sign. The licensee represents the buyer, but the seller still has disclosure obligations to the buyer.

Even when fully representing a buyer against a FSBO seller, the licensee must treat the seller honestly and fairly. The agent must not pressure the seller or take any action that could be construed as coercion. The sales contract should include language identifying the buyer as a licensed real estate agent and confirming the buyer is not representing the seller. The contract should also include a recommendation that the seller seek independent professional counsel before signing.

When a licensee is purchasing FSBO property for themselves rather than for a client, the same disclosure principles apply. The licensee must disclaim any agency relationship with the seller and must never allow the seller to assume the licensee is working on the seller's behalf. Failing to make these disclosures is the first step toward license revocation.

Selling Licensee-Owned Property

When a licensee sells property they own, either entirely or in part, they must disclose their licensed status and ownership interest in writing. The disclosure must be made to the buyer or the buyer's representative. This requirement applies regardless of the size of the ownership interest. A licensee who owns a thirty percent interest in a commercial property has the same disclosure obligation as one who owns it outright.

The licensee must also make clear that they are not acting as the buyer's agent in the transaction and should recommend that the buyer obtain their own professional representation. These disclosures protect both the buyer and the selling licensee. They remove any ambiguity about who represents whom and ensure the buyer is making an informed decision.

Brokers approach licensee-owned property transactions with varying policies. Some limit the number of licensee-owned properties that can be listed under the firm's name, in part to address concerns about reduced-commission arrangements. Others prohibit the practice entirely to avoid any appearance of a conflict of interest. Regardless of the broker's policy, a licensee must inform their broker before listing or selling any property in which they hold an ownership interest.

> ***NAR Code of Ethics, Article 4:*** *REALTORS shall not acquire an interest in or purchase property, or present offers from themselves, their family members, their firm, or any entity in which they hold an ownership interest, without disclosing their true position to the owner or owner's agent. When selling property they own or in which they hold any interest, REALTORS shall disclose that ownership or interest in writing to the buyer or buyer's representative. Agents and brokers typically satisfy this requirement by including a disclosure statement directly in the purchase contract.*

Snapshot Review – Chapter 6

The Evolution of Texas Agency

1. Texas real estate representation evolved from subagency (all agents represent the seller) through buyer agency (each side has its own agent) to intermediary brokerage (one firm represents both sides under a defined statutory framework).
2. Common law dual agency was eliminated in Texas effective September 2005. Section 1101.561 of TRELA requires brokers who represent both buyer and seller in the same transaction to do so as intermediaries. Dual agency is not a permissible model in Texas.
3. A 1983 FTC study found that over 70 percent of buyers believed their agent represented them when in fact the agent represented the seller. This triggered nationwide disclosure reform and eventually the demand for buyer representation.

Key Term Definitions

Subagency: A cooperating broker works with a buyer while legally representing the seller. No fiduciary duties are owed to the buyer.

Dual Agency: One brokerage represents both buyer and seller simultaneously. No longer permissible in Texas. The broker cannot advise either party on negotiating strategy.

Transaction Brokerage: A neutral coordinator model with no fiduciary duties to either party. Legal in some states; not adopted by Texas.

Intermediary: The Texas statutory model for in-house transactions where the same broker represents both buyer and seller. Requires written consent and written compensation from both parties.

Intermediary with Appointments: The broker appoints one agent to represent the seller and a different agent to represent the buyer. Each appointed agent may give full advocacy and advice to their client.

Intermediary without Appointments: One agent represents both buyer and seller under the same broker. The agent may not give advice or opinions to either party.

Pre-Appointment System: A standing office policy that automatically appoints the listing agent to the seller and the buyer's agent to the buyer when an in-house transaction arises, without requiring case-by-case broker action.

Legal Requirements for Intermediary

1. Written consent from both the buyer and the seller. Satisfied by paragraph 9 of the TXR listing agreement and paragraph 8 of the TR buyer representation agreement.
2. Written identification of who will pay the broker. Satisfied by the same agency agreement documents.
3. If either requirement is missing, the broker must obtain the appropriate signed document before intermediary negotiations can proceed.

Appointment Rules

1. The broker can never be appointed to either side of the transaction. The broker remains neutral and provides only administrative support.
2. The same agent cannot be appointed to both the buyer and seller. Appointments require two different agents.
3. The broker may appoint more than one agent to the same side, for example, when agents work in teams.
4. If the broker is absent, a designated person in the office may make appointments, but cannot appoint themselves into the transaction.

Confidentiality

1. Confidentiality survives forever in all agency relationships, including intermediary.
2. The agent appointed to the buyer may not disclose the seller's price floor. The agent appointed to the seller may not disclose the buyer's ceiling offer.
3. The only confidential information that may be shared is information about property condition or information the client has expressly authorized the agent to share.
4. When in doubt, consult the broker before disclosing anything.

Broker Policy and Impact

1. Non-agency is legally available in Texas. The license act does not require someone to be represented.
2. A broker who wants to avoid intermediary should establish a clear policy that when one party is a client, the other will be a customer.
3. Policies that require appointment of a second agent whenever one agent holds both sides can inadvertently discourage agents from converting buyers to clients, which leaves buyers unrepresented.
4. Branch offices under the same broker are treated as one entity. Two clients at different branches of the same brokerage are still in an intermediary transaction.

Specialized Transactions

1. Intermediary obligations apply to all real estate transactions, including 1031 exchanges, syndications, commercial leases, and farm sales. There is no exemption for specialized or commercial transactions.
2. Under TRELA Section 1101.651, any agreement that authorizes the possibility of an intermediary relationship must be in writing, and the intermediary disclosure language must appear in bold print.
3. In any complex transaction involving multiple parties and representatives, every participant must understand who each agent represents. The broker must know every player in the deal before negotiations begin.

Key Term Definitions

Specialized Real Estate Transaction: A transaction involving three or more parties and multiple representatives, such as a 1031 exchange, syndication, commercial lease, or farm sale.

1031 Exchange: A transaction authorized by Section 1031 of the Internal Revenue Code in which the sale of a qualifying property is followed by the acquisition of a like-kind replacement property, deferring recognition of capital gains. A qualified intermediary holds the proceeds between the two closings.

Real Estate Syndicate: A group of investors who pool resources to acquire or develop a property too large or complex for any single investor to handle alone. A general partner manages the investment on behalf of the limited partners.

Undisclosed Dual Agency: An intentional act in which a licensee represents both buyer and seller without disclosing this to either party. Illegal in all states.

Accidental Dual Agency: An unintentional dual representation created by carelessness or conduct that leads the opposing party to believe the agent represents them. Also illegal, and typically arises from an agent becoming too helpful to the non-client side of a transaction.

1031 Exchange Key Deadlines

1. The taxpayer has 45 days from the transfer of the relinquished property to identify the replacement property in writing to the qualified intermediary.
2. The closing on the replacement property must occur within 180 days of the transfer of the relinquished property, or by the due date of the taxpayer's return for the year of transfer, whichever comes first.
3. Missing either deadline disqualifies the exchange and triggers immediate capital gains tax liability. Clients should always work with a qualified intermediary and an independent tax advisor.

Avoiding Unintended Dual Representation

1. Do not give strategic advice to the opposing party. If a customer asks for advice, refer them to seek their own professional counsel.
2. Avoid any statement that suggests the agent is working for the non-client party, including comments about likely seller response, pricing opinions, or negotiating guidance directed at the other side.
3. Do not take on tasks that belong to the opposing party's representative.
4. When a verbal agreement exists with one party and a written agreement with the other, the representation status of both parties is unclear. Use written agreements consistently to prevent this problem.

Disclosure Requirements for Licensee Transactions

1. A licensee purchasing their own company's listing must disclose the price and terms of their offer to competing buyers. Using knowledge of other offers to gain a personal purchasing advantage violates Texas law prohibiting bad faith dealings.
2. A licensee purchasing any property, whether in-house, from the MLS, or FSBO, must disclose their licensed status in writing per Rule 535.144 and must disclaim any agency relationship with the seller.

3. When representing a buyer in a FSBO transaction, the licensee must deliver the TREC IABS 1-2 form to the seller, complete and have the seller sign the TXR Registration Agreement Between Broker and Owner, and provide the Seller's Disclosure Notice.
4. A licensee selling property they own must disclose their ownership interest and license status in writing to the buyer or buyer's representative. This applies to any ownership interest, including partial interests.
5. Licensees must always inform their broker before listing or selling any property in which they hold an ownership interest.

CHAPTER 6 QUIZ — INTERMEDIARY BROKERAGE

1. A 1983 Federal Trade Commission study found that more than 70 percent of buyers incorrectly believed that the agent helping them search for a home was representing their interests. This finding was significant because:

a. It demonstrated that agents in subagency were required to share buyer information with sellers, yet buyers were unaware of that obligation, triggering nationwide disclosure reform.

b. It proved that buyer agency was unnecessary since most buyers felt satisfied with the process.

c. It showed that listing agents were failing to disclose material defects to the buyers they were representing.

d. It established that the MLS cooperative model was causing unfair commission practices across the industry.

2. Under the original subagency model, when a cooperating broker showed a buyer a property listed with a different office, the cooperating broker legally represented:

a. The buyer, because the cooperating broker spent the most time with the buyer.

b. The seller, because all fiduciary duties under subagency ran to the seller-client through the listing broker.

c. Neither party, because both brokers were neutral facilitators.

d. The buyer's lender, because lender qualification was the broker's primary responsibility.

3. Which of the following best describes the key advantage that buyer agency gained over the subagency model?

a. Buyer agency eliminated the MLS cooperation requirement so buyers could negotiate directly with sellers.

b. Buyer agency allowed buyers to avoid paying any commission at closing.

c. Buyer agency gave buyers the same caliber of professional advocacy that sellers had always received, with fiduciary duties running exclusively to the buyer.

d. Buyer agency required sellers to disclose all known defects before listing, creating equal information access.

4. Under Section 1101.561 of the Texas Real Estate License Act, what is required when a broker represents both the buyer and the seller in the same transaction?

a. The broker must refer one party to a different brokerage before negotiations can begin.

b. The broker must obtain written permission from TREC before proceeding as a dual agent.

c. The broker may proceed as a common law dual agent provided both parties sign a disclosure form.

d. The broker must act as an intermediary under the statutory intermediary framework. Common law dual agency is no longer permissible in Texas.

5. For a broker to act as an intermediary under TRELA, which two requirements must be satisfied?

a. Written consent from both parties and written identification of who will pay the broker.

b. Oral consent from both parties and a copy of the contract filed with TREC.

c. A separate intermediary agreement drafted by a real estate attorney and signed at closing.

d. Written consent from TREC and disclosure of the intermediary status in the MLS listing.

6. In the context of Texas intermediary law, where is the written consent to act as intermediary most commonly satisfied in residential transactions?

a. In the TREC Information About Brokerage Services form delivered at first contact.

b. In paragraph 9 of the TR listing agreement and paragraph 8 of the TXR buyer representation agreement.

c. In the Special Provisions section of the earnest money contract.

d. In a separate TREC-promulgated intermediary consent form that must be signed before showings begin.

7. Under intermediary with appointments, each appointed agent is permitted to:

a. Advise both the buyer and the seller on negotiating strategy to help the transaction close efficiently.

b. Share all property condition information about the listing with the buyer without restriction.

c. Give full advocacy and advice exclusively to their own appointed client, even if that advice is not helpful to the other party.

d. Make the final decision about the purchase price if the broker is unavailable.

8. An agent appointed to represent the buyer in an intermediary transaction learns that the seller has told the listing agent they will accept twenty thousand dollars less than the asking price. The appointed buyer's agent:

a. May share this information with the buyer because once appointments are made, full disclosure between sides is permitted.

b. Must share this information with the buyer as part of the fiduciary duty of disclosure.

c. Should report the seller's price floor to TREC as a required disclosure.

d. May not disclose the seller's price floor to the buyer, even under intermediary with appointments.

9. Under intermediary without appointments, the agent working with both the buyer and seller in the same transaction:

a. May not give advice or express opinions to either party on matters involving negotiating strategy.

b. May advise both parties fully because the agent has a professional relationship with each.

c. Must make appointments to at least one side before the buyer can submit an offer.

d. May advise the seller only, because the listing relationship was established first.

10. A broker operating under a pre-appointment system has established a standing office policy. Under this policy, when an in-house buyer makes an offer on a company listing:

a. The broker reviews every transaction individually and makes appointment decisions at the time of each offer.

b. The buyer's agent and listing agent are automatically appointed to their respective clients without requiring the broker to act separately for each transaction.

c. The broker is automatically appointed to the seller and the buyer's agent is appointed to the buyer.

d. No appointments are made and the transaction proceeds as intermediary without appointments by default.

11. In an intermediary transaction with appointments, the broker's role is to:

a. Advise whichever party requests guidance first, then remain neutral for the remainder of negotiations.

b. Be appointed to one side of the transaction to ensure a senior professional oversees the negotiations.

c. Step back from negotiations, provide only administrative support to the appointed agents, and give no strategic advice or opinions to either party.

d. Review and approve every counteroffer before it is delivered to the other party.

12. Which of the following statements about the broker's appointment authority is correct?

a. Brokers may appoint themselves to one side of the transaction as long as they remain neutral with the other side.

b. The broker must be present to make all appointments and cannot delegate the appointment decision to anyone else.

c. The broker may appoint themselves to represent the buyer if no other agents are available in the office.

d. The broker may never be appointed to either side of an intermediary transaction. If absent, a designated person in the office may make appointments but cannot appoint themselves.

13. The Notification of Intermediary Relationships form is a TR form used to:

a. Notify both clients that the intermediary relationship authorized in their original agency agreements has been activated in this specific transaction.

b. Disclose the broker's commission structure to both parties before the listing agreement is signed.

c. Replace the TREC Information About Brokerage Services form when an intermediary situation is anticipated.

d. Request TREC approval for the intermediary transaction before negotiations can proceed.

14. An in-house transaction involves a seller who is a client of the brokerage and a buyer who is a customer of the same brokerage. This transaction is:

a. An intermediary transaction because both parties are connected to the same office.

b. Not an intermediary transaction because intermediary requires two clients. The seller receives full fiduciary representation and the buyer receives only honest and fair treatment.

c. A dual agency transaction because only one brokerage is involved.

d. A transaction brokerage arrangement because neither party receives full representation.

15. A buyer is represented by an agent at one branch office of a large brokerage. The seller is represented by a different agent at a separate branch office of the same brokerage. Under Texas intermediary law, this transaction is:

a. Not an intermediary transaction because the agents work in separate physical locations.

b. Governed by the rules of the branch office where the listing originated.

c. An intermediary transaction because all branch offices under the same broker's license are treated as one entity.

d. A subagency transaction because the buyer's agent is cooperating with a different office.

16. A broker who finds intermediary relationships difficult to administer asks whether they can operate outside the agency framework entirely and simply facilitate transactions without representing anyone. Under Texas law:

a. Non-agency is permitted as long as the broker discloses their neutral status to both parties in writing.

b. Non-agency is available only for commercial transactions, not residential.

c. Non-agency is permitted as long as the broker adopts a written policy and files it with TREC.

d. Non-agency is not legally recognized in Texas. The License Act is an agency law, and someone must be represented in every licensed real estate transaction.

17. Under the 2024 NAR settlement rules adopted in Texas, buyer broker compensation:

a. May no longer be advertised through the MLS and must be negotiated and documented in the buyer representation agreement before any properties are shown.

b. Must be included in the MLS listing so cooperating agents know what they will receive before scheduling showings.

c. Is set by TREC at a uniform percentage for all Texas residential transactions.

d. Is paid directly by the buyer at closing outside the transaction contract.

18. A broker's office policy requires that whenever one agent has both the buyer and seller as clients, a second agent must be brought in to take one client relationship. A potential unintended consequence of this policy is:

a. Agents may earn larger commissions by avoiding intermediary situations entirely.

b. Sellers may object to being assigned a new listing agent mid-transaction.

c. Agents may be discouraged from converting buyers to clients because doing so could require sharing the commission with a second agent, leaving buyers unrepresented as customers instead.

d. The policy creates a dual agency relationship that violates Section 1101.561 of TRELA.

19. Under TRELA Section 1101.651, any agreement that authorizes the possibility of an intermediary relationship must satisfy which specific formatting requirement?

a. The agreement must be notarized and filed with the county clerk before the transaction begins.

b. The agreement must be drafted by a licensed real estate attorney and reviewed by TREC before signing.

c. The intermediary disclosure language must appear on a separate page with a signature line designated for each party.

d. The intermediary disclosure language must appear in bold or underlined print, and the agreement must be in writing.

20. Under a standard 1031 exchange, the taxpayer has how many days from the transfer of the relinquished property to identify the replacement property in writing to the qualified intermediary?

a. 45 days

b. 30 days

c. 60 days

d. 90 days

21. If a taxpayer completing a 1031 exchange misses the 180-day closing deadline for the replacement property, the consequence is:

a. The exchange is automatically extended for an additional 90 days at the IRS's discretion.

b. The exchange is disqualified and deferred capital gains tax becomes immediately due.

c. The qualified intermediary returns all proceeds to the taxpayer tax-free.

d. The taxpayer may substitute a different replacement property without restarting the identification period.

22. A general partner of a real estate syndicate is also a licensed broker. The general partner sells a property owned by the syndicate and receives a commission from the transaction. Under fiduciary duty principles, this arrangement:

a. Is prohibited under Texas law regardless of disclosure, because the general partner cannot receive a commission from the partnership.

b. Does not require disclosure because commission income is separate from the general partner's management duties.

c. Is appropriate only if full and transparent disclosure is made to all partners in the syndicate, removing the element of concealment.

d. Is automatically permissible as long as the commission is at or below the MLS standard rate.

23. The key distinction between undisclosed dual agency and accidental dual agency is:

a. Undisclosed dual agency always results in criminal charges, while accidental dual agency results only in civil liability.

b. Accidental dual agency is legal in Texas as long as the agent discloses it before closing, while undisclosed dual agency is always illegal.

c. Undisclosed dual agency applies only to residential transactions, while accidental dual agency applies only to commercial deals.

d. Undisclosed dual agency is an intentional act of concealment, while accidental dual agency arises unintentionally from carelessness or conduct that leads the opposing party to believe the agent represents them.

24. A seller's agent tells a buyer-customer, "Trust me, I\'ll get you the best possible deal on this property." This statement is problematic because:

a. It signals to the buyer that the agent is working in the buyer's interest, which can create an implied agency relationship and lead to accidental dual agency.

b. Agents are prohibited from making any promises to buyers under Texas license law.

c. The statement constitutes an unauthorized practice of law because it references a contractual outcome.

d. It violates the duty of loyalty to the buyer by implying the agent will negotiate against the seller.

25. A licensee wishes to purchase a property listed with their own brokerage where they have access to the terms of other competing offers. Texas law requires the licensee to:

a. Withdraw from the transaction entirely because licensees are prohibited from purchasing their own firm's listings.

b. Disclose the price and terms of their own offer to competing buyers to level the playing field, since using knowledge of other offers to gain a personal advantage violates the prohibition on bad faith dealings.

c. Submit their offer through an attorney to avoid any appearance of conflict.

d. Obtain written permission from TREC before submitting an offer on an in-house listing.

26. When a buyer's agent represents a client in the purchase of a property being sold directly by the owner without a listing agent, the agent must provide the seller with which of the following documents?

a. The TR Residential Buyer/Tenant Representation Agreement and the buyer's pre-approval letter.

b. The TREC intermediary consent form and a written disclaimer of subagency.

c. The MLS comparable sales report and a written property condition statement from the buyer's inspector.

d. The TREC Information About Brokerage Services form, the TR Registration Agreement Between Broker and Owner, and the Seller's Disclosure Notice.

27. Under Texas Administrative Code Rule 535.144, when a licensee purchases real property, they are required to:

a. Obtain the broker's written approval before any offer is submitted.

b. Disclose their licensed status in writing and disclaim any agency relationship with the seller.

c. Pay full commission to the listing broker regardless of any buyer representation agreement in place.

d. File a disclosure with TREC within ten days of closing.

28. A licensee owns a 25 percent interest in a commercial property that is being sold. Under NAR Code of Ethics Article 4 and Texas law, the licensee must:

a. Disclose the ownership interest only if it exceeds 50 percent, because minority interests do not create a conflict.

b. Withdraw from the transaction and transfer their ownership interest to a family member before the property is listed.

c. Disclose their ownership interest and license status in writing to the buyer or buyer's representative, regardless of the size of the interest, and recommend the buyer obtain independent representation.

d. Disclose only if the broker's company policy requires it, since NAR standards do not apply to commercial transactions.

CHAPTER 7

CREATION AND TERMINATION OF AGENCY

Chapter Objectives

After completing this chapter, you should be able to:

1. Describe the three ways agency is created and explain why a written agreement is always the preferred method.
2. Identify the three types of seller listings and the buyer representation agreement, and distinguish the rights each creates.
3. List and explain the three required disclosures that must be made when creating any agency relationship.
4. Describe the most common ways agency is terminated, including closing, expiration, mutual rescission, revocation, and broker renunciation.
5. Explain which fiduciary duty survives termination of agency, what does not terminate agency, and how courts have interpreted the duration of an agent's duties.

Contents

Broker Renunciation
Death of the Client or Broker
Additional Grounds for Termination
Termination Paperwork
Confidentiality Survives Termination
What the Courts Say
What Does Not Terminate Agency
Ending the Independent Contractor Relationship
Zoning Changes and Agency

How Agency Is Created

Agency is a professional relationship in which a member of the public retains a licensed broker, and the broker's sponsored licensees, to assist in buying, selling, or leasing property. The moment agency begins, the licensee's obligations shift. A customer relationship governed by basic honesty and fair dealing is replaced by a fiduciary relationship in which the agent is bound to act in the client's best interest.

Agency can be created through words, actions, or a written document. The written document is always the correct choice. All skills and obligations of agency rest with the broker, even when a salesperson in the office handles the day-to-day client communication. If the salesperson performs poorly, the broker must step in. If the salesperson needs guidance, the broker must provide it. The broker owns every client relationship in the office.

Agency by Implication

Implied agency occurs when a licensee's words or conduct lead a person to reasonably believe that the agent is representing them, even though no formal agreement was made. This most commonly happens when a licensee inadvertently gives advice, opinions, or guidance to a customer in a way that signals the agent is on that person's side.

A customer cannot accidentally create an implied agency. Only the licensee can do so, and only by saying or doing something that creates the impression of representation. Because this type of agency is unintentional, it is particularly dangerous. The licensee may not realize an implied relationship has been created, while the customer may believe they have an advocate working for them.

Brokers must continually remind licensees in the office that implied agency is not acceptable, that all representation relationships must be established through a written agreement, and that careless communication is one of the most direct paths to unintended legal exposure.

Creating Agency Verbally

Agency can be created verbally, but oral agreements carry significant risks. Tone of voice, word choice, and body language all affect how a spoken message is understood. What the agent intended to communicate may not be what the other person heard. A verbal agency agreement also cannot capture the full range of details a written document addresses: when the relationship begins and ends, what services the agent will provide, how compensation is structured, and what the client's obligations are.

A verbal agreement may be necessary in limited circumstances, such as when a buyer asks for representation while in the field and no written form is available. In that situation, the verbal agreement should be confirmed in writing at the earliest possible opportunity.

Texas law requires certain things to be in writing. A licensee cannot place a sign on a property that is not listed. The intermediary consent paragraphs in both the listing agreement and the buyer representation agreement must be in writing and signed by the client. These requirements exist precisely because verbal understandings are insufficient to establish the legal clarity those provisions require.

Creating Agency in Writing

A written agency agreement is the most reliable foundation for any representation relationship. When a client signs a multi-page document, the act of signing carries a sense of professional commitment for both parties. Each person leaves with a clear reference point that describes their responsibilities, the scope of the relationship, and its beginning and end dates.

Copies of any signed document should be delivered to the client as soon as possible after signing. Licensees must also have explicit authorization before conducting any part of a transaction electronically. That authorization can be given through a signed document, an email confirmation, or a website acknowledgment.

A written agreement should clearly address three core elements: the duties of the agent and the client, the compensation structure and its source, and the protections available to both parties. A written agreement that is complete on these points prevents most disputes before they begin.

Exclusive Right to Sell

The exclusive right to sell is the strongest and most desirable form of seller representation. Under this agreement, the listing broker earns a commission if the property sells during the listing period, regardless of who procures the buyer. Whether the sale is produced by the listing agent, a cooperating broker, or the seller, the listing broker is entitled to the agreed commission.

TREC does not promulgate listing agreement forms. Brokers obtain their listing agreements through the Texas Association of REALTORS or have them prepared by a real estate attorney.

Two situations sometimes test the exclusive right to sell. First, a seller who finds their own buyer may attempt to bypass the broker and avoid paying the commission. If that sale was put together before the listing expired, the broker has a valid commission claim. Second, a cooperating agent who becomes aware that an exclusive listing is in place and works around it to do a direct deal with the seller has violated both the TREC Canon of Professional Ethics and the NAR Code of Ethics. The seller still owes the listing broker a commission in that situation, regardless of any payment made to the other agent.

Exclusive Agency

Exclusive agency is a listing structure in which the broker has the exclusive right to market the property and earn a commission from any sale produced through the brokerage, but the seller retains the right to sell the property independently to specific named individuals without owing the broker a commission.

This structure is most appropriate when a seller was previously marketing the property themselves and has shown it to a defined group of prospective buyers before deciding to engage a broker. To implement exclusive agency in Texas, the licensee uses the TR Exclusive Right to Sell Listing Agreement together with the Named Exclusions addendum. The addendum identifies the specific people the seller may sell to directly. If the property sells to someone on the exclusion list without the broker's involvement, no commission is owed.

The seller and broker are also free to market the property simultaneously. In that case, whoever produces a buyer first earns the sale. The only material difference between exclusive right to sell and exclusive agency is that exclusive agency preserves the seller's ability to complete a transaction outside the broker's involvement under the defined exclusion terms. Some brokers decline to take exclusive agency listings as a matter of policy, accepting only exclusive right to sell agreements.

Open Listings

An open listing is a non-exclusive arrangement in which the seller authorizes any number of brokers to market the property, with the commission going to whichever broker procures the buyer first. If the seller finds a buyer independently, no commission is owed to anyone.

Open listings are the least desirable form of listing for the broker. The agent invests time and marketing resources knowing that a competing licensee or the seller themselves could close the deal and collect nothing. Because of this, many brokers refuse to take open listings as a matter of policy. The MLS does not accept open listings because of the procuring cause disputes they generate.

Open listings appear most commonly in farm, ranch, and commercial transactions. They are frequently oral rather than written, which creates an additional problem: a broker who produces a buyer under an oral open listing has no written document to support a commission claim if the seller refuses to pay. An enforceable commission claim in Texas requires a written listing agreement.

Before working with an open listing, a salesperson must understand and comply with their broker's policy on the matter. The risks are clear, and taking an open listing over the broker's objection creates both professional and legal complications.

Exclusive Right to Buy

The buyer representation agreement in Texas is structured as an exclusive right to buy. The buyer agrees to work solely with the signing broker and not to enter into a representation agreement with any other broker during the agreement's term. This gives the agent a legitimate basis for investing time and effort in the buyer's search without the risk of losing the client mid-transaction.

Most brokers insist on exclusivity. Buyers who want to keep multiple agents working for them simultaneously typically decline to sign any representation agreement and remain as customers, retaining the freedom to move from one agent to another with no obligation to any of them.

Once a buyer signs a representation agreement, the agent should explain two important implications. First, if the buyer encounters an open house while the agreement is in effect, they should inform the host agent that they are already represented before engaging in any substantive conversation about the property. Second, if the buyer discovers a FSBO property they want to see, they should contact their agent first so the agent can accompany them or make the appropriate arrangements. If the buyer must view a FSBO without their agent present, they should at minimum inform the seller that they have a buyer's representative. Some agents provide their buyer-clients with a brief card to present to FSBO sellers confirming the buyer's represented status.

Required Disclosures When Creating Agency

Three specific disclosures must be made when entering into any agency relationship, whether with a seller or a buyer.

1. **Cooperating broker policy.** The client must be informed of the broker's policy on working with other brokers. If the office does not cooperate with outside firms, that will limit the property's market exposure and may extend the time it takes to find a buyer. If the broker shares a smaller portion of the commission with cooperating brokers than is standard in the market, that must also be disclosed.
2. **Source of compensation.** The client must understand where the commission will come from. For a buyer, the agent should explain the three possible sources: the seller pays, the buyer pays, or both contribute. In most transactions the buyer will prefer the seller to pay, but the buyer should understand their obligation if the seller does not cover the full amount. Any arrangement in which both the buyer and the seller are contributing to the broker's compensation must be disclosed to and agreed upon by both parties.
3. **Possibility of intermediary representation.** Each client must be informed that the broker could end up representing both the buyer and the seller in the same transaction and be given the opportunity to consent to or decline that possibility. This disclosure is the basis for the intermediary consent language in the listing agreement and the buyer representation agreement.

Undisclosed Agency

Every licensee should be able to identify clearly who they represent at any given point in a transaction and be comfortable disclosing that representation to every other participant. Undisclosed agency, where an agent has a client relationship that has not been made known to all parties, is one of the most serious professional failures a licensee can commit.

The most common path to undisclosed agency is accidental: a salesperson gives advice or strategic opinions to a buyer-customer, creating an implied agency, and then fails to inform the seller-client that they have inadvertently taken on representation of the opposing party. Both parties are now operating under a false understanding of the agent's loyalties.

When a licensee realizes an undisclosed agency exists, the obligation is to correct it immediately. Options include making the required disclosures to all affected parties, ending agency with one or both clients, or consulting the broker on the best path forward. In real estate, neither agency relationships nor property conditions should ever go undisclosed. Every person with a stake in the transaction is entitled to the information they need to make informed decisions.

How Agency Is Terminated

Agency can end in a variety of ways, some satisfying and some not. The preferred outcome is always a successful transaction that meets the client's goals. But the reality of real estate is that obstacles, market conditions, title problems, financing difficulties, and the sheer unpredictability of negotiations mean that not every listing produces a sale and not every buyer finds a property within the agreement's term.

When the relationship ends without a successful transaction, the goal is to part professionally. A client who leaves without animosity may return in the future or refer others. The licensee's job throughout the relationship is to be a problem solver. When the problems cannot be resolved, both parties move on.

Termination at Closing

The most satisfying way for agency to end is at the closing table. The seller has received acceptable terms and price. The buyer has found a property that meets their needs. The title company processes the transaction and the broker earns a commission. This is what the entire representation relationship is built toward.

A successful closing represents the resolution of countless decisions, showings, negotiations, inspections, and procedural steps that most clients never fully see. The licensee who closes a transaction has walked the client from the beginning of their search or listing all the way through to a completed transfer of ownership. That accomplishment deserves recognition, and it forms the foundation of a professional reputation built on referrals.

Expiration of the Agreement

Both listing agreements and buyer representation agreements contain an end date. When that date arrives without a completed transaction or a mutually agreed extension, the agency expires.

Listing agreements are typically written for six months to one year. As the expiration date approaches, the listing agent should contact the seller to discuss whether an extension is appropriate. A seller who is not regularly informed about the status of the listing, how many showings have occurred, and what feedback has been received is far less likely to extend. Communication failures are consistently cited among the top client complaints about licensees. A seller who feels ignored will let the listing expire without renewing it. The agent who maintains consistent, honest communication gives themselves the best chance of extending the relationship.

Buyer representation agreements are usually written for a shorter period. If an agent has been unable to identify a suitable property for a buyer within a month or two, the issue may be with the buyer's criteria, the market, or the agent's approach. The agreement can be extended by mutual consent if both parties want to continue.

Reasonable Time

The concept of reasonable time as a basis for agency termination applies only in situations where the agency was created verbally and no end date was established. If all agency agreements are in writing with defined terms, this issue never arises. That is precisely the reason written agreements are required.

When a dispute arises over whether an oral agency has expired, the determination of what constitutes a reasonable time is made by a court. A judge would weigh factors such as how long the agent has been working with the client, whether the agent has been actively performing their duties, and whether the client has raised concerns about inactivity. If the court finds that a reasonable period has elapsed without meaningful activity, the agency may be deemed terminated. If not, the agent is still bound by fiduciary duties. This is an entirely avoidable situation: create agency in writing and include a specific end date in every agreement.

Mutual Rescission

Mutual rescission occurs when both the client and the broker agree to end the agency relationship. Because all clients belong to the broker, any request from a client to end the relationship should be directed to the broker, not just the salesperson.

When a seller asks to be released from a listing, the listing agent will naturally wonder whether the seller plans to re-list with another broker. When a buyer asks to end their representation agreement, the salesperson may wonder whether the buyer went elsewhere and completed a purchase. These concerns are understandable but should not prevent a professional and courteous release.

Mutual rescission can also serve the broker's interests. Releasing a client who has a valid reason to exit, such as a serious illness or a change in circumstances, costs the broker less in goodwill and professional reputation than insisting on holding a reluctant client to an agreement. The wise broker considers the circumstances rather than reflexively enforcing the contract.

Revocation by the Client

A client has the power to revoke agency at any time. Whether they have the legal right to do so without liability depends on the terms of the agency agreement and the circumstances of the revocation.

A seller who feels the property is not being shown often enough or marketed effectively may pull the listing and give it to someone else. A buyer who feels their agent is not listening to their preferences or is showing them unsuitable properties may end the relationship and seek different representation. In either case, the client has the authority to take that action.

The broker's response is to meet with both the client and the agent separately to understand what has gone wrong and whether the relationship can be salvaged. If substantial time and marketing expense have already been invested, the broker has a legitimate interest in the conversation. Ultimately, the broker's decision on whether to release the client or assert the agreement's terms depends on the specific facts, the amount at stake, and the professional judgment about what serves the brokerage's long-term reputation.

Broker Renunciation

There are circumstances in which the broker no longer wants to continue the representation relationship even though the client does. The broker may renounce the agency, but must have legitimate cause to do so and must provide proper notice to the client before the termination is effective.

Valid grounds for broker renunciation include a client who consistently behaves in an abusive or threatening manner toward the agent or office staff, a client who asks the agent to violate Fair Housing laws or other legal requirements, or a client who is not negotiating in good faith and is wasting the broker's resources.

> *Example: A property was priced above market in a challenging neighborhood. The seller was advised the price was unrealistic but insisted. The seller began calling the office daily and was verbally abusive with every person who answered the phone, including the broker. After one such call, the broker informed the seller that the brokerage was withdrawing from the representation and would collect the sign and lockbox from the property that day. Good cause existed, and proper notice was given.*

Death of the Client or Broker

The death of the client terminates the agency relationship. When a seller dies, the person who signed the listing agreement is gone, and the agency ends. When a buyer dies, there is no longer a client to represent.

The death of the broker also terminates all agency relationships in the office, since every client relationship belongs to the broker. Agents should remain at the office to determine whether another broker will take over the business. If not, they must locate a new sponsoring broker. TREC and TR have a framework in which a temporary broker may be appointed to the affected office to allow transactions already in escrow to close without disruption.

Additional Grounds for Termination

Several less common circumstances also bring an agency relationship to an end:

Broker Failure: If the broker and their agents fail to perform their duties, the agency relationship is effectively broken. The appropriate response is to acknowledge the failure and release the client through mutual rescission rather than attempting to maintain an agency that has already been abandoned in practice.

Bankruptcy of the Seller: When a seller files for bankruptcy, a court takes legal control of the property. The court determines what happens to it, and the agency with the broker ends at the point of the bankruptcy filing.

Foreclosure: When a property enters foreclosure, the person who signed the listing agreement is no longer the owner. The agency ends because the client no longer has authority over the property. Title passes to the lender or to a buyer at the foreclosure sale.

Destruction of the Property: If the property is destroyed by fire, flood, storm, or other cause, the listing terminates. The land remains but the improvement is gone. If insurance proceeds allow rebuilding and the property was already under contract, the transaction may be able to continue under the terms of the contract's contingency provisions.

Broker's Breach of Fiduciary Duty: A broker who fails to perform required duties, whether by an act of omission such as failing to disclose a material fact, or an act of commission such as sharing confidential client information without authorization, has breached the fiduciary relationship. The client may terminate the agency as a consequence.

Incompetence of Broker or Client: If either the broker or the client becomes legally incompetent and can no longer make rational decisions, the agency terminates. Legal incompetency means the party is no longer capable of fulfilling their obligations under the agreement.

Termination Paperwork

Just as agency should always be created in writing, it should always be terminated in writing. The TXR forms library includes separate forms for terminating agency with sellers and with buyers. Using the correct form matters. Some licensees have mistakenly used an amendment form, which is designed to change a marketing price or extend a listing period, when they intended to terminate the relationship. The termination form has a single purpose: ending the agency. It should be used for that purpose only.

When a buyer representation agreement is written for a short term, such as thirty to sixty days, a formal termination form may never be needed. Both parties can see the expiration approaching if the relationship is not producing results, and the agreement can simply be allowed to expire. When the term is longer, a written termination document provides a clear record and protects both parties.

Confidentiality Survives Termination

When agency ends, every fiduciary duty ends with it except one: confidentiality. A licensee is bound to protect the confidences of a former client indefinitely. There is no expiration date on this obligation.

The only exception is that a client may authorize the agent to share specific information with others. Absent that explicit authorization, the following categories of information remain permanently confidential:

- The reason the seller is selling.
- The lowest price the seller would accept.
- The highest price the buyer would pay.
- Personal circumstances such as a divorce, job loss, or financial difficulty.
- A pending foreclosure or other financial threat.
- The existence or terms of a prior offer that did not result in a contract.
- The amount the buyer would spend on additional or future properties.

These confidences are not merely professionally sensitive. Disclosing them without authorization may harm the former client materially and could result in a complaint to TREC. A licensee who cannot hold client confidences is a liability to the clients they represent, to the brokerage, and to their own license.

What the Courts Say

Courts have been called upon to define exactly when agency ends and how far the broker's duties extend. Several recurring themes appear across the case law:

- When the broker's commission is contingent on the transaction closing, fiduciary duties continue through the closing itself, not merely until the contract is signed.
- Disclosure obligations generally extend through the closing or until the purpose of the agency is fully accomplished.
- In a case where a broker provided down payment assistance to the buyer without disclosing this to the seller, the court found that the loan was inconsistent with the broker's fiduciary duty to the seller and should have been disclosed and approved by the seller in advance.

- A client has the power to end agency at any time, but not necessarily the legal right to do so without consequences. If a client wrongfully terminates the agency before the agreement's end date, the client may be liable for damages caused to the broker.
- The broker may also end the agency, but must give the client proper notice before doing so.
- One court ruled that fiduciary duties do not end simply because the seller rejected an offer. A rejection does not terminate the agency. The agency continues until one or both parties take specific action to end it.

What Does Not Terminate Agency

Several events that might seem significant do not, in fact, terminate agency:

- A salesperson transferring to a different broker. All client relationships belong to the broker, not to the individual salesperson. When a licensee leaves the office and joins a new brokerage, the clients stay with the original broker. The agency continues unchanged.
- Marriage of the client. If a seller lists their property and then gets married, the listing remains intact. Property that was separate before the wedding remains separate property after it, and the agency relationship continues under its original terms.
- Divorce proceedings involving a married seller couple. Texas law does not clearly define what happens to a listing when the sellers are divorcing. The agent must maintain close contact with both parties to understand whether the sale should continue, whether one party intends to keep the property, or whether the property will become entangled in the divorce settlement. The listing may effectively be suspended until the question of ownership is resolved.

Ending the Independent Contractor Relationship

The relationship between a sponsored licensee and their broker is an independent contractor relationship, not an employment relationship. There is no standard form used to end it. The normal process is for the licensee to notify the broker, who then sends the license back to TREC for placement in inactive status. The licensee can reactivate the license at any time by completing applicable education requirements, finding a new sponsoring broker, and submitting the required sponsorship form and fee to TREC.

A broker who wishes to end the independent contractor relationship must also notify the salesperson and return the license to TREC promptly. No advance notice period is required, unlike employment relationships. The relationship ends as soon as the other party has been informed.

A licensee becomes active under a new broker's sponsorship the moment the sponsorship form is placed in the mail. There is no need to wait for the physical license document to arrive at the new broker's office before beginning work.

Zoning Changes and Agency

When a governmental entity changes the zoning classification of a property, questions may arise about whether the listing agent can continue to represent the property under its new use designation.

Many brokerages establish policies limiting their practice to a particular type of real estate, most commonly residential. A residential-only office cannot re-list a property under its new commercial zoning. In that situation, the listing must be referred to a broker authorized to handle commercial transactions. The referring agent may be entitled to a referral fee.

Some offices are structured with separate departments, each authorized for a specific property type. An agent in the residential department may not be permitted to take on a listing that has been rezoned to a commercial classification. The referral would go to the appropriate department within the same office.

Other brokers permit their agents to work across all property types, even when neither the agent nor the broker has direct experience in the newly applicable category. This approach requires the broker to guide the agent through the unfamiliar transaction and carries additional risk if the broker's experience does not cover the property type. The upside is that a well-handled transaction in a new category can become the foundation for expanding the firm's service offerings.

Snapshot Review – Chapter 7

Creating Agency

1. Agency can be created by implication, verbally, or in writing. A written agreement is always the correct method. Implied agency is created by the licensee's conduct, not the customer's.
2. A written agency agreement should address the agent's and client's duties, the compensation structure, and the start and end dates of the relationship. Copies must be delivered to the client promptly.
3. Three disclosures must be made when creating any agency relationship: (1) the broker's policy on cooperating with other firms; (2) the source and structure of the commission; and (3) the possibility that the broker may represent both the buyer and the seller in the same transaction.

Types of Seller Listings

Exclusive Right to Sell: The most desirable listing. The broker earns the commission regardless of who produces the buyer, including the seller. Procuring cause is irrelevant.

Exclusive Agency: The broker has exclusive marketing rights but the seller may sell to specifically named individuals without owing a commission. Implemented using the TXR Exclusive Right to Sell agreement with the Named Exclusions addendum.

Open Listing: Non-exclusive arrangement in which any number of brokers may market the property. The commission goes to whichever broker produces the buyer first. Not accepted by the MLS. Most brokers decline open listings as a matter of policy. Commission claims require a written agreement.

Terminating Agency

Closing: The preferred outcome. Agency ends when the transaction is successfully completed.

Expiration: The agreement's end date arrives without a completed transaction or a mutually agreed extension.

Reasonable Time: Applicable only to oral agreements with no defined end date. A court determines whether a reasonable time has elapsed. Avoidable with a written agreement.

Mutual Rescission: Both the broker and the client agree to end the relationship. All client relationships belong to the broker.

Revocation by the Client: The client has the power to end the agency. Whether they have the legal right without liability depends on the agreement's terms.

Broker Renunciation: The broker ends the agency with proper notice and good cause, such as abusive conduct, a request to violate the law, or bad-faith negotiating.

Death: Death of either the client or the broker terminates the agency. TREC and TXR allow appointment of a temporary broker to close transactions already in escrow.

Broker Failure or Breach: Failure to perform duties or a breach of fiduciary obligation terminates the agency.

Bankruptcy, Foreclosure, or Destruction: Each event removes the client's authority over the property and ends the listing.

Incompetence: Legal incompetence of either the broker or client terminates the agency.

What Does Not Terminate Agency

1. A salesperson leaving the brokerage. The clients belong to the broker and remain with the office.
2. Marriage of the client. Separate property before the wedding remains separate property after it.
3. Rejection of an offer. Agency continues after an offer is rejected unless a specific decision to end it is made.

Confidentiality

1. Confidentiality is the only fiduciary duty that survives termination. It lasts indefinitely unless the client authorizes disclosure.
2. Permanently protected confidences include the seller's lowest acceptable price, the buyer's ceiling offer, personal financial circumstances, the reason for selling, and the terms of prior offers that did not result in a contract.

Courts and Agency Duration

1. When the commission is contingent on closing, fiduciary duties extend through the closing, not just through contract execution.
2. Disclosure obligations generally continue until the purpose of the agency is fully accomplished.
3. A client who wrongfully terminates agency before the agreement's end date may be liable to the broker for resulting damages.
4. A broker who provides undisclosed financial assistance to the buyer may breach fiduciary duty to the seller.

CHAPTER 7 QUIZ — CREATION AND TERMINATION OF AGENCY

1. Implied agency is created in which of the following ways?

a. Either the licensee or the customer may create implied agency through mutual conduct.

b. Implied agency is created by a customer when he or she asks the licensee for advice without first signing a representation agreement.

c. Only the licensee can create implied agency. A customer cannot accidentally create a representation relationship.

d. Implied agency is created automatically when a licensee shows a property to any unrepresented buyer.

2. When a broker takes an exclusive right to sell listing, the commission is earned:

a. Regardless of who produces the buyer, including the seller, as long as the sale occurs during the listing period.

b. Only if the listing broker personally shows the property to the eventual buyer.

c. Only if a cooperating broker from a different office produces the buyer.

d. Only after the property closes and the seller receives net proceeds above the listing price.

3. A seller has been showing his home to a specific group of prospective buyers for several months before deciding to engage a broker. The listing structure best suited to this situation is:

a. An open listing, because it allows the seller to continue showing the property without broker involvement.

b. An exclusive right to sell, because it provides maximum broker protection and should always be used.

c. A net listing, because it allows the seller to set a minimum acceptable price before a commission is owed.

d. An exclusive agency listing using the TXR Exclusive Right to Sell agreement with the Named Exclusions addendum, which preserves the seller's right to sell to those specific individuals without owing a commission.

4. Which of the following correctly states why the MLS does not accept open listings?

a. Open listings involve unrepresented sellers, and MLS rules require all listed properties to have a licensed agent on both sides.

b. Open listings generate procuring cause disputes and do not require an exclusive agreement, making enforcement of commission claims impractical.

c. Open listings are only used in commercial transactions and the MLS is limited to residential properties.

d. MLS rules require all listings to carry a standard commission rate, which open listings do not specify.

5. Three disclosures are required when entering into any agency relationship. Which of the following is one of those three required disclosures?

a. Whether the broker has ever been the subject of a TREC complaint.

b. Whether the broker belongs to the National Association of REALTORS.

c. The broker's policy on cooperating with other firms and how that could affect the property's market exposure.

d. The broker's anticipated marketing timeline for the property.

6. A buyer under an exclusive right to buy agreement encounters a FSBO property while driving through a neighborhood. Before engaging with the seller, the buyer should:

a. Contact his or her agent first so the agent can make appropriate arrangements and inform the seller that they have a buyer's representative.

b. Contact the seller directly and submit an offer without involving their agent, since FSBO sellers negotiate independently.

c. Contact the host of the nearest open house to obtain information about the FSBO property.

d. Terminate the representation agreement before engaging with the seller to avoid a commission obligation.

7. A seller becomes frustrated with the lack of showings and calls the listing salesperson to cancel the listing. The salesperson agrees to cancel it on the spot. Which of the following best describes the problem with this scenario?

a. A salesperson can cancel a listing only with TREC approval, which takes at least ten business days.

b. A listing can only be cancelled if the seller submits a written request to the MLS directly.

c. The salesperson has the authority to cancel the listing but must provide 30 days written notice to the seller before the cancellation is effective.

d. All client relationships belong to the broker, not to the salesperson. A request to end the agency relationship must be directed to and handled by the broker.

8. A broker has a valid listing agreement in place. The seller refuses to cooperate with showings and has been verbally abusive toward the broker and office staff on multiple occasions despite being asked to stop. The broker should:

a. File a complaint with TREC against the seller and allow the listing to expire naturally.

b. Renounce the agency with proper notice and good cause, documenting the abusive conduct as the basis for withdrawal.

c. Do nothing and continue representing the seller, because the broker cannot withdraw from a listing agreement once signed.

d. Refer the listing to another brokerage without notifying the seller.

9. A property is listed with a broker. Before closing, the seller files for bankruptcy. What effect does this have on the listing?

a. The listing continues unchanged because the seller retains possession of the property during bankruptcy proceedings.

b. The listing converts automatically to an open listing until the bankruptcy court rules on the property's disposition.

c. The agency ends because a court takes legal control of the property, and the seller no longer has authority to sell.

d. The listing is suspended for 90 days, after which the broker may relist the property if the bankruptcy has not been resolved.

10. A sponsored salesperson decides to leave the current brokerage and join a different firm. What happens to the salesperson's clients?

a. The clients belong to the broker, not the salesperson. Therefore, they remain with the original brokerage when the salesperson transfers.

b. The clients may choose to follow the salesperson to the new brokerage or stay with the original firm.

c. The clients' agency agreements are automatically terminated when the salesperson leaves.

d. The clients are released from their agreements and are free to engage any broker they choose.

11. A listing agreement expires prior to closing. The listing agent runs subsequently meets the seller at a community event. The seller mentions that they accepted a low offer due to a divorce. The agent later discloses this experience to a colleague. Was this a proper disclosure, and why or why not?

a. The agent acted improperly since he was no longer employed by the seller at the time of the conversation and had no justification for sharing real estate information.

b. The agent needed to obtain TREC permission before sharing any information about a former client.

c. The information was obtained at a social event rather than in a professional context, so it should have been treated as private regardless of the agency relationship.

d. It was improper, since confidentiality is the one fiduciary duty that survives termination of agency indefinitely, and disclosing a former client's personal circumstances without authorization is a permanent obligation.

12. A broker provides down payment assistance to a customer-buyer, without informing the seller, his client, Is this a violation of the various fiduciary duties associated with the agency relationship?

a. Brokers may not provide any financial assistance to buyers under Texas law.

b. Fiduciary duties to the seller require disclosure of any conduct that could affect the seller's interests, including financial assistance given to the opposing party.

c. Buyers are entitled to financial assistance from brokers as part of the fair housing protections under federal law.

d. The seller's agent must approve all financing terms before a buyer can submit an offer.

13. A court ruled that the rejection of an offer did not terminate the agency relationship. This is significant because it demonstrates that:

a. A broker is entitled to a commission even if the seller rejects every offer submitted.

b. The seller must notify TREC within ten days after rejecting an offer if they wish to terminate the listing.

c. The agency continues and fiduciary duties remain in force after an offer is rejected, unless a specific decision is made by one or both parties to end the relationship.

d. After an offer is rejected, the buyer automatically becomes a customer rather than a client of the same brokerage.

14. A property was listed and placed under contract. During the marketing period, the seller died and a successor attorney took over the disposition of the estate. The successor found a buyer, and the closing still proceeded to a successful conclusion. However, in this case, the broker received no commission. This outcome occurred because:

a. Death of the client terminates the agency relationship. The successor had no legal obligation to honor the original listing agreement and chose not to.

b. The death of the executor voided the underlying purchase contract, and the broker was not entitled to a commission without a valid contract.

c. The information was obtained at a social event rather than in a professional context, so it should have been treated as private regardless of the agency relationship.

d. The broker failed to file a commission claim with the title company before the closing took place.

CHAPTER 8

CLARIFYING AGENCY RELATIONSHIPS

Chapter Objectives

After completing this chapter, you should be able to:

1. Describe the steps a licensee should take to clarify agency relationships and eliminate confusion about who represents whom in a transaction.
2. Explain the two separate disclosure requirements a licensee must satisfy under Texas law and describe when each must be delivered.
3. Identify the questions a licensee should ask from both the listing side and the cooperating side to ensure proper agency determination.
4. Explain the purpose and components of a written brokerage agency policy, and describe the steps a broker should follow when developing one.
5. Apply agency disclosure rules to common ambiguous situations, including open houses, in-office tours, and intermediary transitions.

Contents

Clarifying Agency Relationships

Texas law requires agency disclosure in all commercial and residential real estate transactions involving sales or leases. Despite this longstanding requirement, agency misunderstandings remain one of the most common sources of complaints and disputes in the industry. In most transactions, at least one person operates under a mistaken assumption about who represents whom. The licensee bears the responsibility for eliminating that confusion.

Effective agency management requires more than making a disclosure at the right moment. It requires a disciplined professional approach that begins before the first conversation and carries through to the closing. A licensee who takes this seriously will develop strategies that reduce complaints and protect both the client and the brokerage.

The core practices that prevent most agency-related problems are:

- Deciding in each transaction which party the licensee will represent.
- Assessing whether intermediary brokerage is a possibility.
- Disclosing the representation decision to the buyer or seller after the agreement is signed.
- Documenting that disclosure in writing with acknowledgment from the parties.
- Acting consistently throughout the transaction in a manner that matches the disclosed representation.

Inadequate communication is where the greatest risk lives. Every licensee must understand the terms of the signed agency agreement and communicate those terms clearly to the client so that no gap in understanding exists.

Choosing an Agency Relationship

Each transaction presents its own set of parties and circumstances. Before any representation begins, the licensee must decide which party to represent, what services to provide, and what role to play in relation to everyone else involved. Agency is a consensual relationship. A licensee may determine who they are willing to represent, but that determination must be formalized through the other party's written consent before any representation begins.

Defining the role clearly before the work begins prevents the most common source of agency problems: a party who assumes representation existed when the agent never agreed to it. The following working relationships represent the practical range of options available to a licensee in Texas:

- Agent for the seller, but not the buyer.
- Agent for the buyer, but not the seller.
- Intermediary broker representing both buyer and seller with written consent from each.
- Agent exclusively for sellers.

- Agent exclusively for buyers.
- Agent for neither party, functioning as a facilitator with no fiduciary duties.

A licensee may also apply different approaches to different categories of transactions. Commercial transactions may call for a different default relationship than residential ones. First-time buyers may require more structured disclosure conversations than experienced investors. The broker's office policy will establish the framework, and the individual licensee must apply that framework thoughtfully to each situation.

Questions That Guide Proper Disclosure

Before making any representation decisions, a licensee should ask the right questions. The specific questions differ depending on which side of the transaction the licensee is on.

From the Listing Broker's Perspective

- Is the licensee working with a buyer who is only a customer, or has the buyer formed a representation relationship with someone?
- If another licensee presents an offer, is that licensee a non-agent of the seller or a buyer's agent?
- Is the listing salesperson the only licensee from the firm involved, or is there also a buyer's agent in the same office?
- Is this an in-house sale involving another licensee's listing within the same brokerage?
- Is this a sale originating from a branch office of the firm?
- Does the listing agent have any current or prior relationship with the buyer, such as having previously listed the buyer's home, agreed to represent the buyer in a future purchase, or managed one of the buyer's rental properties?

For All Licensees Identifying Their Role

- Who is the customer in this transaction, and what level of service is appropriate?
- Who is the client, and what fiduciary duties are owed?
- If this is an intermediary situation, what services will and will not be performed?

For a Cooperating Licensee from Another Firm

- Does a prior or current business relationship exist with the buyer that could create a contingency or conflict?
- Is this a multiple listing service transaction subject to current MLS compensation rules?

Asking these questions systematically at the start of every transaction is one of the most effective habits a licensee can develop. Most agency disputes arise not from bad intentions but from assumptions that were never tested.

Disclosure Requirements in Agency Relationships

Every Texas licensee is required to discuss proposed agency relationships with buyers, sellers, landlords, and tenants before those parties make decisions about the transaction. This is not simply an ethical expectation. It is a statutory requirement under TRELA. The purpose is to ensure that every person in a transaction can make genuinely informed choices about their representation.

Agency is a consensual relationship. It requires that the principal delegate authority to the agent and that the agent accept that delegation. Without mutual, informed agreement, no valid agency exists. A person who was never told the agent does not represent them is in no position to protect their own interests during negotiations.

TRELA sets out specific disclosure rules:

1. A broker who represents a party in a real estate transaction, or who holds an exclusive listing agreement on a property, is that party's agent.
2. A licensee who represents a party in a proposed transaction must disclose that representation, either orally or in writing, at the time of first contact with another party to the transaction or with another licensee who represents a different party to the transaction.

Disclosure must occur before any party can reasonably claim that an agency relationship has already been established. If disclosure is delayed, the other party may have already formed expectations of representation, acted on those expectations, and shared confidential information in reliance on them. Undoing that harm after the fact is difficult and sometimes impossible.

The Information About Brokerage Services Form

In addition to the agency disclosure described above, TREC requires that licensees deliver a written information statement to prospective buyers, sellers, tenants, and landlords. This statement explains the types of brokerage relationships available in Texas and the roles a broker may take in a transaction. It must be delivered at the first meeting during which substantive information about a specific property is discussed.

TREC has approved a standard form for this purpose: the Information About Brokerage Services form (TREC IABS 1-2). Most brokers require their licensees to use this form consistently. It satisfies the statutory written statement requirement and serves as a starting point for meaningful conversation about the representation options available to the client.

> ***Important distinction:*** *The Information About Brokerage Services form is not the agency disclosure. These are two separate requirements under Texas law. The IABS 1-2 form describes the types of representation available in general terms. The agency disclosure identifies whom the licensee actually represents in the current transaction. Both must be provided. Confusing one for the other leaves the licensee out of compliance with one of the two requirements.*

Exceptions to the written information statement requirement apply in the following circumstances:

- The proposed transaction involves a residential lease and no sale is being contemplated.
- The licensee is meeting with a party who is already represented by another licensee.
- No substantive discussion about a specific property has taken place.
- The contact occurs at an open house.
- The meeting takes place after the parties have already entered into a contract.

Timing of Disclosure

Agency disclosure must occur early in the first substantive meeting about real property. The earlier it happens, the better. Waiting until a relationship has already formed in the client's mind before making the required disclosures creates significant risk.

When attempting to secure a listing, the agent and seller should discuss the following at their first substantive meeting:

- Whether the listing broker will offer compensation to non-agents, to buyer's agents, or to both.
- Who will have access to the listing information.
- Whether the property will be entered into the MLS.
- Whether cooperating licensees will be authorized to assist in finding a buyer.
- Whether cooperating licensees, if involved, will function as non-agents or as buyer's agents.

Timing is particularly challenging with first-time buyers who walk into an office after seeing an advertisement or who meet an agent at an open house. These buyers have often already formed an assumption about the agent's role before any formal disclosure is made. Texas law addresses this directly: a licensee who represents a party must disclose that representation at the time of first contact with another party or with another licensee in the transaction. There is no grace period.

TREC may suspend or revoke a license if a licensee fails to make clear to all parties which party they represent, or if a licensee accepts compensation from more than one party without the full knowledge and consent of all parties. Timely, accurate disclosure is the professional and legal standard, not an optional best practice.

Complying with Both Disclosure Requirements

Both the written information statement and the agency disclosure must be provided. They serve different purposes and neither satisfies the requirement for the other.

A licensee who does not represent any party in a transaction must also disclose that fact. Without that disclosure, a party may reasonably assume they are being represented, or assume that the agent represents the other side. Either assumption could disadvantage the unrepresented party.

A licensee must also be alert to the risk created when a customer begins sharing confidential financial information with an agent who represents the opposing party. The agent who represents the seller is legally required to pass strategically valuable information about the buyer to the seller. If the buyer does not understand this, they may unwittingly provide the seller with a negotiating advantage.

If it is not yet clear at an initial meeting whether a buyer should be treated as a client or a customer, the meeting may still be productive. General topics such as the market, the agent's background, commission structures, and target neighborhoods can be covered without the full client relationship in place. But the required disclosures must still be made before any substantive discussion of specific properties begins. If the relationship will move to formal representation, a written agreement that defines the scope of the relationship and the agent's duties must be put in place before substantive representation work begins.

Brokerage Agency Office Policy

The most effective protection a brokerage has against agency disputes and liability is a thorough, well-written office policy on agency relationships. A written policy that is actively trained, consistently applied, and clearly understood by all licensees in the office reduces the probability of an unauthorized, undisclosed, or illegal agency situation arising.

An agency policy may address all or some of the following topics:

- Definition and explanation of the duties of a buyer's representative.
- Definition and explanation of the duties of a seller's representative.
- Definition and explanation of the duties of an intermediary.
- Listing fees and commission structures.
- Procedures for the first meeting with buyers.
- Requirements for buyer representation presentations.
- Policy on appointed associates in intermediary transactions.
- Policy governing in-house intermediary transactions.
- Policy on working with seller-clients who are also purchasing a subsequent property.
- Policy on representing competing buyers as customers or clients.

- Policy on intermediary authorization in buyer representation agreements.
- Policy on FSBO transactions involving a customer or client.
- Policy on licensees selling their own property or property owned by another agent in the firm.
- Policy on licensees purchasing a company listing or a listing held by another firm.
- Statement on compensation and cooperation with other brokers.
- Procedures for completing and routing required paperwork.
- Policy on disclosing prior working relationships and situations involving close friends or family members.

Developing a Company Policy

Every brokerage should develop its own written agency policy. The process works best when it follows a deliberate, structured approach rather than being assembled informally or borrowed from another market without modification.

A practical development process includes five steps:

1. **Review the available agency options.** These include exclusive seller agency, exclusive buyer agency, intermediary brokerage for in-company transactions, and single agency with no intermediary possibility.
2. **Evaluate the advantages and disadvantages of each option.** Consider which structures create conflicts of interest, which generate the most commission risk, and which best serve the brokerage's client base.
3. **Assess the office's specific situation.** Consider the size and experience level of the staff, the type of property specialization, local market dynamics, and the brokerage's financial model. An office that earns most of its income from selling other brokers' listings has very different needs than a listing-heavy firm.
4. **Draft the written policy.** Begin with a working draft and then circulate it to key staff members, a real estate attorney, and a business advisor. Refine the document based on their input before finalizing.
5. **Train and monitor.** Launch training sessions so all licensees understand the policy and can apply it consistently. Monitor effectiveness over time and update the policy when the law, the market, or the office's circumstances change.

A well-designed and well-trained agency policy gives licensees confidence in their daily practice. Rather than treating agency disclosures as an awkward legal formality, agents who understand the policy can weave agency discussions naturally into their professional presentations.

Components of a Policy and Procedures Manual

The written policy document should be organized into four major sections:

Basic Agency Philosophy

- Statement of commitment to compliance with Texas disclosure laws.
- The firm's specific disclosure guidelines.
- A summary of the firm's overall agency policy.

Handling Common Situations

- Open houses.
- Purchasing property listed in-house.
- Non-agency with cooperating firms.
- In-house sales that do not trigger intermediary status.
- Intermediary representation with licensee appointments.
- Intermediary representation without licensee appointments.
- Requirements for buyer representation presentations.
- Requirements for listing presentations.

Dealing with Outside Companies

- How to interact professionally with buyer's agents from other firms.
- Procedures for fee sharing, property showings, and offer presentation with cooperating brokers.

Forms, Procedures, and Common Questions

- Which forms to use in each situation and how to route them internally.
- Why specific forms are used and what they accomplish.
- Instructions for completing each form correctly.
- The benefits to both the brokerage and the licensee of proper form usage.
- A detailed question-and-answer section covering as many agency scenarios as the brokerage can anticipate. This section should be as comprehensive as possible and updated regularly. New licensees should receive focused training on this section because they will return to it repeatedly.

Building a Comprehensive Policy

A broker who develops a proactive agency disclosure policy takes control of the agency relationships in the office and reduces the risk of unintended or illegal representation situations. Timely, accurate disclosure is the single most important element of a sound agency program.

The policy must comply fully with Texas law. Any policy that is borrowed from another state or adapted from a national template must be carefully reviewed and modified to match Texas rules and regulations before it is used.

Policies are designed to protect the brokerage and its licensees. They are also designed to serve clients and customers. A good policy does both simultaneously by establishing consistent, ethical practices that produce better outcomes for everyone involved.

Documentation procedures deserve specific attention in the policy. For example, the policy should specify that every licensee must document in the client or transaction file that the written information statement was delivered and discussed. The preferred practice is to request the buyer's or seller's signature on the acknowledgment portion of the form, provide the original to the client, and retain copies in both the company file and the individual customer file. When a party declines to sign a form, the licensee must note that refusal in writing and retain documentation of the declined signature.

Sample Policy Section: Open Houses

An open house is one of the most complex agency situations a licensee encounters. The following is an example of how a brokerage policy might address this specific scenario:

> ***Sample Open House Policy*** *When holding a property open, the licensee's duty is to the seller. The agent must use their best efforts to promote the property and assist in finding a buyer. This means that while a visitor has not expressed disinterest in the open house property, the licensee should not suggest competing properties or offer to represent that visitor as a buyer's agent. Once a visitor indicates genuine interest in the property, the licensee should treat them as a customer and make the following disclosures immediately: 1. Provide written confirmation that you represent the seller and answer any questions the visitor has about what that means. 2. Confirm that the visitor is interested in the specific property before proceeding with any substantive discussion. 3. Before discussing the visitor's financial qualifications or offering any specific advice, deliver the company information about brokerage services, including the IABS 1-2 form and any other required materials. If the visitor states that they are not interested in the open house property, the agency discussion may shift to whether you will offer to assist them as a buyer's agent.*

This example illustrates the level of detail a good policy should provide. The same type of scenario-specific guidance should be written for every common situation the brokerage encounters. The more specific the policy, the less room there is for a licensee to misread a situation or improvise in a way that creates liability.

Handling Ambiguous Situations

Not every situation presents a clear agency picture at first. Licensees frequently find themselves in settings where the representation question has not yet been resolved.

A common example is the internal office tour of a new listing. Licensees from the same office often walk through a new company listing to familiarize themselves with the property. At that moment, the touring licensee may not know whether they will eventually show the property to one of their own clients. This ambiguity does not eliminate the disclosure obligation. If the touring licensee meets the seller in person during the tour, they must disclose their agency status. If they meet only with the listing agent, they should at minimum discuss their current role and whether they have clients who might be interested in the property.

The general principle is straightforward: clarify agency status as early as possible in every interaction. When a relationship has not yet been defined, say so. Then define it as quickly as the situation allows. Ambiguity left unaddressed tends to harden into a misunderstanding that becomes difficult to correct later.

Intermediary transitions also require careful handling. Before entering into any intermediary relationship, the broker must obtain written consent from both parties. Once consent is in place, no additional notification is required unless the broker makes agent appointments. When appointments are made, both clients must be informed in writing, with the names of the appointed agents and the parties each represents identified clearly.

Every ambiguous situation is, at its core, an argument for a clearer and more detailed company policy. The more scenarios the policy anticipates, the fewer situations a licensee will face without guidance.

Practical Guidance for Brokers

The following practices have proven effective for brokers working to reduce agency-related miscommunication, misunderstanding, and legal exposure:

1. Prepare licensees to articulate clearly the customer-level services that can be provided to the opposing party while the licensee remains the exclusive agent of their client. Knowing what they can and cannot do for a non-client reduces improvisation in the field.
2. Use the written information statement as a professional tool, not just a legal requirement. Delivering the IABS 1-2 form thoughtfully creates a natural opening for a meaningful conversation about the relationship the licensee is offering.
3. Develop a personalized brokerage disclosure brochure that includes the required written statement and describes the range of professional relationships the firm offers. A branded, professional brochure signals competence and sets clear expectations before any representation decision is made.

4. Use plain, direct language in all disclosure communications. Vague or overly technical language diminishes the value of a disclosure by confusing the person receiving it. The goal is genuine understanding, not technical compliance.
5. Ask every prospective buyer or seller to sign an acknowledgment confirming receipt of the company disclosure form at the time of first contact. Keep a copy in the file.
6. Obtain a separate signed acknowledgment of receipt for the written information statement required by TRELA. If the relationship moves toward formal representation, discuss the client or customer status explicitly and put the agreed relationship in writing before substantive representation work begins.
7. Once agency roles are established, ensure that all participants in the transaction are informed. Full disclosure to all parties is not optional once the representation structure is set.
8. Supervise actively. Brokers are responsible for the conduct of the licensees they sponsor. Throughout each transaction, the broker and the licensees must document every significant step and decision. A well-documented file is the best protection against a complaint or claim after closing.

Snapshot Review – Chapter 8

The Two Separate Disclosure Requirements

Agency Disclosure: A licensee must disclose, orally or in writing, whom they represent at the time of first contact with another party to the transaction or another licensee representing a different party. A licensee who represents no one must also disclose that fact.

Written Information Statement (TREC IABS 1-2): The Information About Brokerage Services form must be delivered to prospective buyers, sellers, tenants, and landlords at the first meeting where substantive discussion about a specific property occurs. This form is not the agency disclosure. Both requirements must be satisfied separately.

Exceptions to the Written Information Statement

1. The transaction involves a residential lease with no sale being contemplated.
2. The licensee is meeting with a party already represented by another licensee.
3. No substantive discussion of a specific property has taken place.
4. The contact occurs at an open house.
5. The meeting takes place after a contract has already been executed.

Disclosure Timing

1. Disclosure must occur at first contact with another party or another party's licensee. There is no grace period.
2. Disclosure that is delayed allows the other party to form expectations, take actions, and share confidences in reliance on an assumed agency that was never formally created. Correcting that after the fact is difficult.
3. Failure to disclose, or accepting compensation from more than one party without full disclosure, may result in license suspension or revocation by TREC.

Developing and Maintaining an Agency Policy

1. Every brokerage must have a written agency policy. A verbal understanding is not sufficient.
2. The policy development process: (1) review agency options, (2) evaluate advantages and disadvantages, (3) assess the firm's specific situation, (4) draft with input from staff and legal counsel, (5) train and monitor.
3. The policy must comply with Texas law. Policies adapted from other states or generic national sources must be modified to conform to TRELA and TREC rules before use.
4. Policies protect the brokerage and licensees. They also protect clients and customers. A good policy serves both purposes simultaneously.

Key Policy Areas

1. Basic agency philosophy and disclosure guidelines.
2. Procedures for common situations: open houses, in-house sales, non-agency, intermediary with and without appointments, buyer and listing presentations.
3. Procedures for working with cooperating firms: buyer's agent interactions, fee sharing, and offer presentation.
4. Forms guidance: which form to use, when to use it, how to complete it, and how to route it internally.
5. A comprehensive question-and-answer section covering every agency scenario the brokerage can anticipate.

Ambiguous Situations

1. Ambiguity in representation status does not suspend the disclosure obligation. If the licensee's status is undecided, that fact must be stated explicitly.
2. Agency status should be clarified as quickly as possible in every interaction. Undefined relationships left unaddressed become misunderstandings.
3. When a broker makes intermediary appointments, both clients must be notified in writing, identifying the name of each appointed agent and the party they represent.

CHAPTER 8 QUIZ — CLARIFYING AGENCY RELATIONSHIPS

1. Under Texas law, when must a licensee who represents one party in a transaction disclose that representation to another party or to another licensee representing a different party?

a. At any point before the purchase contract is signed, as long as disclosure occurs before the transaction closes.

b. At the first meeting in which the licensee is asked directly whether they represent one of the parties.

c. Only when the other party requests a formal written statement of the licensee's role in the transaction.

d. At the time of first contact with the other party or the other party's licensee. There is no grace period.

2. The TREC Information About Brokerage Services form IABS 1-2 and the agency disclosure are often confused. Which of the following correctly distinguishes the two?

a. The IABS 1-2 form describes the types of brokerage representation available in Texas in general terms. The agency disclosure identifies whom the licensee actually represents in the current transaction. Both must be provided separately.

b. The IABS 1-2 form is the agency disclosure. Once it is delivered, both statutory requirements are satisfied.

c. The agency disclosure is required only in commercial transactions, while the IABS 1-2 form is required only in residential sales.

d. The IABS 1-2 form replaces the verbal agency disclosure in transactions where the buyer and seller are already known to each other.

3. At which type of meeting is the licensee exempt from the requirement to deliver the written Information About Brokerage Services form?

a. A first meeting with a first-time buyer who has no prior experience with real estate agents.

b. A meeting at an open house, a meeting with a party already represented by another licensee, or a meeting after a contract has already been executed.

c. Any meeting that takes place at the listing office rather than at the property.

d. A meeting with a buyer who has already toured properties with a different agent in the same firm.

4. A licensee who holds an open house for a seller-client is approached by a visitor who expresses genuine interest in the property. The licensee's primary obligation in this situation is to:

a. Immediately offer to represent the visitor as a buyer's agent since the visitor is unrepresented.

b. Suggest that the visitor hire their own agent before discussing the property in any detail.

c. Disclose to the visitor that the licensee represents the seller, treat the visitor as a customer, and provide the required brokerage services information before discussing the visitor's financial qualifications or offering specific advice.

d. Postpone the agency disclosure until the visitor confirms they want to make an offer.

5. A buyer-customer shares detailed financial information with a listing agent, assuming the agent will keep it confidential. The listing agent's legal obligation is to:

   a. Keep the information confidential as a courtesy, even though no fiduciary duty to the buyer exists.

   b. Immediately refer the buyer to a buyer's agent to avoid any conflict of interest.

   c. Disclose the information to both the seller and to TREC as required by the dual disclosure rule.

   d. Pass the strategically valuable information to the seller-client because the listing agent represents the seller, not the buyer.

6. A licensee walks through a new company listing during an internal office tour. The listing agent is present, but the sellers are also home. Which of the following best describes the touring licensee's obligation?

   a. The touring licensee must disclose his agency status to the sellers when meeting them in person and should discuss hir or her role with the listing agent.

   b. No disclosure obligation exists because the seller is not a party to any transaction with the touring licensee at that point.

   c. The touring licensee must immediately sign a buyer representation agreement to clarify their status before entering the home.

   d. Disclosure is deferred until the touring licensee decides whether they have a client interested in the property.

7. TREC may suspend or revoke a license for which of the following agency-related violations?

   a. Delivering the IABS 1-2 form to a party who is already represented by another licensee.

   b. Failing to make clear to all parties which party the licensee represents, or accepting compensation from more than one party without the full knowledge and consent of all parties.

   c. Using an older version of the IABS 1-2 form that has since been updated by TREC.

   d. Providing a verbal agency disclosure rather than a written one when a written form was available.

8. A broker is developing the brokerage's written agency policy. Which of the following correctly describes the recommended five-step development process?

   a. Copy an existing policy from a successful competing firm, adapt the language for the local market, and distribute it to agents at the next office meeting.

   b. Submit a draft policy to TREC for approval, incorporate TREC's revisions, and publish the final version on the office website.

   c. Ask each licensee in the office to draft a section of the policy based on their personal experience, then compile the sections into a single document.

   d. Review agency options, evaluate advantages and disadvantages, assess the office's specific situation, draft with input from staff and legal counsel, then train and monitor.

9. When a broker makes intermediary agent appointments in a transaction where both the buyer and seller are clients of the same firm, which of the following is required?

a. The broker must notify TREC of the appointment decision within five business days.

b. Both clients must be notified in writing, with the name of each appointed agent and the party they represent identified clearly.

c. The appointed agents must each sign a conflict of interest waiver before proceeding with negotiations.

d. Appointments only take effect after the purchase contract is signed by both parties.

10. A broker's policy requires agents to obtain a separate signed acknowledgment from every prospective client confirming receipt of the written Information About Brokerage Services form. If a party declines to sign the acknowledgment, the agent should:

a. Refuse to continue the representation until the acknowledgment is signed, as an unsigned form has no legal effect.

b. Proceed without documentation since the party's verbal acknowledgment is legally equivalent to a signature.

c. Note the party's refusal in writing and retain that documentation in the file as proof the form was delivered and the party chose not to sign.

d. Contact TREC immediately to report the declination and request guidance on how to proceed.

CHAPTER 9

EMPLOYMENT ISSUES

Chapter Objectives

After completing this chapter, you should be able to:

1. Describe the broker-principal relationship and identify the three types of agreements through which it is created.
2. Explain the legal distinction between an employee and an independent contractor under IRS common law rules and the Section 3508 safe harbor test.
3. Identify the key components of an independent contractor agreement and explain filing and recordkeeping responsibilities.
4. Describe the factors a new licensee should evaluate when choosing a broker, conducting an interview, and negotiating the terms of the relationship.
5. Explain the practical benefits and responsibilities of working as an independent contractor in real estate.
6. Describe the working relationship between brokers and agents, including commission split structures and office models.
7. Explain the differences between licensed and unlicensed assistants and identify which activities each may and may not perform.
8. Describe why a licensee might choose to work as an assistant and how to pursue that role effectively.
9. Calculate commission splits under various brokerage scenarios, including transactions where the buyer is responsible for their own agent's compensation.
10. Explain when a broker may be entitled to a commission on incomplete transactions or after a listing has expired.

Contents

The Broker-Principal Relationship

Every time a licensee creates an agency relationship with a buyer or seller, the broker and office staff are, in effect, hired to serve that client. The agreement between the broker and the client is sometimes referred to as an employment contract, with the broker functioning as the agent and the client functioning as the principal. This terminology describes a service relationship, not an employee-employer relationship in the conventional sense.

The broker is not directed by the client on how to perform their work. A seller does not tell the broker how to market the property. The methods, tools, and timing are left entirely to the broker's professional judgment. The client does not provide benefits, insurance, or retirement contributions. The relationship is a temporary professional engagement with a defined purpose: find a qualified buyer for the seller, or find and negotiate the purchase of a property for the buyer.

Most brokers view the relationship with their clients not as employment but as a goal-oriented professional engagement. Both parties have agreed on an objective. When that objective is accomplished, or the term of the agreement expires, the arrangement ends.

Types of Broker-Principal Agreements

A broker enters into a principal agreement in one of three ways:

Listing and Landlord Agreements

A listing agreement establishes the broker as the agent for a seller. It gives the broker the right to market the property at a specified price for a defined period. If the broker produces a buyer, the commission is typically paid at closing from the sale proceeds. A landlord agreement is structurally similar but involves finding a tenant rather than a buyer.

Buyer and Tenant Representation Agreements

A buyer representation agreement creates an agency relationship in which the broker assists the buyer in finding and negotiating the purchase of a property. Compensation to the buyer's agent may come from a portion of the seller's listing commission or directly from the buyer. A tenant representation agreement follows the same structure but involves locating a rental property rather than a purchase.

Property Management Agreements

A property management agreement occurs when an owner hires a broker to manage an existing property. These agreements typically extend over a longer period than listing or buyer agreements and involve ongoing responsibilities for the operation of the property.

Terms and Compensation

Every broker-principal agreement addresses two fundamental subjects: the terms of the professional engagement and the compensation structure. The broker is responsible for paying any expenses associated with performing the services, and for any income taxes owed on the compensation received.

Brokerage fees are generally paid at closing from the transaction proceeds. However, most courts have held that a broker earns the right to a commission at the moment they produce a ready, willing, and able buyer under the terms of the listing agreement. This means that a seller who decides not to proceed with a sale after the broker has procured a qualified buyer may still owe the broker a commission.

While Texas law does not prohibit creating a broker-client relationship verbally, a verbal agreement provides almost no legal protection for the broker. If a client refuses to pay a commission under a verbal agreement, the broker has very limited recourse under Texas law. All agreements should be in writing and signed by all parties.

Suing for a Commission

When a client refuses to pay a commission as agreed, TRELA Section 1101.806 establishes four requirements that must all be satisfied before a court will hear the broker's claim. If any one of the four is absent, the case is unlikely to proceed. Brokers who pursue commission disputes typically retain an attorney, who will evaluate these four requirements at the outset:

1. A written agreement must exist between the broker and the client. A listing agreement or representation agreement satisfies this requirement.
2. The written agreement must have been signed by the party obligated to pay the commission. Ideally, all owners of record sign the agreement.
3. The broker must be able to show that their license was active at the time of the transaction. This is obtained by requesting a license activity statement from TREC.
4. The buyer must have been advised at the time of making an offer that they should obtain a title search and/or title insurance policy.

In practice, the fourth requirement is straightforward because virtually every lender requires a title search and title insurance as a condition of financing. Documenting that the buyer was informed of this is therefore a routine part of most transactions.

The Broker-Salesperson Relationship

Most brokerages operate with a team of sponsored salespersons rather than the broker working alone. A salesperson is licensed to perform real estate activities on behalf of their sponsoring broker. The broker is ultimately responsible for everything the salesperson does in the name of the brokerage.

A salesperson may only engage in activities assigned by the broker and may only receive compensation from the employing broker. Because the salesperson acts as an agent of the broker, they have no authority to form contracts or accept payment from any other party, whether that is another broker, the buyer, the seller, or a referral service.

A broker may bring a salesperson into the brokerage in one of two ways: as an employee or as an independent contractor. The critical difference between the two is the degree of control the broker may exercise, as defined by income tax law.

IRS Common Law Rules

When determining whether a worker is an employee or an independent contractor, the IRS requires an evaluation of all facts relevant to the degree of control and independence in the relationship. The IRS groups these facts into three categories:

Behavioral Control: Does the company control or have the right to control what the worker does and how they do it? This includes instruction, training, and direction over the method of performing the work.

Financial Control: Does the company control the business aspects of the worker's role? This includes how the worker is paid, whether expenses are reimbursed, and who provides the tools and equipment necessary to perform the work.

Type of Relationship: Are there written contracts or employee-style benefits such as health insurance, pension contributions, or paid time off? Is the relationship ongoing, and is the work a core function of the business?

No single factor is determinative, and no specific number of factors is required to establish either status. The full picture of the working relationship must be considered. A factor that is meaningful in one context may be irrelevant in another.

Employee Status

When a salesperson is classified as an employee, the broker has broad authority to direct the work. The broker may set working hours, require office duty shifts, mandate attendance at meetings, and establish a dress code. The broker may also require the employee to follow a specific work process or to work from a defined location.

Employees typically have their business expenses covered by the broker and are provided with the tools needed to work, which may include a furnished office space, computer access, and administrative support. Some brokers extend health insurance or profit-sharing benefits to employee salespersons.

When paying an employee, the broker must withhold the following from wages:

- Federal income tax
- State income tax
- Social Security tax
- Medicare tax

The broker is also responsible for paying federal and state unemployment taxes, workers' compensation, and disability insurance, and must file quarterly and annual payroll tax reports with the applicable government agencies.

> ***Note:*** *A broker may carry errors and omissions (E&O) insurance on all sponsored licensees, regardless of whether they are employees or independent contractors. The broker may pay the premium or require licensees to contribute to it. This coverage protects the brokerage and the licensees from claims arising out of professional errors or omissions in the performance of real estate services.*

Independent Contractor Status

Independent contractor status is fundamentally different. The broker can direct what the salesperson does, meaning the objectives and goals, but cannot control how they accomplish those objectives. The broker cannot dictate working hours, require attendance at specific office shifts, or mandate participation in meetings.

Independent contractor salespersons are paid by production rather than salary. They pay their own business expenses and supply their own tools. The broker does not withhold income taxes, Social Security, or Medicare from commissions paid to an independent contractor. If the licensee earns more than $2,000 in a calendar year, the broker must file IRS Form 1099-NEC reporting the total earnings paid to that licensee.

A salesperson working as an independent contractor is responsible for paying their own federal and state income taxes, self-employment taxes, Social Security, and Medicare contributions. They cannot receive any benefit from the broker that resembles employee treatment, such as health insurance, paid sick days, or a retirement plan, without risking reclassification of the relationship.

Most real estate brokerages structure their salesperson relationships as independent contractor arrangements. This model eliminates the payroll tax obligations, benefits administration, and government reporting requirements associated with employee status.

IRS Code Section 3508

IRS Code Section 3508 allows licensed real estate agents to be classified as independent contractors for federal tax purposes. To qualify, the arrangement must meet three conditions, collectively called the safe harbor test:

1. The licensee must hold a valid real estate license.
2. The licensee's compensation must be based on production, meaning sales volume or services rendered, and not on hours worked.
3. A written independent contractor agreement must exist between the broker and the licensee, and that agreement must explicitly state that the licensee will not be treated as an employee for federal income tax purposes.

If all three conditions are met, the IRS recognizes the relationship as independent contractor status, and the broker is not responsible for payroll tax withholding or employer-side tax obligations.

Consequences of Misclassification

If an IRS audit determines that a salesperson was incorrectly classified as an independent contractor when they should have been treated as an employee, the consequences for the broker are serious. The broker becomes liable for all back taxes that should have been withheld, including federal and state income tax, Social Security, and Medicare contributions. The broker also becomes responsible for state and federal unemployment insurance premiums, workers' compensation, and disability insurance, and may face substantial tax penalties on top of the unpaid amounts.

This creates a practical tension for brokers: maintaining true independent contractor status requires genuinely relinquishing day-to-day control over the licensee's work methods. Brokers who impose excessive behavioral controls risk having the classification challenged.

The Independent Contractor Agreement

When a broker sponsors a new licensee, the broker submits a sponsorship form to TREC with the required fee. Simultaneously, the broker and licensee should execute a written independent contractor agreement. This document defines the working relationship, sets expectations for both parties, and establishes the legal framework for the engagement.

A well-drafted independent contractor agreement covers the following areas:

Parties: Identifies the broker and the licensee by name.

Term: Specifies the duration of the agreement.

Exclusive Association: States that the licensee will perform all real estate activities exclusively through the sponsoring broker for the duration of the agreement.

Legal and Ethical Compliance: Both parties agree to comply with all applicable laws and professional standards throughout the relationship.

License Maintenance: Both parties commit to maintaining their respective licenses in active and current status.

Independent Contractor Designation: Explicitly confirms that the licensee is not an employee of the broker. This provision is legally required to satisfy the Section 3508 safe harbor test.

Associate's Authority: Defines the scope of authority the licensee has to enter into agency agreements on behalf of the broker, and the requirements for keeping the broker informed of those agreements.

Files and Confidentiality: The licensee is responsible for maintaining complete and accurate transaction files and must not share confidential brokerage information without the broker's authorization.

Contents of the Independent Contractor Agreement

In addition to the provisions listed above, a comprehensive independent contractor agreement addresses the following:

Ownership of Listings and Client Agreements: All listings, buyer representation agreements, and client relationships created by the licensee are owned by and remain with the broker. This is consistent with the principle that all clients belong to the broker.

Receipt of Funds: Establishes how the licensee is to handle any money received from or on behalf of a client, including earnest money and other transaction funds.

Facilities: Describes what office space, technology, and support resources the licensee is authorized to use at the brokerage.

Assignment of Clients: Addresses the licensee's authority to prospect for their own clients and the broker's right to assign clients to licensees within the office.

Compensation and Commission: Sets out the commission split structure, the procedures to follow if a client fails to pay, and the process for resolving commission disputes between licensees.

Expenses: Generally each party is responsible for their own operating expenses, but the agreement may specify any shared expenses such as office fees, technology fees, or franchise assessments.

Disputes and Litigation: Describes the procedures and respective obligations of the broker and licensee if either becomes involved in a complaint, regulatory proceeding, or civil lawsuit arising from the brokerage relationship.

Termination: Either party may terminate the agreement by providing written notice. The agreement should specify how outstanding commissions will be handled at the time of termination to avoid disputes after the relationship ends.

The format, length, and tone of the independent contractor agreement will vary from one brokerage to another. What matters is that the key provisions are present, clearly written, and understood by both parties before the agreement is signed.

Filing and Recordkeeping

Both the broker and the licensee should retain copies of all agreements in a secure location. The sponsorship form submitted to TREC contains the licensee's Social Security number and other personal information. It must be stored securely to protect privacy. The local real estate board will also request a copy when the licensee applies for MLS membership.

The licensee should keep a personal copy of both the sponsorship form and the independent contractor agreement. Disputes between brokers and licensees sometimes arise months or years after the agreement was signed. Reading the agreement again during a disagreement often clarifies the broker's position and may resolve the misunderstanding without further conflict.

Brokers are strongly advised to maintain a comprehensive office policy manual that applies the independent contractor agreement in practical terms. A well-drafted policy manual supplements the agreement, guides the initial training of new licensees, and serves as a reference document for more experienced agents when questions arise.

Supervision, Form 1099, and Balance

Brokers must file IRS Form 1099-NEC for any independent contractor licensee who receives more than $2,000 in earnings during the calendar year. A copy of this form must be provided to the licensee for their personal tax records. Licensees should maintain their own detailed earnings records and verify that what the broker reports to the IRS matches their own records before filing their annual tax returns.

Even with an independent contractor agreement in place, the broker retains a legal duty to supervise sponsored licensees. This supervisory responsibility exists regardless of the independent contractor classification and is a fundamental obligation under TRELA. The agreement does not relieve the broker of this duty.

In practice, supervisory needs vary considerably. A newly licensed salesperson requires close guidance on forms, procedures, client interaction, and transaction management. An experienced agent with years of productive closings may need only periodic check-ins and access to the broker for unusual situations. The broker must exercise judgment in calibrating the level of oversight to the licensee's experience and demonstrated competence.

Choosing a Broker

Selecting a sponsoring broker is among the most consequential decisions a new licensee makes. Because all client relationships belong to the broker, a licensee who leaves one brokerage for another starts over without any of the clients developed during the prior relationship. A poor fit chosen at the beginning can cost a licensee significant time, momentum, and income.

Several factors are worth evaluating before committing to a brokerage:

- Consider the management style that brings out your best performance. Some licensees thrive under close mentorship. Others do better with independence and minimal oversight.
- Understand the office structure. A larger office may offer formal training programs and support systems but may provide less direct access to the broker. A smaller office may provide more personalized mentorship and easier access to the broker but fewer formal resources.
- When visiting the office, pay attention to how the broker and the salespersons interact with each other. A collegial, communicative culture is a positive indicator. Tension or disengagement among the staff is worth noting.
- Review the brokerage's online presence. A well-maintained, professionally designed website suggests an organization that takes its brand and its tools seriously. While a strong website alone does not make a good broker, it is one data point about the firm's approach to the business.

Interviewing a Broker

A new licensee should approach the broker interview with the perspective that the decision flows both ways. The question is not only whether the broker will accept the licensee, but whether the brokerage is a good fit for the licensee's goals and working style. Choosing a broker who does not align with your needs can limit your development significantly.

Research the target geographic area first and identify several brokerages operating in the markets where you want to build your practice. Schedule appointments in advance rather than arriving unannounced. Prepare specific questions in writing before each interview so that important topics are not overlooked in the conversation.

Request a tour of the office during or after the interview. Observe the interaction between the broker or manager and the sales staff, and among the staff themselves. Also confirm that the office displays two required items: the Fair Housing poster and TREC Form CN 1-5, which identifies the office as regulated by TREC and provides contact information for filing a complaint. The presence of both items indicates the office is meeting basic regulatory compliance standards.

Negotiating Key Terms

Before signing the independent contractor agreement, the licensee should discuss and clarify the following:

Training and Support

Ask specifically what onboarding and ongoing training looks like. Some brokerages provide a structured initial training period. Others use experienced licensees as mentors who accompany new agents on appointments and answer questions as they arise. Knowing what support is available helps set realistic expectations from the start.

Commission Structure

Understand how commissions are split, when they are paid, and under what circumstances the split may change. Some brokerages offer a higher commission percentage after the licensee reaches a defined production threshold. This type of graduated structure creates a meaningful financial incentive for sustained productivity.

Lead Flow and Phone Coverage

Determine how inbound leads and phone inquiries are handled. In offices where licensees take turns covering the phones, those on duty receive direct access to prospective clients who call in response to advertising. Understanding the lead distribution system tells you a great deal about the opportunity available at that brokerage.

Additional Benefits and Fees

Ask whether the brokerage offers access to continuing education, professional development seminars, or other licensee benefits. Some brokers allow licensees to purchase their own personal residence through the office at a reduced or waived commission. Any benefits or unique arrangements should be documented in the independent contractor agreement rather than left as an informal understanding.

Working Under a Broker

When a licensee joins a brokerage, the broker provides initial training on the tools, forms, and procedures used in the office. This training covers the practical aspects of working with buyers and sellers that are not fully addressed in pre-licensing education. It takes time to become truly proficient, and the learning continues well beyond the first transaction.

After the initial training period, the broker remains available for questions, problem-solving, and guidance. An experienced broker who has worked through many different transaction types can often provide a quick and practical answer to a situation that seems complex or unfamiliar to a newer agent. The broker functions as a professional resource during this phase, not as a supervisor in the traditional employment sense.

The broker may accompany a new licensee on listing appointments or buyer showings when it would be helpful to do so. As the licensee gains experience and confidence, the need for that direct involvement naturally diminishes. The key is that the relationship between broker and licensee during this period should feel collaborative rather than hierarchical.

Life as an Independent Contractor

Freedom and flexibility are the most frequently cited benefits of the independent contractor model. Licensees set their own schedules, manage their own time, and are accountable primarily to their results rather than to a clock or a set of workplace conduct rules. There is no manager watching whether you look busy. There are no mandatory check-in times.

This independence, however, comes with real responsibility. A licensee who does not structure their time effectively and invest consistent effort in building their business will see that directly reflected in their income. The freedom to work as you choose is also the freedom to underperform without anyone stopping you.

The other practical reality is that the independent contractor's schedule is ultimately shaped by the needs of clients. Buyers and sellers operate on their own timetables, and a licensee who is unavailable when a client needs them will find that client working with someone else. The flexibility of the independent contractor model does not mean unlimited discretion about when to respond. Responsiveness and availability are professional obligations that the market enforces more reliably than any employment rule ever could.

Working for a Broker

Most salespersons affiliate with a broker as independent contractors rather than employees. The independent contractor agreement between the broker and salesperson covers commission splits, expense responsibilities, office procedures, and the scope of the working relationship. Because the broker is not the salesperson's employer in the legal sense, no income taxes are withheld, and no employment benefits such as health insurance or retirement contributions are provided. Each licensee is responsible for setting aside funds for taxes, funding their own retirement, and securing their own health coverage.

The degree of day-to-day interaction between a broker and salesperson varies considerably. Some licensees prefer to operate independently, essentially affiliating with a broker for licensing purposes while managing their own business. Others rely on the broker for regular guidance, training, and problem-solving support. Both approaches are legitimate, and a good broker is prepared to serve both types.

Technology has expanded the flexibility of the independent contractor model. Licensees can access transaction management platforms, MLS systems, and client communication tools from anywhere, so they are not required to be physically present at the brokerage office to conduct productive work. Most offices still benefit from periodic in-person interaction, however, and provide structured opportunities for exactly that.

Sales Meetings

Many brokerages schedule regular sales meetings, often weekly, as a way to disseminate important information and build cohesion among the office's licensees. New listings, changes to office procedures, market updates, and compliance reminders are typical agenda items. These meetings also provide one of the few regular occasions for licensees who spend most of their time in the field to connect with colleagues.

An important limitation applies: because salespersons are independent contractors, a broker cannot require attendance at sales meetings as a condition of affiliation. Mandatory attendance would be characteristic of an employer-employee relationship. Instead, brokers use voluntary incentives to encourage participation. Common approaches include door prize drawings for those who attend, guest speakers on topics of professional interest, or simply providing a meal. Attendance generally reflects how much value the broker creates in the meeting.

Some offices follow sales meetings with an office caravan, where licensees travel together to preview newly listed properties. This serves both as a practical tool for building inventory knowledge and as an informal team-building activity in an industry where individual schedules rarely align.

Commission Splits Between Brokers and Salespersons

Commission splits between a broker and affiliated salesperson take many forms. A traditional 50/50 split, in which the salesperson and broker each receive half of the commission dollars brought into the office, remains common but is no longer the universal standard. Competitive pressure has pushed many brokerages to offer more agent-favorable arrangements.

A 60/40 split, with the salesperson keeping 60 percent, is now fairly standard at many offices. Some firms offer new licensees a 70/30 arrangement to attract talent. The most productive brokerages typically use a progressive split structure: the agent's percentage of commission increases as their annual sales volume grows, creating a direct financial incentive for higher production. The reset point, whether yearly or quarterly, and the thresholds that trigger the step-ups should be clearly defined in the independent contractor agreement.

Beyond the basic split, salespersons should be aware of additional fees that may be deducted before or after the split is calculated. These can include transaction coordination fees, marketing fees, technology fees, and franchise fees. As a general principle, offices that offer higher agent splits tend to offset the reduced broker revenue by charging per-transaction or monthly fees.

Franchise Fees

A broker who operates under a national franchise brand has a contractual obligation to pay a royalty fee to the franchisor on each transaction. This fee is non-negotiable: failure to pay it risks loss of the franchise. The fee is typically calculated as a percentage of the gross commission and is deducted before the broker-salesperson split is applied.

For example, if a transaction generates a brokerage commission of $15,000 and the franchise royalty rate is 8 percent, the broker retains $1,200 before distributing the remaining $13,800 according to the agreed split. Salespersons at franchise offices should factor this deduction into their income projections.

Some franchisors also require brokers to purchase branded materials, signage, and supplies exclusively through the franchise system. This requirement serves to maintain brand consistency across all affiliated offices nationally, and it generates additional revenue for the franchisor. Salespersons joining a franchise office should ask about all such costs before signing an independent contractor agreement.

100% Commission Offices

Some brokerages allow salespersons to keep the full commission on every transaction. In exchange, the broker charges a flat monthly desk fee, which is due regardless of whether the salesperson closes any transactions that month. Monthly fees at some offices can exceed $2,000. Salespersons may also be responsible for all of their own advertising and marketing costs.

This model works best for experienced licensees with an established client base who can reliably generate enough transaction volume to cover the fixed monthly cost and still profit. A newer agent with inconsistent closings may find the monthly obligation financially stressful.

Some 100% commission offices operate under recognizable national franchise brands, which provides the salesperson with brand-awareness benefits without a traditional split. The perception that the broker provides less problem-solving support at these offices is somewhat overstated: licensees who gravitate toward the 100% model tend to be experienced enough that they require less frequent broker guidance.

Rent-a-Broker Offices

Texas law does not require a license to own a real estate company. However, every brokerage must have a licensed broker of record who is responsible for the activities of all affiliated salespersons. Some licensees who have built their own client base and operational infrastructure, but who do not yet hold a broker's license, contract with an outside broker to serve as the broker of record for a fee.

The arrangement typically involves either a per-transaction fee or a flat monthly charge paid to the broker. In most cases the broker provides no training, mentorship, or active problem-solving. The role is purely to satisfy the legal requirement of broker oversight. When the salesperson accumulates sufficient education hours to qualify for a broker's license, they typically transition to becoming the sponsoring broker of their own office.

The financial advantage of this model is that the salesperson retains more commission income than they would under a traditional split arrangement. The significant disadvantage is the absence of experienced broker guidance, which can be particularly costly when a difficult transaction arises. There is also a real supervisory liability risk: a broker who lends their license without genuinely supervising the affiliated salespersons exposes that license to discipline by TREC for failing to fulfill the broker's legal duty of supervision.

Deciding to Hire an Assistant

A productive licensee eventually reaches a point where the volume of administrative and coordination work begins to compete with the higher-value activities of securing listings, working with buyers, and building the business. When routine tasks consume time that would otherwise generate income, hiring a personal assistant becomes a sound business decision.

Common tasks an assistant can handle include answering and directing calls, scheduling appointments, preparing transaction documents, producing newsletters and marketing materials, managing the agent's website, attending open houses, and maintaining client databases.

Delegation does not come naturally to every agent. A licensee who has built a reputation by handling everything personally may find it difficult to trust another person with client-facing tasks. The transition is easier once the assistant has learned the agent's systems and standards. The goal is to reach the point where the assistant handles the routine work reliably enough that the agent is freed to focus on activity that produces revenue.

Real estate assistants may be either licensed or unlicensed. The distinction has significant legal implications.

Unlicensed Assistants

An unlicensed assistant may perform purely administrative tasks: answering phones, filing documents, maintaining client records, preparing non-licensee documents such as correspondence, building and updating databases, and creating marketing materials. These activities do not require a real estate license.

However, an unlicensed assistant may not perform any activity that requires a license under Texas law. Specifically, an unlicensed assistant may not host or conduct an open house independently, show properties, interpret contract language or supporting documents, attend a closing without supervision, or negotiate commission on any transaction.

Texas law prohibits a broker from employing or compensating, directly or indirectly, an unlicensed person for performing acts that require a license. An agent who allows an unlicensed assistant to perform licensed activities is creating legal exposure for both the assistant and the brokerage. Unlicensed assistants must be supervised carefully and their activities must stay strictly within the administrative category. Many unlicensed assistants in real estate are family members or personal acquaintances of the licensee and work part-time from the brokerage office or from home.

Licensed Assistants

A licensed assistant holds an active Texas real estate license and can therefore perform virtually any task the supervising agent assigns, including conducting open houses independently, discussing specific properties with buyers and sellers, preparing and reviewing contract documents, and attending closings.

Many licensees work as assistants on a part-time basis while developing their own client base, gaining practical experience, and supplementing their income. Others work full-time as assistants for a highly productive agent or team. In either case, a licensed assistant provides the supervising agent with far greater operational flexibility than an unlicensed one, and an agent looking to hire should strongly prefer a licensed candidate.

The scope of a licensed assistant's responsibilities typically expands over time as the assistant becomes familiar with the agent's standards, clients, and systems. Responsibilities commonly fall into six areas: office administration, data management, appointment coordination, client communication, technology support, and escrow coordination.

Licensed Assistant Responsibilities

Office Administration

Real estate transactions are paperwork-intensive. One of an assistant's first priorities is learning the firm's document flow: what forms are generated at each stage of a transaction, who receives copies, and where originals are filed. A well-organized, cross-referenced filing system that any member of the team can navigate quickly is an essential operational tool.

Data Management

Keeping listing statuses current in the MLS, updating the office inventory, and maintaining the agent's website are time-consuming tasks that a licensed assistant can handle efficiently. Accurate, up-to-date data is a professional credibility issue, and delegating these updates to an assistant frees the agent to focus on client relationships.

Appointment Coordination

A busy agent moving through multiple showings, listing appointments, inspections, and closings in a single day is at risk of running late or missing an engagement entirely. An assistant who monitors the schedule and maintains phone contact throughout the day reduces that risk. Assistants can also prepare appointment folders with all relevant documents before the agent heads to a listing presentation or buyer meeting, and can attend appraisals, inspections, or pre-closing walkthroughs as the agent's representative.

Client Communication

Maintaining personal contact with a growing client list becomes harder as a business expands. The agent remains responsible for meaningful face-to-face interactions, but an assistant can sustain the relationship through routine communications such as seasonal greetings, market newsletters, and follow-up messages that keep the agent's name in the client's awareness between transactions.

Technology Support

A licensed assistant can photograph new listings and upload images to the MLS and the agent's website. High-quality listing photography has become a minimum professional standard, and delegating this task to an assistant ensures it gets done consistently. These images also serve as evidence for sellers of the work being done to market their property.

Escrow Coordination

The period between contract execution and closing is where transactions most commonly fail. An assistant who actively monitors the escrow process, tracking which documents have been returned, which contingencies remain open, and which conditions still need to be satisfied, significantly reduces the probability of a transaction falling apart due to an overlooked detail. Regular communication with the escrow or title officer keeps everyone aligned and ensures the closing proceeds without last-minute surprises.

Why Become a Licensed Assistant

Obtaining a Texas real estate license requires genuine effort: completing hours of coursework and passing a demanding state examination. It may seem counterintuitive to apply that effort toward an assistant role rather than independent listing and selling. There are, however, legitimate and practical reasons a licensee might choose this path, at least initially.

Some new licensees discover quickly that the entrepreneurial, self-directed nature of selling real estate does not match their personality. Prospecting for clients, handling rejection, and sustaining motivation through unpredictable income cycles are real challenges that not everyone is suited for. Working as an assistant provides a structured income stream while keeping the licensee professionally active.

Others choose the assistant role as a deliberate learning strategy. Working alongside an experienced, high-producing agent provides an accelerated education in transaction management, client communication, and market knowledge that no classroom can replicate. Once the assistant has built the confidence and professional fluency to go out independently, the transition is far smoother.

Financial predictability is a third factor. An hourly wage or salary is more manageable for someone with fixed household obligations than the income volatility of a commission-only structure. Some agents structure assistant compensation as a base wage plus a percentage of commissions on transactions the assistant helped close, providing a path toward commission income without full exposure to its unpredictability.

Getting Hired as an Assistant

Applying for an assistant position follows the same professional standards as any job search. A well-organized, carefully proofread resume is the first impression a candidate makes. The resume should address:

Work history: List positions in which the skills acquired are transferable to a real estate support role. Customer service, administrative work, and client-facing experience are all directly relevant.

People skills: Real estate involves constant interaction with buyers, sellers, vendors, and other agents. Any experience dealing with the public professionally should be highlighted.

Education and licensing: An active Texas real estate license should be prominently featured if held. Other relevant coursework such as business writing, spreadsheet applications, or contract administration is worth including.

Real estate experience: Any prior transaction experience, whether as an agent, a transaction coordinator, or in a title or mortgage role, is valuable context.

Technical skills: Proficiency with transaction management platforms, MLS systems, Microsoft Office, AI platforms, digital photography, and social media tools are all relevant in the modern real estate environment.

References: Two or three professional references who can speak to the candidate's reliability and work quality are important. Instructors from real estate licensing courses can serve this purpose effectively.

The visual presentation of the resume matters. A well-designed, clean document that is free of typographical and grammatical errors signals professionalism before the interview begins.

Assistant Employment Arrangements

An assistant position may be structured in one of three ways:

Part-Time Employee

An agent hiring an assistant for the first time may begin with a part-time arrangement to assess workload and fit before committing to more hours. Part-time assistants typically work 20 to 24 hours per week at an hourly wage. Benefits are generally not provided, but the employer must carry workers' compensation coverage. Positions that start part-time frequently grow into full-time roles as the agent's reliance on the assistant increases.

Full-Time Employee

Full-time assistants generally work 35 to 40 hours per week and receive a regular salary plus benefits. Agents who require evening and weekend availability may supplement the base salary with a percentage of the commission on transactions the assistant helped manage.

Independent Contractor

An assistant operating as an independent contractor sets their own schedule, pays their own taxes, and is subject to minimal behavioral oversight. This arrangement provides flexibility for both parties but requires a properly drafted independent contractor agreement to satisfy IRS classification rules. Some high-demand assistants operate as independent contractors and serve multiple agents or teams simultaneously.

Some agents prefer assistants who are primarily field-based rather than office-based. These on-call assistants handle property visits, vendor coordination, and client-facing tasks on an as-needed basis. Hours can vary dramatically, with peak transaction periods requiring significantly more time. On-call assistants working irregular hours should still receive compensation that reflects actual hours worked, plus a share of commissions on closings they supported.

Compensation and Compliance Considerations

A recurring compliance problem in the industry involves agents who employ assistants as hourly or salaried workers but fail to withhold the required taxes. The issue is not how much the assistant is paid, but whether the payment structure conforms to federal and state employment tax law. An employee paid without proper withholding of income tax and Social Security contributions creates tax liability for the assistant, the salesperson, and potentially the broker.

Any agent who employs an assistant should consult with an attorney or CPA before the first paycheck is issued. The cost of that professional guidance is modest compared to the penalties associated with mismanaging payroll taxes. Structuring the employment correctly from the start eliminates the problem entirely.

Sharing Commissions

A salesperson may receive compensation only from their sponsoring broker. The salesperson cannot accept a commission directly from a buyer, seller, another broker, or any third party. The broker is the only permissible source of compensation for a sponsored licensee.

Brokers, however, may share commissions with other licensed Texas brokers and with brokers licensed in other states. Brokers may also share with individuals who are exempt from the licensing requirement.

A broker may not share a commission with any unlicensed person who is not otherwise exempt. Compensating an unlicensed person for performing or facilitating a real estate transaction is known as a kickback and is a violation of TRELA. Penalties can include license suspension or revocation.

Many transactions involve a cooperating broker who identifies and represents the buyer while the listing broker represents the seller. The cooperating broker has no direct agreement with the seller and must rely on an arrangement with the listing broker for their compensation. Each licensee's share of the commission received by their employing broker is determined by the split specified in their individual independent contractor agreement.

Commission Calculations

> ***2024 NAR Settlement Update:*** *Effective August 2024, the National Association of REALTORS settlement changed the rules for how buyer broker compensation is handled in MLS-connected transactions. Buyer broker compensation can no longer be advertised or offered through the MLS. Instead, compensation for a buyer's agent must be negotiated directly between the buyer and their broker and documented in the buyer representation agreement before showings begin. Sellers may still voluntarily offer to pay the buyer's broker as a concession or contract term, but this is now a separate negotiation rather than a standard MLS practice. In transactions where the seller does not cover the buyer's agent fee, the buyer pays their agent directly or through a credit structure negotiated in the purchase contract. Texas licensees must be prepared to work through both compensation models.*

The practical effect of this change is that buyer representation agreements must now address compensation explicitly. The fee agreed between the buyer and their broker must be stated in the representation agreement before any showing takes place. If the seller agrees to cover that fee as a contract concession, the buyer's obligation may be offset. If not, the buyer pays their agent directly.

The following examples illustrate commission calculations under both models. Brokerage names, agents, and splits are illustrative.

Commission Split Examples

Example 1: Seller Pays Listing Commission Only; Buyer Pays Own Agent

Broker Diana owns Ridgeline Realty. Agent Marcus has a 65/35 split with Diana (Marcus keeps 65%). The seller listed with Marcus at a 2.5% listing-side commission. The seller is offering no compensation to the buyer's agent. The buyer separately agreed in their buyer representation agreement to pay their agent, Agent Priya of Clearview Properties (Broker Chen), a 2.5% fee. The home sells for $620,000.

Listing Side (Seller Pays)

Sale Price: **$620,000**
Listing Commission (2.5%): **$15,500 ($620,000 x 0.025)**
Marcus's share (65%): **$10,075 ($15,500 x 0.65)**
Diana's share (35%): **$5,425 ($15,500 - $10,075)**

Buyer Side (Buyer Pays Directly)

Buyer agent fee (2.5%): **$15,500 ($620,000 x 0.025)**
Priya's share (60% split with Chen): **$9,300 ($15,500 x 0.60)**
Broker Chen's share (40%): **$6,200 ($15,500 - $9,300)**

In this transaction, the total commission cost is the same as a traditional transaction, but the two sides are negotiated and paid separately. The seller paid only for the listing side, and the buyer paid for their own representation.

Example 2: Seller Pays Both Sides as Contract Concession

Agent Marcus lists a property for $750,000 at a 2.5% listing commission. The seller agrees, as a separate contract concession, to cover the buyer's agent fee of 2.5%. The home sells for $735,000. Agent Priya represents the buyer with a 60% split with Broker Chen. Marcus retains a 65% split with Broker Diana.

Total Commission Paid by Seller

Sale Price: **$735,000**
Listing commission (2.5%): **$18,375 ($735,000 x 0.025)**
Buyer agent concession (2.5%): **$18,375 ($735,000 x 0.025)**
Total seller pays: **$36,750**

Listing Side Split

Marcus's share (65%): **$11,944 ($18,375 x 0.65)**
Diana's share (35%): **$6,431 ($18,375 - $11,944)**

Buyer Side Split (paid as concession from seller to buyer's broker)

Priya's share (60%): **$11,025 ($18,375 x 0.60)**
Chen's share (40%): **$7,350 ($18,375 - $11,025)**

This structure mirrors the pre-2024 model economically, but it is now documented as a specific seller concession in the purchase contract rather than an automatic MLS-based co-brokerage offer.

Example 3: In-House Sale, Two Agents from the Same Brokerage

Both sides of this transaction involve Ridgeline Realty agents. Agent Marcus listed the property. Agent Sofia represents the buyer. Both have a 65% split with Broker Diana. The seller agreed to pay a 2.5% listing commission. The seller also agreed as a contract concession to cover a 2.5% buyer agent fee. Sale price is $880,000.

Total Commission

Sale Price: **$880,000**
Listing commission (2.5%): **$22,000 ($880,000 x 0.025)**
Buyer agent concession (2.5%): **$22,000 ($880,000 x 0.025)**
Total brokerage receives: **$44,000**

Listing Side

Marcus's share (65%): **$14,300 ($22,000 x 0.65)**
Diana's share (35%): **$7,700 ($22,000 - $14,300)**

Buyer Side

Sofia's share (65%): **$14,300 ($22,000 x 0.65)**
Diana's share (35%): **$7,700 ($22,000 - $14,300)**

Diana's total from both sides: **$15,400 ($7,700 + $7,700)**

Example 4: Agent Sells Own Listing

Agent Marcus listed a home for $1,100,000 and it received an accepted offer at $1,050,000 from an unrepresented buyer. The listing agreement provided for a 2.5% commission. The buyer is purchasing without an agent and no buyer-side compensation is involved.

Commission Calculation

Sale Price: **$1,050,000**
Commission (2.5%): **$26,250 ($1,050,000 x 0.025)**
Marcus's share (65%): **$17,063 ($26,250 x 0.65)**
Diana's share (35%): **$9,187 ($26,250 - $17,063)**

Note that referral fees, transaction coordination fees, franchise assessments, and other agreed-upon expenses are deducted from the agent's share before the final net is calculated.

Commissions and Incomplete Transactions

A broker may still be entitled to a commission even when a transaction does not close, provided the failure to close resulted from the client's default rather than the broker's failure to perform. A seller may owe a commission to the listing broker despite the sale not completing if the seller:

- Decides not to proceed with the sale after accepting an offer.
- Cannot obtain the required signature of a co-owner on the deed.
- Has a title defect that cannot be corrected.
- Engages in fraudulent conduct related to the transaction.
- Cannot deliver possession of the property.
- Insists on terms inconsistent with the listing agreement.
- Mutually agrees with the buyer to cancel the contract.

Similarly, a buyer who signed a representation agreement and agreed to pay a commission is obligated for that commission even if they decide not to purchase, acquire a FSBO property directly, or work with a different broker to complete a purchase. In any of these scenarios, the broker would need to initiate a lawsuit to recover the commission if the client refuses to pay voluntarily.

Commission After Listing Expiration

A listing agreement that expires does not necessarily extinguish the broker's right to a commission. Most listing agreements include a carryover clause, sometimes called a safety clause or holdover provision, which entitles the broker to a commission for a specified period after the listing expires if the property is sold to a buyer the broker introduced during the listing period.

For example: Agent Marcus listed a home at $975,000 and showed it to Buyer Andrea during the listing period. The listing expired without a sale. Within the carryover period specified in the listing agreement, the seller accepted Andrea's offer and closed the transaction privately. Marcus is still entitled to his commission, because Andrea was introduced to the property during the active listing period.

> ***Important procedural note:*** *Only a broker may initiate legal action against a seller or buyer to recover a commission under a written agency agreement. A salesperson cannot sue a client directly for commission. However, if the broker has received a commission that includes the salesperson's earned share and refuses to pay it, the salesperson may bring an action against the broker to recover their portion.*

Snapshot Review – Chapter 9

The Broker-Principal Relationship

1. Broker-principal agreements are professional service engagements, not employment relationships in the conventional sense. The broker is not directed by the client on how to perform their work.
2. The three types of broker-principal agreements are: listing and landlord agreements, buyer and tenant representation agreements, and property management agreements.
3. All broker-principal agreements should be in writing and signed by all parties. A verbal agreement provides almost no legal protection if a commission dispute arises.

Commission Dispute Requirements (TRELA Section 1101.806)

To pursue a commission claim in court, all four of the following must be present:

1. A written agreement between the broker and the client.
2. The agreement was signed by the party obligated to pay.
3. The broker's license was active at the time of the transaction (confirmed by TREC license activity statement).
4. The buyer was advised to obtain a title search and/or title insurance policy at the time of making the offer.

Employee vs. Independent Contractor

Employee: Works under the direct supervision and control of the broker. The broker may set hours, require office duty, mandate meetings, and direct how work is performed. The broker must withhold federal income tax, state income tax, Social Security, and Medicare from wages, and pay unemployment and workers' compensation taxes.

Independent Contractor: Performs real estate activities without the broker controlling how they are accomplished. Paid by production (commission), not salary. Pays own taxes and expenses. The broker files Form 1099-NEC if earnings exceed $2,000 per year. Cannot receive employee-style benefits.

IRS Section 3508 Safe Harbor Test

To qualify for independent contractor classification, all three conditions must be met:

1. The licensee holds a valid real estate license.
2. Compensation is based on production, not hours worked.
3. A written independent contractor agreement exists and states the licensee will not be treated as an employee for federal income tax purposes.

Misclassification discovered in an IRS audit exposes the broker to back taxes, payroll tax obligations, and significant penalties.

Key Independent Contractor Agreement Provisions

Exclusive Association: The licensee performs all real estate activities exclusively through the sponsoring broker.

Independent Contractor Designation: Confirms the licensee is not an employee. Required by Section 3508.

Associate's Authority: Defines the licensee's authority to enter into agency agreements and requirements to keep the broker informed.

Ownership of Listings: All client relationships and listings belong to the broker, not the individual licensee.

Compensation and Commission: Documents the commission split, procedures if a client fails to pay, and dispute resolution between licensees.

Termination: Either party may terminate with written notice. The agreement must address handling of outstanding commissions at termination.

Choosing and Evaluating a Broker

1. Because all clients belong to the broker, a licensee who leaves a brokerage starts over without the clients developed there. Choosing the right broker from the start matters enormously.
2. Evaluate training and support, commission structure, lead flow and phone coverage, and any additional benefits or fees.
3. Approach the interview as a mutual evaluation. The licensee is deciding whether the brokerage is a good fit, not just seeking acceptance.
4. Confirm the office displays the Fair Housing poster and TREC Form CN 1-5 (regulatory compliance notice). Their absence is a compliance concern.
5. All agreed terms should be documented in the independent contractor agreement, not left as informal understandings.

Office Models

Traditional Split Office: The broker and salesperson divide commission according to an agreed percentage. Common starting splits are 60/40 or 65/35 in the agent's favor. Progressive split structures increase the agent's percentage as annual production grows.

100% Commission Office: The salesperson retains the full commission and pays the broker a fixed monthly desk fee regardless of production volume. Best suited for experienced agents with a reliable transaction base.

Rent-a-Broker: A salesperson who owns their own office contracts with a broker solely to satisfy the broker-of-record requirement. The contracted broker provides no training or support. Supervisory liability risk for the broker is significant.

Franchise Fee: A percentage of each commission deducted before the broker-salesperson split and remitted to the national franchisor. Must be factored into income projections by agents at franchise offices.

Assistants

Unlicensed Assistant: May perform administrative tasks only. Cannot host open houses, show property, interpret contract documents, attend closings unsupervised, or negotiate commissions. Texas law prohibits compensating an unlicensed person for performing licensed acts.

Licensed Assistant: Holds an active Texas real estate license and may perform any task assigned by the supervising agent. Preferred over unlicensed assistants because of the greatly expanded scope of permissible activities.

Assistant Employment Structures

1. Part-time employee: 20 to 24 hours per week, hourly wage, no benefits, workers' compensation required.
2. Full-time employee: 35 to 40 hours per week, salary plus benefits, possible commission percentage for transactions supported.
3. Independent contractor: sets own schedule, pays own taxes, requires a properly drafted independent contractor agreement.
4. All employees (part-time and full-time) require proper payroll tax withholding. Failure to withhold income tax, Social Security, and Medicare creates liability for the agent and the broker.

Commission Rules

1. A salesperson may receive compensation only from their sponsoring broker, not from buyers, sellers, or other brokers directly.
2. Brokers may share commissions with other licensed brokers (Texas or out-of-state) and with licensure-exempt persons such as attorneys.
3. Paying commission to an unlicensed, non-exempt person is a kickback and a violation of TRELA.
4. Since the 2024 NAR settlement, buyer broker compensation may no longer be advertised through the MLS. It must be negotiated between buyer and buyer's broker and stated in the buyer representation agreement before showings begin. Sellers may still voluntarily offer to cover buyer agent fees as a contract concession.

Commission on Incomplete Transactions and Expired Listings

1. A broker may be entitled to commission on a transaction that does not close if the failure results from the seller's or buyer's default.
2. Most listing agreements include a carryover (holdover) clause entitling the broker to commission for a defined period after expiration if the property is sold to a buyer the broker introduced during the listing term.
3. Only a broker may sue to collect a commission from a client. A salesperson who has not received their share of an earned commission may sue the broker to recover it.

CHAPTER 9 QUIZ — EMPLOYMENT ISSUES

1. Under Texas law, a seller-broker agreement is sometimes called an employment contract. In this context, the term "employment" most accurately describes:
    a. A formal employer-employee relationship in which the broker receives benefits and the client withholds taxes.
    b. An arrangement in which the client directs the broker's work schedule, marketing activities, and pricing decisions.
    c. A salaried position in which the broker is compensated by the client regardless of whether the transaction closes.
    d. A goal-oriented professional service engagement in which the broker provides expertise toward a defined objective without being directed on methods by the client.

2. Under TRELA Section 1101.806, which of the following is one of the four requirements that must be satisfied before a court will hear a broker's commission claim?
    a. A written agreement must exist between the broker and the client, signed by the party obligated to pay the commission.
    b. The broker must have placed the property in the MLS and held at least one open house during the listing period.
    c. The broker must have provided the seller with a written comparative market analysis before the listing was signed.
    d. The broker must have attempted mediation before filing any claim in court.

3. A licensee earns commissions, pays her own business expenses, sets her own schedule, and has a written agreement with the broker confirming she will not be treated as an employee. This licensee is most accurately classified as:
    a. An employee, because they work exclusively through the sponsoring broker and cannot accept commissions from other sources.
    b. An independent contractor, because they are compensated by production, bear their own expenses, and have a written agreement confirming their non-employee status.
    c. A statutory employee, because the real estate industry requires payroll tax withholding regardless of written agreements.
    d. A subagent, because they are not directly supervised by the listing broker on a daily basis.

4. When a broker classifies a salesperson as an employee, the broker is required to withhold which of the following from the salesperson's wages?
    a. Federal income tax only, because state income tax is the licensee's personal responsibility.
    b. Self-employment tax and errors and omissions insurance premiums.
    c. Federal income tax, state income tax, Social Security tax, and Medicare tax.
    d. Commission advances, TREC renewal fees, and professional dues.

5. To qualify for independent contractor classification under the IRS Section 3508 safe harbor test, all three of the following conditions must be met. Which of the following correctly lists all three?

   a. The licensee holds a valid license, earns a salary plus commission, and works from an office provided by the broker.

   b. The licensee holds a valid license, files quarterly estimated taxes independently, and belongs to the local board of REALTORS.

   c. The licensee holds a valid license, does not receive a company vehicle, and does not work regular office hours.

   d. The licensee holds a valid real estate license, compensation is based on production rather than hours worked, and a written independent contractor agreement exists stating the licensee will not be treated as an employee for federal tax purposes.

6. An IRS audit determines that a broker incorrectly classified several salespersons as independent contractors when they should have been treated as employees. The broker's most likely consequence is:

   a. Liability for all back taxes that should have been withheld, including income tax, Social Security, and Medicare contributions, plus state and federal unemployment premiums and potential tax penalties.

   b. A fine equal to the amount of commissions paid to the misclassified licensees during the audit period.

   c. Suspension of the broker's TREC license until the licensee classification issue is corrected.

   d. A requirement to renegotiate and re-execute all independent contractor agreements with current licensees.

7. A salesperson receives $42,000 in commission income from his or her sponsoring broker during the calendar year. The broker's IRS reporting obligation is to:

   a. Withhold federal and state income taxes from each commission check and submit them to the appropriate agencies.

   b. File IRS Form 1099-NEC reporting the total earnings and provide a copy to the licensee for his or her personal tax records.

   c. File IRS Form W-2 because the amount exceeds the threshold for independent contractor status.

   d. Take no action because independent contractors are solely responsible for reporting their own income to the IRS.

8. A key provision of the independent contractor agreement states that all listings, buyer representation agreements, and client relationships created by the licensee belong to and remain with the broker. This provision reflects which broader principle of Texas agency law?

   a. Subagency law, which requires all client contacts to flow through the listing broker before the cooperating agent can be compensated.

   b. The NAR Code of Ethics requirement that all representation agreements be held by the MLS to prevent commission disputes.

   c. The principle that all client relationships belong to the broker, not to the individual licensee, which is why clients remain with the brokerage when a licensee leaves.

   d. TREC's promulgated escrow rules, which require all earnest money to be held in the broker's name rather than the salesperson's name.

9. Despite a written independent contractor agreement, the broker retains a legal duty under TRELA to:

a. Set the licensee's working hours to ensure client availability during peak showing periods.

b. Provide health insurance and paid time off as required compensation for sponsored licensees.

c. Attend every transaction closing to verify that contracts were prepared according to brokerage standards.

d. Supervise the sponsored licensee's real estate activities, regardless of the independent contractor classification.

10. A new licensee is interviewing at a brokerage and wants to confirm the office is meeting basic regulatory compliance standards. Which two items should they confirm are displayed in the office?

a. The Fair Housing poster and TREC Form CN 1-5, which identifies the office as regulated by TREC and provides complaint contact information.

b. The broker's personal license certificate and a copy of the current NAR Code of Ethics.

c. The office's MLS membership certificate and a current copy of the Texas Property Code.

d. A copy of the broker's errors and omissions insurance policy and the most recent TREC inspection report.

11. A licensee leaves a brokerage after two years and joins a competing firm. Which of the following correctly describes what happens to the clients the licensee was working with?

a. All clients follow the licensee to the new firm because the licensee personally established and maintained those relationships.

b. The clients remain with the original broker because the independent contractor agreement establishes that all client relationships belong to the broker.

c. Clients may choose independently whether to follow the licensee or remain at the original brokerage.

d. The clients are assigned to a new licensee within the original office only if they have active listing or representation agreements still in effect.

12. A new licensee is negotiating terms with a prospective broker and is told verbally that the commission split will increase after reaching a defined production threshold. The most professionally appropriate response is to:

a. Accept the verbal promise since the broker has a strong reputation in the market.

b. Ask a more experienced agent in the office to confirm the broker has honored similar promises in the past.

c. Request that the graduated commission structure and all other agreed terms be documented in the written independent contractor agreement before signing.

d. Decline the offer entirely because graduated commission structures violate TREC compensation rules.

13. A broker schedules a weekly sales meeting and tells all affiliated salespersons that attendance is mandatory. Why is this policy problematic?

a. TREC rules prohibit brokers from holding meetings during standard business hours.

b. Weekly meetings violate the MLS cooperation agreement by taking salespersons away from showing properties.

c. TXR rules require that all office meetings be held quarterly rather than weekly.

d. Requiring attendance at sales meetings is characteristic of an employer-employee relationship and is inconsistent with independent contractor status.

14. A broker operating under a national franchise brand closes a transaction with a gross commission of $18,000. The franchise royalty rate is 8 percent. After the royalty is deducted, what amount remains to be split between the broker and the salesperson?

a. $16,560

b. $18,000

c. $1,440

d. $14,400

15. Which of the following best describes the 100% commission office model and the type of licensee it is best suited for?

a. The broker retains all commissions and pays each salesperson a fixed monthly salary regardless of production. Best suited for new agents who need income stability.

b. The salesperson keeps the full commission but pays the broker a fixed monthly desk fee. Best suited for experienced licensees with an established client base who can reliably cover the fixed cost.

c. The broker and salesperson split all commissions equally after deducting a monthly technology fee. Best suited for part-time agents.

d. The salesperson keeps all commissions and pays no fees to the broker. Best suited for licensees who want maximum independence.

16. An unlicensed assistant working for a licensee independently hosts an open house and discusses specific contract terms with prospective buyers. Under Texas law, this situation:

a. Is permissible as long as the supervising licensee is reachable by phone during the open house.

b. Is acceptable if the unlicensed assistant limits contract discussions to general information and does not give specific advice.

c. Is a violation of TRELA because hosting an open house independently and interpreting contract documents are activities that require a license, and compensating an unlicensed person for performing licensed acts is prohibited.

d. Is permitted under the broker's supervision license as long as the assistant is a family member of the licensee.

17. Which of the following tasks may a licensed assistant perform that an unlicensed assistant may not?

a. Answering the office phone and directing calls to the appropriate agent.

b. Maintaining the agent's client database and preparing marketing newsletters.

c. Uploading listing photographs to the MLS and updating the agent's website.

d. Conducting an open house independently, reviewing contract documents with buyers, and attending a closing as the agent's representative.

18. A salesperson hires a full-time assistant and pays them a weekly salary without withholding any income taxes, Social Security, or Medicare contributions. The primary risk of this arrangement is:

a. The failure to withhold required payroll taxes creates tax liability for the assistant, the salesperson, and potentially the broker, and may result in penalties.

b. TREC may revoke the salesperson's license for failing to submit the required assistant registration form.

c. The assistant may file a grievance with the local board of REALTORS for the failure to provide required employment benefits.

d. The arrangement is automatically reclassified as an independent contractor relationship, which eliminates the withholding requirement retroactively.

19. Under the post-2024 NAR settlement rules in effect in Texas, which of the following correctly describes how buyer broker compensation must be handled?

a. Buyer broker compensation must be posted in the MLS listing before any showing is scheduled so cooperating agents can review it.

b. Buyer broker compensation must be negotiated between the buyer and their broker and stated in the buyer representation agreement before showings begin. Sellers may still choose to cover it as a contract concession.

c. Buyer broker compensation is set by the local board of REALTORS at a uniform rate and applied automatically to all MLS transactions.

d. Buyer broker compensation is paid exclusively from the listing broker's commission, with no input from or obligation to the buyer.

20. Agent Sofia lists a property at a 2.5% listing commission, and the seller agrees as a contract concession to cover a 2.5% buyer agent fee. The home sells for $500,000. Sofia has a 65% split with her broker. How much does Sofia earn from the listing side of this transaction?

a. $16,250

b. $12,500

c. $8,125

d. $6,500

21. A salesperson receives a commission check directly from a seller who wanted to thank the agent personally. Under Texas law, this arrangement:

a. Is permissible as long as the salesperson reports the payment to their sponsoring broker within five business days.

b. Is acceptable if the salesperson endorses the check over to the broker before depositing it.

c. Is permissible because a seller's gratitude payment is not technically a commission and falls outside TRELA's compensation rules.

d. Is a violation because a salesperson may receive compensation only from their sponsoring broker, not directly from a buyer, seller, or any third party.

22. A listing broker pays a portion of the commission to an individual who referred the buyer but who does not hold a Texas real estate license and is not otherwise exempt from the licensing requirement. This arrangement is:

a. A kickback and a violation of TRELA, which may result in license suspension or revocation.

b. Permissible if the referral fee is disclosed in writing to both the buyer and the seller before closing.

c. Permissible as long as the payment is structured as a gift rather than a referral fee.

d. Permissible if the amount paid does not exceed one percent of the sales price.

23. A listing agent showed a property to a buyer during the active listing period. The listing expired without a sale. Six weeks later, still within the carryover period specified in the listing agreement, the seller accepted that same buyer's offer privately and closed the transaction without notifying the broker. The broker is:

a. Not entitled to a commission because the listing had already expired at the time of the sale.

b. Entitled to a commission because the carryover clause protects the broker's right to compensation when the property sells to a buyer the broker introduced during the listing period.

c. Not entitled to a commission because the seller and buyer negotiated directly without the broker's involvement.

d. Entitled to only half a commission because the transaction closed after the listing expired.

24. A salesperson believes his sponsoring broker received a commission that included the salesperson's earned share but the broker has refused to pay the salesperson's portion. Under Texas law, the salesperson's correct course of action is to:

a. File a complaint with the local board of REALTORS and request that the MLS freeze the broker's listings until the dispute is resolved.

b. Contact the seller directly and ask them to issue a separate check to the salesperson for the unpaid share.

c. Bring a legal action against the broker to recover the salesperson's portion of the commission, since only the broker may sue a client for commission but a salesperson may sue the broker to recover their earned share.

d. File a claim with TREC's Real Estate Recovery Trust Account to recover the unpaid commission from state funds.

CHAPTER 10

AGENCY, ETHICS, AND THE LAW

Chapter Objectives

After completing this chapter, you should be able to:

1. Distinguish between ethics, morals, and laws, and explain why ethical conduct matters to a real estate practice beyond simple legal compliance.
2. Describe the origin and purpose of the NAR Code of Ethics, explain its structure, and identify how it is enforced through association complaint processes.
3. Identify key federal and state laws governing advertising conduct, lending discrimination, and deceptive trade practices as they apply to Texas licensees.
4. Describe the five Texas Administrative Code canons of professional ethics and explain the TREC complaint and advisory letter process.
5. Explain the ethical rules governing fees from service providers, commission sharing, the Real Estate Recovery Trust Account, and escrow account management.
6. Explain the minimum ethical standards that apply to real estate licensees and describe the structure of the NAR Code of Ethics.
7. Describe the informal and formal dispute resolution processes used to enforce the Code of Ethics.
8. Explain Article 1 and its key Standards of Practice, including obligations regarding offer presentation, confidentiality, and disclosure of multiple offers.
9. Explain Articles 2 and 3 and their Standards of Practice, including the 2026 changes to compensation and cooperation obligations.
10. Apply Articles 1, 2, and 3 to real-world case studies to identify ethical violations and supporting Standards of Practice.

Contents

Internet Advertising and the Fair Housing Act
Federal Lending Discrimination: The Equal Credit Opportunity Act
The Texas Deceptive Trade Practices Act
The Texas Administrative Code Canons of Professional Ethics
The TREC Complaint Process
TREC Advisory Letters
Association Complaints and the Citation Program
Receiving Fees from Service Providers
Residential Service Company Disclosure
Disclosure of Shared Commissions
The Real Estate Recovery Trust Account
Escrow Account Ethics and Rules
TAC Rule 535.159: Depositing Escrow Funds
TAC Rule 535.146: Accounting and Commingling
Minimum Ethical Standards
Structure of the Code of Ethics
The Preamble
The Articles: An Overview
Standards of Practice
Enforcing the Code of Ethics
Informal Dispute Resolution: Ombudsman
Informal Dispute Resolution: Mediation
Formal Dispute Resolution: Ethics Complaints
Grievance Committee Review
Ethics Hearing Panel
Arbitration
Arbitration Hearing Panel
Article 1: Protecting Client Interests
Key Standards of Practice Under Article 1
Article 2: Truthfulness and Disclosure
Article 3: Cooperation and Compensation
Case Studies

Ethics, Morals, and Laws

Ethics are the accepted standards of conduct that guide behavior within a group or profession. They are rooted in moral principles and extend beyond mere legal compliance to reflect the values of the professional community. Business ethics, as an organized field of study, emerged in the 1960s and has since become a recognized discipline in professional education.

Ethical behavior is not just a philosophical ideal. It is good for business. An organization that conducts itself ethically tends to reduce legal exposure, maintain compliance with regulations, attract capable employees, earn client trust, and draw investment. Conversely, companies that disregard ethical standards face regulatory fines, civil liability, and reputational damage that can far exceed any short-term advantage gained.

Ethics are context-sensitive. The standards appropriate for one situation or profession may differ from another, and applying them requires judgment about the specific circumstances. This is why ethics complaints in real estate are evaluated case by case rather than by a mechanical checklist.

Morals and Principles

Morals are a person's individual standards of right and wrong. They derive from deeply held principles, which are the foundational beliefs that shape how a person views and responds to the world. Morals define personal character from within, while ethics describe the external standard of behavior that a profession, community, or society expects of its members.

The relationship between personal morals and professional ethics is not always simple. A criminal defense attorney may personally believe that a client is guilty of a serious crime, yet professional ethics require a vigorous and zealous defense. In that case, professional ethics must take precedence over personal moral discomfort to preserve the integrity of the legal system. Real estate professionals encounter similar tensions when client interests, market pressures, or personal relationships create competing pulls on conduct.

Moral reasoning is complex. A person may hold certain principles as absolute while justifying other behaviors because the outcome appears to serve a greater good. These tensions are why codes of ethics in professional practice provide explicit guidance rather than relying on each practitioner to reason through every situation independently.

Laws and Their Sources

Laws represent the minimum standard of conduct a society requires and enforces. An action may be legal yet unethical, or ethical yet technically illegal under a given legal system. Historical examples illustrate this plainly: practices that were lawful in one era are now recognized as profoundly wrong. Ethical reasoning asks more of a professional than simply staying on the legal side of the line.

Law in the United States derives from five principal sources:

- Constitutional law, which establishes the framework and limits of government authority.
- Statutory law, which consists of laws enacted by legislatures at the federal, state, or local level.
- Treaties, which govern relationships between the United States and other nations.

- Administrative regulations, which are rules issued by government agencies such as TREC under authority delegated by statute.
- Common law, which develops through court decisions over time and fills gaps not addressed by statute.

Real estate law is a branch of civil law governing the rights to possess, use, and enjoy land and the structures permanently attached to it. It encompasses ownership rights and interests, sales and purchases, transfers of title, landlord-tenant relationships, zoning, development, mortgage lending, and foreclosure. Texas licensees operate within a layered framework of federal, state, and local law, and must remain current on developments in all three.

The NAR Code of Ethics: Background

The National Association of REALTORS was founded in 1908. In 1913, the Association adopted the first industry-wide code of ethical conduct in American real estate practice. At that time, no state licensing laws yet governed the profession. The Code of Ethics was created to establish a professional standard where none existed, and it subsequently served as a model for the license laws that states began enacting in subsequent decades.

The Code of Ethics serves multiple purposes. It protects the public by requiring truthful and honest communication and by placing client interests above the licensee's own. It benefits REALTORS, brokerage firms, and local associations by elevating the profession's credibility and integrity. It requires disclosure of material facts relevant to properties and transactions, and it ensures that competitive behavior among licensees remains secondary to client interests.

> *The NAR Code of Ethics is reviewed and updated annually. The current version, effective January 2026, reflects the most recent revisions approved by the NAR Board of Directors. Texas licensees who are REALTORS are bound by this version. Courts have also applied Code of Ethics principles to non-REALTOR licensees when evaluating professional standards in litigation.*

Code of Ethics and General Business Ethics

General business ethics in any industry encompass values, principles, and the judgment to act on them even when doing so is not legally required. Educators, physicians, accountants, attorneys, and many other professions maintain formal codes of ethical conduct. The NAR Code of Ethics shares that tradition but applies it specifically to the conduct of REALTOR members in real estate transactions.

NAR was a pioneer: it established a code of ethics before laws governed the profession. Most industries developed their codes of conduct after regulation was already in place. This history reflects the real estate industry's early recognition that professional self-governance was essential to public trust.

Within a brokerage, ethical culture starts at the top. When the broker and office leadership demonstrate high ethical standards consistently, the agents and staff in the office are far more likely to follow that example. Ethics training, policy documentation, and active supervision are the tools that translate a commitment to ethics into consistent day-to-day practice.

Articles, Standards of Practice, and Case Interpretations

The NAR Code of Ethics is organized into three components:

Articles: Broad statements of ethical principle that define the obligations of REALTOR members. Only the Articles may serve as the basis for a formal ethics violation complaint.

Standards of Practice: Specific statements that explain, support, and amplify the Articles. Standards of Practice may be cited to support an alleged Article violation but cannot stand alone as the basis for a complaint.

Case Interpretations: Published decisions from actual ethics proceedings that illustrate how the Articles have been applied in specific situations. They may not be used as a basis for a complaint but provide useful context for understanding how the Code is enforced in practice.

The Code of Ethics is a living document, revised annually by NAR as the profession evolves. Technology changes, new business models, shifting compensation practices, and evolving standards of consumer protection have all prompted additions and revisions over the years. Article 17 of the Code requires that REALTOR members resolve monetary disputes through arbitration rather than litigation, reflecting the profession's longstanding preference for internal resolution of financial conflicts.

Federal Laws Governing Conduct

Texas licensees must be aware of several federal laws that directly govern their conduct in real estate transactions. The Fair Housing Act of 1968, significantly strengthened by the 1988 amendments, prohibits discrimination based on race, color, religion, national origin, sex, disability, and familial status in the sale, rental, and financing of housing.

The Department of Housing and Urban Development (HUD) administers and enforces the Fair Housing Act through its Office of Fair Housing and Equal Opportunity (FHEO). HUD actively investigates potential violations, including through the use of trained testers who contact real estate offices as prospective buyers or renters. Offices may be visited by testers of different backgrounds on separate occasions to determine whether the service provided is consistent.

When a complaint is filed, FHEO investigates and determines whether reasonable cause exists to believe discrimination occurred. If reasonable cause is found, a Charge of Discrimination is issued and a hearing before a HUD administrative law judge is scheduled. Either party may instead elect to have the matter heard in federal court, in which case the Department of Justice assumes the enforcement role. All proceedings are subject to review by the U.S. Court of Appeals. Licensees must treat all customers consistently and all clients consistently. The distinction between client and customer treatment that arises from fiduciary duties does not justify any difference in treatment based on a protected class.

Advertising Guidelines Under the Fair Housing Act

Section 804(c) of the Fair Housing Act prohibits any notice, statement, or advertisement related to the sale or rental of housing that indicates a preference, limitation, or discrimination based on any protected class. Both the advertiser and the publisher of a discriminatory advertisement may be held liable. Discriminatory housing advertising is not protected under the First Amendment because housing advertising is classified as commercial speech.

The following principles apply to advertising compliance:

- Advertisements must not express any preference or limitation based on race, color, religion, national origin, sex, disability, or familial status.
- Describing a property in racially or ethnically coded language is discriminatory, regardless of whether the language appears overtly discriminatory on its face.
- Advertisements may not include explicit religious preferences such as "Christian home only" or "no members of a particular faith."
- Describing a property's features, such as a chapel on the premises, does not constitute discriminatory advertising if no preference for a particular religion is explicitly stated.
- The term "master bedroom" does not constitute a gender or race-based violation. Common descriptive terms like "mother-in-law suite" or "bachelor apartment" describe physical configurations and are not considered discriminatory.
- Advertisements may not exclude or discourage persons with disabilities. Advertisements that describe accessible features are lawful.
- Advertisements may not limit the number or ages of children, state a preference for adults only, or discourage families.
- Descriptions of property features, services, facilities, or neighborhood characteristics are generally not discriminatory. Conduct-based requirements such as "no smoking" are also acceptable.

Internet Advertising and the Fair Housing Act

The Fair Housing Act's advertising prohibition applies to all media without exception. Newspapers, television, radio, and websites are all subject to the same standard. HUD has determined that websites may not publish discriminatory housing advertisements and will investigate and issue a Determination of Reasonable Cause when there is evidence that a website has done so.

Some website operators have argued that Section 230 of the Communications Decency Act (CDA) provides immunity from Fair Housing Act liability for third-party content posted by users. HUD has concluded that the CDA does not exempt websites from Fair Housing Act obligations or from liability under state and local fair housing laws that HUD has certified as substantially equivalent to the federal Act. Licensees who maintain websites or use digital platforms to advertise properties should ensure that all content, including user-generated content on their platforms, complies with fair housing standards.

Federal Lending Discrimination: The Equal Credit Opportunity Act

The Equal Credit Opportunity Act (ECOA) is a federal lending law that prohibits discrimination in any aspect of a credit transaction. While it is primarily directed at lenders, it affects how property is acquired and financed, and Texas licensees should understand its scope.

The ECOA prohibits discrimination based on race, color, religion, national origin, sex, marital status, age (when the applicant has legal capacity to contract), receipt of public assistance income, or good-faith exercise of rights under the Consumer Credit Protection Act. The Act applies to all forms of credit, including loans to individuals, businesses, partnerships, and trusts.

Under the ECOA, a lender may not withhold or vary the information or services it provides in the lending process based on any of the prohibited factors. This includes application procedures, credit standards, loan terms, interest rates, collateral evaluation, servicing practices, or secondary market treatment. Licensees who observe or suspect lending discrimination in connection with a transaction should advise the affected client to seek counsel or file a complaint with the Consumer Financial Protection Bureau.

The Texas Deceptive Trade Practices Act

The Texas Deceptive Trade Practices-Consumer Protection Act (DTPA), enacted in 1973, is a general consumer protection statute that applies across industries, including real estate. Brokers and agents can be held liable under the DTPA for false, misleading, or deceptive business practices, unconscionable conduct, and breaches of warranty.

The DTPA identifies 25 specific practices as illegal without requiring proof of intent. This no-fault structure makes violations easier to establish and creates a strong incentive for all service providers to avoid the enumerated prohibited acts. If a defendant acted intentionally, the court may award additional damages up to three times the actual damages suffered by the consumer.

Enforcement of the DTPA occurs through two channels:

Public enforcement: The Consumer Protection Division of the Texas Attorney General's Office may seek temporary restraining orders, temporary or permanent injunctions, and civil penalties of up to $2,000 per violation, not to exceed $10,000 in total. Courts may also order restitution to affected consumers. Violating an injunction carries an additional civil penalty of up to $10,000 per violation, with a cap of $50,000. Enforcement actions require at least seven days' prior written notice to the alleged violator.

Private remedies: An individual consumer may bring a private action for damages caused by prohibited conduct. If the defendant acted intentionally, treble damages may be awarded.

The DTPA provides a limited exemption for publishers, broadcasters, and similar media when the false statement originated with the advertiser and the media outlet had no actual knowledge of it and no substantial financial interest in the transaction.

The Texas Administrative Code Canons of Professional Ethics

Title 22 of the Texas Administrative Code, Chapter 531, sets out five canons of professional ethics and conduct that apply to all Texas real estate licensees. These canons are part of TREC's rules and carry the force of law. They are consistent with federal fair housing requirements, common law agency principles, and the ethical standards established by professional trade associations.

The five canons are:

Fidelity

A licensee must represent the interests of their client and subordinate their own interests to those of the client. In carrying out those duties, the licensee must make their position clear to all parties in the transaction, treat other parties fairly, honor the trust placed in them, perform their duties carefully and thoroughly, and never place personal interests above the client's interests.

Integrity

A licensee must perform their responsibilities with care and honesty, and must take particular caution to avoid misrepresentation through both acts of commission, such as making false statements, and acts of omission, such as failing to disclose material information that the licensee knew or should have known.

Competence

A licensee must maintain working knowledge of real estate practice, stay current on market conditions, pursue continuing education, remain informed on national, state, and local developments in the industry, and apply sound judgment and skill in performing their work. Competence is an ongoing obligation, not a one-time standard achieved at licensing.

Consumer Information Form

Every active Texas real estate broker licensed by TREC must display Consumer Information Form 1-1 prominently in each business location maintained by the broker. This form informs consumers of their rights and provides contact information for TREC.

Discriminatory Practices

No Texas real estate licensee may inquire about, respond to, facilitate, or disclose information that indicates or is intended to indicate any preference, limitation, or discrimination based on a protected class.

Protected classes under Texas law include race, color, religion, sex, national origin, ancestry, familial status, and disability. The disability category expressly includes persons who have or have had AIDS, HIV-related illness, or HIV infection as defined by the U.S. Centers for Disease Control and Prevention.

The TREC Complaint Process

Any person who believes a licensee has violated TRELA may file a complaint with TREC. If TREC has jurisdiction, its enforcement division will investigate by interviewing the parties and witnesses and gathering relevant documentation. If the investigation supports a finding of a violation, TREC will notify the licensee and initiate a disciplinary proceeding.

TREC prioritizes its complaint workload using a risk-based approach that weighs:

- The degree and immediacy of potential harm to the consumer.
- The overall severity of the alleged conduct.
- The number of licensees potentially involved.
- The prior complaint history of the licensee.
- The number of potential violations alleged.

Consumer complaints receive priority consideration. Following a hearing or settlement, TREC may impose a reprimand, license suspension, license revocation, a monetary fine, probation, or any combination of these sanctions. TREC may also order a licensee to pay a refund to the affected consumer as part of an informal settlement or enforcement order, in addition to any other sanction imposed (TRELA Section 1101.659).

TREC Advisory Letters

In cases where the conduct identified in a complaint does not rise to the level warranting formal discipline, TREC may close the complaint file by issuing an advisory letter to the licensee. An advisory letter is appropriate when the matter is technical in nature, when the rule at issue is newly adopted, or when procedural obstacles such as unavailable witnesses make formal proceedings impractical.

An advisory letter is not a disciplinary sanction. It serves as a formal notice that the investigation revealed conduct that, while not warranting immediate discipline, could lead to future complaints and eventual disciplinary action if not corrected. Licensees who receive an advisory letter should treat it as a signal to review and correct their practices.

TREC is also required to adopt procedures for informal disposition of contested cases. These proceedings must provide both the complainant and the licensee an opportunity to be heard and must include a public member of the Commission when the case involves a consumer complaint. In cases where the evidence suggests the licensee poses a risk to the public, TREC's presiding officer may convene a three-member disciplinary panel to determine whether a temporary license suspension is warranted (TRELA Sections 1101.660 and 1101.662).

Association Complaints and the Citation Program

Ethics complaints against REALTOR members may be filed with the local association to which the member belongs. The Texas REALTORS, the National Association of Real Estate Brokers (NAREB), and other trade associations maintain their own complaint resolution processes. A grievance panel conducts an initial review to determine whether the complaint alleges a violation of the applicable code of ethics. If it does, a hearing panel is convened to receive testimony and evidence, determine whether a violation occurred, and impose any warranted discipline.

Association disciplinary sanctions may include a reprimand, a fine, probation, suspension of membership, revocation of membership, or any combination. The parties are notified of their appeal rights following any panel decision.

The Texas REALTORS implemented a citation program to provide a faster resolution pathway for ethics complaints involving certain NAR Code of Ethics articles. A grievance tribunal first determines whether the complaint qualifies for the citation track. If a citation is issued, the respondent is informed of their right to request a full due process hearing rather than pay the citation fine. Agreed-to citations result in fines and required educational coursework.

Receiving Fees from Service Providers

When a licensee receives a commission, rebate, or other fee from a service provider in connection with a transaction, two obligations apply. First, the licensee must obtain consent from their principal. Second, the licensee must disclose to the person being referred that the licensee is receiving compensation from the service provider.

As a general rule, a licensee may not share a commission or fee with an unlicensed person. However, TREC rules recognize specific limited exceptions:

1. A licensee may give a gift certificate valued at no more than $50 to an unlicensed person. The gift certificate may not be exchangeable for cash, and the licensee may not give cash in lieu of the certificate.
2. A licensee may pay a rebate to a buyer or seller in a transaction, provided the licensee first obtains written consent from the party they represent.
3. A business entity licensed as a broker may share income with an unlicensed owner of that entity, provided the unlicensed owner does not personally engage in real estate brokerage activity. This recognizes that passive ownership of a licensed brokerage entity does not require a real estate license.

Residential Service Company Disclosure

Brokers and salespersons are sometimes paid fees by residential service companies for advertising and promotional services rendered on the company's behalf. These arrangements are separate from the agent's ordinary transaction services and must be disclosed.

TREC requires licensees to use form RSC-3, Disclosure of Relationship with Residential Service Company, to disclose such fees in writing to their client. If the licensee is not receiving any fee from a residential service company, the form is not required. However, if the licensee or their sponsoring broker is being compensated by a residential service company for advertising services unrelated to any single transaction, the licensee must disclose those payments to any client in a transaction that falls within the compensation period.

The RSC-3 form should not be attached to the purchase contract as an addendum. It should be retained in the transaction file maintained by the broker as documentation that the required disclosure was made.

Disclosure of Shared Commissions

TAC Section 535.147 addresses the limits on commission sharing and the disclosure obligations that apply:

- A licensee may not share a commission with an unlicensed person except as specifically authorized by TRELA or TREC rules.
- An unlicensed person may share in the income of a licensed business entity so long as the unlicensed person does not personally perform brokerage activities.
- A licensee may not share a commission with an unlicensed corporation or LLC that was created for the purpose of collecting compensation on the licensee's behalf. Such entities are not a permissible vehicle for routing commission income around licensing requirements.
- A licensee may not enter into an exclusive service contract with a service provider that prohibits the licensee from also contracting with competing providers. Licensees must retain their freedom to recommend competing services.
- A licensee may not accept a fee from a service provider when the fee is contingent on the buyer or seller actually purchasing a product or service from that provider. Contingent referral fees create an undisclosed conflict of interest.

The Real Estate Recovery Trust Account

TREC maintains the Real Estate Recovery Trust Account, funded by fees collected from licensees, to compensate members of the public who have suffered financial harm caused by a licensee's misconduct and have obtained a final court judgment that cannot otherwise be collected.

Eligible claims must involve a person who was licensed by TREC as a salesperson, broker, or easement and right-of-way agent at the time of the conduct at issue. If the licensee was acting as a buyer, seller, landlord, or tenant in the transaction, the claim must involve fraud, misrepresentation, or dishonest conduct. If the licensee was acting as an agent or broker representing a party, the claim may also involve negligence, incompetence, or conduct prohibited by TRELA Section 1101.652(b).

Conduct that does not involve the licensee acting in a real estate capacity, such as a breach of a construction contract, a failed investment arrangement unrelated to brokerage, or a default on a personal promissory note, is not covered by the Trust Account.

Many claims are resolved without a court hearing once TREC has reviewed the documentation and determined that the statutory requirements are met. TREC will request additional documentation as needed and, if the requirements are satisfied, may authorize payment without a contested proceeding. The maximum payment from the Trust Account is $125,000 for a single transaction and $250,000 for all claims arising from the conduct of a single licensee.

Escrow Account Ethics and Rules

Mishandling of escrow funds is among the most frequently cited real estate regulatory violations nationwide. The category of mishandling covers a range of conduct, including mixing escrow money with business operating funds, failing to maintain required records, neglecting to collect required deposits, borrowing from escrow accounts, and making unauthorized disbursements.

Escrow funds are money provided by a buyer with an offer to demonstrate good faith. Once an offer is accepted, these funds are held in trust for both parties until settlement, at which point they are applied to the purchase price in exchange for the deed. The escrow holder has a fiduciary obligation to safeguard and accurately account for all funds entrusted to their care.

Two TAC rules govern escrow account management for Texas licensees: Rule 535.159, which addresses the deposit of escrow funds, and Rule 535.146, which addresses proper accounting and the prohibition on commingling.

TAC Rule 535.159: Depositing Escrow Funds

The key provisions of TAC Rule 535.159 are:

- A broker is not required to maintain a trust account unless the broker accepts trust funds belonging to others.
- When a broker accepts funds for deposit in escrow, the broker becomes a trustee accountable to both the depositing party and the party for whose benefit the funds are held.
- The principals to a transaction determine who will serve as escrow agent. A broker may not require the parties to designate the broker as their escrow agent.
- Nonresident brokers conducting transactions in Texas who accept trust funds must deposit those funds in a trust account at a banking institution or title company authorized to do business in Texas.

- A broker may use a savings account as a trust account, provided funds can be withdrawn at the appropriate time. Any interest earned on a savings account trust must be distributed to the equitable owners of the funds during the period the interest accrued, unless the depositing parties have agreed otherwise in writing.
- A salesperson may not maintain a trust account and may not act as escrow agent. All trust funds received by a salesperson in connection with a real estate transaction must be delivered immediately to the sponsoring broker for deposit in accordance with the principals' agreement.
- A broker may maintain separate trust accounts for earnest money deposits, security deposits from property management, and other trust funds, but is not required to do so.
- Any trust account maintained by a broker must be clearly identified as a trust account.
- Unless the parties have expressly agreed in writing to a different timeline, "reasonable time" for deposit means by the close of business on the second working day after the contract is executed by the principals.
- A broker who accepts a check as escrow agent and later learns the check has been dishonored must immediately notify all parties to the transaction in writing.

TAC Rule 535.146: Accounting and Commingling

TAC Rule 535.146 governs how brokers account for trust funds and prohibits the mixing of trust funds with other money:

- A broker who holds trust funds must maintain a separate trust account or use a title company as escrow agent.
- A broker may authorize a salesperson to sign on a trust account, but the broker remains solely responsible and accountable for all deposits to and withdrawals from the account.
- A salesperson must immediately deliver to their sponsoring broker any trust funds received in connection with a real estate transaction that have not been deposited directly with a title company.
- A licensee maintaining a trust account must retain records of every deposit and withdrawal for a minimum of four years.
- A licensee may not commingle trust funds with personal funds or business operating funds. Depositing or holding trust funds in any account other than a specifically designated broker trust account is prohibited.
- A licensee who holds money belonging to others holds those funds in a fiduciary capacity.
- If any party to a transaction makes demand for the money, the licensee must properly account for or remit the funds within 30 days. If it cannot be determined to whom the funds should be paid, the licensee may pay the money into the registry of the court and interplead the parties.
- When a broker makes a disbursement that all parties have not expressly authorized in writing, the broker must immediately notify all parties in writing.
- Placing trust funds in a licensee's operating account is prima facie evidence of commingling.

- Once the licensee acquires ownership of funds held in the trust account, such as an earned commission, those funds must be removed from the trust account within 30 days.
- The trust account balance must at all times equal the total of all trust funds for which the broker is accountable. A broker may deposit and maintain a reasonable amount of personal funds in the trust account solely to cover bank service fees, but detailed records of any such deposit must be maintained.

Minimum Ethical Standards

A code of ethics is a set of conduct principles, grounded in ideas of what is right and wrong, that guides professional decision-making and behavior. Its purpose is to give members and the public a clear framework for evaluating whether conduct meets professional standards. Professional integrity is central to any practitioner's credibility, and adopting a formal code is how an organization publicly declares its values and standards.

An important distinction separates law from ethics. Obeying the law is the floor of acceptable conduct in society. Ethics demand more than legal compliance. Lying, for example, is unethical in virtually all circumstances, but it becomes illegal only in specific contexts, such as perjury under oath. Business ethics and the codes that define them always reach beyond strict legality and hold practitioners to a higher standard.

The sources that have shaped the real estate code of ethics fall into three categories: federal and state anti-discrimination and fair trade laws; state-level real estate licensing regulations governing agency and disclosure; and self-regulation by professional associations that establish standards of conduct beyond what law requires.

The NAR Code of Ethics was created to give REALTORS a higher standard to pursue than the law alone provides. Many state real estate commissions, including Texas through the TAC canons, have incorporated similar principles into their governing regulations. The Code requires disclosure of material facts about properties and transactions, protects client interests, and insists that competitive behavior between licensees remain subordinate to client welfare.

Structure of the Code of Ethics

The NAR Code of Ethics is organized into four sections:

Preamble: Sets out guiding principles and aspirational statements about professional conduct. Contains no specific, enforceable requirements. May not be cited in an ethics complaint.

Duties to Clients and Customers: Articles 1 through 9. Defines the obligations licensees owe to the people they represent and work with in transactions.

Duties to the Public: Articles 10 through 14. Defines the broader obligations licensees owe to the public, including non-discrimination, truthful advertising, and compliance with the law.

Duties to REALTORS: Articles 15 through 17. Defines how REALTOR members must treat one another, including honesty about colleagues and resolution of financial disputes.

The Code currently consists of 17 Articles, each supported by one or more Standards of Practice. The Code is a living document, reviewed and amended annually by the NAR Professional Standards Committee.

The Preamble

The Preamble articulates the values and aspirations that should guide a REALTOR's conduct. Among the principles it addresses, a REALTOR should:

Stay informed on issues affecting the real estate industry and the communities they serve.

Identify and work to eliminate practices that damage the public or bring discredit to the industry.

Share professional knowledge and experience with colleagues.

Report to the appropriate association any knowledge of misappropriation of client funds, willful discrimination, or fraud.

Avoid seeking unfair competitive advantage over other licensees.

Refrain from making unfair or disparaging comments about other professionals.

Represent clients loyally and exclusively.

Offer professional opinions in an objective, impartial manner, free from personal interest or anticipated gain.

The Preamble concludes with a pledge to observe the spirit of the Code in all professional and personal activities and to conduct business in accordance with the Articles. Because the Preamble contains no specific enforceable obligations, it may never be cited in an ethics complaint. Only the Articles may be named as the basis for a violation.

The Articles: An Overview

Duties to Clients and Customers (Articles 1-9)

Article 1: Protect and promote the client's interests while treating all parties honestly.

Article 2: Avoid exaggeration, misrepresentation, or concealment of pertinent facts about properties or transactions.

Article 3: Cooperate with other real estate professionals to advance the client's best interests.

Article 4: Disclose true position or interest when buying or selling on the REALTOR's own account, for family members, or for their firm.

Article 5: Disclose any present or contemplated personal interest in a property before providing professional services related to it.

Article 6: Disclose any fee, rebate, or financial benefit received from recommending related real estate products or services.

Article 7: Accept compensation from only one party in a transaction except with full disclosure to all parties and the informed consent of the REALTOR's client.

Article 8: Hold client and customer funds in a separate escrow account.

Article 9: Ensure that all contract terms are in writing and that all parties receive copies.

Duties to the Public (Articles 10-14)

Article 10: Provide equal professional services to all without regard to race, color, religion, sex, disability, familial status, national origin, sexual orientation, or gender identity. Do not harass any person based on these protected characteristics.

Article 11: Be competent in every area of practice, or disclose limitations and obtain appropriate professional assistance.

Article 12: Present a truthful and accurate picture in all advertising and public representations.

Article 13: Do not engage in the unauthorized practice of law.

Article 14: Cooperate fully with ethics investigations and enforcement proceedings.

Duties to REALTORS (Articles 15-17)

Article 15: Make only truthful, objective statements about other real estate professionals.

Article 16: Respect the exclusive representation or exclusive brokerage relationship agreements that other REALTORS have with their clients.

Article 17: Resolve financial disagreements with other REALTORS and with clients through mediation and, if unresolved, arbitration rather than litigation.

> ***2026 Update: Article 10 and SOP 10-5 (effective June 5, 2025).*** *SOP 10-5 was revised to create a more specific and enforceable definition of harassment, aligned with the NAR Member Code of Conduct. Under the revised standard, REALTORS are prohibited from harassing any person based on a protected characteristic in their capacity as real estate professionals, in association with their real estate businesses, or in their real estate-related activities. Harassment is defined as unwelcome behavior directed at an individual or group based on a protected characteristic where the purpose or effect is to create a hostile, abusive, or intimidating environment that adversely affects equal access to professional services or employment. Additionally, Policy Statement 29 was amended to focus the entire Code of Ethics' application on conduct occurring in a professional context, consistent with how other major trade associations apply their ethical codes.*

Standards of Practice

Each Article is a broad statement of ethical principle. Accompanying each Article are one or more Standards of Practice that explain, support, and amplify the Article's meaning in specific situations. The number of Standards of Practice per Article varies widely, from none for some Articles to as many as 16 or more for others.

A REALTOR cannot be found to have violated a Standard of Practice directly. Violations are always of the Article itself. A Standard of Practice may, however, be cited to support and clarify the basis for an alleged Article violation. Case interpretations from prior ethics proceedings may illustrate how an Article has been applied but also cannot be named as the basis for a complaint.

Enforcing the Code of Ethics

Local Associations of REALTORS are responsible for enforcing the Code of Ethics. Only NAR members are subject to it. Associations that receive and decide ethics complaints and arbitration requests must be the associations of which the respondent is a member or through which the respondent accesses MLS services.

Associations do not determine whether a licensee has violated any law or real estate regulation. That authority belongs to TREC, courts, and other regulatory bodies. The association's role is limited to the Code of Ethics.

Many disputes between real estate professionals originate in misunderstanding or poor communication rather than intentional misconduct. When those situations arise, direct professional discussion often resolves the matter without formal proceedings. When that fails, licensees have two paths: informal dispute resolution or formal action through an ethics complaint or arbitration request.

Informal Dispute Resolution: Ombudsman

Ombudsman services offer a voluntary, informal pathway for resolving misunderstandings before they become formal complaints. An ombudsman does not adjudicate disputes or render judgments about who is right or wrong. The focus is entirely on communication, helping the parties understand each other's positions and reach a mutually acceptable resolution without coercion.

Ombudsmen do not determine whether an ethics violation occurred. Their role is preventive: to identify, address, and defuse misunderstandings before they escalate into formal proceedings. Ombudsman programs are available only if the local association offers the service, and participation by all parties is voluntary.

A real estate ombudsman should be knowledgeable about the Code of Ethics, state real estate regulations, and standard industry practices. The ombudsman may be a REALTOR, an association staff member, or another qualified individual. If the dispute is resolved through the ombudsman process, the complaint is considered discharged. If one party refuses to participate or fails to honor a mutually agreed resolution, the other party may file or re-file a formal ethics complaint.

Informal Dispute Resolution: Mediation

Mediation is an informal, voluntary process in which a trained neutral third party, the mediator, facilitates a conversation between the disputing parties. Each side presents its view of the issue. The mediator works with both parties to identify common ground and assist them in reaching a negotiated settlement. Mediation is non-binding: the mediator does not impose a decision but instead helps the parties arrive at an outcome they can both accept.

Mediation is the preferred dispute resolution method of REALTOR organizations because it produces a mutually agreed outcome without requiring a hearing panel to impose a judgment. Local associations may offer mediation before or after a grievance committee's review of an arbitration request. If the association offers pre-review mediation, it must also offer mediation again after the grievance committee makes its determination. When mediation results in a settlement, the parties document the agreement in writing and a formal arbitration hearing becomes unnecessary.

Formal Dispute Resolution: Ethics Complaints

Any person, whether a member of the public or a licensee, may file a formal ethics complaint with the local association against a REALTOR member. Filing through the association gives consumers an alternative to civil litigation and provides a faster, less expensive resolution pathway.

An ethics complaint must identify the specific Article or Articles of the Code that the complainant believes were violated. Standards of Practice may be cited to support the Article, but the complaint is built around the Article. Once filed, the complaint goes first to the grievance committee and, if it passes initial review, to a full hearing panel.

Grievance Committee Review

The grievance committee conducts a preliminary review of every ethics complaint. This is not a hearing on the merits. The committee's role is to determine whether the complaint alleges facts that, if taken as true, could constitute a violation of the Code of Ethics and whether the procedural requirements for the complaint have been met.

The committee confirms the following before forwarding a complaint to a hearing panel:

- The complaint is in the proper format.
- The appropriate parties are identified.
- The complaint was filed within 180 days of the alleged conduct.
- Specific Articles are cited.
- The association can provide an impartial hearing panel.

- The respondent is a member and was a member at the time of the alleged violation.
- If related criminal or civil proceedings are pending, the committee determines the appropriate course. For pending criminal matters, the file is held until legal proceedings conclude. For pending civil matters, the association's legal counsel reviews whether the ethics hearing should proceed.
- The alleged facts, taken as true, describe a possible Code violation.

If all conditions are satisfied, the complaint proceeds to a full ethics hearing panel.

Ethics Hearing Panel

The ethics hearing panel conducts a full due-process proceeding that includes sworn testimony, the opportunity to present evidence and witnesses, and the right to be represented by counsel. Panel members are drawn from the association's professional standards committee.

After the hearing, the panel determines whether a violation occurred. Any finding of violation must be supported by clear, strong, and compelling evidence. If a violation is found, the panel determines the appropriate disciplinary sanction. Possible sanctions include:

- Letter of warning
- Letter of reprimand
- Required education
- Fine not to exceed $5,000
- Probation for a period of up to one year
- Suspension of membership for not less than 30 days and not more than one year
- Expulsion from membership for a period of one to three years
- Suspension or termination of MLS privileges

An administrative processing fee not to exceed $500 may also be assessed. The panel may impose more than one form of discipline. More severe or repeated violations warrant more serious sanctions. The primary purpose of discipline is to create awareness of and respect for the Code, not to punish.

> ***Important:*** *The ethics hearing panel does not have authority to suspend or revoke a real estate license. That authority belongs exclusively to TREC. The panel's jurisdiction is limited to association membership and MLS access.*

Arbitration

While ethics complaints address violations of the Code of Ethics, arbitration is used primarily to resolve monetary disputes between broker members of an association. Article 17 of the Code requires REALTOR members to resolve contractual disputes and specified non-contractual disputes through mediation first, and if unresolved through mediation, through arbitration rather than litigation.

The grievance committee also performs an initial screening of arbitration requests, similar to its review of ethics complaints. The key question is whether, if the claims in the arbitration request are accepted as true, the matter involves a real estate transaction that is appropriate for arbitration and could support a monetary award. This initial review is not a hearing on the merits.

Arbitration Hearing Panel

An arbitration hearing follows the same due-process structure as an ethics hearing: sworn testimony, evidence, witnesses, and the right to counsel. Panel members are drawn from the professional standards committee.

The panel determines which party is entitled to the disputed commission or other monetary award, based on a preponderance of the evidence. The panel applies NAR's Arbitration Guidelines from the Code of Ethics and Arbitration Manual. The central question in most arbitration cases is procuring cause: which licensee initiated and maintained an uninterrupted series of events that resulted in the completed transaction.

No single factor establishes procuring cause. The panel considers all pertinent conduct, including the first showing of the property, the circumstances under which any offer was written and accepted, continuity of contact with the buyer or seller, and the nature of the relationships between the parties. After considering all relevant evidence, the panel awards the commission to the party whose claim is better supported. Awards may be judicially enforced if not paid voluntarily by the non-prevailing party.

Article 1: Protecting Client Interests

Article 1 states that REALTORS protect and promote their clients' interests while treating all parties honestly. This primary obligation exists whether the REALTOR is acting as a conventional agent or in a legally recognized non-agency capacity such as a transaction broker or facilitator. The obligations of the Code apply even when the REALTOR is a principal to the transaction rather than a representative of a party.

Article 1 establishes the following key definitions:

Client: The person or entity with whom the REALTOR or the REALTOR's firm has an agency or legally recognized non-agency relationship.

Customer: A party to a transaction who receives information, services, or benefits but has no contractual relationship with the REALTOR or the REALTOR's firm.

Prospect: A purchaser, seller, tenant, or landlord who is not subject to a representation relationship with the REALTOR or the REALTOR's firm.

Agent: A real estate licensee, including brokers and sales associates, acting in an agency relationship as defined by state law or regulation.

Broker: A real estate licensee, including brokers and sales associates, acting as an agent or in a legally recognized non-agency capacity.

Key Standards of Practice Under Article 1

Truthfulness About Value (SOP 1-3)

REALTORS are prohibited from deliberately misleading property owners about market value. Overstating value to secure a listing, understating value to facilitate a quick sale, or misleading buyers or tenants about savings or other financial benefits all constitute violations.

Dual Agency (SOP 1-5)

A REALTOR may act as a disclosed dual agent only with the full disclosure and written, informed consent of both parties. This Standard is consistent with Texas intermediary requirements under TRELA.

Offer Presentation (SOP 1-6)

REALTORS must present all offers and counter-offers to their clients objectively and as quickly as possible. A listing broker must continue to present all offers until closing or execution of a lease unless the seller or landlord specifically waives this obligation in writing. A REALTOR is not obligated to continue marketing a property after an offer has been accepted.

Recommending Legal Counsel (SOPs 1-7 and 1-8)

REALTORS must advise clients to seek legal counsel whenever the circumstances warrant it. Sellers and landlords must be advised to consult an attorney before accepting a subsequent offer unless that acceptance is contingent on termination of the existing contract or lease. Buyer and tenant clients should similarly be advised to obtain legal counsel when there is any uncertainty about whether a prior contractual obligation has been terminated.

Confidentiality (SOP 1-9)

REALTORS are obligated to protect the confidential information provided by their clients throughout the agency relationship and after it ends. Confidential information may not be disclosed or used to the disadvantage of a former client without authorization, except under the following circumstances:

- When required by a court order.

- To prevent the client from committing a crime.
- To defend the REALTOR against an allegation of wrongful conduct.

Information about latent material defects in the property is not treated as confidential under the Code and must be disclosed.

Property Management (SOPs 1-10 and 1-11)

REALTORS who manage property must do so competently and with due regard for the rights, safety, and health of tenants and others lawfully on the premises, in compliance with real estate license laws and the terms of the management agreement. REALTORS must also exercise due diligence in working to protect clients against foreseeable contingencies and losses.

Advising About Cooperation and Compensation (SOPs 1-12 and 1-13)

When entering into a listing agreement, a REALTOR must advise the seller or landlord of the firm's policy on cooperation with other brokers, the total compensation to be paid by the client, and the amount, if any, that will be offered to cooperating brokers. The seller must also be advised that other agents may represent the buyer's interests even while receiving compensation from the listing side, and that the REALTOR may act as a disclosed intermediary.

Buyer clients must be informed that sellers or their representatives may not treat the existence, terms, or conditions of their offer as confidential.

Appraisal Fees (SOP 1-14)

Fees for appraisals or other valuations may not be contingent upon the dollar amount of the appraisal. Appraisal fees may be based on the size or complexity of the assignment. This principle is also embodied in the Uniform Standards of Professional Appraisal Practice (USPAP).

Disclosing Existence of Other Offers (SOPs 1-15 and 1-16)

When buyers or cooperating brokers ask whether other offers exist on a property, the listing REALTOR must, with the seller's approval, disclose that other offers are present. If the seller approves disclosure and the inquiry is made, the REALTOR must also disclose, if asked, whether the existing offer was obtained by the listing agent, another agent in the listing firm, or a cooperating broker.

SOP 1-16 prohibits a REALTOR from accessing, using, or permitting others to access or use a listed property on any terms or conditions other than those authorized by the owner. Buyers and tenants should always be accompanied by a REALTOR when viewing listed property.

Article 2: Truthfulness and Disclosure

Article 2 requires REALTORS to avoid exaggeration, misrepresentation, and concealment of pertinent facts related to a property or transaction. Facts defined as non-material by law, or that law expressly excludes from disclosure obligations, are not considered pertinent under this Article.

REALTORS are not obligated to discover latent defects, to advise on matters outside their license authority, or to disclose information that is properly treated as confidential. Their disclosure obligation is limited to adverse facts that would be reasonably apparent to a professional with the level of expertise required by their licensing authority. REALTORS are not engineers, attorneys, environmental consultants, or structural experts, and should not attempt to render opinions in those fields. Instead, they should recognize red flags that call for professional inspection or consultation and make appropriate referrals.

REALTORS are prohibited from presenting false consideration in any document, except in documents where nominal consideration is clearly identified as such. Indicating a false sale price on a contract constitutes mortgage fraud, a criminal offense extending well beyond a Code of Ethics violation.

Article 3: Cooperation and Compensation

Article 3 requires REALTORS to cooperate with other real estate professionals when cooperation advances the client's best interests. Cooperation is not required when it would work against the client's interests. The duty to cooperate encompasses sharing information about listed property and making property available for showing to other brokers when doing so serves the seller or landlord.

REALTORS may not refuse to cooperate on the basis of another broker's race, color, religion, sex, disability, familial status, national origin, sexual orientation, or gender identity.

Cooperation and Compensation Are Separate (SOP 3-1, as amended June 5, 2025)

An offer of cooperation does not automatically include an offer of compensation. Listing brokers and property managers work with sellers and landlords to establish the terms and conditions of offers to cooperate. Unless expressly stated in the offer to cooperate, cooperating brokers may not assume that the offer includes compensation. Before accepting an offer of cooperation, a cooperating broker must verify its terms. This change directly reflects the compensation practice framework established by the 2024 NAR settlement.

Changes to Offered Compensation (SOP 3-2, as amended June 5, 2025)

If the listing broker has offered compensation to cooperating brokers, any change to that offered compensation must be communicated as soon as practicable. A listing broker may not unilaterally modify offered compensation after a REALTOR has already submitted a purchase or lease offer. REALTORS are prohibited from delaying or withholding delivery of a buyer's or tenant's offer for the purpose of negotiating compensation. These ethical obligations do not prevent either party from negotiating compensation in the client's best interest, including within the terms of an offer to purchase or lease.

Dual or Variable Rate Commission Disclosure (SOP 3-4)

Listing brokers have a duty to disclose the existence of dual or variable rate commission arrangements, meaning listings where the commission payable differs depending on whether the listing firm is the procuring cause versus a cooperating broker or the seller acting independently. This disclosure must be made to potential cooperating brokers as soon as practicable. When asked, the listing broker must describe the differential that would result from a cooperative transaction. If the cooperating broker represents a buyer, that broker must disclose the information to the buyer before the buyer makes an offer.

Article 7 and Multi-Party Compensation (2026 Amendment)

Article 7 has been clarified to address compensation scenarios that have become common following the 2024 settlement. When a buyer has agreed in writing to compensate their broker at a specific amount, and some portion of that compensation comes from the listing side while the buyer is responsible for the remainder, the buyer's broker is technically receiving compensation from more than one source. The amended Code requires disclosure to all parties and the informed consent of the REALTOR's client. However, there is no obligation to disclose the contents of the buyer-broker agreement to the seller or the seller's broker, as they are not parties to that agreement.

Subagent Disclosure

Subagents must promptly disclose all pertinent facts to the principal's agent both before and after a purchase or lease agreement is executed. REALTORS must disclose the existence of accepted offers, including those with unresolved contingencies, to brokers who are seeking cooperation.

Property Access (SOP 3-9, as amended June 5, 2025)

When acting as a cooperating broker or in any capacity other than as a listing broker or property manager, a REALTOR may not access, use, or permit others to access or use a property on any terms or conditions other than those established by the owner or seller. All access must comply with the instructions provided in the listing.

Case Studies

The following case studies illustrate the application of Articles 1, 2, and 3. For each situation, consider which Articles were violated, if any, and which Standards of Practice support the analysis.

Case Study 1: The Multiple Offer Situation

Agent Rosa had an active listing with multiple showings over a short period. Agent Marco from another brokerage called Rosa to let her know he was preparing an offer and asked to schedule a presentation as soon as possible. Rosa explained that her seller was out of state and all offers would need to be presented by phone conference call. Marco asked Rosa to schedule the call and confirm a time.

Marco learned through a contact at Rosa's office that Rosa was herself writing an offer for a buyer she was also representing. By the time Marco had not heard back from Rosa by late afternoon, he went to her office and found her in the conference room with her buyer, in the process of placing a call to present her own offer.

Marco entered the room and insisted on presenting his offer simultaneously. Rosa's buyer became upset, tore up his offer, and left. Rosa called her seller and Marco presented his offer. The seller promised to respond within a few hours. After Marco left, Rosa contacted another buyer who had viewed the property and wrote an offer for that buyer at a price slightly above Marco's offer. Rosa then called the seller again with the new offer. The seller accepted this second offer.

Analysis. Marco's conduct does not present an obvious violation of Articles 1, 2, or 3. Rosa, however, committed multiple violations. By failing to present Marco's offer promptly after receiving it, she violated Article 1 and SOP 1-6, which requires offers to be submitted objectively and as quickly as possible. She appears to have disclosed the seller's willingness to accept less than list price to her own buyer without the seller's authorization, a violation of Article 1 supported by SOP 1-9, which protects confidential client information. Rosa also failed to disclose to Marco that another offer was being presented and that it was her own, a violation of SOP 1-15, which requires disclosure of existing offers with the seller's approval. If Rosa had the seller's permission to disclose, the failure to do so was a missed procedural obligation. If she did not have permission, presenting her own offer without informing the other party was a significant breach.

Case Study 2: The Overpriced Listing

Agent Diane presented a comparative market analysis to a seller showing a recommended list price of approximately $625,000. The seller insisted on listing at $699,000, citing a competing agent who had suggested a higher price. Diane explained the CMA a second time and advised the seller that listing at market value was in their best interest. After discussion, she listed the property at $699,000.

A month later, Diane was working with a buyer interested in the property. She had disclosed to both the buyer and the seller that she was acting as a disclosed dual agent in compliance with Texas intermediary requirements. Diane prepared an offer for the buyer at $610,000 without advising the buyer whether this amount was strong, weak, or appropriate. The seller refused the offer and countered at $685,000. The buyer countered at $622,000. The seller rejected that offer as well.

Analysis. Diane presented accurate market data and made a sound recommendation. Taking the listing at the seller's insistence above the CMA-suggested price did not violate the Code of Ethics. A Code violation would have occurred only if Diane had misled the owner about true market value, which she did not. Although Diane may have absorbed time and marketing costs marketing an overpriced property, her conduct was consistent with Article 1.

Case Study 3: The Undisclosed Rezoning Potential

Broker Grant listed a residential property on a large lot near a commercial corridor. He believed the home could sell for as much as $975,000 but recommended listing below $900,000 because he wanted a quick sale. The seller was unaware that the property could potentially be rezoned for commercial use, which could significantly increase its value. After listing the property, Grant learned of the rezoning potential. Rather than disclose this to the seller, he began showing the property to Phil, a commercial investor.

Grant also offered a reduced commission if he produced the buyer himself. He did not indicate the existence of this dual or variable rate commission arrangement in the listing information. A cooperating agent from another firm called to schedule a showing. Grant did not return the call and had no intention of doing so until he determined whether Phil would be writing an offer.

Analysis. Grant's failure to disclose the rezoning potential to his seller, information that materially affected the property's value, was a violation of Article 2. He also misrepresented the property's value by recommending a price well below what the market might support, which could also be construed as a violation of Article 2 and Article 1 (SOP 1-3). Grant's failure to disclose the dual commission arrangement to potential cooperating brokers violated Article 3, supported by SOP 3-4. His refusal to return the cooperating agent's call and make the property available for showing was a violation of Article 3.

Snapshot Review – Chapter 10

Ethics, Morals, and Laws Defined

Ethics: Standards of conduct expected of members of a group or profession, based on moral principles and extending beyond legal minimum requirements.

Morals: An individual's personal beliefs about what is right and wrong, derived from fundamental principles.

Laws: The minimum standards of conduct that a society requires and enforces. An action may be legal but unethical, or ethical but technically illegal.

NAR Code of Ethics

1. Adopted in 1913, before state licensing laws existed. The current version is effective January 1, 2025.
2. Only Articles may form the basis for an ethics violation complaint. Standards of Practice support Articles but cannot stand alone as a basis for a complaint.
3. The Code is a living document revised annually. Article 17 requires monetary disputes between REALTOR members to be resolved through arbitration.
4. Courts have applied Code of Ethics principles to non-REALTOR licensees as evidence of professional standards.

Federal Laws

Fair Housing Act (1968, amended 1988): Prohibits discrimination in the sale, rental, and financing of housing based on race, color, religion, national origin, sex, disability, and familial status. HUD enforces through investigation, testing, administrative hearings, and federal court referrals.

Section 804(c): Advertising: Applies to all media including websites. Both the publisher and advertiser may be held liable. Not protected by the First Amendment. The CDA does not exempt websites from Fair Housing Act liability.

Equal Credit Opportunity Act (ECOA): Prohibits discrimination in any aspect of a credit transaction. Covers race, color, religion, national origin, sex, marital status, age, public assistance income, and exercise of consumer credit rights.

Texas Laws

DTPA (1973): Protects consumers against false, misleading, or deceptive business practices. Identifies 25 prohibited practices without requiring proof of intent. Treble damages available for intentional violations. Public penalties up to $2,000 per violation, maximum $10,000. Injunction violations carry up to $10,000 per violation, maximum $50,000.

Texas Administrative Code: Five Canons

1. Fidelity: Represent the client's interests faithfully. Place no personal interest above the client's.
2. Integrity: Avoid misrepresentation by both acts of commission and omission.
3. Competence: Maintain current market knowledge, pursue continuing education, and exercise professional judgment.
4. Consumer Information Form: Display Consumer Information Form 1-1 prominently in every business location.
5. Discriminatory Practices: No inquiry about, facilitation of, or disclosure of preferences based on any protected class.

TREC Enforcement

1. Sanctions available: reprimand, suspension, revocation, fine, probation, consumer refund, or any combination.
2. An advisory letter is not disciplinary action. It identifies conduct that should be corrected to avoid future formal proceedings.
3. Consumer complaints receive priority. TREC uses a risk-based approach to prioritize investigation.

Fees, Commissions, and Disclosures

1. Fees from service providers require principal consent and disclosure to the referred party.
2. Unlicensed persons may not receive commissions. Exceptions: gift certificate up to $50 (non-cash), buyer/seller rebate with principal consent, passive income sharing by an unlicensed owner of a licensed entity.
3. RSC-1 form required to disclose residential service company compensation. Retained in transaction file, not attached to the contract.
4. Contingent referral fees and exclusive service provider contracts are prohibited.

Recovery Trust Account

1. Funded by licensee fees. Pays final judgments against licensees for fraud, misrepresentation, negligence, or incompetence in licensed activities.
2. Maximum payment: $50,000 per transaction; $100,000 total per licensee.

Escrow Accounts: Core Rules

1. A salesperson may not maintain a trust account or act as escrow agent. All trust funds must be delivered immediately to the sponsoring broker.
2. Deposit deadline: close of business on the second working day after contract execution, unless the parties agree otherwise in writing.
3. Trust funds must never be commingled with personal or business operating funds. Placing trust funds in an operating account is prima facie evidence of commingling.
4. Records of all deposits and withdrawals must be retained for a minimum of four years.

5. Earned commissions and other funds the broker acquires ownership of must be removed from the trust account within 30 days.
6. Trust account balance must at all times equal the total of all funds held in trust.

Code of Ethics Structure

Preamble: Aspirational guidance only. May not be cited in an ethics complaint.

Articles: Enforceable obligations. Only Articles may form the basis of a complaint. The Code contains 17 Articles.

Standards of Practice: Explain and amplify Articles. May support an alleged violation but cannot stand alone as a basis for a complaint.

Case Interpretations: Illustrate how Articles have been applied. Cannot be cited in complaints.

2026 Key Updates (Effective June 5, 2025)

1. SOP 10-5 (Article 10): Harassment is now defined as unwelcome behavior based on a protected characteristic that creates a hostile, abusive, or intimidating professional environment. The Code applies to REALTORS acting in their professional capacity and in connection with their real estate businesses.
2. SOP 3-1 (Article 3): An offer of cooperation no longer includes an offer of compensation unless expressly stated. Cooperating brokers must verify compensation terms before accepting an offer of cooperation.
3. SOP 3-2 (Article 3): Listing brokers may not unilaterally change offered compensation after an offer has been submitted. REALTORS may not delay or withhold an offer to negotiate compensation.
4. Article 7 (multi-party compensation): When buyer-side compensation is funded partly from the listing side and partly by the buyer, full disclosure and client consent are required. No obligation to share buyer-broker agreement contents with sellers or their brokers.
5. SOP 3-9 (Article 3): Cooperating brokers and others not acting as listing brokers or property managers may not access a property except on terms established by the owner or seller.

Dispute Resolution Pathways

Ombudsman: Voluntary, informal. Focuses on communication and mutual agreement. Does not determine whether a violation occurred. Complaint is discharged if resolved.

Mediation: Voluntary, informal. Trained mediator facilitates a negotiated resolution. Non-binding. Preferred method of REALTOR organizations. Eliminates need for arbitration if settlement is reached.

Ethics Complaint: Formal. Filed with the local association. Grievance committee conducts preliminary review. Ethics hearing panel conducts full due-process hearing if review passes. Sanctions are limited to membership and MLS access. TREC retains exclusive authority over license sanctions.

Arbitration: Formal. Used for monetary disputes between REALTOR members. Governed by Article 17. Panel determines which party is entitled to a commission or other award based on procuring cause and preponderance of evidence.

Ethics Hearing Panel Sanctions

Any combination of: letter of warning, letter of reprimand, required education, fine up to $5,000, probation up to one year, suspension 30 days to one year, expulsion one to three years, suspension or termination of MLS privileges, and an administrative processing fee up to $500. License suspension and revocation are exclusively within TREC's authority.

Article 1 Key Rules

1. Client interests are primary. Treat all parties honestly.
2. Present all offers promptly and objectively until closing, unless seller waives in writing.
3. Confidential client information is protected during and after the agency relationship. Exceptions: court order, preventing a crime, defending against a professional conduct allegation.
4. Latent material defects are not confidential and must be disclosed.
5. Disclose existence of other offers when authorized by seller and when inquiry is made.
6. Appraisal fees may not be contingent on the appraisal amount.

Article 2 Key Rules

1. No exaggeration, misrepresentation, or concealment of pertinent facts.
2. REALTORS are not obligated to discover latent defects or advise on matters outside their license scope, but must recognize red flags and refer clients to appropriate experts.
3. False consideration in a contract document is fraud and potentially a criminal offense.

Article 3 Key Rules

1. Cooperate with other brokers when doing so serves the client. Not required when cooperation is against the client's interest.
2. Cooperation does not imply compensation. Terms must be verified before accepting an offer to cooperate.
3. Compensation terms may not be unilaterally changed after an offer has been submitted.
4. Disclosure of dual or variable rate commission arrangements is required as soon as practicable.
5. REALTORS may not refuse to cooperate based on a broker's membership in a protected class.

CHAPTER 10 QUIZ — AGENCY, ETHICS, AND THE LAW

1. The NAR Code of Ethics was first adopted in 1913, well before state real estate licensing laws existed. This historical fact is significant because it demonstrates that:

a. REALTORS are exempt from state licensing requirements because their professional code predates those laws.

b. The NAR Code of Ethics supersedes Texas Administrative Code rules whenever the two conflict.

c. The real estate industry established a professional ethical standard through self-governance before the law required it, and the Code subsequently served as a model for state licensing laws.

d. Only REALTOR members are bound by ethical conduct standards because non-members were not part of the original code.

2. In the structure of the NAR Code of Ethics, which of the following may serve as the sole basis for a formal ethics violation complaint?

a. An Article, because only Articles may form the basis for a complaint. Standards of Practice may support an alleged violation but cannot stand alone.

b. A Standard of Practice, because it provides specific guidance on how agents should behave in common situations.

c. A Case Interpretation, because it represents a prior finding of an actual ethics violation.

d. Any combination of Articles and Standards of Practice cited together in the same complaint.

3. Section 804(c) of the Fair Housing Act prohibits discriminatory housing advertising. Which of the following is a correct statement about the legal status of such advertising?

a. Discriminatory housing advertising is protected by the First Amendment as commercial free speech.

b. Only the person who placed the advertisement may be held liable, not the publication or website that ran it.

c. Discriminatory housing advertising is not protected by the First Amendment, and both the advertiser and the publisher may be held liable.

d. The Fair Housing Act advertising prohibition applies only to print media and does not extend to websites or digital platforms.

4. HUD has determined that websites that publish user-generated discriminatory housing content may be held liable under the Fair Housing Act. Website operators who argue that Section 230 of the Communications Decency Act shields them from liability should understand that:

   a. Section 230 provides complete immunity from Fair Housing Act liability for all third-party content posted on a website.

   b. HUD has concluded that the Communications Decency Act does not exempt websites from Fair Housing Act obligations or from liability under certified state and local fair housing laws.

   c. Section 230 immunity applies only to state fair housing laws and not to the federal Fair Housing Act.

   d. Websites are automatically exempt from the Fair Housing Act as long as the discriminatory content was posted by a user rather than by the site operator.

5. The Texas Deceptive Trade Practices Act identifies 25 prohibited practices as illegal without requiring proof of intent. If a licensee committed one of those prohibited acts intentionally and a court so finds, the consumer may receive:

   a. Actual damages only, because the DTPA does not authorize punitive awards in real estate cases.

   b. A fixed statutory penalty of $10,000 per violation regardless of actual damages.

   c. A refund of the commission paid as the exclusive remedy available under the DTPA.

   d. Up to three times the actual damages suffered, because intentional violations may support a treble damages award.

6. Under the Texas Administrative Code Canon of Competence, a real estate licensee's obligation to maintain current market knowledge and pursue continuing education is best described as:

   a. A one-time standard satisfied at the time of initial licensure and renewal.

   b. An ongoing professional obligation that continues throughout the licensee's career.

   c. Required only for brokers, since salespersons work under the supervision of a broker who maintains competence on their behalf.

   d. Satisfied automatically by completing the minimum continuing education hours required for license renewal.

7. TREC closes an investigation by issuing an advisory letter to a licensee. Which of the following correctly describes what an advisory letter means?

   a. It is a formal disciplinary sanction equivalent to a reprimand and will appear on the licensee's public record.

   b. It suspends the licensee's ability to accept new listings until the identified conduct is corrected.

   c. It requires the licensee to pay a fine to the TREC Recovery Trust Account within 30 days.

   d. It is not a disciplinary sanction. It formally notifies the licensee that the investigation found conduct that, while not warranting immediate discipline, should be corrected to avoid future formal proceedings.

8. A licensee wants to thank a neighbor who referred a buyer client. The licensee would like to give the neighbor something of value. Under TREC rules, which of the following is permissible?

a. A cash payment of up to $100, provided it is disclosed to the sponsoring broker.

b. A gift certificate valued at no more than $50 that cannot be exchanged for cash.

c. A referral fee of up to $500 if the referred buyer successfully closes a transaction.

d. Any gift of personal property as long as its value does not exceed the amount allowed by the principal's written consent.

9. A licensee is receiving periodic payments from a residential service company for advertising services. A buyer-client in a current transaction is considering purchasing a home warranty from that same company. Under TREC rules, the licensee must:

a. Disclose the compensation arrangement to the client using TREC form RSC-1 and retain the form in the transaction file, not attach it to the purchase contract.

b. Decline to recommend the service company to any client while the advertising compensation arrangement is in effect.

c. Attach the RSC-1 form to the purchase contract as an addendum so all parties are aware of the relationship.

d. Terminate the advertising agreement with the service company before recommending it to any client.

10. The maximum payment from the TREC Real Estate Recovery Trust Account is $125,000 for a single transaction. If multiple claims arise from the misconduct of a single licensee, the total payout from the Trust Account across all claims is capped at:

a. $50,000, because the per-transaction cap applies to all claims involving the same licensee.

b. $150,000, which represents the maximum civil penalty available under TRELA.

c. An unlimited amount, because the Trust Account is funded by licensee fees and is not subject to a per-licensee cap.

d. $250,000 for all claims arising from the conduct of a single licensee.

11. A salesperson receives a buyer's earnest money check at a showing on a Friday afternoon. Under TAC Rule 535.159, assuming no written agreement specifies a different timeline, by when must the funds be deposited?

a. By the close of business on the second working day after the contract is executed by the principals.

b. By the close of business on the same day the check is received.

c. Within five business days of the effective date of the purchase contract.

d. Within 10 days of the effective date of the contract, consistent with standard option period practice.

12. A broker earns a commission on a transaction that has now closed. The earned commission is currently sitting in the broker's trust account. Under TAC Rule 535.146, the broker must:

a. Leave the earned commission in the trust account indefinitely because it was derived from a trust transaction.

b. Transfer the earned commission to the salesperson's personal account within five business days of closing.

c. Remove the earned commission from the trust account within 30 days of acquiring ownership of those funds.

d. Obtain written authorization from both the buyer and the seller before withdrawing any funds from the trust account.

13. The Preamble of the NAR Code of Ethics contains statements and guiding principles for REALTOR conduct. Which of the following correctly describes the Preamble's role in the enforcement process?

a. The Preamble may not be cited in an ethics complaint because it contains no specific, enforceable obligations. Only the Articles may form the basis of a complaint.

b. The Preamble may be cited in an ethics complaint when the conduct at issue is too general to be covered by a specific Article.

c. The Preamble may be cited to support an alleged Article violation in the same way a Standard of Practice is used.

d. The Preamble governs all disputes between REALTOR members and the public, while the Articles govern disputes between REALTOR members only.

14. Which section of the NAR Code of Ethics contains the Articles that define the obligations REALTORS owe specifically to each other, including honesty about colleagues and resolution of financial disputes?

a. Duties to Clients and Customers (Articles 1 through 9).

b. Duties to the Public (Articles 10 through 14).

c. Duties to REALTORS (Articles 15 through 17).

d. The Preamble, which addresses all professional relationships in the industry.

15. An ombudsman and a mediator both provide informal dispute resolution pathways for REALTOR members. Which of the following correctly distinguishes the two?

a. An ombudsman facilitates a negotiated settlement with a binding outcome, while a mediator focuses only on communication without imposing a resolution.

b. An ombudsman focuses entirely on improving communication between parties and does not determine whether a violation occurred, while a mediator facilitates a negotiated but non-binding settlement that the parties agree to in writing.

c. Mediation is mandatory before any ethics complaint may be filed, while the ombudsman process is optional.

d. An ombudsman may impose a fine of up to $500 as part of the resolution, while a mediator may not award any monetary amount.

16. A formal ethics complaint is submitted to a local association. Before forwarding the complaint to a full hearing panel, the grievance committee must confirm that several procedural requirements have been met. Which of the following is one of those requirements?

a. The complainant must have first attempted ombudsman services and received a written determination that no resolution was possible.

b. The respondent must have been formally warned about the alleged conduct before the complaint was filed.

c. The complainant must be a licensed real estate agent in the same association as the respondent.

d. The complaint must have been filed within 180 days of the alleged conduct and must cite specific Articles.

17. After a full ethics hearing, a panel finds that a REALTOR violated Article 1. The panel determines that the violation was serious and imposes the maximum available fine. That fine may not exceed:

a. $500, which is the administrative processing fee cap established by the Code.

b. $2,000, which is the per-violation limit set by the Texas Deceptive Trade Practices Act.

c. $5,000, which is the maximum fine the ethics hearing panel may impose.

d. $10,000, which is the maximum fine available under TRELA Section 1101.659.

18. An ethics hearing panel finds that a REALTOR committed a serious violation and wants to impose the most severe sanction available within its authority. Which of the following is the most serious action the panel may take?

a. Expel the REALTOR from association membership for a period of one to three years and suspend or terminate MLS privileges, since the panel has no authority to suspend or revoke a real estate license.

b. Revoke the REALTOR's Texas real estate license for a period of up to three years.

c. Suspend the REALTOR's Texas real estate license and refer the matter to TREC for permanent revocation.

d. Require the REALTOR to pay restitution to the harmed party and submit to TREC oversight for five years.

19. Arbitration under Article 17 of the NAR Code of Ethics is primarily used to resolve which type of dispute?

a. Consumer complaints about misrepresentation or failure to disclose material facts.

b. Monetary disputes between REALTOR broker members, with the central question typically being which licensee is entitled to a commission based on procuring cause.

c. Licensing violations that TREC has referred to the local association for peer review.

d. Disputes between a REALTOR and a seller over the terms of the listing agreement.

20. Under SOP 1-6, a listing REALTOR's obligation to present offers to the seller continues:

a. Only until the listing agent's own offer has been submitted and reviewed by the seller.

b. Until the listing agreement expires, after which no offer presentation obligation applies.

c. Only during the first 30 days of the listing period, which is when most serious offers are submitted.

d. Until closing or execution of a lease, unless the seller has specifically waived this obligation in writing.

21. Under SOP 1-9, a REALTOR's obligation to protect a former client's confidential information continues after the agency relationship ends. Which of the following is a recognized exception that would allow a REALTOR to disclose confidential client information without the client's authorization?

a. When a subsequent buyer of the same property requests the information as part of their due diligence process.

b. When the client has purchased another property and the original transaction has been closed for more than one year.

c. When the REALTOR is defending themselves against an allegation of wrongful professional conduct, when required by court order, or to prevent the client from committing a crime.

d. When a competing agent requests the information to complete their own CMA on the same property.

22. Under Article 2, a REALTOR's obligation to disclose is limited to adverse facts that would be reasonably apparent to a professional with the expertise required by their licensing authority. This means a REALTOR is:

a. Not required to discover latent defects or advise on matters outside his or her license scope, but must recognize red flags that call for professional inspection

b. Required to hire an engineer or environmental consultant to inspect every property before listing it.

c. Obligated to discover and disclose all latent defects, because their professional status creates a higher duty of investigation than that of an ordinary person.

d. Exempt from any disclosure obligation for physical defects because sellers bear sole responsibility for completing the Seller's Disclosure Notice.

23. Under SOP 3-1 as amended effective June 5, 2025, which of the following correctly describes the relationship between an offer of cooperation and an offer of compensation?

a. An offer of cooperation automatically includes an offer of compensation at the standard market rate unless the listing specifies otherwise.

b. Cooperation and compensation are separate. An offer of cooperation does not include an offer of compensation unless compensation is expressly stated, and a cooperating broker must verify terms before accepting.

c. Cooperating brokers may assume compensation is included whenever the listing broker is a member of the same local association.

d. An offer of cooperation includes compensation only when the transaction involves a buyer who is represented by a written buyer representation agreement.

24. In Case Study 3, Broker Grant listed a residential property and recommended a price below what the market would support because he wanted a quick sale. He later learned the property could potentially be rezoned for commercial use and did not disclose this to the seller. He also failed to disclose to cooperating brokers that his commission arrangement was variable depending on who produced the buyer. Which Articles of the Code did Grant most clearly violate?

a. Articles 8 and 9 only, because Grant failed to maintain proper escrow records and did not put all terms in writing.

b. Article 10 only, because Grant's conduct reflected a preference for one type of buyer over another.

c. Article 3 only, because the failure to return a cooperating agent's call is the only conduct that directly affected another REALTOR.

d. Articles 1, 2, and 3: Article 2 for concealing the rezoning potential and misrepresenting value, Article 1 for misleading the seller about market value in violation of SOP 1-3, and Article 3 for failing to disclose the variable commission arrangement and refusing to cooperate with a competing agent.

CHAPTER 11

DECEPTIVE TRADE PRACTICES AND CONSUMER PROTECTION

Chapter Objectives

After completing this chapter, you should be able to:

1. Define fraud and misrepresentation and explain how they differ from each other and from DTPA violations.
2. Describe the purpose of the Texas Deceptive Trade Practices Act, the Section 17.46 laundry list, and the violations most likely to affect licensees.
3. Explain the DTPA's notice and inspection requirements, available damages, and circumstances under which the DTPA may be waived or does not apply.
4. Identify the defenses available to licensees, the statute of limitations, and the limits of what a court may impose on a licensee.
5. Describe the legal issues associated with selling property "as is," commission and omission, and how to minimize exposure to DTPA claims.
6. Explain the history, scope, and causation standard of the Texas DTPA.
7. Describe economic damages, mental anguish damages, and additional damages available under the DTPA, including the conditions that trigger each.
8. Identify the defenses available under the DTPA, including the pre-suit notice process, mediation, arbitration, settlement options, and the statute of limitations.
9. Describe the ethical and legal responsibilities of Texas licensees, including examples of unlawful conduct and unethical practices.
10. Explain procuring cause, how arbitration panels evaluate it, and the standard of proof that applies.

Contents

Fraud

Fraud is a deliberate act of deception committed to gain an unfair advantage over another person. Intent is the defining element. A mistake, even a serious one, is not fraud because it lacks the element of purposeful wrongdoing. This distinction makes fraud significantly more difficult to prove in court than misrepresentation.

To succeed on a fraud claim, the plaintiff's attorney must establish three things: that the plaintiff suffered actual damage, that those damages were caused by the licensee's conduct, and that the licensee acted intentionally. Proving intent is the hardest of these three elements. Demonstrating that someone did something on purpose, rather than through negligence or carelessness, requires evidence that courts scrutinize carefully.

For this reason, most claims against real estate licensees are brought under misrepresentation rather than fraud. Misrepresentation is easier to establish and does not require proof of intent. That said, any licensee can be sued regardless of actual wrongdoing. Anyone may file a lawsuit for virtually any reason. The legal system presumes innocence until guilt is proven, and a licensee who is sued has not necessarily done anything wrong. The practical goal is to avoid the conduct that creates exposure in the first place.

Misrepresentation

Misrepresentation occurs when a licensee makes a false or misleading statement that is accepted as fact by a client or customer and that person suffers harm as a result of relying on it. Intent is not required. The licensee may have believed the statement was accurate, but if it was wrong and caused damage, a misrepresentation claim may still succeed.

One of the most common sources of accidental misrepresentation is the uncritical repetition of data. A licensee who copies room measurements or square footage from a prior MLS entry without independently verifying the information inherits any error that entry contained. If that figure is wrong and the buyer relies on it, the copying licensee can face liability for repeating the mistake.

The same risk applies to information found online. Property data aggregated on real estate websites is frequently outdated, inaccurate, or sourced from unverified records. A licensee who quotes figures from an internet source without citing it creates the impression of firsthand knowledge. The better practice is to attribute every factual statement to a verifiable source: "According to the Bexar County Appraisal District, the recorded square footage of this property is 2,180 square feet." Citing the source protects the licensee and gives the consumer the ability to verify the information independently.

The professional standard has evolved from telling buyers nothing to avoid liability to providing accurate, sourced information to reduce it. Sharing facts with proper attribution is now the expected practice, and it is a more effective defense than silence.

Recommending Service Providers

Buyers and sellers regularly ask their agents to recommend ancillary professionals: home inspectors, lenders, title companies, attorneys, surveyors, plumbers, electricians, and general contractors. How a licensee handles these requests has legal significance.

When a licensee recommends a single provider and that provider later causes harm to the consumer, the attorney representing the consumer will almost certainly name the referring licensee as a co-defendant. The theory is that the licensee created a representation, implied or explicit, about the quality of the recommended provider.

The appropriate approach is for the broker to maintain a curated list of qualified providers across the relevant service categories. When a consumer asks for a referral, the licensee hands them the list. When pressed for a personal recommendation, the licensee's response should be something like: "I can share a name whose work I have seen, but I don't recommend any one provider over the others on this list." By offering a list rather than a single recommendation, and by explicitly declining to endorse one over the others, the licensee significantly reduces personal exposure and the broker's exposure.

The broker must also exercise care in assembling the referral list. Simply having a list does not eliminate all responsibility if the providers on it consistently perform poorly. The list should reflect providers whose work the office has had reason to trust.

The Texas Deceptive Trade Practices Act

The Texas Deceptive Trade Practices Act (DTPA) is a state consumer protection law that applies broadly across industries, not only to real estate. When a Texas licensee is named in a civil lawsuit, the claim is most commonly brought under the DTPA. Brokers invest substantial training effort in helping their agents understand and avoid conduct that triggers DTPA liability.

A large portion of DTPA risk in real estate is managed through disclosure. Ensuring that buyers and sellers have accurate, complete information about the property and about who represents whom reduces the chance that a consumer later claims they were misled. The guiding principle has shifted from "let the buyer beware" to "make the buyer aware." Real estate professionals are now expected to facilitate informed decision-making, not to exploit information gaps.

Purpose of the DTPA

The DTPA exists to protect Texas consumers from false, misleading, and deceptive business practices, from unconscionable conduct, and from breaches of warranty. It also functions as a deterrent against bad actors who might otherwise calculate that the benefit of dishonest conduct outweighs the risk.

For real estate licensees, DTPA exposure typically arises in two ways: a licensee who makes inaccurate representations about a property to induce a buyer to enter into a contract, or a consumer who believes they lost value or suffered harm because of something a licensee said or failed to say. Both TREC and the

DTPA share the same protective purpose: shielding the public from licensees who cause harm, whether through fraud, negligence, or carelessness.

The consistent preventive practice is straightforward: state only facts, identify the source of those facts, and when a question falls outside the licensee's knowledge or expertise, say so and refer the consumer to someone qualified to answer it.

Section 17.46: The Laundry List

Section 17.46 of the DTPA contains what practitioners call the "laundry list": a catalog of specific acts and practices that constitute violations. The list is not exhaustive. A court may find conduct unlawful even if the specific act does not appear on the list, as long as the conduct is substantially similar in nature to a listed violation.

Selected items from the laundry list include:

- Misrepresenting the source, sponsorship, approval, or certification of goods or services.
- Claiming that goods or services have characteristics, benefits, qualities, or quantities they do not have.
- Representing that goods are new or original when they are used, deteriorated, or reconditioned.
- Misrepresenting the quality, standard, grade, or style of goods or services.
- Disparaging the goods, services, or business of another through false or misleading statements of fact.
- Advertising goods or services with no intention of selling them as advertised.
- Making false or misleading statements about the basis or extent of price reductions.
- Misrepresenting the rights, remedies, or obligations created by a contract.
- Falsely claiming that work or repairs have been performed when they have not.
- Failing to disclose information known at the time of the transaction when that failure was intended to induce the consumer into a transaction they would not have entered had the information been disclosed.
- Price gouging on necessities such as food, fuel, or medicine during a governor-declared disaster.

Not every item on the list seems immediately relevant to real estate, but several have direct application. Failing to disclose known information to induce a transaction is particularly significant. Misrepresenting the authority of a salesperson to negotiate final terms is another. Even the repair-related entries can affect licensees who steer clients toward a specific contractor.

The Violation Licensees Are Most Likely to Commit

Among all the items on the Section 17.46 list, the one real estate licensees are most likely to violate is disparaging the goods, services, or business of another through false or misleading statements.

The situation typically arises at the end of a listing presentation. The agent has made their pitch and asks whether there is any reason not to begin marketing the property today. The seller responds that another agent from a competing firm is scheduled to interview as well. The temptation in that moment is to criticize the competing firm to eliminate the competition.

Making false or disparaging statements about a competing brokerage to persuade a seller to sign with you instead is a DTPA violation. The appropriate response is to acknowledge the competitor professionally and return to the substance of your own presentation. Following up a few days later to ask whether a decision has been made is entirely acceptable. Attacking the competition is not.

Case Study: Orkin v. LaSassier

A homeowner contracted with a pest control company for termite treatment services. A technician visited the property, and the homeowner allowed him in before leaving for work. Nearly a year later, she found evidence of active termite damage. When the pest control company returned and treated the property, problems continued, and she ultimately hired a different company. After having the damage repaired, she sued the original pest control company under the DTPA, alleging that the company had represented that treatment services were performed when they had not been properly completed.

The company argued that it had made no verbal statement that the treatment was finished. The court rejected this defense. It held that the technician's conduct, visiting the home, beginning treatment, and then leaving without completing it, constituted a representation through conduct that the necessary services had been performed.

The real estate lesson is direct: if a licensee had recommended this company as the only pest control provider they trusted, that licensee and their broker could well have been named as co-defendants. The cost and disruption of defending that claim, even if ultimately resolved in the licensee's favor, would have been substantial. Providing a list of options rather than a single recommendation is the practical protection against exactly this kind of exposure.

Waiving DTPA Rights

Properties in poor condition present a higher-than-average risk of post-closing disputes. The buyer who purchases a distressed property, completes repairs, and later discovers undisclosed defects has an obvious motivation to pursue a claim. For this reason, some sellers refuse to close a transaction unless the buyer executes a written Waiver of Rights under the DTPA, agreeing not to pursue DTPA claims arising from the condition of the property.

This is particularly common in foreclosure sales. Lenders selling REO properties typically have no independent knowledge of the property. Most will not proceed with a sale unless the buyer signs a DTPA waiver.

Whether a DTPA waiver is legally effective is a matter of ongoing debate among Texas attorneys. The prevailing view is that waivers are enforceable only when they meet specific statutory requirements, discussed in the following section. Most brokers still prefer to have a signed waiver in place when selling distressed property, even if its enforceability is uncertain. The act of signing the waiver may itself discourage a buyer from pursuing litigation over issues the buyer accepted in writing at the time of purchase.

Notice and Inspection

Before filing a DTPA lawsuit, the plaintiff is required to give the potential defendant at least 60 days written notice of the intent to sue. The notice must describe the specific complaint in reasonable detail and identify the damages being claimed, including both economic losses and any mental anguish. It must also include anticipated attorney fees and court costs.

During the 60-day notice period, the defendant has the right to inspect the property at issue and the opportunity to make a settlement offer without admitting liability. A settlement offer does not constitute an admission of wrongdoing. If the plaintiff refuses the offer and proceeds to trial, the defendant may present the offer to the court as evidence of a reasonable attempt to resolve the dispute.

If the court determines that the refused settlement offer was reasonable and approximated the actual damages and legal fees that had accrued by the time the offer was made, the court may close the case and award the amount in the offer. The plaintiff in this scenario would not be entitled to attorney fees incurred after the date the reasonable offer was extended.

Exemptions to the DTPA

Since a 1995 amendment, certain transactions may be exempt from the DTPA's anti-waiver provisions under Section 17.49(f). To qualify for an exemption, a written contract must meet all of the following conditions:

1. The transaction or project involves total consideration by the consumer exceeding $100,000.
2. The consumer is independently represented by legal counsel who was not identified, suggested, or selected, directly or indirectly, by the defendant or the defendant's agent.
3. The transaction does not involve the consumer's primary residence.
4. All transactions involved, whether written or oral, have consideration exceeding $500,000.

The third requirement explains why many attorneys argue that a residential DTPA waiver is not worth the paper it is written on. Even a well-drafted waiver signed in connection with the sale of someone's home does not meet the exemption criteria if the property is the buyer's residence. The exemption is far more relevant to large commercial transactions where all four conditions can be satisfied.

The practical takeaway for licensees is that the best protection against a DTPA claim is not a waiver but accurate disclosure. Always state the facts. Always cite the source. When in doubt about whether something should be disclosed, disclose it. Providing more information than legally required is far less risky than providing too little.

Case Study: Weitzel v. Barnes

A developer sold a remodeled home to buyers who had the contractual right to inspect the property before closing. An addendum provided that if the buyers failed to conduct an inspection and submit a repair request, they would be deemed to have accepted the property as is. The buyers did not have the property independently inspected. The developer had verbally represented to the buyers that the plumbing and air conditioning systems were up to current city code.

After closing, the buyers discovered that the air conditioning system was inoperable and did not meet city code standards. The developer argued that the buyers' failure to inspect meant they had accepted the property as is and could not now complain about its condition. The developer also pointed out that the buyers had seen a city condemnation notice posted on the property before closing.

The court ruled in favor of the buyers. The court held that the verbal representations made about the plumbing and air conditioning were admissible evidence and that the seller could not use the as-is clause to shield a misrepresentation that had already been made. If the developer had made no statements at all about the mechanical systems, the as-is clause might have been sufficient protection. But once a specific factual representation was made and proven false, the as-is language did not extinguish the claim.

Damages Under the DTPA

A consumer who prevails in a DTPA action may recover economic damages, attorney fees, and court costs. Economic damages are those that can be calculated with reasonable certainty, such as the cost to repair a defect, the difference in value between what was promised and what was delivered, or out-of-pocket losses directly caused by the violation.

If the defendant acted knowingly, meaning the defendant was aware that the conduct was false, deceptive, or misleading, the court or jury may award additional damages for mental anguish. If the defendant acted intentionally, the court may multiply those damages. The maximum multiplier under the DTPA is three times the economic damages.

The court must evaluate what the licensee knew, what they did, and whether their conduct was deliberate. These determinations directly affect the magnitude of any damages award.

Some brokers include a provision in their independent contractor agreement allowing the broker to recover DTPA-related costs and judgments from future commissions earned by the salesperson responsible for the conduct. While this provision is a practical business protection for the broker, it predictably creates tension between the broker and the licensee during and after any litigation.

Successful Defenses

A seller who makes complete and accurate disclosures and who gives the buyer a fair opportunity to inspect the property has generally done what the law requires. Unknown defects cannot be disclosed. A seller who genuinely did not know about a problem cannot be held liable for failing to reveal it.

Consider a seller who had lived in a home for a decade without ever accessing a particular section of the attic. A home inspector during the transaction discovered that rafters in that area had never been properly fastened. Because the seller had no physical access to that part of the attic, they had no reason to know the defect existed. The seller was not liable for failing to disclose what they could not reasonably have known.

The same defense is available to licensees. An agent who has no knowledge of a material defect is not held responsible for that defect. However, this defense does not reduce the importance of carefully reviewing the Seller's Disclosure Notice with the seller, ensuring that all known conditions are accurately reported, and asking the seller for clarification on any entry that appears incomplete or inconsistent with what the agent observed during their visits to the property. A thorough disclosure process is both a legal obligation and the licensee's best protection.

Case Study: Alvarado v. Bolton

A buyer purchased 50 acres of land under a sales contract that did not reserve any mineral rights for the seller. However, the deed executed at closing did reserve 50 percent of the mineral rights in the seller's favor. Oil was subsequently discovered on the property. The buyers filed suit under the DTPA when they learned of the mineral rights they had unknowingly transferred.

The seller argued that under the doctrine of merger, the buyers' acceptance of the deed had extinguished all prior contract rights, including the right to receive full mineral ownership. The court rejected this argument, holding that the doctrine of merger cannot override a DTPA claim. The buyers could pursue their case if they could demonstrate that the seller had breached the terms of the sales contract.

The lesson for licensees is clear: any transaction involving mineral rights, either a conveyance of them or a reservation of them, should prompt an immediate recommendation to both parties to retain separate legal counsel. The mineral rights provisions in a deed are complex legal matters. A licensee who attempts to draft or interpret mineral rights language risks being accused of the unauthorized practice of law, and a licensee who fails to flag the issue at all risks being blamed when the transaction goes wrong.

Groundless Lawsuits

Some lawsuits are filed with no legitimate basis, purely to harass the defendant or to extract a settlement. The time, energy, legal fees, and distraction from income-producing work that defending even a meritless lawsuit creates are real costs. Defendants in baseless cases are robbed of significant resources regardless of the eventual outcome.

The DTPA provides some protection against this. If a court determines that a lawsuit was groundless, filed in bad faith, or brought primarily to harass the defendant, the court may award the defendant reasonable attorney fees and court costs. The defendant will not, however, recover lost income or compensation for time consumed in the litigation.

TREC maintains the Real Estate Recovery Trust Account to compensate consumers who win judgments against licensees who cannot satisfy those judgments. The fund is funded by licensee fees and exists solely to protect the public. Licensees are not eligible to recover anything from the fund. A consequence of the fund's existence is that some attorneys are willing to file marginal claims because the prospect of recovery from the Trust Account makes collection more likely. The judge must evaluate the merits of every claim, and baseless ones can be dismissed, but the filing itself causes harm to the defendant in the meantime.

Avoiding DTPA Liability

Preventing DTPA claims requires consistent professional habits rather than any single protective action. The most effective practices are:

1. Point out known deficiencies in a property. Licensees are not construction experts, but experience with many properties makes pattern recognition easier. When something looks wrong, say so and recommend professional evaluation.
2. Recommend and encourage a professional home inspection for every buyer. The inspection report may identify concerns that warrant referral to a structural engineer or licensed contractor for further review and cost estimation.
3. Advise buyers to include a termination option in the contract. This gives the buyer a clean and inexpensive exit if the inspection reveals conditions that make the purchase inadvisable.
4. Obtain a DTPA waiver when selling a property in poor condition, understanding that its enforceability may be limited in residential transactions.
5. Attribute every factual statement to a verifiable source. Quoted figures without attribution create implied representations.
6. Refer questions outside the licensee's knowledge or expertise to qualified professionals. Stating facts accurately and acknowledging the limits of your knowledge is a more effective defense than guessing.

When a complaint arises, the licensee should consult an attorney promptly. The first consultation is typically at no charge and allows the licensee to understand the exposure and options before making any decisions about how to respond.

Statute of Limitations

The DTPA imposes a two-year statute of limitations on consumer claims. The limitation period begins running from the date of the underlying event or from the date the consumer discovered, or reasonably should have discovered, the existence of the claim, whichever is later.

This discovery rule has important practical implications. Consider a buyer who purchases a home and lives in it for several years before undertaking a renovation. During demolition, evidence of a prior fire is found behind wall panels. The Seller's Disclosure Notice completed at the time of purchase had indicated no prior fires. The two-year limitation period does not begin until the moment the buyer discovered the concealed evidence, not the date of the original closing.

In the scenario above, the court dismissed the claim against the listing agent, concluding that a reasonable person in the agent's position would not have known about the concealed fire damage. The claim against the sellers, who had been aware of the fire and had covered the evidence, was allowed to proceed. The court ordered the sellers to pay for the necessary repairs.

The discovery rule means that exposure to a DTPA claim does not necessarily end at closing or even within the first few years of a buyer's ownership. This reinforces the importance of thorough disclosure at the time of the transaction rather than relying on the hope that problems will not be discovered later.

What a Court Cannot Do

Being named in a lawsuit triggers two simultaneous proceedings in most cases. An attorney representing an aggrieved consumer will typically file a civil lawsuit in district court and file a concurrent complaint with TREC. The licensee must respond to both at the same time, doubling the burden and expense of the defense.

Defending against a DTPA claim is expensive. Attorney fees for a contested case can reach tens of thousands of dollars even in matters that are ultimately resolved in the licensee's favor. Defense attorneys who have strong track records in real estate litigation still acknowledge that even winning cases are financially and emotionally costly, and that many clients later wish they had explored settlement before litigation escalated.

Among all the sanctions and remedies available to a court in a DTPA or related civil proceeding, there is one the court cannot impose: it cannot revoke or suspend a real estate license. License revocation and suspension are exclusively within the authority of TREC, the agency that issued the license. A court may award damages, impose fines, and award attorney fees, but the licensee's ability to practice real estate is determined by TREC, not by civil courts.

Selling Property As Is

The phrase "as is" has a specific and often misunderstood meaning in Texas real estate. In consumer goods transactions, an as-is sale typically signals that the seller makes no warranty about the condition of the item. In real estate, however, the as-is concept does not relieve the seller of the obligation to disclose known defects.

When a Texas seller markets a property as is, what they are actually communicating is that they will not make repairs or contribute to the cost of corrections. They are not representing that the property is defect-free, and they are not released from their disclosure obligations. The phrase is therefore somewhat misleading when used in real estate advertising.

Licensees should avoid using "as is" in MLS descriptions, advertising materials, or verbal communications with prospective buyers without immediately clarifying its actual meaning. The appropriate message to deliver to a buyer is this: the seller will not make repairs, and any corrections identified during the inspection period will be the buyer's responsibility to address. It is also important to note that lenders may require certain repairs before approving a loan on the property, which can affect the buyer's ability to finance the purchase.

Case Study: Prudential v. Jefferson Associates

A commercial buyer purchased a four-story office building from a large insurance company on a fully negotiated as-is basis. The contract gave the buyer complete access to the property, and multiple independent inspections were conducted by an engineering firm, the buyer's maintenance supervisor, and the buyer's property manager. None of the inspections identified asbestos. The buyer purchased the property and later transferred ownership to a limited partnership. Years after the transfer, asbestos fireproofing material was discovered in the building.

The case reached the Texas Supreme Court. The court found no evidence that the seller had known about the asbestos at the time of sale, and therefore could not have disclosed it. The court also observed that the purchase price reflected the as-is terms and that the buyer had accepted the associated risk by proceeding without discovering the condition.

The court established four tests for evaluating an as-is clause in a real estate transaction:

1. All defects known to the seller must be disclosed.
2. The seller must not interfere with or obstruct the buyer's inspection efforts.
3. The as-is provision must be a meaningful, integral element of the contract, not a minor boilerplate clause.
4. The buyer and seller must not be in substantially unequal bargaining positions.

When all four conditions are present, an as-is clause can provide meaningful protection to a seller. When any one of them is absent, particularly the disclosure of known defects, the clause offers far less protection.

Attorney Fees

Legal costs accumulate quickly in disputed real estate matters. Even before a lawsuit is formally filed, having an attorney respond to a demand letter or a complaint can involve several hours of billable time. Once litigation begins, fees in a contested case can reach significant sums before the matter is resolved.

Brokers are well-advised to maintain a relationship with a real estate attorney who has courtroom experience. Having counsel available reduces response time when issues arise and ensures that early communications are handled in a way that does not inadvertently worsen the broker's position.

One important boundary: the broker's attorney should not be on the list of attorneys the office provides to buyers and sellers. If a client later decides to pursue a claim against the broker, the shared attorney would face a conflict of interest that could complicate the defense.

When a licensee believes they may be personally exposed in a claim, they should consult their own separate attorney rather than relying solely on the broker's representation. The interests of the broker and the individual salesperson may diverge during litigation, and each party benefits from independent legal advice. Most attorneys offer an initial consultation at no charge, which gives the licensee a chance to understand their exposure before making any commitments.

Commission and Omission

In a misrepresentation claim, the attorney must demonstrate either that the licensee did something that caused a false impression, or that the licensee failed to do something they were obligated to do, and that either action or inaction caused the consumer harm. These two categories are known as commission and omission.

Commission: An act that causes misrepresentation. The licensee did something affirmatively wrong, such as telling a buyer that a home contains 2,800 square feet when the actual figure is 1,900.

Omission: A failure to act that causes misrepresentation. The licensee failed to disclose something they knew or should have known, such as not informing a buyer that the property experienced flooding in a prior year.

When a buyer purchases a property and later discovers an undisclosed condition, a complaint to TREC and a civil lawsuit against both the seller and the licensee typically follow. Courts apply what is called the reasonable person standard: the judge evaluates whether a reasonable licensee with ordinary professional knowledge and diligence would have been aware of the problem. If the answer is yes, the licensee is expected to have disclosed it.

A seller sometimes fails to disclose a known condition, either on the Seller's Disclosure Notice or in conversation with the listing agent. This places the listing agent in a difficult position: they cannot disclose what they were not told, but their professional observation of the property may create an expectation that they noticed and acted on visible signs of the issue. An experienced licensee reviews the Seller's Disclosure Notice carefully, compares it to what they observed during their visits to the property, and asks the seller follow-up questions when something appears incomplete or inconsistent. When appropriate, the listing agent may make additional disclosures to the buyer based on their own observations, independent of what the seller has reported.

History and Scope of the Texas DTPA

The Texas Legislature enacted the Texas Deceptive Trade Practices Act in 1973 as a consumer protection measure. At the time of its passage, the DTPA was considered one of the strongest consumer protection statutes in the country. Courts at all levels interpreted it broadly, consistent with its stated purpose: to protect consumers against false, misleading, and deceptive business practices, breaches of warranty, and unconscionable actions, and to provide efficient and economical procedures to secure that protection.

By the early 1990s, consumer attorneys were applying the DTPA successfully across a wide range of commercial disputes. Actual damages in individual cases sometimes reached seven figures, treble damages were frequently awarded, and attorney fees were mandatory for prevailing plaintiffs. In response to concerns about the scope of liability, the Legislature amended the DTPA in 1995, limiting the damages available, narrowing the class of qualifying consumers, and creating additional settlement opportunities for defendants.

The DTPA applies broadly. It covers any individual who purchases or leases goods or services, as well as most businesses that purchase for business purposes. To qualify as a consumer entitled to bring a DTPA claim, the person or entity must have sought or acquired goods or services through a purchase or lease. Persons who have not made such a transaction cannot use the Act.

Causation: Producing Cause

Before a consumer can recover any damages under the DTPA, they must establish that the defendant's conduct was a producing cause of their harm. This is the causation standard the Act requires.

> **Producing cause**: A contributing cause that, in a natural sequence, produced the damages complained of. It is a factor that both caused the harm and without which the harm would not have occurred.

Causation is a significant element in every DTPA case. A consumer may be able to prove that a defendant engaged in deceptive conduct, but if the conduct was not the producing cause of the consumer's specific losses, the claim will not succeed. The Act is designed to compensate losses that flow directly from the wrongful conduct, not losses attributable to other causes.

Damage Remedies: Overview

The DTPA is structured to provide liberal recovery for consumers who succeed on a claim. The damage framework serves three purposes: to fully compensate injured consumers, to give attorneys an economic incentive to take consumer cases, and to deter wrongful conduct by making it financially unwise.

A prevailing consumer may be entitled to three categories of damages, each with different conditions for recovery:

1. Economic damages, recoverable in all successful cases.
2. Mental anguish damages, recoverable when the defendant acted knowingly.
3. Additional damages of up to three times the base award, recoverable when the defendant acted knowingly or intentionally.

Economic Damages

Every consumer who prevails under the DTPA is entitled to recover economic damages. The 1995 amendments replaced the earlier term "actual damages" with "economic damages," narrowing the recoverable base.

> **Economic damages**: Compensatory damages for measurable financial loss, including costs of repair and replacement. Economic damages expressly exclude mental anguish, physical pain and suffering, loss of consortium, disfigurement, physical impairment, and loss of companionship.

A prevailing consumer recovers the full amount of their pecuniary loss as economic damages. This includes out-of-pocket costs and both direct and consequential financial losses flowing from the violation. It does not include non-economic losses, which are governed by separate damage categories.

Mental Anguish Damages

Mental anguish damages are available in addition to economic damages when the defendant acted knowingly. They are evaluated under the same standard applied in other Texas civil cases and require more than general frustration or unhappiness with a transaction outcome.

> **Knowingly**: Actual awareness, at the time of the conduct, of the falsity, deception, or unfairness of the act giving rise to the claim. Actual awareness may be inferred from objective evidence indicating the defendant knew what they were doing was wrong.

To support a mental anguish award, the consumer must demonstrate a substantial disruption in daily routine or a high degree of mental pain and distress. Mere disappointment, frustration, embarrassment, or anger is not sufficient. Qualifying mental anguish may be expressed through grief, shame, despair, or public humiliation, provided the distress meets the substantial disruption threshold.

Mental anguish damages do not require the consumer to have suffered physical injury, and they are not contingent on the consumer having first recovered economic damages. Knowingly is treated as a question of fact, and once the fact finder determines the defendant acted knowingly, it may consider an award of mental anguish damages.

Additional Damages

The DTPA authorizes additional damages, sometimes called punitive or multiplied damages, when the defendant acted knowingly or intentionally. These damages serve a deterrent purpose beyond compensation.

The current framework, established by the 1995 amendments, limits multiplied damages as follows:

> **Knowing conduct:** The court may award a total recovery of up to three times the consumer's economic damages. For example, if the jury awards $10,000 in economic damages and finds the defendant acted knowingly, the court may award a total between $10,000 and $30,000.
>
> **Intentional conduct:** The court may award a total of up to three times the combined economic damages and mental anguish damages. Intentional conduct carries the highest potential exposure.

Before the 1995 amendments, the DTPA automatically tripled all damages. The current framework gives the court discretion to set the multiplier anywhere from one to three times the applicable base, rather than requiring automatic trebling. This change was a significant limitation on the pre-1995 exposure defendants faced.

Attorney Fees

The DTPA makes attorney fees mandatory for a prevailing consumer. The use of the word "shall" in the statute leaves no discretion: if the consumer wins, the court must award reasonable and necessary attorney fees and court costs. This provision ensures that consumers with legitimate smaller claims can obtain qualified legal representation, because the attorney's fee recovery does not depend solely on the size of the damages award.

The DTPA also provides for mandatory attorney fees in favor of a defendant. If the court finds that the lawsuit was groundless and filed in bad faith, or was brought primarily to harass the defendant, the court must award the defendant reasonable and necessary attorney fees and court costs. Either bad faith or harassment is independently sufficient to trigger a fee award for the defendant. This provision is intended to deter the filing of meritless claims.

Defenses to a DTPA Claim

The DTPA provides limited defenses to defendants, and the 1995 amendments did not significantly expand them. One of the few statutory defenses available is reliance on written information provided by a third party. To use this defense successfully, the defendant must demonstrate two things: that the defendant's conduct was based on written information received from someone other than the defendant's own organization, and that the defendant gave the consumer reasonable and timely written notice of that reliance.

Because the DTPA operates outside the common law, common law defenses generally do not apply to DTPA claims. The following doctrines have been found inapplicable in DTPA proceedings:

- Substantial performance
- The parol evidence rule
- Waiver and estoppel

Negating causation is another path to defeating a DTPA claim. If a consumer knowingly and voluntarily signs a contract stating that the buyer is not relying on any representation of the seller, and that agreement was the product of genuine arm's-length negotiation freely and intelligently entered into, the consumer may have eliminated producing cause and with it the basis for damages. However, a court will scrutinize such a clause carefully. In a transaction between an unsophisticated consumer and a sophisticated commercial party, the same clause may not carry the same weight.

The most effective practical defense in any DTPA matter is ensuring that reliable, independent information from qualified sources has been made available throughout the transaction. Encouraging buyers and sellers to use appraisers, licensed inspectors, engineers, and government data sources reduces dependence on the licensee's personal representations and creates a documented record that the parties had access to accurate information.

Pre-Suit Notice

Before filing a lawsuit under the DTPA, a consumer is required to give the prospective defendant written notice at least 60 days before the suit is filed. The notice must describe the consumer's specific complaint in reasonable detail and state the amount of economic damages being claimed. It must also identify anticipated attorney fees and court costs.

If the consumer fails to provide proper notice, the defendant may file a plea in abatement no later than 30 days after filing an original answer. The case will be paused to give the consumer the opportunity to deliver proper notice. Once notice is correctly given, the 60-day period begins.

The pre-suit notice requirement is one of the most underused and misunderstood features of the DTPA. When used as intended, it creates a structured opportunity for early settlement and reduces the volume of cases that proceed to full litigation.

Mediation and Arbitration

Mediation

Either party to a DTPA case may request mediation. Under the 1995 amendments, a motion for mediation must be filed within 90 days after service of a pleading seeking relief under the Act. Mediation must be conducted within 30 days of the request. The parties share the cost of mediation equally, unless the total amount in dispute is less than $15,000, in which case the party requesting mediation bears the cost.

Arbitration

Contractual provisions requiring arbitration of DTPA claims are enforceable on the same basis as arbitration clauses in any other agreement. Agreeing to arbitrate a DTPA dispute does not constitute a waiver of rights under the Act.

Settlement Options

Once a consumer has given proper pre-suit notice, the defendant has four options:

1. Pay the amount requested and resolve the matter without further proceedings.
2. Ignore the notice and take no action.
3. Propose a settlement offer and deliver it to the consumer within 60 days of receiving the notice.
4. Wait until suit is filed and then submit a settlement proposal during the period that begins when an original answer is filed and ends on the 90th day after that date.

If mediation is held, a party may also tender a settlement during the 20-day period following the close of mediation.

A valid settlement offer under the DTPA must include two components: a dollar amount offered to settle the consumer's actual damages, and a separate amount to cover the consumer's reasonable attorney fees incurred up to the date of the offer. A settlement offer that does not address attorney fees does not satisfy the statutory requirements.

The practical significance of a reasonable settlement offer is substantial. If the consumer refuses the offer and the eventual court award is not materially better than what was offered, the consumer's recovery of attorney fees incurred after the offer date may be limited or denied. Defense attorneys should always be prepared to put some amount on the table as an offer, because doing so preserves access to these penalty provisions.

Case Study: Kennemore v. Bennett

Two brothers contracted with a builder for construction of a home. When they refused to pay the remaining balance and an additional amount for extra work, the builder placed a mechanic's lien on the property and sued to enforce it. The brothers countersued, asserting that the builder had failed to construct the home in a workmanlike manner, and brought their claim under the DTPA.

Before trial, the brothers paid the builder's claim in full. They nonetheless proceeded to trial on their own DTPA counterclaim. The builder argued that by moving into the house and paying the full amount claimed, the brothers had waived their DTPA rights.

The Texas Supreme Court rejected this argument. It held that a consumer's acceptance of a defective product and payment of the purchase price do not constitute a waiver of DTPA claims arising from the defect. A consumer who has been harmed by defective goods or services retains DTPA rights even after accepting delivery and paying in full.

The broader takeaway for real estate licensees mirrors the lesson from the original DTPA chapter: a buyer who closes on a property does not automatically waive future claims. The best protection against a DTPA case is ensuring that qualified independent professionals, including appraisers, licensed inspectors, and engineers, are involved in the transaction and that their findings are documented.

Statute of Limitations

A consumer must bring a DTPA claim within two years of the relevant event. The Act applies what Texas courts call a discovery rule of limitations, which means the two-year clock does not necessarily start on the date of the transaction. The period begins running from whichever of the following occurs first:

- The date the false, misleading, or deceptive act occurred.
- The date the consumer actually discovered the act.
- The date the consumer, exercising reasonable diligence, should have discovered the act.

The discovery rule serves consumers who could not have known of the violation at the time it occurred. It also has an objective component: a consumer cannot indefinitely delay the limitations period simply by claiming ignorance when the facts were reasonably available. The court will evaluate whether a reasonable person in the consumer's circumstances would have discovered the violation earlier.

In terms of attorney fees, the statute of limitations interacts with the settlement process in an important way. A consumer who refuses a reasonable settlement offer and proceeds to trial may find their attorney fee recovery limited to fees incurred up to the date of the offer. Plaintiff's attorneys must therefore craft notice letters that are genuinely designed to encourage settlement, and defense attorneys must always position themselves to argue that any eventual recovery did not materially exceed an offer that was on the table.

Preemption

In some situations, other state or federal laws take precedence over the DTPA and limit its application. Texas courts have recognized that the DTPA is indirectly preempted by the Texas Antitrust Act in certain circumstances. State law also specifically exempts certain conduct by health care providers and veterinarians from DTPA coverage.

Federal law can also preempt the DTPA when the two conflict. Courts have found that federal statutes including the Employee Retirement Income Security Act, the Airline Deregulation Act, and the Carmack Amendment preempt DTPA claims in cases where their provisions directly conflict with the Act. In other circumstances, preemption arguments have not succeeded. The analysis turns on whether the federal statute expressly provides for preemption, whether preemption is implied by the regulatory scheme, and whether the facts of the particular case fall within the scope of the federal law.

Preemption can work in either direction for the parties involved. A licensee facing a DTPA claim should work closely with legal counsel to identify any applicable federal or state law that might limit or eliminate DTPA exposure in the specific circumstances of the case.

Ethical and Legal Responsibilities of Licensees

Texas real estate licensees operate within overlapping layers of obligation. Common law fiduciary duties apply to agency relationships. TRELA and the Texas Administrative Code impose statutory and regulatory requirements. Contracts create binding commitments to clients and other parties. Professional associations add voluntary ethical codes. Understanding and consistently meeting these obligations across all of these sources is what it means to practice real estate professionally in Texas.

The following conduct constitutes a violation of Texas real estate license law:

- Making a material misrepresentation or false promise to influence a party to enter into a transaction.
- Acting for more than one party in a transaction without the knowledge and consent of all parties.
- Commingling funds received from or on behalf of clients with personal or business operating funds.
- Demanding a commission under an exclusive listing or exclusive buyer agency agreement that does not contain a specific, definite termination date.
- Demonstrating negligence or incompetence in the performance of licensed activities.
- Acting as a broker while holding only a salesperson's license.
- Accepting compensation from any source other than the sponsoring broker.
- Failing to ensure that financial obligations and commitments in a real estate transaction are in writing and that all parties receive copies of relevant documents.

Examples of Unlawful Conduct

Continuing education beyond the minimum required hours is a practical investment for any licensee. The following are examples of conduct that constitute unlawful behavior in the practice of real estate:

- Presenting competing offers to a seller in a manner calculated to steer the seller toward the offer that generates the highest commission to the broker, without regard to the seller's interests.
- Making a false or misleading representation to the seller about the amount of an earnest money deposit or the financial qualifications of a buyer.
- Adding to or modifying the terms of a signed contract without the knowledge and consent of all parties.
- Knowingly misrepresenting the market value of a property, whether for the purpose of securing the listing or to facilitate the licensee's own acquisition of an interest in the property.
- Falsely telling a seller that the licensee has already obtained a purchase offer when attempting to secure a listing.
- Failing to disclose known material facts that affect a property's value when the licensee has reason to believe those facts are not readily apparent to the buyer or seller.

Examples of Unethical Practices

Beyond outright legal violations, Texas licensees are also subject to ethical standards that prohibit conduct harmful to clients, customers, and the profession, even when the conduct does not rise to the level of a TRELA violation. Examples of unethical practices include:

- Representing the condition of a property's interior or exterior features without actually having knowledge of that condition.
- Demanding or expecting a commission discount or reduction when purchasing property for the licensee's own account, after a price agreement has been reached with the seller, without having disclosed that expectation upfront.
- Failing to disclose the licensee's personal ownership interest in a property at the earliest point in any discussion about purchasing it.
- Failing to respond in a timely way to a client's reasonable inquiries about the marketing of their exclusively listed property.
- Representing that a specific service is provided at no cost to the client when in fact the cost is embedded in the transaction fees.
- Recommending a lender, title company, or escrow service in which the broker has a material financial interest without disclosing that interest at the time of the recommendation.

Avoiding Misrepresentation Claims

The most effective protection against misrepresentation claims is a consistent practice of thorough inquiry, accurate disclosure, and appropriate referral to experts. The following approach provides a practical framework:

1. **Complete the Seller's Disclosure Notice carefully.** Ask the seller follow-up questions about ownership interests, the condition of improvements and utility systems, any known or potential zoning changes, applicable special ordinances, and boundary or encroachment issues. Do not simply accept yes or no answers on items where the property's condition suggests more investigation is warranted.
2. **Conduct an independent assessment of the property.** A licensee's job is not merely to relay whatever the seller says. Experience with many properties makes it possible to identify conditions that warrant further investigation. When a matter is complex or requires technical knowledge, recommend that the seller engage an expert.
3. **Investigate external factors.** Consider conditions outside the property that could affect its value or a buyer's decision, such as pending zoning changes, infrastructure projects, or neighborhood developments.
4. **State only what you know, and know where it comes from.** Do not speculate or offer opinions on matters outside your knowledge or expertise. Every factual representation should be attributable to a reliable, verifiable source.
5. **Use government and public resources.** Maintain a working list of agencies and databases that can provide authoritative information on property taxes, flood zones, permits, zoning classifications, and comparable sales.
6. **Do not participate in nondisclosure.** If a seller refuses to disclose a known material condition, the appropriate response is to decline the listing. No commission is worth the risk of license revocation or a DTPA judgment.
7. **Put everything in writing.** Obtain and document pertinent disclosures in the transaction file. Maintain thorough records that could support a defense if a complaint arises months or years after closing.

Procuring Cause

Procuring cause: In real estate, the broker or agent whose actions, by introducing and maintaining a relationship with a buyer, brought about the completion of a transaction. The procuring cause is the cause that results in the attainment of the intended goal: a completed sale or lease.

Procuring cause is the central question in most real estate commission arbitration disputes. When two cooperating brokers both assert a right to a commission on the same transaction, the arbitration panel must determine which one actually produced the buyer and maintained the relationship that led to the closing.

The analysis focuses on the nature and continuity of the relationship between each broker and the buyer. Key questions include whether the broker who first introduced the buyer to the property continued to maintain active and meaningful contact, or whether that broker's inactivity or disengagement gave the buyer a reasonable basis to conclude the relationship had ended.

If a buyer shifted from one broker to another, the panel will want to understand why. The issue may be that the first broker's conduct, whether through neglect, an apparent loss of interest, or some form of friction, caused the buyer to seek assistance elsewhere. If so, that break in the relationship may shift procuring cause to the second broker who continued the transaction through to closing.

Arbitration Panel Considerations in Procuring Cause Disputes

When cooperating brokers cannot resolve a commission dispute on their own, the matter proceeds to arbitration before a professional standards panel. The party requesting arbitration bears the burden of proof by a preponderance of the evidence. Panel members may ask questions to ensure they understand the full sequence of events that led to the transaction.

Because every transaction is different, no fixed checklist determines procuring cause in every case. The following are among the questions a panel will typically explore:

- What was the nature of the transaction: a purchase, a lease, a commercial deal?
- Was the property listed or subject to a management agreement, and was that agreement in writing and in effect at the time of the dispute?
- Who were the cooperating brokers and how were all parties represented?
- Is the matter also the subject of pending civil litigation?
- Who first introduced the buyer to the property?
- Was there an interruption or break in the original series of events connecting the buyer to the transaction? If so, how did it occur and who caused it?
- Did any party interfere with the relationship between the buyer and the first broker?
- If a compensation offer was made, how and when was it communicated?
- Was the second broker's involvement the result of genuine abandonment or estrangement between the buyer and the first broker, or was it an intrusion into an existing active relationship?

No single factor is determinative. The panel must consider the complete picture of the parties' conduct throughout the transaction, from the first introduction of the buyer to the property through the signed agreement and closing, and weigh all relevant events in reaching its award.

Snapshot Review – Chapter 11

Key Definitions

Fraud: A deliberate act of deception intended to gain an unfair advantage. Intent must be proven. Harder to establish in court than misrepresentation.

Misrepresentation: A false or misleading statement accepted as fact by a client or customer who suffers harm as a result. Intent is not required.

Commission (in misrepresentation): An affirmative act that causes a false impression, such as stating incorrect square footage.

Omission (in misrepresentation): A failure to disclose known information that the consumer needed to make an informed decision.

DTPA: The Texas Deceptive Trade Practices Act. Protects consumers from false, misleading, and deceptive business practices. Applies broadly across industries.

The Section 17.46 Laundry List

1. Contains specific prohibited acts. Courts may extend DTPA liability to conduct that is substantially similar to a listed act even if not explicitly enumerated.
2. The violation licensees are most commonly at risk of committing: disparaging the goods, services, or business of a competitor through false or misleading statements.
3. Failing to disclose known material information that would have caused the consumer to decline the transaction is also a listed violation.

Procedural Requirements

Pre-suit Notice: The plaintiff must give the defendant at least 60 days written notice before filing, describing the complaint and all claimed damages including mental anguish and attorney fees.

Inspection Right: During the notice period, the defendant has the right to inspect the property and may make a settlement offer without admitting liability.

Reasonable Offer: If a court finds that the plaintiff rejected a reasonable settlement offer and the trial result was not materially better, the court may limit further fee recovery.

Statute of Limitations: Two years from the date of the event or from the date the consumer discovered or reasonably should have discovered the harm.

Damages

1. Base recovery: economic damages, attorney fees, and court costs.
2. Knowing violations: additional damages for mental anguish may be awarded.
3. Intentional violations: damages may be multiplied up to three times the economic damages.
4. Licensees are not held liable for material defects they had no knowledge of.

DTPA Waiver and Exemptions

1. Sellers and lenders selling distressed or foreclosure properties may require buyers to sign a Waiver of Rights under the DTPA. Enforceability is limited.
2. The Section 17.49(f) exemption applies to commercial transactions over $500,000 where the consumer is independently represented, and the property is not the consumer's residence.
3. The exemption does not apply to transactions involving a buyer's primary residence, making residential DTPA waivers generally unenforceable.

Selling As Is

1. As is in Texas real estate means the seller will not make repairs. It does not eliminate the seller's duty to disclose known defects.
2. Courts uphold as-is clauses only when the seller disclosed all known defects, did not obstruct inspections, the clause was a material element of the contract, and the parties were not in substantially unequal bargaining positions.
3. Licensees should avoid using as-is in advertising without immediately explaining its actual meaning to prospective buyers.

What Courts Cannot Do

1. A court cannot revoke or suspend a real estate license. Only TREC, the issuing authority, may take that action.
2. Courts may award economic damages, mental anguish damages, multiplied damages for intentional conduct, attorney fees, and court costs.
3. If a lawsuit is found to be groundless or filed for the purpose of harassment, the court may award the defendant reasonable attorney fees and court costs, but not lost income.

Best Practices for Avoiding DTPA Claims

1. State facts and cite the source of every factual statement.
2. Provide a list of service providers rather than endorsing a single one.
3. Recommend and encourage independent professional inspections on every transaction.
4. Advise buyers to include a termination option.
5. Review the Seller's Disclosure Notice carefully and ask follow-up questions when entries appear inconsistent with the condition of the property.
6. Disclose when in doubt. Providing too much information is never the basis for a DTPA claim. Providing too little frequently is.

DTPA History and Scope

1. Enacted in 1973. Amended in 1995 to limit damages, narrow consumer eligibility, and expand settlement opportunities for defendants.
2. Applies to consumers who purchase or lease goods or services. Persons who have not made such a transaction cannot use the Act.

3. Purpose: protect consumers against false, misleading, and deceptive business practices; breaches of warranty; and unconscionable conduct.

Key Definitions

Producing cause: A contributing cause that, in a natural sequence, produced the harm. A necessary element of every DTPA damages claim.

Economic damages: Compensatory damages for measurable financial loss, including repair and replacement costs. Excludes mental anguish, physical pain, loss of consortium, and disfigurement.

Knowingly: Actual awareness of the falsity, deception, or unfairness of the conduct at the time it occurred. May be inferred from objective evidence.

Procuring cause: The broker whose actions introduced the buyer and maintained the relationship that resulted in a completed transaction.

Damages Framework

1. Economic damages: available in every successful DTPA case.
2. Mental anguish damages: available when the defendant acted knowingly. Requires proof of substantial disruption in daily routine or a high degree of mental pain and distress.
3. Additional damages: up to three times economic damages for knowing conduct; up to three times combined economic and mental anguish damages for intentional conduct.
4. Attorney fees: mandatory for a prevailing consumer. Also mandatory for a prevailing defendant when the suit was groundless and filed in bad faith or for harassment.

Pre-Suit Notice and Settlement

1. Consumer must give 60 days written notice before filing suit, identifying the complaint and all claimed damages and fees.
2. Failure to give proper notice allows the defendant to seek abatement of the suit until notice is given.
3. The defendant may settle at any time: immediately, within 60 days of the notice, or within 90 days of filing an answer.
4. A valid settlement offer must cover both the consumer's damages and attorney fees incurred to that date.
5. Mediation: either party may request it within 90 days of service of the pleading. Must be held within 30 days of the request. Costs are shared unless the amount at issue is under $15,000.

Defenses

1. Reliance on written third-party information: effective only if the defendant gave the consumer timely written notice of that reliance.
2. Common law defenses (substantial performance, parol evidence rule, waiver, estoppel) do not apply to DTPA claims.
3. Negating producing cause: an arm's-length contractual disclaimer of reliance may defeat causation in commercially balanced transactions.

4. Statute of limitations: two years from the date of the act, date of discovery, or date the consumer reasonably should have discovered the act.

Procuring Cause Arbitration

1. The party requesting arbitration bears the burden of proof by a preponderance of the evidence.
2. Panels consider the full sequence of events: who first introduced the buyer, whether an ongoing relationship was maintained, whether a break occurred and why, and whether the second broker's involvement was the result of the first broker's abandonment or an intrusion into an active relationship.
3. No single factor is determinative. The panel weighs all relevant conduct from introduction through closing.

Avoiding Misrepresentation: Core Practices

1. Question sellers thoroughly when completing the Seller's Disclosure Notice.
2. Conduct an independent assessment of the property's condition and visible features.
3. State only facts and attribute every factual statement to a verifiable source.
4. Refer technical matters to qualified experts.
5. Decline listings from sellers who refuse to disclose known material conditions.
6. Document all disclosures in writing and retain records in the transaction file.

CHAPTER 11 QUIZ — DECEPTIVE TRADE PRACTICES AND CONSUMER PROTECTION

1. The primary distinction between fraud and misrepresentation in a real estate claim is:

a. Fraud applies only to sellers, while misrepresentation applies only to real estate licensees.

b. Fraud requires proof that the licensee acted with deliberate intent to deceive, while misrepresentation does not require proof of intent and is therefore easier to establish in court.

c. Misrepresentation requires proof of actual damages, while fraud does not require any showing of financial harm.

d. Fraud may be pursued only in federal court, while misrepresentation claims must be filed with TREC before litigation may begin.

2. A licensee copies square footage data from an old MLS entry without independently verifying the figure and presents it to a buyer as the size of the property. The recorded square footage later turns out to be significantly overstated. The licensee's exposure in this situation arises from:

a. Accidental misrepresentation, because repeating unverified data that turns out to be false can create liability even without intent, since the licensee created the impression of firsthand knowledge.

b. Fraud, because the licensee knowingly presented inaccurate data to the buyer.

c. No legal exposure, because MLS data is provided by third parties and licensees are not responsible for its accuracy.

d. A TREC Canon violation only, because misrepresentation based on copied data is an administrative matter rather than a civil one.

3. A buyer asks his agent for a recommendation for a home inspector. The agent provides the buyer with one name and says, "This is the only inspector I trust." The inspector the agent recommends later misses a major structural defect. The agent's recommended approach to referral requests, and the practice that would have best reduced this exposure, is to:

a. Decline to provide any referral at all and tell the buyer to find their own inspector independently.

b. Provide a single trusted referral but require the buyer to sign a waiver confirming they chose the inspector independently.

c. Recommend only service providers who are affiliated with the broker's office so the broker can monitor their performance directly.

d. Provide the buyer with a list of qualified providers while declining to endorse one over the others, to avoid creating a representation about any single provider's quality.

4. Section 17.46 of the DTPA contains the "laundry list" of prohibited acts. Among all the listed violations, which prohibited act are real estate licensees most likely to commit?

   a. Price gouging on necessities during a governor-declared disaster.

   b. Falsely claiming that work or repairs have been completed when they have not.

   c. Disparaging the goods, services, or business of a competing brokerage through false or misleading statements, typically at a listing presentation.

   d. Misrepresenting the rights, remedies, or obligations created by an insurance policy.

5. In the case study Orkin v. LaSassier, the pest control company argued that no verbal statement was made that the treatment had been completed. The court rejected this defense and held that:

   a. The technician's conduct of visiting the home and leaving without completing the treatment constituted a representation through conduct that the services had been performed, which was sufficient to support a DTPA claim.

   b. A DTPA violation requires a written representation, and the company's conduct therefore did not meet the threshold for liability.

   c. The homeowner assumed the risk by leaving the property before the technician finished, which relieved the company of any obligation to notify her that the job was incomplete.

   d. A statement must be both false and intentional to create DTPA liability, and the company's omission was neither.

6. Before filing a DTPA lawsuit, a plaintiff is required to provide the defendant with written notice of intent to sue. Which of the following correctly describes the notice requirement?

   a. The plaintiff must provide 30 days written notice citing only the dollar amount of claimed damages.

   b. The plaintiff must provide at least 60 days written notice that describes the complaint in reasonable detail and identifies all claimed damages, including economic losses, mental anguish, anticipated attorney fees, and court costs.

   c. Notice must be filed simultaneously with TREC and the defendant's broker before the 90-day pre-suit window begins.

   d. Written notice is required only when the plaintiff intends to seek treble damages for an intentional violation.

7. In the case study Weitzel v. Barnes, a developer made verbal representations that the plumbing and air conditioning were up to city code. After closing, the buyers discovered the air conditioning was inoperable. The developer argued the as-is clause in the contract shielded them from liability. The court ruled that:

   a. The as-is clause was enforceable because the buyers had a contractual opportunity to inspect the property and chose not to exercise it.

   b. The as-is clause shielded the developer from liability for all physical conditions because a condemnation notice was visible on the property before closing.

   c. An as-is clause cannot be used to shield a misrepresentation that was already made. Once the developer made specific factual statements about the systems, the as-is language did not extinguish the claim.

   d. The verbal representations were inadmissible because the written contract superseded all prior oral statements under the parol evidence rule.

8. A DTPA defendant acted knowingly, meaning they were aware the conduct was false or deceptive. In addition to economic damages and attorney fees, the court may also award:

a. Damages for mental anguish.

b. Automatic treble damages equal to three times the economic loss.

c. A civil penalty payable to the Texas Attorney General rather than to the plaintiff.

d. Punitive damages equal to the defendant's gross commission income for the calendar year.

9. The DTPA statute of limitations is two years. Under the discovery rule, the two-year period begins running:

a. On the date of closing, regardless of when the defect or harm becomes apparent to the consumer.

b. On the date the Seller's Disclosure Notice was signed.

c. On the date the consumer first consulted an attorney about the potential claim.

d. From the date of the underlying event or from the date the consumer discovered or reasonably should have discovered the harm, whichever is later.

10. In the case study Prudential v. Jefferson Associates, the Texas Supreme Court established four tests for evaluating whether an as-is clause is enforceable in a real estate transaction. Which of the following is one of those four conditions?

a. The buyer must waive the right to an independent inspection before the as-is clause can take effect.

b. The sale price must reflect a discount of at least 10 percent below appraised value to demonstrate the parties understood the as-is risk.

c. All defects known to the seller must be disclosed, the seller must not obstruct inspections, the as-is provision must be a meaningful element of the contract, and the parties must not be in substantially unequal bargaining positions.

d. The property must be sold through a foreclosure or estate proceeding, since as-is clauses are enforceable only in distressed property sales.

11. A court has found a licensee liable under the DTPA and is considering what sanctions to impose. Which of the following actions is outside the authority of a civil court in a DTPA proceeding?

a. Awarding economic damages and attorney fees to the prevailing consumer.

b. Multiplying damages up to three times the economic damages for an intentional violation.

c. Awarding the defendant reasonable attorney fees and court costs if the lawsuit was groundless and filed for harassment.

d. Revoking or suspending the licensee's Texas real estate license.

12. The terms "commission" and "omission" describe the two ways a misrepresentation claim may be established. Which of the following correctly defines each term?

a. Commission refers to the broker's compensation, while omission refers to the failure to include commission terms in the listing agreement.

b. Commission is an affirmative act that causes a false impression, such as stating incorrect square footage. Omission is a failure to disclose known or discoverable information, such as not informing a buyer about prior flooding on the property.

c. Commission and omission are synonymous terms in DTPA practice, both describing conduct that falls below the reasonable person standard.

d. Commission describes a licensee's conduct before a contract is signed, while omission describes conduct that occurs after the contract is executed but before closing.

13. The Texas Legislature amended the DTPA in 1995 in response to concerns about the scope of liability under the original Act. Which of the following correctly describes the effect of those amendments?

a. The 1995 amendments expanded the class of qualifying consumers and increased the automatic trebling of all damages.

b. The 1995 amendments removed mental anguish damages entirely and capped attorney fees at $5,000 per case.

c. The 1995 amendments applied the DTPA only to residential real estate transactions and excluded commercial deals from coverage.

d. The 1995 amendments limited available damages, narrowed the class of qualifying consumers, and created additional settlement opportunities for defendants.

14. Before a consumer can recover any damages under the DTPA, they must establish that the defendant's conduct was the producing cause of their harm. Which of the following correctly defines producing cause?

a. A contributing cause that, in a natural sequence, produced the damages complained of — a factor that both caused the harm, and without which, the harm would not have occurred.

b. Any conduct by the defendant that occurred within 60 days of the consumer's loss, regardless of whether a direct connection to the harm can be proven.

c. A cause recognized by the court that exceeded the consumer's reasonable expectations at the time of the transaction.

d. Any misrepresentation proven at trial, whether or not the consumer can demonstrate that they personally relied on it.

15. Under the current DTPA framework, economic damages expressly **exclude** which of the following categories of loss?

a. Costs of repair and replacement of defective goods or services.

b. Mental anguish, physical pain and suffering, loss of consortium, disfigurement, and physical impairment.

c. Out-of-pocket financial losses directly flowing from the violation.

d. Consequential financial losses that were foreseeable at the time of the transaction.

16. Mental anguish damages are available under the DTPA when a defendant acted "knowingly." Which of the following correctly defines knowingly as used in the Act?

a. The defendant had a general awareness that real estate transactions carry risk and proceeded anyway.

b. The defendant's license history included at least one prior TREC complaint related to the same type of conduct.

c. The defendant had actual awareness, at the time of the conduct, of the falsity, deception, or unfairness of the act giving rise to the claim.

d. The defendant signed a written representation that was later proven to contain a factual error.

17. A jury finds that a licensee acted intentionally in a DTPA case and awards the consumer $20,000 in economic damages and $10,000 in mental anguish damages. Under the current DTPA framework, what is the maximum total damages the court may award?

a. $90,000, because intentional conduct allows up to three times the combined economic and mental anguish damages.

b. $30,000, because additional damages may not exceed the amount of economic damages alone.

c. $60,000, because intentional conduct allows up to three times the economic damages only.

d. $20,000, because the 1995 amendments capped total recovery at the amount of actual economic loss.

18. The DTPA requires a consumer to give written pre-suit notice to the defendant at least 60 days before filing a lawsuit. If the consumer fails to provide proper notice, the defendant's correct procedural response is to:

a. File a motion for summary judgment because the failure to give notice is a complete bar to the consumer's claim.

b. Contact TREC immediately and request that the consumer's complaint be transferred to the regulatory system.

c. Proceed to trial on the merits because the notice requirement is procedural and does not affect the consumer's substantive rights.

d. File a plea in abatement no later than 30 days after filing an original answer, which pauses the case until the consumer delivers proper notice.

19. Under the DTPA, a valid settlement offer made by a defendant after receiving pre-suit notice must include which two components?

a. A written admission of liability and a payment equal to the full amount claimed by the consumer.

b. A notarized statement of the defendant's net worth and a payment schedule for the proposed settlement amount.

c. A dollar amount offered to settle the consumer's actual damages and a separate amount to cover the consumer's reasonable attorney fees incurred up to the date of the offer.

d. A warranty against future defects in the property and a cash payment for the consumer's documented out-of-pocket losses.

20. In the case study Kennemore v. Bennett, two brothers moved into a newly constructed home and paid the builder's full invoice before proceeding to trial on their own DTPA counterclaim for defective construction. The builder argued the brothers had waived their DTPA rights by accepting delivery and paying in full. The Texas Supreme Court ruled that:

a. Accepting a defective product and paying the purchase price constitute a waiver of all DTPA claims arising from that product.

b. A consumer's acceptance of a defective product and payment of the purchase price do not constitute a waiver of DTPA claims arising from the defect.

c. The brothers were barred from pursuing DTPA claims because they had already obtained a remedy through the civil counterclaim process.

d. Moving into the property and paying in full created an implied warranty of acceptance that precluded any DTPA recovery..

21. A licensee lists a property and discovers that the seller has failed to disclose on the Seller's Disclosure Notice that the home experienced a significant foundation failure three years ago. The seller refuses to amend the form or allow the licensee to make any additional disclosure to prospective buyers. The licensee's most appropriate response is to:

a. Decline the listing, because no commission justifies the risk of license revocation or a DTPA judgment that could result from participating in a nondisclosure of a known material condition.

b. List the property and rely on the buyer's inspection to identify the prior foundation issue.

c. Attach a separate rider to the MLS listing noting that the Seller's Disclosure Notice may be incomplete.

d. Accept the listing but insert a general as-is clause into the purchase contract to protect the seller and the brokerage from claims based on the undisclosed condition.

22. In a procuring cause arbitration, the panel must determine which broker is entitled to the commission. The party requesting arbitration bears the burden of proof by which standard?

a. Beyond a reasonable doubt, because commission disputes involve potential financial penalties similar to civil fines.

b. A preponderance of the evidence, meaning the panel must find that the requesting party's claim is more likely true than not.

c. Clear and convincing evidence, which is the same standard applied in all NAR Code of Ethics proceedings.

d. Substantial evidence, which requires the panel to find that a reasonable jury could have reached the same conclusion.

CHAPTER 12

IMPLEMENTATION AND PRESENTATION: BROKER WORKING WITH SELLERS

Chapter Objectives

After completing this chapter, you should be able to:

1. Describe the key components of listing service, including seller communication, activity reports, advertising, showings, and open houses.
2. Explain how to modify or extend a listing agreement and communicate those changes effectively.
3. Counsel a seller through the offer process, including presenting buyer information, reviewing offer terms, and making recommendations.
4. Explain the counteroffer process and the legal effect of offer acceptance.

Contents

Servicing the Listing

The most common complaint sellers have about their agents is not that the property failed to sell. It is that the agent disappeared after the listing agreement was signed. Sellers describe a pattern they find frustrating: an enthusiastic listing presentation, a sign installed on the lawn, and then very little contact until the listing either expires or an offer appears. A business card left on the kitchen counter after a showing is not feedback.

The root cause is usually a failure to prepare sellers for what the listing period actually looks like. In the first days after a listing is secured, the agent is genuinely busy: entering the property into the MLS, preparing marketing materials, coordinating photography, scheduling tours, and setting up advertising. Sellers sitting at home do not see any of this activity and may assume nothing is happening.

Treating sellers as partners in the marketing process, keeping communication frequent and substantive, and setting clear expectations at the outset will prevent most of the frustration that damages the agent-seller relationship during a listing period.

Setting Seller Expectations

Before leaving the property after signing the listing agreement, cover the following with the sellers:

- Install the lockbox immediately. Explain how agents will access it, whether by a standard lockbox key or an electronic keycard, and attach it to a fixed, secure location such as a door handle or metal railing.
- Let sellers know they will receive an introductory letter from the broker welcoming them as clients and inviting them to contact the broker directly with any concerns.
- Schedule a follow-up meeting within the first day or two to walk through the specific marketing plan, do a second walkthrough of the property, and deliver written preparation tips.
- Explain that the first few days of a new listing rarely bring a surge of buyer traffic. Activity typically builds after MLS exposure, advertising, and agent tours have had time to circulate.

Homeowner Preparation Tips

Providing sellers with written guidance on how to present their property gives them a productive way to participate in the marketing effort and typically improves the showing experience for buyers. Tips should cover both the exterior and interior of the home.

Exterior

- Keep grass trimmed and shrubs shaped.
- Repair and repaint fencing if needed.

- Add potted flowering plants near the entry.
- Inspect and refinish the front door and trim if the finish is worn or peeling.
- Arrange outdoor furniture attractively.
- Address any visible roof damage.
- Keep pet areas clean and contained.

Interior

- Keep the home consistently neat and orderly throughout the listing period.
- Ensure floors, bathrooms, the kitchen, and appliances are thoroughly clean.
- Be mindful of cooking odors during the listing period. Strong smells from frying or vinegar can linger and create a negative impression. Pleasant aromas from baking can have the opposite effect.
- Fix leaky faucets in the kitchen and bathrooms.
- Have carpets professionally cleaned.
- Maximize light in every room through natural sources or higher-wattage bulbs.
- Clear closets of excess items so they appear spacious.
- Remove unnecessary furniture to make rooms feel larger.
- Organize and declutter the garage. Move overflow to storage if needed.

Weekly Activity Reports

Regular written communication with sellers is one of the most important habits a listing agent can develop. A weekly activity report serves two purposes: it demonstrates that work is being done on the seller's behalf, and it maintains the relationship during slow periods when there is little to report.

Some agents prefer monthly reports because the accumulation of activity appears more impressive. The better practice is weekly contact, even during slow periods, because consistent communication prevents the seller from concluding that nothing is happening.

A typical weekly activity report includes:

- Number of inquiries received that week
- Number of showings conducted
- Advertising placed during the week, with copies of ads where applicable
- Open houses held and the number of visitors
- Feedback from agents or prospective buyers who viewed the property
- Copies of current MLS pages and any web listings

> ***Important:*** *Even in a week with no showings and no new inquiries, contact the sellers. Silence during slow periods is one of the fastest ways to erode seller confidence.*

The Advertising Plan

Sellers want to know when and how their property will be marketed. Presenting a clear advertising plan at the outset reduces uncertainty and gives sellers a concrete picture of what the agent is doing on their behalf.

For-Sale Sign

Place the sign immediately after leaving the property. If a temporary sign goes up first, tell the sellers when the permanent sign will arrive.

Property Flyers

A well-designed property flyer, sometimes called a property brief, describes the home's key features, includes quality photographs, and provides a website address where buyers can learn more. Leave a large supply at the property for visitors to take. Flyers can also be distributed at open houses, delivered to agents at other offices, placed in sign tubes, sent to cooperating agents within your firm, and mailed or emailed to inquiring buyers.

MLS Entry

Submit the listing to the MLS as quickly as possible after the agreement is signed. Once it is live, print a copy and send it to the sellers as part of the initial activity report. When a price change occurs, notify MLS members directly rather than relying on them to notice the update on their own.

Online Presence

Upload the listing to your website and your company's website promptly. Provide the sellers with a copy showing how the property appears online. Most buyers begin their search online, making a complete and accurate digital presence essential.

Agent Tours and Caravans

Arranging for agents to tour a new listing, either within your own firm or as part of an MLS caravan, expands exposure quickly. Ask touring agents to complete a written property evaluation form. These evaluations give you objective feedback to share with sellers and often surface improvement suggestions the sellers will take more seriously coming from other professionals than from their own agent.

Advertising Compliance

All advertising must comply with Texas license law and federal requirements. Under TREC rules, all advertising must be truthful and not misleading, and must include the sponsoring broker's name as licensed. If a licensee advertises their own personally-owned property, the ad must state that the owner holds a real estate license. Advertising that references financing terms must also comply with the federal Truth in Lending Act. All property advertising is subject to the Fair Housing Act and may not contain any preference, limitation, or discrimination based on a protected class.

Managing Showings

Prepare sellers for the full range of showing situations they may encounter, including those that fall outside the typical scheduled appointment.

Agents actively showing property sometimes identify a home that matches their buyer's needs and request a same-day or next-hour showing. Buyers riding through a neighborhood may call while parked in front of the home and ask to see it immediately. Neither scenario is ideal, but both have produced sales. Sellers who are flexible and prepared for short-notice situations are far less likely to turn away an interested buyer.

If someone arrives unannounced at the door requesting a showing, the seller should politely get the person's name and contact information, then call the listing agent's office immediately so a licensed agent can come to the property to conduct the showing. Sellers should never conduct showings themselves.

Canceled showings are also a reality. Agents occasionally fail to appear for scheduled appointments without notifying anyone. Reassure sellers that you will investigate whenever this occurs and report back. Encourage sellers to treat both short-notice showings and canceled appointments as normal parts of the process rather than causes for alarm.

Open Houses

Agent Open House

An open house limited to real estate professionals gives agents from other firms extended, focused time with a listing. This is particularly useful for properties with unusual features or configurations that benefit from a walkthrough rather than photos alone. Agents who attend are potential sources of qualified buyers, and their feedback is professionally credible.

Incentives such as a drawing for a restaurant gift card or other prize encourage attendance. Collect business cards from everyone who comes through and follow up afterward to ask for feedback and to inquire whether they have buyers who might be interested.

Public Open House

Public open houses are the format most familiar to buyers and sellers. Before the event, remind sellers to have the home clean, uncluttered, and in its best showing condition.

Use a sign-in sheet to capture each visitor's contact information, what brought them to the open house, and whether they are currently working with another agent. This information helps you identify potential buyer clients and allows you to follow up appropriately. Give every visitor a property flyer and your business card. Have information available on comparable homes in the same and nearby price ranges for buyers who may be interested in alternatives.

Include a summary of open house visitor comments in your next weekly activity report to the sellers.

Modifying or Extending a Listing

Modifying the Price

If market conditions shift during the listing period, or if the initial pricing assessment turns out to be optimistic, the agent has an obligation to bring this to the sellers' attention promptly. Sellers may resist a price reduction, but a well-supported recommendation grounded in current market data is easier to accept than an appeal to emotion alone.

Sellers generally do not want to watch their property sit on the market without activity while the listing clock runs down. Present updated comparable sales, days-on-market figures for comparable properties, and any buyer feedback that addresses pricing. When MLS members need to be notified of a price change, contact them directly by email rather than assuming they will catch the update on their own.

Extending the Listing

Meet with sellers a few weeks before the listing is set to expire. Review everything done to market the property and present any additional ideas or strategies for the extension period. If the relationship has been characterized by consistent communication and diligent effort, sellers will typically agree to extend.

When an extension is secured, have the broker send an acknowledgment letter to the sellers and update the MLS with the new expiration date.

Counseling the Seller Through an Offer

When an offer arrives, schedule a meeting with the sellers as promptly as possible. Choose a comfortable, private setting where all parties can sit together, spread out the documents, and have a focused conversation without distractions.

Structure the presentation in three parts:

1. A brief recap of listing activity to date, including advertising, showings, open houses, and any prior offers. Keep this section concise since the sellers are eager to hear the offer itself, but it provides essential context for evaluating the offer that follows.
2. A summary of the buyers and their situation.
3. A thorough review of the offer itself.

Reviewing the Offer

Provide each seller with their own copy of the offer documents so everyone can follow along. Review the offer term by term and invite questions throughout. If any question involves a legal interpretation, direct the seller to consult an attorney. Never attempt to provide legal advice.

While the purchase price typically draws the most attention, it is not always the most consequential term. Make sure sellers understand that the following provisions can be equally or more significant depending on their circumstances:

- **Proposed closing date.** Affects when the seller must vacate and when funds are received.
- **Proposed possession date.** May differ from the closing date and affects the seller's move-out planning.
- **Personal property inclusions.** Lists fixtures, appliances, or other items the buyer expects to convey with the property.
- **Contingencies.** Common contingencies include financing approval, satisfactory inspection results, and the buyer's sale of their current home. Each contingency represents a condition that must be met for the contract to proceed.
- **Seller obligations prior to closing.** May include specific repairs, removal of personal property, or other actions the seller agrees to complete before the transaction closes.

Once every provision has been reviewed and questions answered, ask the sellers whether they are prepared to sign. If the offer is at full price with acceptable terms, move to acceptance. If it is not, discuss the options.

Making Recommendations

After presenting the offer, the sellers have three options:

1. Accept the offer as written.
2. Reject the offer outright.
3. Reject the offer and respond with a counteroffer.

Your role is to help the sellers evaluate each option clearly. If you believe the offer is fair given current market conditions, your goal is to secure acceptance rather than a counteroffer whenever possible. Outright rejection is rarely advisable unless the offer is so far below market value or contains terms so unfavorable that no reasonable counter could bridge the gap. Make clear to sellers that once an offer is rejected without a counter, the parties have no further contractual connection. The buyers are free to move on.

Counteroffers

It is the exception rather than the rule for an offer to be accepted exactly as written. Most buyers submit an opening offer below asking price, expecting to negotiate. Most sellers will respond to the first offer by countering on one or more terms. The most commonly contested elements are:

- Purchase price
- Earnest money deposit amount
- Proposed closing date
- Proposed possession date
- Personal property included in the sale
- Financing terms or contingencies

A counteroffer is a legal rejection of the original offer. Once a counteroffer is submitted, the original offer is no longer on the table. The buyers may accept the counteroffer, counter again, or walk away entirely. Sellers need to understand this clearly before countering.

When sellers are tempted to counter at the original asking price, caution is warranted. Many buyers will not pay full list price if they feel negotiation is possible, and a full-price counter can read as inflexibility rather than firmness. A more effective approach is often to suggest that sellers meet the buyers partway, splitting the difference between the offer price and the asking price, which allows the buyer to perceive a negotiating win while moving the price meaningfully toward the seller's goal.

Offer Acceptance

When an offer or counteroffer is accepted, a binding contract is formed. Both parties are legally obligated to perform.

Three conditions must be met for acceptance to be legally effective:

1. The party who made the offer or counteroffer must receive actual notice of the acceptance.
2. The acceptance must be communicated in the manner specified by the offer.

3. The terms of the offer must be accepted exactly as written, without any modification. Any change, however minor, converts the acceptance into a new counteroffer.

After Acceptance: The Contract Period

Contract execution is not the finish line. In many transactions, the most complex and consequential work begins after the offer is accepted. The commission is not earned until closing actually occurs, and closings fail during the contract period far more often than buyers or sellers expect.

During the contract period, the agent should actively monitor the timeline, track contingency deadlines, verify that lender requirements are being met, confirm that inspection issues are being addressed, and maintain regular contact with both parties. Small problems caught early are manageable. The same problems identified at the last minute can unravel a transaction. Proactive follow-through during this period is one of the clearest ways to demonstrate professional value.

Snapshot Review – Chapter 12

Seller Communication

Primary seller complaint: Lack of communication from the agent after the listing agreement is signed. Not failure to sell.

Weekly activity report: The core communication tool during the listing period. Should include inquiry count, showing count, advertising summary, open house results, and buyer or agent feedback. Send every week, even in slow periods.

Setting expectations: Tell sellers at the outset what the first days of the listing period look like: lockbox installation, broker welcome letter, follow-up meeting within 48 hours, and a realistic picture of when buyer activity typically begins.

Marketing the Listing

1. Sign goes up immediately after leaving the property.
2. MLS entry should be submitted as soon as possible after listing. Notify MLS members directly of any price changes.
3. Property flyers should be left at the home for visitors and distributed to agents, at open houses, and in response to inquiries.
4. Agent tours and caravans build awareness among cooperating brokers. Use evaluation forms to generate feedback for sellers.
5. All advertising must be truthful, must include the sponsoring broker's name as licensed, must comply with the Truth in Lending Act where financing is mentioned, and must comply with the Fair Housing Act.

Showings

1. Prepare sellers for last-minute showing requests and for occasional canceled appointments.
2. If a stranger arrives unannounced wanting to see the property, the seller should get the person's name and immediately contact the office so an agent can come conduct the showing.
3. Sellers should never conduct showings themselves.

Open Houses

Agent open house: Invites real estate professionals for extended property preview. Generates feedback and exposes the listing to a network of potential buyers. Use sign-in and business cards for follow-up.

Public open house: Open to all visitors. Use a sign-in sheet to identify representation status. Provide flyers and business cards to every visitor. Report visitor feedback in the weekly activity report.

Modifying or Extending the Listing

1. If the market shifts or the initial price was too high, advise the sellers promptly with data to support the recommendation.
2. Schedule a meeting several weeks before the listing expires to review results and present an extension plan.
3. Notify MLS members directly of price changes and extensions.

Presenting an Offer

1. Structure the presentation: recap of listing activity, buyer background, then the offer itself.
2. Provide every seller present with their own copy of the offer documents.
3. Review every term. Direct legal questions to an attorney.
4. Important terms beyond price: closing date, possession date, personal property inclusions, contingencies, and seller pre-closing obligations.
5. Fair housing rules apply when describing buyers. Do not mention race, national origin, religion, disability, familial status, or other protected characteristics.

Seller Options and Counteroffers

Accept: The offer becomes a binding contract. Acceptance must be communicated to the offeror, in the required manner, with no changes to any term.

Reject: The offer is dead. No further contractual relationship with those buyers.

Counteroffer: A legal rejection of the original offer and submission of a new one. Countering at full list price is often counterproductive. Splitting the difference is frequently more effective.

After Acceptance

1. A binding contract is formed when all three acceptance conditions are met: notice to the offeror, acceptance in the required manner, and no modification to any term.
2. The agent's work does not end at contract execution. Monitor contingency deadlines, lender progress, inspection responses, and timeline compliance throughout the contract period.
3. The commission is not earned until the transaction closes. Active management of the contract period protects that outcome.

CHAPTER 12 QUIZ — IMPLEMENTATION AND PRESENTATION: BROKER WORKING WITH SELLERS

1. Research and professional experience consistently show that the most common complaint sellers have about their listing agents is:

a. That the agent disappeared after the listing agreement was signed and provided little or no communication during the listing period.

b. That the agent set the initial listing price too low, resulting in a sale below the property's market value.

c. That the agent spent too much of the marketing budget on print advertising rather than online platforms.

d. That the agent pressured the sellers into accepting the first offer received rather than waiting for better terms.

2. A listing agent sends sellers a weekly activity report during a week when there were no showings and no buyer inquiries. Which of the following best explains why contacting sellers even in a slow week is important?

a. TREC rules require agents to document weekly contact with all listing clients regardless of market activity.

b. Weekly reports protect the agent from commission disputes by creating a paper trail of marketing efforts.

c. Most sellers interpret a lack of contact as a signal that the agent has already secured a buyer and is finalizing the offer privately.

d. Silence during slow periods is one of the fastest ways to erode seller confidence. Consistent weekly communication prevents sellers from concluding that nothing is being done on their behalf.

3. An agent hosting a public open house asks every visitor to complete a sign-in sheet. In addition to contact information, the sign-in sheet should ask visitors:

a. Their household income and current mortgage balance, so the agent can determine their buying power quickly.

b. What brought them to the open house and whether they are currently working with another agent.

c. Whether they intend to make an offer on the property before leaving the open house.

d. The address of the home they currently own or rent, to assess their ability to relocate quickly.

4. A stranger arrives unannounced at a listed home while the sellers are present and asks to see the property. According to proper listing protocol, the sellers should:

a. Conduct the showing themselves and report it to the listing agent afterward so the visitor's information can be captured.

b. Ask the visitor to schedule an appointment through the MLS showing service before any access is granted.

c. Get the visitor's name and contact information and immediately call the listing agent's office so a licensed agent can come to the property to conduct the showing.

d. Allow the visitor to tour the home unaccompanied as long as the sellers remain on the premises throughout.

5. Under TREC advertising rules and federal law, which of the following is a requirement that applies to all property advertising placed by a Texas licensee?

a. All advertising must include the listing price and the property tax rate for the current year.

b. All advertising must be submitted to TREC for review at least five business days before publication.

c. All advertising must include the expiration date of the listing agreement and the total commission rate.

d. All advertising must be truthful, must include the sponsoring broker's name as licensed, must comply with the Fair Housing Act, and must comply with the Truth in Lending Act when financing terms are referenced.

6. A listing agent believes the sellers' current asking price is too high based on updated comparable sales and extended days-on-market data for similar properties. The agent's most appropriate course of action is to:

a. Contact the sellers promptly with current market data to support a pricing recommendation, and notify MLS members directly of any agreed price change rather than relying on them to notice the update on their own.

b. Wait until the listing expires and then discuss pricing when the sellers request a renewal.

c. Reduce the price in the MLS without consulting the sellers since the agent has a fiduciary duty to price the property competitively.

d. Advise the sellers to withdraw the listing temporarily and re-enter it at a later date to reset the days-on-market counter.

7. When presenting an offer to sellers, the agent should structure the meeting in three parts. Which of the following correctly identifies those three parts in the recommended order?

a. Review of the offer terms, review of comparable sales data, and a summary of the sellers' net proceeds at the proposed price.

b. A brief recap of listing activity to date, a summary of the buyers and their situation, and a thorough review of the offer itself.

c. An introduction of the buyers' agent, a summary of the buyers' financing, and a line-by-line review of the purchase contract.

d. A review of the listing agreement terms, a discussion of the agent's commission, and a presentation of the offer.

8. While presenting an offer to a seller couple, the agent wants to describe the buyers to help the sellers feel comfortable with the transaction. Which of the following describes the fair housing boundary the agent must observe?

a. The agent may describe the buyers in any terms that put the sellers at ease, since the intent is to facilitate the sale rather than to discriminate.

b. The agent may share protected class information about the buyers only if both sellers sign a written acknowledgment that the information will not affect their decision.

c. The agent must decline to provide any personal information about the buyers and should present only the financial terms of the offer.

d. The agent may not describe the buyers in terms of race, national origin, religion, disability, familial status, or any other protected characteristic, even when the intent is to reassure the sellers.

9. A seller receives an offer $18,000 below the asking price. After reviewing the offer and current market data, the seller decides to submit a counteroffer. Which of the following correctly describes the legal effect of submitting that counteroffer?

a. The original offer remains open as a backup until the buyers formally withdraw it in writing.

b. The original offer is suspended for 48 hours while the counteroffer is being considered and automatically becomes binding if the buyers do not respond within that period.

c. The original offer is legally terminated. The buyers may accept the counteroffer, counter again, or walk away, but the original offer is no longer available to either party.

d. The original offer becomes a backup contract that takes effect automatically if the counteroffer is rejected.

10. After an offer is accepted and a binding contract is formed, a licensee's professional obligations during the contract period include which of the following?

a. The licensee should monitor contingency deadlines, verify that lender requirements are being met, confirm that inspection issues are being addressed, and maintain regular communication with both parties.

b. No further obligations apply, since the commission is secured at contract execution and closing is the title company's responsibility.

c. The licensee's only remaining obligation is to attend the final walkthrough and the closing table.

d. The licensee must file a copy of the executed contract with TREC within five business days of the effective date.

CHAPTER 13

IMPLEMENTATION AND PRESENTATION: BROKER WORKING WITH BUYERS

Chapter Objectives

After completing this chapter, you should be able to:

1. Explain how to qualify buyers and plan productive showing schedules.
2. Describe effective techniques for conducting showings and helping buyers evaluate properties.
3. Identify the signals that indicate a buyer is ready to make an offer and explain how to address last-minute objections.
4. Explain the process of preparing, reviewing, and presenting a purchase offer, including the licensee's legal boundaries.

Contents

Meeting and Qualifying Buyers

The first meeting with prospective buyers serves two purposes: understanding what they want and determining what they can afford. Showing properties that are outside a buyer's financial reach wastes everyone's time and sets unrealistic expectations.

Prepare a written list of questions before the meeting so nothing important is overlooked. Topics to cover include:

- Whether they currently own or rent, and whether an existing home needs to sell first.
- Their motivation for the move and timeline.
- Features they consider essential versus preferred.
- Whether they have spoken with a lender or obtained a pre-qualification or pre-approval letter.

A pre-qualification letter from a lender gives the most reliable picture of purchase capacity. As a general guideline, total monthly housing costs should not exceed roughly 28 percent of the buyer's gross monthly income, though individual lenders and loan programs vary. Ask buyers what they plan to put down and how much they expect to finance. If they are hesitant to share this, explain that the information helps you identify properties in the right range so their time is not wasted on homes they cannot close.

Use open-ended questions throughout the conversation. Buyers who feel heard and understood are far more likely to work exclusively with you and to move forward with confidence.

Planning the Showings

Thorough preparation before any showing appointment signals professionalism and keeps buyers focused. Disorganized showings frustrate clients and reflect poorly on the agent.

Listen carefully during the initial meeting to identify what buyers truly need versus what they say they want. Buyers generally reveal their non-negotiable requirements, the conditions that will end their interest in a property, early in the conversation. Note these deal-breakers and filter your property selections accordingly.

If the buyers must sell a current home before purchasing, temper expectations about the number of properties worth viewing. Most sellers are reluctant to accept an offer contingent on the buyer's home selling, except when the home is unusual or difficult to move. Showing a large number of homes to buyers who cannot act quickly can create confusion and false attachment.

Prepare a presentation package for each showing appointment. A good package includes a property information sheet, photographs, a map of the area, space for buyer notes, and information about school districts, nearby shopping, parks, recreational facilities, and commute routes. School districts deserve particular emphasis because strong district ratings affect resale values even for buyers without children.

Preparing for the Showings

Before the appointment, preview every property you plan to show if you have not visited it recently. Map a logical route between properties that also allows you to highlight neighborhood features along the way. Note the specific attributes of each property you want to draw attention to during the walkthrough.

Limit showings to three or four properties per outing when possible. A shorter list allows buyers to form clear impressions of each home and give you useful feedback on what is working and what is not. Confusion and decision fatigue set in quickly when too many properties are stacked back to back.

When circumstances require more showings, such as when buyers are visiting from out of town and have limited time, provide printed flyers with photos of each property and schedule brief breaks every three or four homes to give buyers time to absorb what they have seen. After every showing, ask buyers to share their reactions while the property is still fresh.

Conducting the Showings

Driving buyers to showings rather than having them follow in their own vehicle reduces no-shows and gives you uninterrupted time to build rapport and set the stage for each property.

Use the drive to sell the neighborhood before the buyers ever walk through the door. Point out features you know will matter to them: the nearby park, the elementary school, the community recreation center. Ask questions that connect the neighborhood to the buyers' lives. If a parent mentioned that their child plays soccer, ask that child what they think of the new sports fields as you drive past. Personal connection to a neighborhood accelerates the emotional attachment that leads to an offer.

Pointing out recent sales of comparably priced homes in the area also serves two purposes: it establishes your market knowledge, and it helps anchor buyers to a realistic price range before they see the listing price.

Inside the home, focus on the features that matter most to these particular buyers. Very few homes offer everything a buyer wants, and drawing attention to every detail regardless of relevance dilutes the impact of the genuinely important features. When children accompany buyers, involve them by asking which space would be theirs. When friends or family members come along, treat them as helpful participants rather than distractions.

Asking the Right Questions During a Showing

Effective showing technique uses questions to draw buyers into the home rather than narrating features at them. Stating the obvious, such as announcing that you are standing in the kitchen, adds no value. Instead, describe a specific feature and invite a reaction.

Questions that ask who, what, where, or how for each room and feature help buyers mentally inhabit the space. Rather than saying "this is a large pantry," ask whether the pantry would be large enough to hold everything currently crammed into the buyer's current kitchen. The goal is to have buyers picturing their own belongings and routines in the home.

A useful technique is the positive affirmation question, sometimes called a tie-down, which frames a known buyer priority as a statement and invites confirmation. For example:

- "Having a workspace for your woodworking was at the top of your list, and this garage delivers exactly that, right?"
- "Being within walking distance of the middle school was important to you, and this location checks that box, correct?"
- "This kitchen has the room your family needs for everyone to be in there at once, doesn't it?"

A series of small confirmations builds positive momentum and helps buyers articulate why a property works for them. Inviting comparisons between properties is also productive: ask whether buyers preferred a feature in a home they saw earlier or the version in the current property. These comparisons surface priorities and prepare buyers for the decision ahead.

Additional Showing Tips

- The features that appeal to you as an agent may not be the ones that matter to the buyer. Let buyer priorities drive the tour, not your own preferences.
- Plan the path through the home in advance. Buyers tend to follow the agent, so a logical sequence avoids backtracking and confusion.
- Address objections when they arise rather than letting them accumulate. If a buyer comments that a room feels dark, immediately note that recessed lighting can be added at modest cost.
- Position yourself to the side of small rooms rather than standing in the center. This preserves sightlines and makes rooms appear more spacious.
- Avoid overselling any single feature. Excessive enthusiasm for one aspect can make buyers feel you are steering them away from something, or create unreasonable expectations about other properties.
- Bring a tape measure. Buyers frequently have questions about whether furniture will fit or whether a room meets a specific size requirement. Being able to measure on the spot eliminates doubt and demonstrates preparation.
- Turn on lights in every room, even during daylight hours. A well-lit home photographs better in the buyer's memory.
- Do not rush buyers through a property. A buyer who lingers is a buyer who is interested. Give them room to explore and imagine.
- Begin and end the tour in the room or space that has the greatest appeal for these specific buyers. A strong finish reinforces the positive impression and creates a natural setting for a closing conversation.

Recognizing Buying Signals

After showings are complete and a buyer has narrowed their focus to a favorite property, the next step is converting interest into an offer. Buyers rarely announce that they are ready to make an offer. Instead, they signal readiness through behavior:

- Expressing visible excitement or enthusiasm during or after a showing.
- Asking to schedule a second visit to the same property.
- Bringing measuring tape, a contractor, or a family member back for a second look.
- Asking specific questions about the seller's timeline or motivation.
- Discussing how they would use specific rooms or where their furniture would go.

When these signals appear, be ready to move into the offer process smoothly. Waiting for the buyer to announce readiness often means waiting too long.

Overcoming the Reluctant Buyer

Some buyers fall into the habit of waiting, believing there is no urgency and that the right home will still be available whenever they decide to act. In a slow market this may occasionally be true, but well-priced homes in desirable areas frequently receive multiple showings in the first days on the market and may go under contract quickly.

When a buyer is hesitating, use factual information to convey realistic urgency without applying pressure. Share how long comparable homes in the area have been staying on the market, how many times the subject property has already been shown, and whether price reductions in the neighborhood suggest that well-priced listings are selling before adjustments become necessary. Facts are more persuasive than urgency for its own sake.

Last-Minute Objections

Last-minute objections are a positive sign. A buyer who raises specific concerns about a property is a buyer who has narrowed their thinking to that property and is working through the remaining reservations before committing. Silence and indifference are harder to work with than articulated concerns.

Common late-stage objections include concerns about the listing price, the condition of a kitchen or bathroom, property tax amounts, or the need to sell a current home first. Each objection tells you something important about what the buyer needs in order to move forward. Acknowledge the concern genuinely, then address it with information or a practical path forward.

Your advisory role in preparing the offer covers several practical areas:

- **Earnest money.** Advise buyers on customary earnest money amounts for their price range and explain how the deposit is applied toward the purchase price at closing.
- **Personal and real property.** Buyers can specify in the offer which items of personal property they want to convey with the sale and which real property items, if any, they want excluded.
- **Home warranty.** Buyers can request that the seller provide a home warranty covering major systems and appliances through the first year of ownership.
- **Closing date.** Help buyers think through a realistic closing timeline that accounts for lender processing, inspection contingency periods, and the seller's own moving plans.

Offering a Reasonable Price

The most consistent buyer objection is that the asking price is too high. In most cases, buyers assume some negotiating room is built into the list price. Your job is to help them offer a price that is competitive enough to be taken seriously without overpaying.

A comparative market analysis prepared for the buyer gives an objective picture of what similar properties have actually sold for and where the subject property sits relative to the market. If the property is priced fairly, share the data and advise accordingly. If it is genuinely overpriced, tell the buyer that as well.

When a buyer wants to submit a very low offer, consider whether the offer risks insulting the seller into refusing to negotiate at all. An offer that reads as uninformed or disrespectful can close down a negotiation before it starts. Encourage buyers to anchor their offer in comparable sales data rather than an arbitrary discount from the list price.

Closing the Deal with the Buyer

When a buyer has signaled readiness, move forward rather than waiting for an explicit declaration. Several practical techniques help convert buyer interest into a signed offer:

1. **Proceed as if the decision has been made.** When you detect readiness, begin filling out the offer form. Waiting for the buyer to formally announce the decision often creates unnecessary hesitation. Momentum is your ally.
2. **Offer a choice between two positive options.** Rather than asking whether the buyer wants to make an offer, ask a question that assumes an offer and focuses attention on a specific term: "Do you want to propose a closing date of 30 days or 45 days?" This keeps the buyer engaged in the details of the offer rather than the threshold question of whether to make one.
3. **Use a relevant inducement when appropriate.** If interest rates have dipped or a competing offer is expected, share factual information that creates a concrete reason to act now. Only offer incentives you can actually deliver. Promising something you cannot produce destroys trust and may create legal exposure.

Explaining the Purchase Contract

Before a buyer signs the offer, review every provision of the contract with them. Buyers need to understand that an accepted offer is a binding contract. Take as long as needed. Do not leave any section unexplained or allow a buyer to initial something they have not read.

A useful memory tool for the seller's three options after receiving an offer is the acronym ARC: Accept, Reject, or Counter. Remind buyers that sellers typically counter on only a few specific points, leaving the rest of the offer intact. For this reason, every provision of the offer should reflect exactly what the buyer wants because a clean acceptance is always possible.

An offer remains open until it is either withdrawn by the buyer or responded to by the seller. If a buyer does not want their offer to remain open indefinitely, they may include an expiration date and time in the offer after which it is automatically withdrawn. This prevents the seller from holding the offer while waiting to see whether better options emerge.

Getting a Signature

Signing a contract that represents a commitment of hundreds of thousands of dollars is an intimidating moment for most buyers. Two approaches help ease this transition.

First, encourage buyers who want additional reassurance to have the contract reviewed by a real estate attorney before signing. This recommendation builds trust and increases the buyer's confidence in the document. The practical concern is speed: attorneys are not always available immediately, and a well-priced listing may not wait. If a buyer takes this path, impress on them and their attorney the importance of a fast turnaround.

Second, remind buyers that a signed offer is not yet a binding contract. Until the seller accepts every term without modification and communicates that acceptance, both parties remain free to walk away. Framing the signature as one step in a process rather than a final commitment reduces the anxiety around the moment.

Considerations During the Offer Process

Throughout the offer and contract period, keep the following obligations in mind:

- Help buyers select a closing date that is realistic for both sides. A closing date that creates hardship for the seller can derail an otherwise acceptable offer.
- Explain the inspection process clearly: what it covers, how the option period works, and what the buyer's rights are if deficiencies are found.
- Walk through every addendum or rider attached to the contract. Buyers are bound by terms they did not read as fully as terms they did.
- Remind buyers of the importance of a final walkthrough before closing to verify that the property is in the expected condition.

> ***Important:*** *Never advise a buyer on how to take title to property. Vesting and ownership structures carry legal and tax consequences that require attorney guidance. This is not a topic within the licensee's scope of practice.*

When to Consult an Attorney

There are circumstances where licensees should seek legal counsel before proceeding:

- The sponsoring broker is unavailable and the situation involves a question with legal consequences that cannot wait.
- Buyers are requesting contract language that addresses a situation not covered by the standard TREC-promulgated forms or approved addenda. Licensees are not authorized to draft custom contract clauses.
- The transaction requires a legal document outside the scope of a real estate sales contract, such as a road easement or access agreement. A real estate licensee does not have authority to prepare or interpret these documents.

Presenting the Offer

Once the buyers have signed the offer, the listing agent presents it to the sellers. Before that presentation takes place, the buyer's agent should review the complete offer with the listing agent to ensure the listing agent fully understands what the buyers are proposing, including any special circumstances or context that would help the sellers evaluate the offer fairly.

If the buyer's agent believes their presence at the presentation meeting would be helpful, they may ask to attend. A buyer's agent who attends a seller meeting can answer questions about the buyers or the offer directly. If the buyer's agent does attend, they must disclose their agency status to the sellers at the outset.

After the presentation is complete, the buyer's agent should leave and give the sellers private time to deliberate with their listing agent. Once the sellers have decided, the listing agent communicates their decision to the buyer's agent, who then reports back to the buyers. The sellers may accept, reject, or counter the offer. In each case, the buyer's agent is responsible for promptly conveying the response and advising their clients on next steps.

Snapshot Review – Chapter 13

Qualifying Buyers

Pre-qualification: Determining purchase capacity before selecting properties to show. Use a written question list covering current housing situation, motivation, desired features, and lender status.

28% guideline: A common rule of thumb: total monthly housing costs should not exceed approximately 28 percent of gross monthly income. Individual loan programs vary.

Deal-breakers: Non-negotiable buyer requirements identified early in the relationship. Use these to filter property selections and avoid wasted showings.

Planning and Preparing Showings

1. Limit showings to three or four properties per outing when possible to reduce confusion and get clearer buyer feedback.
2. Preview every property before showing it. Map a logical route that incorporates relevant neighborhood features.
3. Prepare a presentation package for each appointment: property information, photographs, area map, school district data, and buyer note space.
4. For out-of-town buyers requiring more showings, provide printed materials for each property and schedule breaks every three or four homes.

Conducting Showings

1. Drive buyers to showings. Use the drive to sell the neighborhood before arriving at the property.
2. Focus on features that match what these buyers said they need. Do not narrate the obvious.
3. Use who, what, where, and how questions to help buyers imagine themselves living in the home.
4. Use positive affirmation questions to build momentum toward a decision.
5. Invite comparisons between properties to surface buyer priorities.
6. Address objections immediately. Use a tape measure for size questions. Turn on lights in every room. Do not rush.
7. Begin and end the tour in the room with the strongest appeal for these buyers.

Moving to an Offer

Buying signals: Returning for a second visit, taking measurements, bringing a contractor, asking about the seller's timeline, or discussing room use. When signals appear, move into the offer process.

Reluctant buyer: Use factual market data, including average days on market and showing activity, to convey realistic urgency. Avoid applying pressure without facts.

Last-minute objections: A positive indicator that the buyer is focused on this property. Acknowledge the concern and address it. Objections signal readiness, not rejection.

Preparing the Offer

1. Review every contract provision with the buyer. An accepted offer is a binding contract.
2. ARC: sellers may Accept, Reject, or Counter. Buyers should ensure every term reflects their actual intentions because a clean acceptance can happen at any time.
3. Include an expiration date if the buyer does not want the offer to remain open indefinitely.
4. Do not draft custom clauses or prepare legal documents outside the TREC-approved forms. Refer those situations to an attorney.
5. Never advise a buyer on how to take title to property. That advice requires an attorney.

Getting a Signature

1. Encourage buyers who want reassurance to have an attorney review the contract. Stress the importance of a quick turnaround.
2. Remind buyers that a signed offer is not yet binding. Both parties remain free to withdraw until acceptance is communicated on all terms.

Presenting the Offer

1. Review the complete offer with the listing agent before the seller presentation.
2. The buyer's agent may attend the seller presentation. If so, agency status must be disclosed to the sellers.
3. After presentation, leave to give sellers private deliberation time with their listing agent.
4. The listing agent reports the seller's decision to the buyer's agent, who then advises their buyers.

CHAPTER 13 QUIZ — IMPLEMENTATION AND PRESENTATION: BROKER WORKING WITH BUYERS

1. When meeting with prospective buyers for the first time, a common general guideline is that total monthly housing costs should not exceed approximately what percentage of the buyer's gross monthly income?
   a. 20 percent
   b. 36 percent
   c. 43 percent
   d. 28 percent

2. An agent is preparing for a day of showings and wants to give buyers the clearest possible impressions of each property. According to best practice, the ideal number of properties to show in a single outing is:
   a. As many as possible to maximize the buyer's exposure to available inventory before the market shifts.
   b. No more than ten properties, since most buyers can evaluate that many before losing focus.
   c. Three or four properties, which allows buyers to form clear impressions of each home and provide useful feedback without decision fatigue.
   d. Exactly two properties per outing, which forces buyers to make a direct comparison and reach a decision more quickly.

3. During a showing, an agent uses a technique called a positive affirmation question. Which of the following is an example of this technique used correctly?
   a. "Having a home office on the main level was at the top of your list, and this layout delivers exactly that, right?"
   b. "Would you say this home is in the price range you were hoping for, or is it too expensive?"
   c. "What do you think about the condition of the kitchen? Does it need work in your opinion?"
   d. "How does this home compare overall to what you were expecting when you started your search?"

4. A buyer who asks about a second visit to a property, discusses where their furniture would go, and asks specific questions about the seller's move-out timeline is most likely demonstrating:
   a. Decision fatigue from viewing too many properties in a short period.
   b. A reluctance to commit and a need for more properties to compare before deciding.
   c. Buying signals that indicate readiness to move into the offer process.
   d. A concern about the property's condition that should be addressed by a licensed home inspector before any offer is submitted.

5. A buyer raises a last-minute concern about the listing price during the offer preparation meeting. The agent's best interpretation of this objection is that it represents:

a. A clear indication that the buyer has decided not to make an offer and is looking for a way to exit the conversation.

b. Evidence that the agent showed the buyer too many properties and created unrealistic price expectations.

c. A fair housing issue that must be escalated to the broker before the agent can respond.

d. A positive sign that the buyer is focused on this property and is working through remaining reservations before committing. It is not a signal of rejection.

6. When acting as an intermediary in a transaction and helping a buyer evaluate what price to offer, the licensee's correct approach is to:

a. Provide the buyer with comparable sales data but refrain from recommending a specific offer price, treating both principals with impartiality.

b. Recommend a specific offer price based on the comparable sales analysis, since providing that guidance is the agent's primary value.

c. Decline to discuss pricing at all while acting as an intermediary, since both price and terms must be set by the buyer independently.

d. Recommend an offer price to the buyer only after obtaining written consent from the seller to do so.

7. A buyer wants to include language in their offer addressing a specific situation not covered by any TREC-promulgated form or approved addendum. The agent's correct response is to:

a. Draft the needed language directly in the special provisions section of the contract, since that section exists precisely for non-standard circumstances.

b. Refer the buyer to a real estate attorney, because licensees are not authorized to draft custom contract clauses and doing so could constitute unauthorized practice of law.

c. Contact TREC to request a variance allowing the non-standard clause to be added to the offer.

d. Ask the listing agent to draft the language on the buyer's behalf, since the listing agent has authority to prepare contract documents for both sides of the transaction.

8. The acronym ARC is a useful memory tool for reminding buyers of the three possible seller responses to a purchase offer. The three responses represented by ARC are:

a. Accept, Reject, or Counter.

b. Acknowledge, Review, and Confirm.

c. Approve, Revise, or Cancel.

d. Agree, Respond, or Continue.

9. A buyer's agent attends the seller presentation meeting to answer questions about the offer. Which of the following correctly describes the buyer's agent's obligations and appropriate conduct during and after that meeting?

a. The buyer's agent may attend and advocate actively for the buyer's position throughout the seller's deliberations, since doing so ensures the offer is fairly represented.

b. The buyer's agent must obtain written permission from the sellers before attending any seller presentation meeting.

c. The buyer's agent should remain present throughout the sellers' deliberations to answer any follow-up questions that arise during their discussion.

d. The buyer's agent must disclose his or her agency status to the sellers at the outset, then leave after the presentation to give the sellers private deliberation time with their listing agent before the listing agent communicates the sellers' decision.

CHAPTER 14

IMPLEMENTATION AND PRESENTATION: PRACTICAL GUIDE TO EVERYDAY PRACTICE

Chapter Objectives

After completing this chapter, you should be able to:

1. Identify best practices and daily routines that support agency compliance in a brokerage.
2. Explain the broker's obligations regarding consistent training, information delivery, and client follow-up.
3. Describe proper handling of offer presentation, including single offers, multiple offers, and backup offers.
4. Explain the current framework for broker compensation in a post-NAR settlement environment and how earnest money defaults are handled.
5. Describe a structured approach to risk management, including identifying risk, evaluating claims, avoiding misrepresentation, and reducing exposure.

Contents

Questions to Ask When a Potential Claim Arises

Avoiding Misrepresentation Claims

Risk Avoidance

Best Practices for Agency Compliance

Running a compliant brokerage requires more than good intentions. It requires systems. When evaluating a firm for agency compliance, a broker should address the following foundations:

- A written best practices model that all licensees are trained on and held accountable to.
- A dedicated section in the company policy manual covering agency compliance specifically.
- An internal review routine for all paperwork flow: listing agreements, buyer representation agreements, contracts, and addenda.
- A working relationship with a real estate attorney available for document review and legal questions.
- A complete training program that is updated as laws and rules change.
- A clearly defined internal chain of responsibility so everyone knows who handles what.
- A process for monitoring and distributing information about new laws, court decisions, and regulatory updates.
- Follow-up with clients after signed agency agreements to confirm understanding.
- Post-closing contact with clients to assess satisfaction, answer remaining questions, and cultivate referrals.

Most of a broker's day involves either preventing problems before they arise, catching them early, or resolving them before they escalate. A well-built compliance infrastructure is what makes that possible.

Establishing a Daily Review Routine

The most effective tool a broker has for maintaining daily compliance is a comprehensive written policy and procedures manual. When agents know what is expected and have a written reference, accountability becomes straightforward.

Daily compliance habits should include:

- Thorough licensee review of all buyer representation agreements, listing agreements, contracts, and transaction paperwork before submission.
- Verification of MLS entries for accuracy, with corrections made immediately when errors are found.

- Broker review of advertising for all newly listed properties, checking for accuracy, fair housing compliance, and agency disclosure requirements.
- Adherence to written paperwork submission deadlines. Real estate transactions are time-sensitive at every stage. Delayed paperwork creates downstream problems in financing, appraisals, title work, and inspections.

Open communication between the broker and every licensee in the office is not optional. Licensees need to know that guidance is always accessible. A culture where agents feel comfortable raising questions early is far less expensive than one where they handle problems quietly and report them late.

Consistent Training for All Licensees

Training programs across brokerages vary dramatically. Some offer very little structure, leaving new licensees to figure things out on their own. Others require weeks of classroom preparation before allowing any client contact. Most licensees benefit from something in between, calibrated to their background.

A new licensee who brings substantial people skills and self-motivation from a prior career may need less hand-holding than someone entering real estate with no comparable background. However, all new licensees benefit from observing experienced agents in action: listening to phone conversations, watching client presentations, and sitting in on offer presentations as silent observers.

New licensees should ask experienced agents whether they can accompany them on appointments. Observing real transactions, then analyzing what happened and why, compresses the learning curve more effectively than any classroom instruction. Every experienced agent in the office is a training resource.

Finding, Reviewing, and Delivering Information

A brokerage has an ongoing obligation to monitor the real estate landscape for developments that affect how the firm operates. The following categories deserve regular attention:

- Changes in Texas real estate laws, rules, and TREC regulations.
- Marketing and practice updates affecting how properties are listed and shown.
- Training program updates from professional associations.
- Continuing education requirements and compliance deadlines.
- Court decisions that may affect brokerage liability or agency obligations.
- Shifts in the competitive environment affecting fee structures, service models, or technology.

When a relevant change is identified, the management team should determine how it affects company policy, whether forms or manuals need revision, and how to communicate the change to all licensees. Delivery should match the significance of the update: some items belong in a weekly or monthly staff meeting, others require a signed acknowledgment from each licensee. Policy manuals must be kept current because an outdated policy creates as much exposure as having no policy at all.

Key information sources for Texas real estate professionals include the National Association of Realtors at realtor.org, TREC at trec.texas.gov, and the Texas Realtors at texasrealestate.com.

Establishing Follow-Up Routines with Clients

After closing, every buyer and seller involved in a transaction should be added to the licensee's sphere of influence list, regardless of which side the licensee represented. Buyers become future sellers. Sellers become future buyers. Even former clients who move out of state can generate referrals when someone asks them who helped them buy or sell locally.

A minimum of five meaningful contacts per year is a reasonable starting point for maintaining sphere relationships. Monthly contact is better. These contacts can take the form of market updates, postcards, email newsletters, or holiday greetings. Licensees who do not want to manage this personally can work with a real estate marketing service that specializes in sphere-of-influence outreach.

Building and maintaining a database that includes email addresses for as many contacts as possible reduces the cost per contact and allows for targeted, timely communication. Consistent outreach over years is what converts a past client into a repeat client and a referral source.

Preventive Brokerage

Regardless of which party a broker represents, every licensee in the firm should follow three core practices in every transaction:

1. Use written disclosures. The most common basis for complaints against Texas licensees is failure to disclose material facts. Every material disclosure should be documented in writing and retained.
2. Clarify the licensee's role. Both buyer and seller should understand clearly who the licensee represents, what the licensee can do on their behalf, and what is outside the licensee's scope. If a licensee has no experience with a particular property type, say so and recommend qualified professionals.
3. Use experts when needed. Presenting oneself as having expertise one does not possess exposes the licensee to DTPA liability and potential license revocation. When a situation calls for an engineer, attorney, inspector, or other specialist, make the referral.

The distinction between duties owed to a client versus a customer also matters in daily practice. A buyer's agent reviewing a seller-financing arrangement with a buyer client will examine the terms in detail, including prepayment rights, grace periods, and due-on-sale clauses, where a seller's agent dealing with a buyer-customer would merely disclose the relevant facts. A buyer's agent discovering an easement will review the grant document for restrictions affecting the buyer's intended use, not just mention that an easement exists. The higher standard of care flows from the agency relationship, and licensees must understand where that line falls in each transaction.

Presentation of Offers

The duty to present every offer is one of the most important obligations in the listing relationship. The listing broker does not have discretion over which offers reach the seller. Every offer, regardless of price or terms, must be presented to the seller promptly unless the seller has provided written instructions specifying otherwise.

If a seller requests that the licensee filter offers and bring only those meeting certain criteria, the licensee must obtain that instruction in writing. Before doing so, the licensee should have a direct conversation with the seller about the risks: deals that appear unacceptable on first review sometimes contain room to negotiate, and circumstances change. A seller who seemed certain they would never accept a contingent offer may later be more flexible than anticipated.

The listing broker's duty includes explaining the offer clearly to the seller and providing an estimate of the net proceeds the seller would receive if the offer is accepted. Offer terms are confidential and must not be disclosed to other licensees or potential competing buyers. Unauthorized disclosure of offer terms is an ethical violation and can result in a professional standards complaint.

Case Study: Refusing to Present an Offer

A listing agent had a property on the market at $525,000. The seller had stated verbally that he would accept only a full-price cash offer with no seller-paid closing costs. Several offers below those terms had already been rejected.

A buyer's agent submitted an offer for $510,000 with the seller paying closing costs. The listing agent refused to present it, telling the buyer's agent that the seller had rejected similar offers before and would certainly reject this one too.

This was a violation of the listing agent's duty. The listing agent had no authority to make that determination. Sellers' circumstances and priorities shift. An offer that was unacceptable three weeks ago may be the basis for a successful negotiation today. Every offer deserves to reach the seller's hands. Many transactions that looked impossible at the start have been successfully negotiated precisely because the agent did not pre-screen offers based on personal judgment about their likely reception.

Presentation of Multiple Offers

When two or more offers arrive before any have been presented, or when a second offer arrives while the seller is already considering a first, the listing broker must handle the situation carefully and equitably.

The broker should prepare a complete presentation for each offer, including a net proceeds estimate for each. The goal is to give the seller as much useful information as possible so the decision is fully informed. No offer should be prioritized based on the order in which it was received, the office that submitted it, or any other factor unrelated to the seller's best interests.

When a second offer arrives while the seller is deliberating on the first, the listing agent should notify the seller immediately. The seller should be advised not to execute the first contract until they have had an opportunity to review both. Once a contract is signed, the seller's options become significantly more limited.

All parties whose offers are pending should generally be made aware that competing offers exist, without disclosing the specific terms of any other offer. This allows each buyer's agent to advise their client whether to strengthen or stand on the existing offer.

Case Study: Multiple Offers on the Roberts Property

A listing agent secured a listing at $1,600,000. At 9 a.m. Wednesday, a buyer's agent from another firm submitted an offer for $1,500,000. The listing agent scheduled a 6 p.m. appointment with the sellers to present it.

At 2 p.m., a colleague within the same firm submitted an offer for $1,520,000 on the same property. At 4 p.m., a prospect the listing agent had personally shown the property called and asked to come in and write an offer.

Three issues deserve attention:

The in-house offer. The colleague's offer should be acknowledged to the first buyer's agent in general terms. The existence of other offers may be disclosed, though specific terms of competing offers should not be shared.

Notifying the first buyer. The buyer who submitted the 9 a.m. offer should be informed that other offers are also pending. This gives that buyer the opportunity to reassess and potentially strengthen their position.

The listing agent's own prospect. When the listing agent's personal prospect wants to submit an offer, a conflict of interest arises. Best practice is to bring the managing broker into the transaction at this point so that all offers can be presented without any appearance of influence favoring the agent's own prospect. Transparency protects all parties.

Backup Offers

A backup offer is submitted by a buyer when the property is already under contract with another buyer. The backup offer does not take effect unless the primary contract fails to close.

Backup offers create legal and ethical complexity. Once a contract is executed, the buyer under contract holds equitable title, meaning the right to receive the property upon satisfying all contractual conditions. A seller who entertains a backup offer without the primary buyer's knowledge or consent risks interfering with those contractual rights, which can expose the seller to legal liability.

Equitable title: The buyer's legal right to receive title to a property once all conditions of the purchase contract are fulfilled. This right attaches at contract execution and precedes the actual transfer of deed.

The TREC One to Four Family Residential Contract permits a seller to continue marketing the property and accept backup offers during the contract period, provided the primary contract does not prohibit this. If a buyer does not want the seller soliciting backup offers, the buyer must include a specific provision in the contract restricting that activity.

The listing agent's first step when a backup offer situation arises is to determine whether the seller wishes to accept backup offers at all, and then confirm whether the existing contract permits it. If both conditions are met, the backup offer may be accepted in writing, with its effectiveness explicitly conditioned on the failure of the primary contract to close.

Earnest Money Disbursement in the Event of Default

Most earnest money disputes arise when one party believes the other caused the transaction to fail. These situations often involve strong emotions and a determination to hold the other side accountable. In practice, however, the subjective question of fault is rarely the controlling legal issue. The TREC One to Four Family Residential Contract and its addenda specify how earnest money is to be disbursed when a default occurs. The problem is not usually the contract language. It is that the aggrieved party refuses to follow it.

Standard TREC forms do not include a provision entitling the listing broker to share in the earnest money retained by the seller as liquidated damages when the buyer defaults. Most listing agreements, however, do contain a broker protection clause addressing this scenario. Whether the buyer's broker has any claim to a share of the retained earnest money depends on the terms of the commission agreement between the brokers and, in some cases, whether the buyer's broker agreed to such an arrangement in writing.

When an earnest money dispute cannot be resolved by agreement between the parties, the broker holding the funds may be required to interplead the deposit, placing it with a court and letting the parties litigate their respective claims. Brokers should consult legal counsel when a disbursement dispute cannot be resolved promptly.

Commissions

> ***Practice Update:*** *The following section reflects the compensation framework that took effect following the August 2024 NAR settlement and subsequent MLS rule changes. Practices that were standard before 2024 have changed significantly, and licensees must be familiar with the current requirements.*

All real estate brokerage commissions are negotiable. This has always been true under Texas and federal law. What has changed since 2024 is the framework for how buyer broker compensation is offered, communicated, and paid.

Written Buyer Representation Agreements Are Now Required

Under the terms of the NAR settlement and the MLS policy rules that followed, a buyer's broker must have a signed written buyer agreement in place before showing a home listed on an MLS. This agreement must specify the compensation the buyer's broker expects to receive, stated as a definite dollar amount or a clearly defined percentage. Vague or open-ended compensation descriptions are no longer acceptable.

Offers of Compensation Are No Longer Made Through the MLS

MLS systems may no longer include fields for sellers or listing brokers to offer compensation to cooperating buyer brokers. The practice of advertising a buyer-side commission on the MLS, which was standard for decades, ended with the August 2024 rule changes. Offers of buyer broker compensation may still be made, but they must occur outside the MLS, such as through direct negotiation between brokers or within the terms of the purchase contract itself.

How Buyer Broker Compensation Is Now Structured

Compensation for a buyer's broker now typically comes from one of three sources or a combination of them: the buyer pays the broker directly pursuant to their written agreement, the seller agrees to contribute toward the buyer's broker compensation as a concession negotiated within the purchase contract, or the listing broker agrees to share a portion of the listing-side commission with the buyer's broker through direct negotiation between the two firms. Any seller concession toward buyer broker compensation must be disclosed and included in the contract terms.

The key principle is that compensation no longer determines representation. A seller may agree to pay the buyer's broker compensation as part of the transaction without that payment creating any agency obligation to the seller. The buyer's broker owes undivided loyalty to the buyer regardless of who writes the check.

Listing Broker Counseling Obligations

The listing broker should counsel the seller about the current compensation landscape before the listing goes on the market. Sellers need to understand that buyer broker compensation is negotiable, that they may be asked to contribute to it as part of an offer, and that their decision about how to handle that issue can affect the pool of buyers willing to submit offers. A seller who refuses to contribute anything toward buyer broker compensation in a market where buyers are not accustomed to paying their own broker directly may receive fewer offers or lower prices.

The buyer's broker, for their part, must ensure their client understands what the broker is owed under the representation agreement and how any gap between the seller's concession and the agreed compensation will be handled. Transparency between the broker and the buyer client is now a formal requirement, not merely a best practice.

Risk Management

Litigation and arbitration are realities of the real estate business. Fiduciary relationships create elevated trust obligations, and elevated trust obligations create elevated liability. The goal is not to eliminate risk entirely, which is impossible, but to manage it systematically so that exposure is minimized and problems are caught before they become claims.

Every brokerage of meaningful size should consider establishing a quality assurance function, whether a formal committee or a designated managing broker, with the specific responsibility of overseeing risk management and handling client complaints. A brokerage without a structured protocol for reporting and addressing potential claims is vulnerable in ways that can be avoided.

Identifying Risk

Risk identification should be a regular, ongoing process at the brokerage level. Changes in law and regulation create new exposures. Agent behavior patterns create others. The following questions help surface risk areas that warrant attention:

- Are any agents accumulating multiple complaints or client dissatisfaction incidents?
- Does any agent's practice area carry elevated risk, such as REO listings, commercial transactions, or property management?
- When the brokerage lists bank-owned or REO properties, are agents aware that the bank's disclaimer of knowledge does not eliminate the agent's own disclosure obligations?
- Does the firm address ethical issues in regular meetings, or do potential problems accumulate without discussion?
- Are agents encouraging clients to seek expert advice, such as inspections, legal counsel, and structural evaluations, when appropriate?
- Is all agent advertising reviewed for accuracy? Are agents allowed to make unsupported claims about their experience or qualifications?
- Does the broker's file review process genuinely evaluate document completeness, or does it function as a rubber stamp?
- Are confidentiality obligations clearly defined in writing and consistently enforced?
- Are new agents given a thorough orientation that includes risk management topics before they begin independent client work?
- How many licensees is the principal broker directly supervising? Is that ratio manageable?

- Do any agents have personal business interests, such as home construction or rental properties, that could create undisclosed conflicts in transactions?
- Are agents with licensed assistants providing adequate supervision of those assistants' activities?
- Are agents required to promptly report client complaints to the broker, or are they handling complaints independently without escalation?

After identifying risks, the next step is implementing corrective action. A realistic assessment of where the brokerage is vulnerable is the starting point. Policies, training, supervision structures, and file review processes can then be adjusted to address the exposures identified.

Claims Evaluation

The single most important factor in risk management is the ability to identify and evaluate a potential claim as early as possible. Early awareness allows early intervention, and early intervention prevents most complaints from becoming formal claims or litigation.

Two preconditions are necessary: agents must be required to report any client dissatisfaction or potential problem to the principal broker immediately, and the principal broker must have the skills and temperament to handle complaints effectively. A broker who dismisses or minimizes complaints does not reduce risk. Effective claims management begins with someone who takes every complaint seriously, regardless of initial severity.

When a complaint surfaces, the recommended sequence is:

1. Contact the unhappy client promptly to acknowledge the issue and let them know you are reviewing it. Do not make commitments or admissions in this call. Its purpose is to demonstrate responsiveness.
2. Debrief the agent thoroughly and separately. Understand exactly what happened from the agent's perspective.
3. Review every document in both the agent's personal file and the office transaction file. Ensure nothing has been separated from the official record.
4. Instruct the agent to have no further contact with the client on this matter unless the issue is fully resolved. All communication should route through the broker.
5. Once the facts are assembled, arrange a face-to-face meeting with the client where possible. Listen carefully and take thorough notes. Many complaints that begin as potential claims can be resolved through a candid, respectful conversation.

Good listening, courtesy, and genuine willingness to address the problem prevent a significant share of complaints from escalating further.

Questions to Ask When a Potential Claim Arises

When a potential claim is being evaluated, the following questions help the managing broker assess exposure and determine next steps:

- Is the agent providing a complete and honest account of events, or does the explanation leave gaps?
- Is the managing broker willing to ask difficult, direct questions of both the agent and the client?
- Are all transaction documents present, fully executed, and consistent with one another?
- Did the agent have any undisclosed personal interest in the transaction beyond the stated commission?
- Is this a claim that may or may not fall within the firm's errors and omissions insurance coverage? What are the policy's reporting requirements and deadlines?
- Are the managing brokers familiar enough with the E&O policy to know which activities are covered, which are excluded, and what the firm's reporting obligations are?

After gathering all available facts, the matter should be reviewed by the most experienced managing brokers available. Multiple perspectives help calibrate the severity of the claim and identify legal exposure that a single reviewer might miss.

Avoiding Misrepresentation Claims

Misrepresentation claims typically stem from one of two failures: the agent made an inaccurate statement about the property, or the agent failed to disclose something material. Both can be avoided through careful practice.

When working with sellers, the agent should question them thoroughly about the property's condition and use the Seller's Disclosure Notice to capture their responses in writing. The agent should review the completed form carefully and compare it to what they have personally observed during their walkthroughs of the property. If something the seller says appears inconsistent with what the agent saw, or if an entry seems incomplete, ask for clarification.

Additional practices that reduce misrepresentation exposure include:

Recommend independent inspections. Encourage the buyer to hire a licensed property inspector. The licensee's job is not simply to relay the seller's representations. It is to help all parties make informed decisions based on accurate information.

Watch for cosmetic concealment. New paint, fresh flooring, or recently repaired surfaces in isolated areas can indicate that a defect was covered rather than corrected. When something appears inconsistent with the age or condition of the surrounding area, note it and recommend professional evaluation.

Refer technical questions to qualified experts. Foundation concerns, structural questions, drainage issues, and environmental matters all require specialists. The agent who ventures an opinion outside their area of competence creates liability without adding value.

Only state facts you can support. Every factual statement about a property should be attributable to a specific, verifiable source. If you cannot support the statement with documentation, do not make it.

Never participate in nondisclosure. If a seller refuses to disclose a material defect the agent is aware of, the agent should consider declining the listing. Protecting a seller's desire to conceal a problem is not a service worth the risk. A single listing is not worth losing a license.

Risk Avoidance

While risk cannot be eliminated entirely in real estate practice, it can be reduced to manageable levels through a combination of insurance, expert referrals, and strong internal policy.

Errors and omissions insurance provides financial protection when mistakes occur despite reasonable care. Brokers should ensure every licensee in the firm is covered and that the coverage limits are appropriate for the transaction volume and types of properties handled. Recommending that buyers purchase a home warranty shifts some risk from the seller and the agent to a third-party provider.

Referring principals to qualified experts, including attorneys, licensed inspectors, title companies, lenders, appraisers, and surveyors, distributes the burden of specialized knowledge appropriately. Agents who attempt to provide guidance in areas outside their expertise create risk without delivering value.

Ultimately, the most effective single risk management tool in a brokerage is a well-written, consistently applied, and regularly updated office policy. The policy should address agency requirements in detail, specify disclosure procedures, set documentation standards, and define escalation protocols for complaints and potential claims. Every licensee should review the policy at onboarding and whenever it is materially updated. Each acknowledgment of review should be signed and placed in the licensee's personnel file.

An outdated policy is not a safe harbor. A policy that has not been revised to reflect the latest TREC rules, MLS changes, or court decisions can expose the firm to liability just as readily as no policy at all.

Snapshot Review – Chapter 14

Agency Compliance Framework

Policy manual: The primary tool for daily compliance. Should include a dedicated agency compliance section, be updated regularly, and be reviewed and signed by every licensee.

Daily review routine: Includes paperwork review, MLS accuracy checks, advertising compliance review, and enforcement of document submission timelines.

Sphere of influence: The list of past clients, referral sources, and contacts maintained for ongoing marketing. Minimum five contacts per year; monthly is better.

Preventive Brokerage

1. Use written disclosures in every transaction. Failure to disclose material facts is the most common basis for complaints against licensees.
2. Clarify the licensee's role explicitly to both buyer and seller.
3. Refer to experts whenever a matter falls outside the licensee's competence.
4. The agent's duty to a client is deeper than the duty to a customer. A client receives active advocacy, strategic advice, and protection of interests. A customer receives honesty and accurate information.

Offer Presentation

1. Every offer must be presented to the seller promptly, regardless of the agent's view of its likely reception.
2. The seller alone has the right to accept, reject, or counter.
3. If a seller instructs the agent to filter offers, get the instruction in writing only after counseling the seller on the risks.
4. Offer terms are confidential. Unauthorized disclosure is an ethical violation.
5. Multiple offers must be presented without preference by order of receipt or submitting office.
6. When competing offers exist, all buyers' agents should be informed of the competition generally, without disclosing specific terms of any other offer.

Backup Offers and Earnest Money

Backup offer: An offer accepted by a seller while already under contract with another buyer. Becomes effective only if the primary contract fails to close.

Equitable title: The buyer's right to receive title upon satisfaction of all contract conditions. Attaches at contract execution.

Earnest money default: Governed by the express terms of the TREC contract. Problems arise when an aggrieved party refuses to follow the contract's disbursement provisions.

Commissions

1. Written buyer representation agreements are required before showing MLS-listed property and must specify compensation in definite terms.
2. Offers of buyer broker compensation may no longer be communicated through MLS listings.
3. Buyer broker compensation may be paid by the buyer directly, offered by the seller as a contract concession, or negotiated between brokers outside the MLS.
4. Who pays the buyer's broker does not determine representation. Compensation and agency are separate.
5. Listing brokers should counsel sellers on the current compensation landscape before listing.

Risk Management

Quality assurance function: A designated managing broker or committee responsible for risk identification, complaint handling, and claims evaluation.

Risk identification: An ongoing process evaluating agent behavior, practice areas, supervision ratios, policy currency, and complaint history.

Claims evaluation: Prompt acknowledgment, agent debriefing, complete document review, communication restriction, and face-to-face resolution meeting with the client.

E&O insurance: Errors and omissions coverage protecting the brokerage when professional mistakes occur despite reasonable care. Coverage scope and reporting requirements must be well understood by managing brokers.

Avoiding Misrepresentation

1. Use the Seller's Disclosure Notice thoroughly and compare it to personal observations of the property.
2. Watch for cosmetic improvements that may conceal underlying defects.
3. Only state facts that can be attributed to a specific verifiable source.
4. Refer all technical and legal questions to qualified professionals.
5. Decline listings where sellers refuse to disclose known material defects.

CHAPTER 14 QUIZ — IMPLEMENTATION AND PRESENTATION: PRACTICAL GUIDE TO EVERYDAY PRACTICE

1. The most common basis for complaints filed against Texas real estate licensees is:

a. Failure to disclose material facts about a property or transaction.

b. Charging a commission rate that exceeds the amount disclosed in the listing agreement.

c. Conducting showings without a signed buyer representation agreement in place.

d. Submitting MLS entries with inaccurate property descriptions or square footage.

2. A seller verbally tells her listing agent that she will only accept full-price cash offers and to stop bothering her with anything less. The agent later receives a written offer for $310,000 on a property listed at $325,000. The agent's correct course of action is to:

a. Decline to forward the offer since the seller's verbal instruction is binding and the agent is obligated to follow it.

b. Contact the buyer's agent and ask them to resubmit the offer at full price before scheduling any presentation meeting.

c. Notify TREC of the seller's filtering instruction before proceeding with the transaction.

d. Present the offer to the seller promptly, because the listing agent has no authority to pre-screen offers based on personal judgment about their likely reception. A verbal instruction to filter offers is not sufficient.

3. When two offers on the same property arrive before the seller has responded to either one, the listing broker's obligation when presenting them is to:

a. Present the higher offer first and hold the other in reserve in case the seller counters unsuccessfully.

b. Present the offer that arrived first, since the order of receipt determines which offer takes priority.

c. Prepare a complete presentation for each offer, including a net proceeds estimate for each, and advise the seller not to execute any contract until both have been reviewed. No offer should be prioritized by order of receipt or the office that submitted it.

d. Disclose the specific terms of each offer to the other buyers' agents so all parties can submit their best and final offers simultaneously.

4. In the Roberts Property case study, the listing agent's own personal prospect called at 4 p.m. wanting to submit an offer on a property that already had two competing offers pending. The recommended best practice in this situation is to:

a. Decline the prospect's offer entirely to avoid any appearance of favoritism toward the listing agent's own buyer.

b. Bring the managing broker into the transaction so all offers can be presented without any appearance of influence favoring the listing agent's own prospect, protecting all parties through transparency.

c. Present all three offers simultaneously and allow the seller to select without any input from the listing agent.

d. Schedule the prospect's offer presentation for the following day so that the two existing offers can be resolved before the conflict of interest arises.

5. A buyer under a signed TREC One to Four Family Residential Contract holds what is known as equitable title. Which of the following correctly defines equitable title?

a. The buyer's right to occupy and use the property during the option period before deciding whether to proceed with the purchase.

b. The seller's remaining ownership interest in the property after the contract is executed but before the deed is transferred.

c. A shared title interest held jointly by the buyer and the title company during the escrow period.

d. The buyer's legal right to receive title to the property once all conditions of the purchase contract are fulfilled, which attaches at contract execution and precedes the actual transfer of deed.

6. Following the August 2024 NAR settlement and MLS rule changes, which of the following correctly describes the current requirement for written buyer representation agreements?

a. A written buyer agreement is recommended but not required until the buyer submits a formal offer.

b. A buyer's broker may begin showings without a written agreement as long as the compensation terms are verbally agreed upon within 24 hours of the first showing.

c. A buyer's broker must have a signed written buyer agreement in place before showing a home listed on an MLS, and the agreement must specify compensation in a definite dollar amount or clearly defined percentage.

d. Written buyer agreements are required only in transactions where the buyer is financing the purchase through a federally insured mortgage.

7. Under the post-2024 NAR settlement framework, how may a buyer broker's compensation now be structured?

a. From the buyer paying the broker directly, from the seller contributing as a concession negotiated in the purchase contract, or from the listing broker sharing a portion of the listing-side commission through direct negotiation between firms — or a combination of these.

b. Exclusively through a buyer-paid fee, since the settlement prohibits sellers from contributing to buyer broker compensation under any circumstances.

c. Only through the listing-side commission shared between the two firms, as was the standard practice before August 2024.

d. Only through MLS-advertised cooperative compensation fields, which must now be updated to reflect the settlement guidelines.

8. When a client complaint surfaces at a brokerage, the chapter identifies a recommended five-step sequence for handling it. Which of the following correctly describes the first step?

a. Immediately notify the firm's errors and omissions insurance carrier and await instructions before taking any action.

b. Contact the unhappy client promptly to acknowledge the issue and let them know it is being reviewed, without making commitments or admissions. The purpose of the call is to demonstrate responsiveness.

c. Instruct the agent to call the client immediately and resolve the matter directly before it is escalated to the broker.

d. Review all transaction documents first so the broker is fully informed before making any contact with the client.

9. A listing agent is previewing a property and notices that one corner of the living room has fresh paint and new flooring in an otherwise older home. The rest of the flooring and walls show normal wear consistent with the property's age. Which of the following best describes the appropriate professional response?

a. Note the improvement in the property description as a recent upgrade and include it in the MLS entry as a selling point.

b. Disregard the observation since the seller is responsible for completing the Seller's Disclosure Notice and any defects will be identified during the buyer's inspection.

c. Ask the seller directly whether the new surfaces conceal a defect, and if the seller says no, take that answer at face value and proceed without further inquiry.

d. Recognize the isolated improvement as a potential sign of cosmetic concealment, a defect covered rather than corrected.

10. The chapter states that an outdated office policy manual is not a safe harbor and can expose a firm to liability just as readily as having no policy at all. This principle means that:

a. A well-written policy that has not been revised to reflect current TREC rules, MLS changes, or court decisions provides no meaningful protection and may itself create exposure if agents follow an outdated procedure.

b. A firm that has never had a written policy is at lower risk than one with an outdated policy, because the absence of a policy cannot be used against the broker in a complaint proceeding.

c. Policy manuals are required only for brokerages with more than ten licensees, since smaller firms can manage compliance through direct broker supervision.

d. Once a policy is signed by all licensees at onboarding, it does not need to be updated unless TREC formally publishes a notice requiring revisions.

Answer Key to Chapter Quizzes

Answer Key for Chapter 1

1. **a** — A broker who has a formal legal relationship with a principal such as a buyer or seller
2. **b** — The person who hires the broker and grants authority to act on their behalf
3. **c** — A customer
4. **d** — Universal agency
5. **a** — Special agency, because the broker is hired to complete one specific transaction
6. **b** — It cannot be revoked by the principal and survives the principal's death
7. **c** — The broker level, with salespeople acting as representatives of the broker
8. **d** — Before the licensee shows the buyer any property
9. **a** — The seller may share in the liability for the agent's misrepresentation
10. **b** — Acting solely in the client's best interest above all others, including the agent's own interests
11. **c** — Dual agency in which the broker secretly represents both parties without disclosure
12. **d** — Disclosing to the buyer that the seller will accept a price lower than the listing price
13. **a** — At the time of the first substantive dialogue about a specific property
14. **b** — A meeting at an open house with a prospective buyer
15. **c** — It must be negotiated and documented in the buyer representation agreement before properties are shown
16. **d** — Suspension or revocation of their license and other sanctions as determined by TREC
17. **d** — A broker who takes legal responsibility for the real estate activities of salespersons working under their supervision
18. **a** — Interchangeable, both refer to a person formally represented by a broker
19. **b** — The licensee may have unintentionally created an implied agency relationship with the customer
20. **c** — An independent contractor agreement
21. **d** — The agreements belong to the broker, so the clients and agreements stay with the original brokerage
22. **a** — Special agency, because the broker is authorized to complete one specific task
23. **b** — The client is responsible only for actions they specifically authorized and knew the broker was taking
24. **c** — Gratuitous agency
25. **d** — An agency relationship declared by a court based on how a licensee behaved, even without a formal agreement
26. **a** — An unauthorized act by the licensee, followed by the principal accepting the benefit without objection
27. **b** — The broker has implied authority to show, market, and negotiate on the seller's behalf, while the client retains final decision-making authority
28. **c** — Written notice of the licensee appointments
29. **c** — The buyer is legally unable to contract because they are a minor

Answer Key for Chapter 2

1. **a** — The agent is obligated to act in the principal's best financial interest because the relationship involves money or property.
2. **d** — A formal agency relationship is established, such as through a listing or buyer representation agreement.
3. **c** — Special agency
4. **a** — Universal agency
5. **b** — Market the property, conduct showings, and negotiate offers.
6. **d** — General agency created by the independent contractor agreement.
7. **c** — Refuse the request because it violates the Federal Fair Housing Act, and explain the legal limits to the seller.
8. **a** — Through the buyer representation agreement, negotiated and documented before any properties are shown.
9. **b** — Violation of the agent's fiduciary duty of confidentiality to the buyer-client.
10. **d** — Confidentiality continues permanently, even after the agency relationship ends.
11. **b** — Not liable for the client's direct misrepresentation during the showing, as the broker is entitled to rely on the truthfulness of their client.
12. **c** — Evaluate whether the buyer is genuinely committed to purchasing and, if not, consider ending the representation relationship.
13. **d** — Care, Obedience, Accountability, Loyalty, Disclosure
14. **a** — Disclosure, because the agent should have identified and disclosed a condition that could affect a buyer's decision.
15. **b** — Directs the agent to conceal a known water intrusion problem from prospective buyers.
16. **c** — Must keep this information confidential and may not disclose it without the seller's express permission.
17. **d** — Continues permanently, even after the agency relationship has ended.
18. **a** — Customer, who receives factual information but not professional advice or advocacy.
19. **b** — At the time of first substantive dialogue about a specific property.
20. **c** — A buyer visits an open house and asks general questions about the property.
21. **d** — Notify all buyers that competing offers exist without revealing specific terms, present both offers to the seller promptly, and advise the seller on how to respond.
22. **a** — Shopping an offer.
23. **b** — Negotiated and documented in the buyer representation agreement before any properties are shown.
24. **c** — Recommend that the buyer consult a licensed attorney, as licensees are prohibited from providing legal advice.

Answer Key for Chapter 3

1. **a** — Customer, and the licensee must disclose their buyer agency status to the seller at the outset.
2. **d** — The last licensee whose client signed the final counteroffer contacts the other agent and communicates that everything has been accepted.

3. **b** — Is legally the same as notifying the buyer-client directly, requiring the salesperson to communicate acceptance to the buyer immediately.
4. **c** — Direct the buyer to the local law enforcement agency's website or office to research crime statistics independently.
5. **a** — Information that a buyer could not discover independently and that would likely influence their decision about the transaction.
6. **d** — A violation of the duty to disclose material facts to the buyer, applying the reasonable person standard.
7. **b** — Fairness means honest, transparent conduct with the customer while still providing full fiduciary advocacy for the client.
8. **c** — Disclose the flooding condition to buyers regardless, and inform the seller that concealing known defects is not permitted.
9. **a** — Must disclose to the prospective buyer that confidential information from the prior listing cannot be shared, and may refer the buyer to another licensee if the buyer is uncomfortable with that limitation.
10. **d** — A customer who is a minor and lacks the legal capacity to enter a real estate contract.
11. **b** — A reminder that buyers will eventually learn the truth about a property, and it is better for the agent to disclose known issues before closing than for the buyer to discover them afterward.
12. **c** — A violation of the duty of loyalty, because it gives the buyer a negotiating advantage at the seller's expense.
13. **d** — Negligent misrepresentation, because the agent offered a structural opinion without the expertise to support it.
14. **a** — A history of basement flooding that the seller has known about for several years.
15. **b** — The buyer suffered actual damages as a result of relying on a false statement of material fact made to induce the transaction.
16. **c** — Not visible or discoverable through a reasonable inspection, while a patent defect is obvious to anyone who looks.
17. **d** — A patent defect that the seller actively concealed, which would likely support a buyer claim against the seller.
18. **a** — A transfer of property acquired through a court-ordered foreclosure sale.
19. **b** — Decline to complete the form and explain that the seller must complete and sign it, suggesting a family member, friend, or personal attorney assist instead.
20. **d** — A murder that occurred on the property.
21. **b** — Decline to respond, explain that the firm's policy is not to answer such inquiries as the information is immaterial to the transaction, and advise the buyer to pursue the inquiry independently if desired.
22. **c** — Is a material fact that must be disclosed, and the parties must decide how to address the discrepancy before closing.

Answer Key for Chapter 4

1. **a** — Exclusive right to sell
2. **d** — Exclusive agency, which authorizes one broker while allowing the seller to sell to specific buyers without a commission.
3. **c** — That an implied agency was created by the conduct of the parties, and full fiduciary duties apply.

4. b — A shared database that allows participating brokers to search and publish listing information across a broad network.
5. a — Active listings, recently sold properties, and expired listings.
6. d — Buyer broker compensation must be negotiated and documented in the buyer representation agreement before any property is shown, and may no longer be advertised through the MLS.
7. c — The broker has earned the commission by producing a ready, willing, and able buyer, and may need to pursue it through legal action.
8. b — Decline to share that information, because the duty of loyalty requires the agent to protect the seller's negotiating position.
9. a — Disclose in the purchase contract that they are a licensed agent purchasing the property for their own account and are no longer acting as the seller's representative.
10. d — Answer honestly, acknowledge the limited experience, and emphasize the commitment and effort they will bring to the listing.
11. a — May no longer be advertised through the MLS and must instead be negotiated and documented in the buyer representation agreement before any property is shown.

Answer Key for Chapter 5

1. a — Through a written agreement, orally, or through the conduct of the parties, though a written agreement is strongly preferred.
2. b — Does the buyer have the financial ability to obtain a mortgage?
3. c — The buyer has made a professional commitment, allowing the licensee to invest time and resources with confidence of being at the closing table.
4. d — In the buyer representation agreement, negotiated and documented before any properties are shown.
5. a — The buyer is responsible for covering the difference between what the listing broker offers and the agreed commission amount.
6. b — Proceed with the transaction and disclose the dual representation to TREC within 48 hours.
7. c — There is no TREC-promulgated buyer representation form. Licensees use TXR forms, local board forms, or broker-developed forms reviewed by legal counsel.
8. d — The buyer purchases any property during the agreement term, even one the broker did not show.
9. a — Advise the buyer to contact their current agent directly or send a letter to the first office themselves, and not complete the termination paperwork on the buyer's behalf.
10. b — The agent whose efforts were the direct cause of the buyer's decision to purchase a specific property.
11. c — Offer both clients the choice to continue with the current broker or transfer to representation at a different office, and document all communications carefully.
12. d — A single-property buyer representation agreement limited to that one address.
13. a — The buyer's agent owes the same full COALD fiduciary duties but directed toward the buyer-client rather than a seller-client.
14. b — A signed buyer representation agreement reduces procuring cause risk by clearly documenting the agency relationship.
15. c — Execute an amendment to the representation agreement identifying the additional territory, signed by both parties, before showing any properties in the new area.
16. a — Professional analysis, strategic advocacy, and guidance through every stage of the transaction.

17. **d** — Disclose this finding to the buyer-client as part of the proactive inquiry the fiduciary relationship requires.
18. **b** — Negotiated and documented in the buyer representation agreement before any properties are shown, and may no longer be advertised through the MLS.
19. **c** — Credit the retainer toward the final commission or refund it at closing to avoid double compensation and preserve the buyer's available cash.
20. **a** — Refer the drafting of any non-standard clause to a licensed real estate attorney to avoid unauthorized practice of law.
21. **d** — Is not yet legally effective because acceptance must be communicated in writing to the buyer or the buyer's agent.
22. **b** — The source of payment does not alter the agency relationship as long as it is clearly documented in writing and both parties understand who represents whom.
23. **c** — Presents a clean purchase price to lenders and appraisers without embedded commission adjustments, while producing equivalent economics for all parties.
24. **a** — Any existing agency relationships the broker has with sellers whose properties the buyer may wish to consider, along with the TREC IABS 1-2 form.
25. **d** — The seller and their agent must disclose known hazards, provide the EPA pamphlet, retain signed buyer acknowledgments for three years, and allow a ten-day testing window.
26. **b** — $11,000
27. **c** — Does not obligate the seller to make any repairs; if the buyer requests a repair, the contract moves into counteroffer status and the seller may refuse.
28. **a** — Permission to show the property to prospective tenants before closing.

Answer Key for Chapter 6

1. **a** — It demonstrated that agents in subagency were required to share buyer information with sellers, yet buyers were unaware of that obligation, triggering nationwide disclosure reform.
2. **b** — The seller, because all fiduciary duties under subagency ran to the seller-client through the listing broker.
3. **c** — Buyer agency gave buyers the same caliber of professional advocacy that sellers had always received, with fiduciary duties running exclusively to the buyer.
4. **d** — The broker must act as an intermediary under the statutory intermediary framework. Common law dual agency is no longer permissible in Texas.
5. **a** — Written consent from both parties and written identification of who will pay the broker.
6. **b** — In paragraph 9 of the TXR listing agreement and paragraph 8 of the TXR buyer representation agreement.
7. **c** — Give full advocacy and advice exclusively to their own appointed client, even if that advice is not helpful to the other party.
8. **d** — May not disclose the seller's price floor to the buyer, even under intermediary with appointments.
9. **a** — May not give advice or express opinions to either party on matters involving negotiating strategy.
10. **b** — The buyer's agent and listing agent are automatically appointed to their respective clients without requiring the broker to act separately for each transaction.

11. **c** — Step back from negotiations, provide only administrative support to the appointed agents, and give no strategic advice or opinions to either party.
12. **d** — The broker may never be appointed to either side of an intermediary transaction. If absent, a designated person in the office may make appointments but cannot appoint themselves.
13. **a** — Notify both clients that the intermediary relationship authorized in their original agency agreements has been activated in this specific transaction, and document who has been appointed to each side.
14. **b** — Not an intermediary transaction because intermediary requires two clients. The seller receives full fiduciary representation and the buyer receives only honest and fair treatment.
15. **c** — An intermediary transaction because all branch offices under the same broker's license are treated as one entity.
16. **d** — Non-agency is not legally recognized in Texas. The License Act is an agency law, and someone must be represented in every licensed real estate transaction.
17. **a** — May no longer be advertised through the MLS and must be negotiated and documented in the buyer representation agreement before any properties are shown.
18. **c** — Agents may be discouraged from converting buyers to clients because doing so could require sharing the commission with a second agent, leaving buyers unrepresented as customers instead.
19. **d** — The intermediary disclosure language must appear in bold or underlined print, and the agreement must be in writing.
20. **a** — 45 days
21. **b** — The exchange is disqualified and deferred capital gains tax becomes immediately due.
22. **c** — Is appropriate only if full and transparent disclosure is made to all partners in the syndicate, removing the element of concealment.
23. **d** — Undisclosed dual agency is an intentional act of concealment, while accidental dual agency arises unintentionally from carelessness or conduct that leads the opposing party to believe the agent represents them.
24. **a** — It signals to the buyer that the agent is working in the buyer's interest, which can create an implied agency relationship and lead to accidental dual agency.
25. **b** — Disclose the price and terms of their own offer to competing buyers to level the playing field, since using knowledge of other offers to gain a personal advantage violates the prohibition on bad faith dealings.
26. **d** — The TREC Information About Brokerage Services form, the TXR Registration Agreement Between Broker and Owner, and the Seller's Disclosure Notice.
27. **b** — Disclose their licensed status in writing and disclaim any agency relationship with the seller.
28. **c** — Disclose their ownership interest and license status in writing to the buyer or buyer's representative, regardless of the size of the interest, and recommend the buyer obtain independent representation.

Answer Key for Chapter 7

1. **c** — Only the licensee can create implied agency. A customer cannot accidentally create a representation relationship.
2. **a** — Regardless of who produces the buyer, including the seller, as long as the sale occurs during the listing period.

3. **d** — An exclusive agency listing using the TXR Exclusive Right to Sell agreement with the Named Exclusions addendum, which preserves the seller's right to sell to those specific individuals without owing a commission.
4. **b** — Open listings generate procuring cause disputes and do not require an exclusive agreement, making enforcement of commission claims impractical.
5. **c** — The broker's policy on cooperating with other firms and how that could affect the property's market exposure.
6. **a** — Contact their agent first so the agent can accompany them or make appropriate arrangements, and at minimum inform the seller that they have a buyer's representative.
7. **d** — All client relationships belong to the broker, not to the salesperson. A request to end the agency relationship must be directed to and handled by the broker.
8. **b** — Renounce the agency with proper notice and good cause, documenting the abusive conduct as the basis for withdrawal.
9. **c** — The agency ends because a court takes legal control of the property, and the seller no longer has authority to sell.
10. **a** — The clients belong to the broker, not the salesperson. They remain with the original brokerage when the salesperson transfers.
11. **d** — Confidentiality is the one fiduciary duty that survives termination of agency indefinitely, and disclosing a former client's personal circumstances without authorization is a permanent obligation.
12. **b** — Fiduciary duties to the seller continue beyond contract signing and require disclosure of any broker conduct that could affect the seller's interests, including financial assistance given to the opposing party.
13. **c** — The agency continues and fiduciary duties remain in force after an offer is rejected, unless a specific decision is made by one or both parties to end the relationship.
14. **a** — Death of the client terminates the agency relationship. The successor had no legal obligation to honor the original listing agreement and chose not to.

Answer Key for Chapter 8

1. **d** — At the time of first contact with the other party or the other party's licensee. There is no grace period.
2. **a** — The IABS 1-2 form describes the types of brokerage representation available in Texas in general terms. The agency disclosure identifies whom the licensee actually represents in the current transaction. Both must be provided separately.
3. **b** — A meeting at an open house, a meeting with a party already represented by another licensee, or a meeting after a contract has already been executed.
4. **c** — Disclose to the visitor that the licensee represents the seller, treat the visitor as a customer, and provide the required brokerage services information before discussing the visitor's financial qualifications or offering specific advice.
5. **d** — Pass the strategically valuable information to the seller-client because the listing agent represents the seller, not the buyer.
6. **a** — The touring licensee must disclose their agency status to the seller when meeting them in person and should discuss their role with the listing agent.

7. **b** — Failing to make clear to all parties which party the licensee represents, or accepting compensation from more than one party without the full knowledge and consent of all parties.
8. **d** — Review agency options, evaluate advantages and disadvantages, assess the office's specific situation, draft with input from staff and legal counsel, then train and monitor.
9. **b** — Both clients must be notified in writing, with the name of each appointed agent and the party they represent identified clearly.
10. **c** — Note the party's refusal in writing and retain that documentation in the file as proof the form was delivered and the party chose not to sign.

Answer Key for Chapter 9

1. **d** — A goal-oriented professional service engagement in which the broker provides expertise toward a defined objective without being directed on methods by the client.
2. **a** — A written agreement must exist between the broker and the client, signed by the party obligated to pay the commission.
3. **b** — An independent contractor, because they are compensated by production, bear their own expenses, and have a written agreement confirming their non-employee status.
4. **c** — Federal income tax, state income tax, Social Security tax, and Medicare tax.
5. **d** — The licensee holds a valid real estate license, compensation is based on production rather than hours worked, and a written independent contractor agreement exists stating the licensee will not be treated as an employee for federal tax purposes.
6. **a** — Liability for all back taxes that should have been withheld, including income tax, Social Security, and Medicare contributions, plus state and federal unemployment premiums and potential tax penalties.
7. **b** — File IRS Form 1099-NEC reporting the total earnings and provide a copy to the licensee for their personal tax records.
8. **c** — The principle that all client relationships belong to the broker, not to the individual licensee, which is why clients remain with the brokerage when a licensee leaves.
9. **d** — Supervise the sponsored licensee's real estate activities, regardless of the independent contractor classification.
10. **a** — The Fair Housing poster and TREC Form 1, which identifies the office as regulated by TREC and provides complaint contact information.
11. **b** — The clients remain with the original broker because the independent contractor agreement establishes that all client relationships belong to the broker.
12. **c** — Request that the graduated commission structure and all other agreed terms be documented in the written independent contractor agreement before signing.
13. **d** — Requiring attendance at sales meetings is characteristic of an employer-employee relationship and is inconsistent with independent contractor status.
14. **a** — $16,440
15. **b** — The salesperson keeps the full commission but pays the broker a fixed monthly desk fee. Best suited for experienced licensees with an established client base who can reliably cover the fixed cost.
16. **c** — Is a violation of TRELA because hosting an open house independently and interpreting contract documents are activities that require a license, and compensating an unlicensed person for performing licensed acts is prohibited.

17. **d** — Conducting an open house independently, reviewing contract documents with buyers, and attending a closing as the agent's representative.
18. **a** — The failure to withhold required payroll taxes creates tax liability for the assistant, the salesperson, and potentially the broker, and may result in penalties.
19. **b** — Buyer broker compensation must be negotiated between the buyer and their broker and stated in the buyer representation agreement before showings begin. Sellers may still choose to cover it as a contract concession.
20. **c** — $8,125
21. **d** — Is a violation because a salesperson may receive compensation only from their sponsoring broker, not directly from a buyer, seller, or any third party.
22. **a** — A kickback and a violation of TRELA, which may result in license suspension or revocation.
23. **b** — Entitled to a commission because the carryover clause protects the broker's right to compensation when the property sells to a buyer the broker introduced during the listing period.
24. **c** — Bring a legal action against the broker to recover the salesperson's portion of the commission, since only the broker may sue a client for commission but a salesperson may sue the broker to recover their earned share.

Answer Key for Chapter 10

1. **c** — The real estate industry established a professional ethical standard through self-governance before the law required it, and the Code subsequently served as a model for state licensing laws.
2. **a** — An Article, because only Articles may form the basis for a complaint. Standards of Practice may support an alleged violation but cannot stand alone.
3. **c** — Discriminatory housing advertising is not protected by the First Amendment, and both the advertiser and the publisher may be held liable.
4. **b** — HUD has concluded that the Communications Decency Act does not exempt websites from Fair Housing Act obligations or from liability under certified state and local fair housing laws.
5. **d** — Up to three times the actual damages suffered, because intentional violations may support a treble damages award.
6. **b** — An ongoing professional obligation that continues throughout the licensee's career.
7. **d** — It is not a disciplinary sanction. It formally notifies the licensee that the investigation found conduct that, while not warranting immediate discipline, should be corrected to avoid future formal proceedings.
8. **b** — A gift certificate valued at no more than $50 that cannot be exchanged for cash.
9. **a** — Disclose the compensation arrangement to the client using TREC form RSC-1 and retain the form in the transaction file, not attach it to the purchase contract.
10. **d** — $250,000 for all claims arising from the conduct of a single licensee.
11. **a** — By the close of business on the second working day after the contract is executed by the principals.
12. **c** — Remove the earned commission from the trust account within 30 days of acquiring ownership of those funds.
13. **a** — The Preamble may not be cited in an ethics complaint because it contains no specific, enforceable obligations. Only the Articles may form the basis of a complaint.
14. **c** — Duties to REALTORS (Articles 15 through 17).

15. **b** — An ombudsman focuses entirely on improving communication between parties and does not determine whether a violation occurred, while a mediator facilitates a negotiated but non-binding settlement that the parties agree to in writing.
16. **d** — The complaint must have been filed within 180 days of the alleged conduct and must cite specific Articles.
17. **c** — $5,000, which is the maximum fine the ethics hearing panel may impose.
18. **a** — Expel the REALTOR from association membership for a period of one to three years and suspend or terminate MLS privileges, since the panel has no authority to suspend or revoke a real estate license.
19. **b** — Monetary disputes between REALTOR broker members, with the central question typically being which licensee is entitled to a commission based on procuring cause.
20. **d** — Until closing or execution of a lease, unless the seller has specifically waived this obligation in writing.
21. **c** — When the REALTOR is defending themselves against an allegation of wrongful professional conduct, when required by court order, or to prevent the client from committing a crime.
22. **a** — Not required to discover latent defects or advise on matters outside their license scope, but must recognize red flags that call for professional inspection and refer clients to appropriate experts.
23. **b** — Cooperation and compensation are separate. An offer of cooperation does not include an offer of compensation unless compensation is expressly stated, and a cooperating broker must verify terms before accepting.
24. **d** — Articles 1, 2, and 3: Article 2 for concealing the rezoning potential and misrepresenting value, Article 1 for misleading the seller about market value in violation of SOP 1-3, and Article 3 for failing to disclose the variable commission arrangement and refusing to cooperate with a competing agent.

Answer Key for Chapter 11

1. **b** — Fraud requires proof that the licensee acted with deliberate intent to deceive, while misrepresentation does not require proof of intent and is therefore easier to establish in court.
2. **a** — Accidental misrepresentation, because repeating unverified data that turns out to be false can create liability even without intent, since the licensee created the impression of firsthand knowledge.
3. **d** — Provide the buyer with a curated list of qualified providers across the relevant category, explicitly declining to endorse one over the others, to avoid creating a representation about any single provider's quality.
4. **c** — Disparaging the goods, services, or business of a competing brokerage through false or misleading statements, typically at a listing presentation.
5. **a** — The technician's conduct of visiting the home and leaving without completing the treatment constituted a representation through conduct that the services had been performed, which was sufficient to support a DTPA claim.
6. **b** — The plaintiff must provide at least 60 days written notice that describes the complaint in reasonable detail and identifies all claimed damages, including economic losses, mental anguish, anticipated attorney fees, and court costs.
7. **c** — An as-is clause cannot be used to shield a misrepresentation that was already made. Once the developer made specific factual statements about the systems, the as-is language did not extinguish the claim.
8. **a** — Damages for mental anguish.

9. **d** — From the date of the underlying event or from the date the consumer discovered or reasonably should have discovered the harm, whichever is later.
10. **c** — All defects known to the seller must be disclosed, the seller must not obstruct inspections, the as-is provision must be a meaningful element of the contract, and the parties must not be in substantially unequal bargaining positions.
11. **d** — Revoking or suspending the licensee's Texas real estate license.
12. **b** — Commission is an affirmative act that causes a false impression, such as stating incorrect square footage. Omission is a failure to disclose known or discoverable information, such as not informing a buyer about prior flooding on the property.
13. **d** — The 1995 amendments limited available damages, narrowed the class of qualifying consumers, and created additional settlement opportunities for defendants.
14. **a** — A contributing cause that, in a natural sequence, produced the damages complained of — a factor that both caused the harm and without which the harm would not have occurred.
15. **b** — Mental anguish, physical pain and suffering, loss of consortium, disfigurement, and physical impairment.
16. **c** — The defendant had actual awareness, at the time of the conduct, of the falsity, deception, or unfairness of the act giving rise to the claim. Actual awareness may be inferred from objective evidence.
17. **a** — $90,000, because intentional conduct allows up to three times the combined economic and mental anguish damages.
18. **d** — File a plea in abatement no later than 30 days after filing an original answer, which pauses the case until the consumer delivers proper notice.
19. **c** — A dollar amount offered to settle the consumer's actual damages and a separate amount to cover the consumer's reasonable attorney fees incurred up to the date of the offer.
20. **b** — A consumer's acceptance of a defective product and payment of the purchase price do not constitute a waiver of DTPA claims arising from the defect.
21. **a** — Decline the listing, because no commission justifies the risk of license revocation or a DTPA judgment that could result from participating in a nondisclosure of a known material condition.
22. **b** — A preponderance of the evidence, meaning the panel must find that the requesting party's claim is more likely true than not.

Answer Key for Chapter 12

1. **a** — That the agent disappeared after the listing agreement was signed and provided little or no communication during the listing period.
2. **d** — Silence during slow periods is one of the fastest ways to erode seller confidence. Consistent weekly communication prevents sellers from concluding that nothing is being done on their behalf.
3. **b** — What brought them to the open house and whether they are currently working with another agent, to help identify potential buyer clients and guide appropriate follow-up.
4. **c** — Get the visitor's name and contact information and immediately call the listing agent's office so a licensed agent can come to the property to conduct the showing.
5. **d** — All advertising must be truthful, must include the sponsoring broker's name as licensed, must comply with the Fair Housing Act, and must comply with the Truth in Lending Act when financing terms are referenced.

6. **a** — Contact the sellers promptly with current market data to support a pricing recommendation, and notify MLS members directly of any agreed price change rather than relying on them to notice the update on their own.
7. **b** — A brief recap of listing activity to date, a summary of the buyers and their situation, and a thorough review of the offer itself.
8. **d** — The agent may not describe the buyers in terms of race, national origin, religion, disability, familial status, or any other protected characteristic, even when the intent is to reassure the sellers.
9. **c** — The original offer is legally rejected. The buyers may accept the counteroffer, counter again, or walk away, but the original offer is no longer available to either party.
10. **a** — The licensee should monitor contingency deadlines, verify that lender requirements are being met, confirm that inspection issues are being addressed, and maintain regular communication with both parties to catch problems early before they can unravel the transaction.

Answer Key for Chapter 13

1. **d** — 28 percent
2. **c** — Three or four properties, which allows buyers to form clear impressions of each home and provide useful feedback without decision fatigue.
3. **a** — "Having a home office on the main level was at the top of your list, and this layout delivers exactly that, right?"
4. **c** — Buying signals that indicate readiness to move into the offer process.
5. **d** — A positive sign that the buyer is focused on this property and is working through remaining reservations before committing, not a signal of rejection.
6. **a** — Provide the buyer with comparable sales data but refrain from recommending a specific offer price, treating both principals with impartiality.
7. **b** — Refer the buyer to a real estate attorney, because licensees are not authorized to draft custom contract clauses and doing so could constitute unauthorized practice of law.
8. **a** — Accept, Reject, or Counter.
9. **d** — The buyer's agent must disclose their agency status to the sellers at the outset, then leave after the presentation to give the sellers private deliberation time with their listing agent before the listing agent communicates the sellers' decision.

Answer Key for Chapter 14

1. **a** — Failure to disclose material facts about a property or transaction.
2. **d** — Present the offer to the seller promptly, because the listing agent has no authority to pre-screen offers based on personal judgment about their likely reception. A verbal instruction to filter offers is not sufficient.
3. **c** — Prepare a complete presentation for each offer, including a net proceeds estimate for each, and advise the seller not to execute any contract until both have been reviewed. No offer should be prioritized by order of receipt or the office that submitted it.
4. **b** — Bring the managing broker into the transaction so all offers can be presented without any appearance of influence favoring the listing agent's own prospect, protecting all parties through transparency.

5. d — The buyer's legal right to receive title to the property once all conditions of the purchase contract are fulfilled, which attaches at contract execution and precedes the actual transfer of deed.

6. c — A buyer's broker must have a signed written buyer representation agreement in place before showing a home listed on an MLS, and the agreement must specify compensation in a definite dollar amount or clearly defined percentage.

7. a — From the buyer paying the broker directly, from the seller contributing as a concession negotiated in the purchase contract, or from the listing broker sharing a portion of the listing-side commission through direct negotiation between firms — or a combination of these.

8. b — Contact the unhappy client promptly to acknowledge the issue and let them know it is being reviewed, without making commitments or admissions. The purpose of the call is to demonstrate responsiveness.

9. d — Recognize the isolated improvement as a potential sign of cosmetic concealment, a defect covered rather than corrected, and recommend professional evaluation, since new surfaces in isolated areas inconsistent with the surrounding condition warrant further investigation.

10. a — A well-written policy that has not been revised to reflect current TREC rules, MLS changes, or court decisions provides no meaningful protection and may itself create exposure if agents follow an outdated procedure.

INDEX

If you liked Fundamentals of Agency in Texas, check out the other titles of Performance Programs Company!

Looking for a Texas-specific real estate principles textbook? Get what all the students love -- Principles of Real Estate Practice in Texas!

Principles of Real Estate Practice in Texas is invaluable reference material for real estate professionals. Its 625-pages contain the essentials of real estate law, principles, and practices taught in real estate schools and colleges across Texas.

Where can you buy Principles of Real Estate Practice in Texas?
Principles Real Estate Practice in Texas is available as a printed book or e-book through nearly all online retailers.

Cramming for the Texas real estate exam? You need Texas Real Estate License Exam Prep!

Texas Real Estate License Exam Prep (TX-RELEP) is a 300-page modern learning tool designed to prepare real estate candidates to pass Texas' Pearson Vue licensing exam. TX-RELEP contains six different sections to provide the knowledge and practice necessary to succeed with both Texas and national questions.

Where can you buy Texas Real Estate License Exam Prep?

Texas Real Estate License Exam Prep is available as a printed book or e-book through nearly all online retailers.

Struggling with real estate math? The solution to that equation is Real Estate Math Express!

Real Estate Math Express is a concise, easy-to-study test preparation guide to help real estate students improve their real estate math scores to pass the state licensing test. The primary feature of Real Estate Math Express is that it contains all necessary formulas and practice questions in 100+ pages.

Where can you buy Real Estate Math Express?
Real Estate Math Express is available as a printed book or e-book through nearly all online retailers.

Publisher Contact
Ryan Mettling
Performance Programs Company
6810 190th Street East, Bradenton, FL 34211
941-677-6043
ryan@performanceprogramscompany.com
www.performanceprogramscompany.com

www.ingramcontent.com/pod-product-compliance
Ingram Content Group UK Ltd.
Pitfield, Milton Keynes, MK11 3LW, UK
UKHW051510290926
15471UKWH00008B/1539

9 781965 482575